Shadowed
Reflections,

Japanese Views

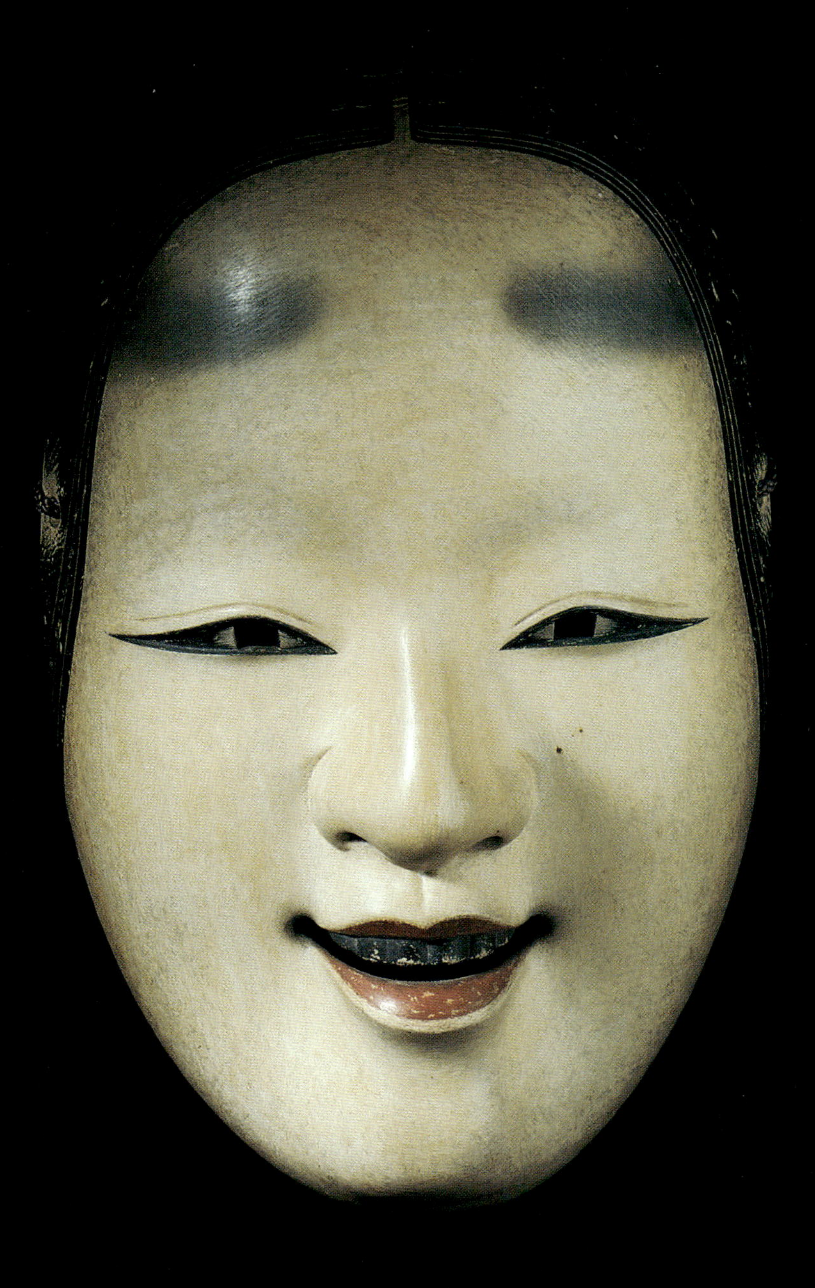

Catalogue by Jeffery Cline & William Knospe
Design by Rosanne Chan
Photography by Dick Busher
Color Separation by Goody Color Separation (Scanner) Ltd.
Produced by (C A Design) Communication Art Design & Printing Ltd., Hong Kong

ISBN 962-7502-25-1

Shadowed Reflections,

Japanese Views

Kagedo Japanese Art
520 First Avenue South
Seattle, Washington 98104
USA

Zuihitsu, *To Follow the Brush*, denotes a type of miscellany or informal collection of jottings. The Japanese have written such books since Heian, following an unpremeditated inspiration to brush onto the page ideas, reflections or simply things to be admired. Here we offer you a kind of *zuihitsu*, a visual compilation of things we like. All but a few of these are from Japan, and those few are Chinese scholar's objects treasured by the Japanese. Many mirror the natural world. Many speak to one another.

You will find all of the text or background information referenced by page and item number in the back of the catalogue, beginning on page 128. Reduced photographs of the illustrated pages float with the text as a visual guide.

The collections section we devoted entirely to photographs of the objects, linked to the text by number. The objects themselves suggested the order they should take. Implicitly, many of them relate to others by way of style, material, or in the way they comment on the world. Ceramics will generally be together, as will furniture, trays, baskets and painting. Some categories keep generally to a time line, but others abandon this for purposes of comparison, or suggestion. Metalwork for example we divided into flower containers or vases, splitting off *okimono* as a mixed media category of its own. Other metal pieces found kinship with objects elsewhere in the catalogue. Images are grouped as we see them, rather idiosyncratically.

To offer you these objects by way of a book seemed a way to let them speak more naturally for themselves. For us, their voices are distinct, and we often hear them conversing among themselves. We hope they speak to you as well.

Kagedo Japanese Art   Jeffery Cline

Seattle, 1997   William Knospe

Our deep thanks are due our many friends:

All of the people who help us find things, and to the people who value them.

Our photographer,
Dick Busher for his art, his dedication and an eye that sees beyond the surface.

Sachiko Furuya for her devoted translation.

Our wonderful staff for everything:
Greg Lulay, Lilly Sako, Wendy Wees, Maria Wing

And for their mad encouragement:
Rodney & Patrizia of Belkonia

Always our love to:
Tink

かげろう

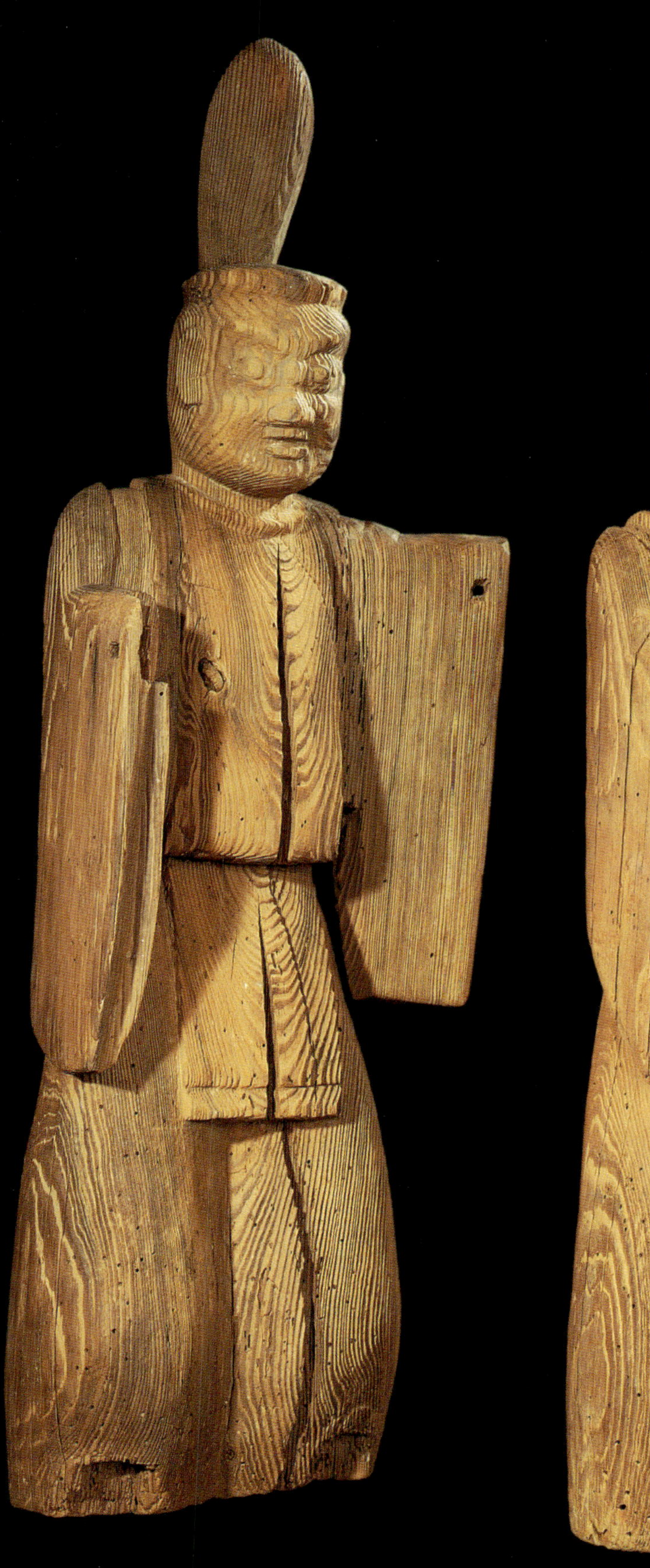
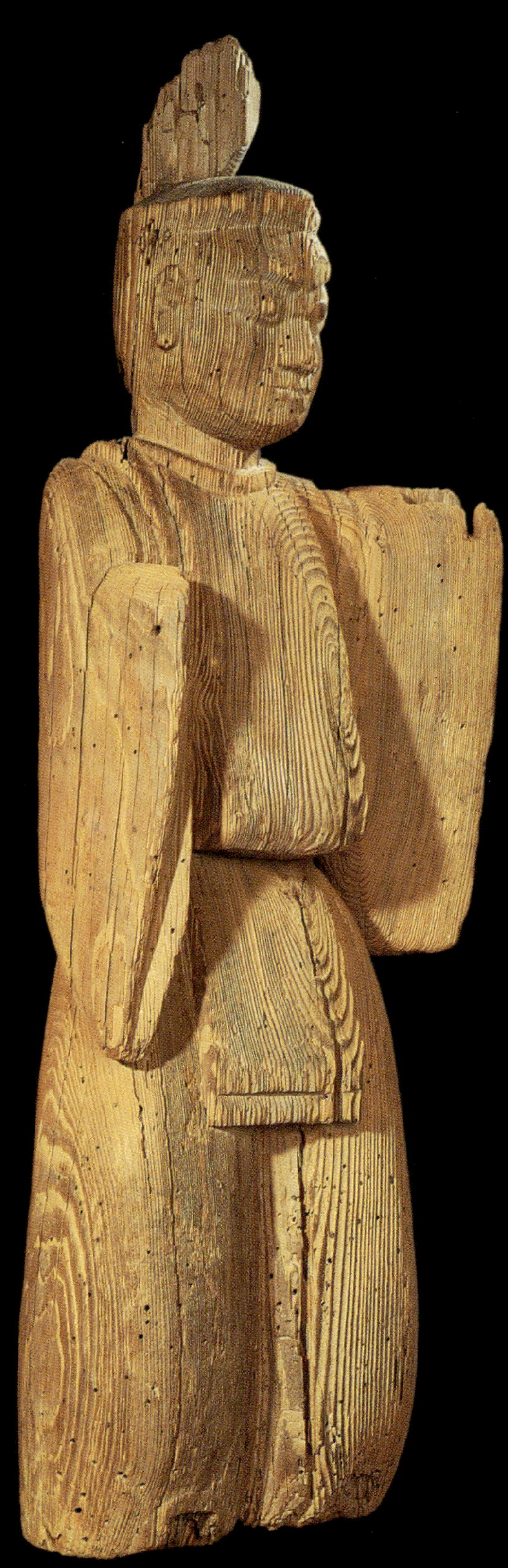

1

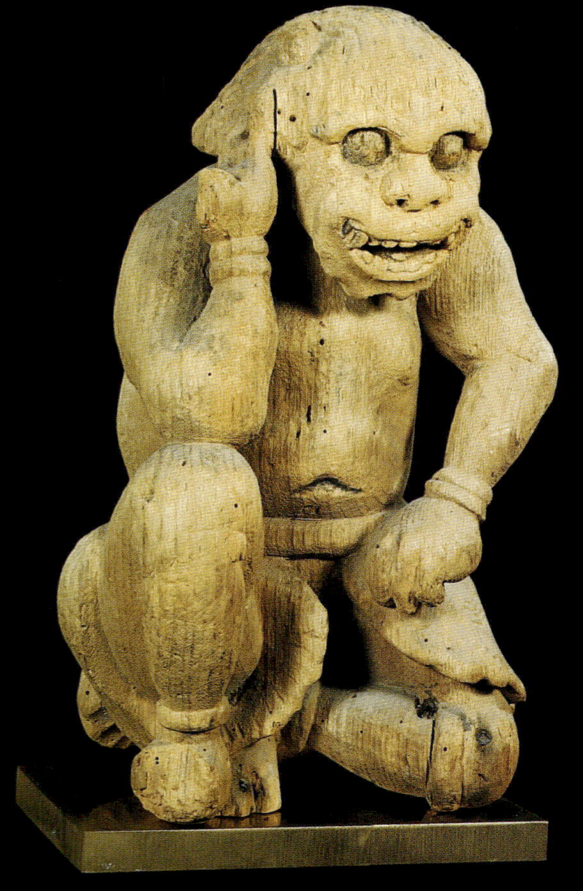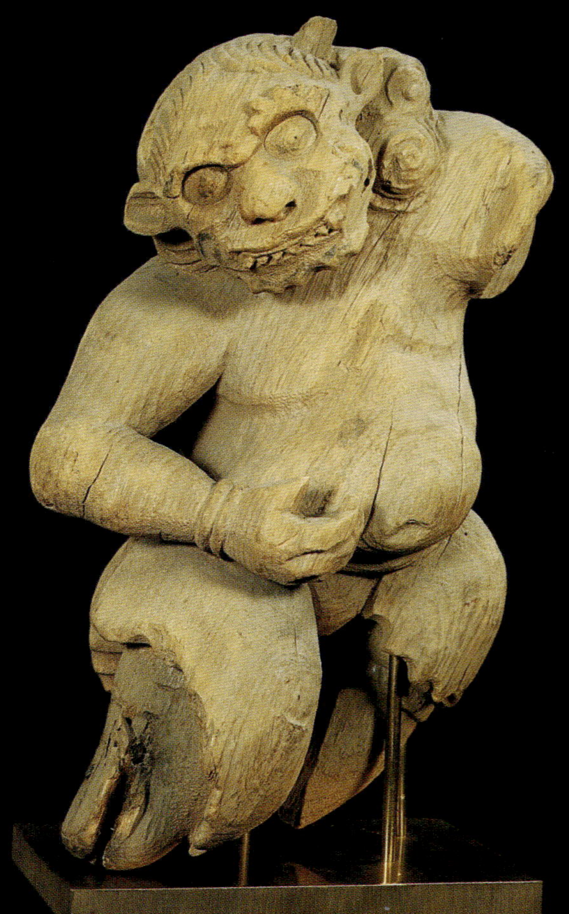

2

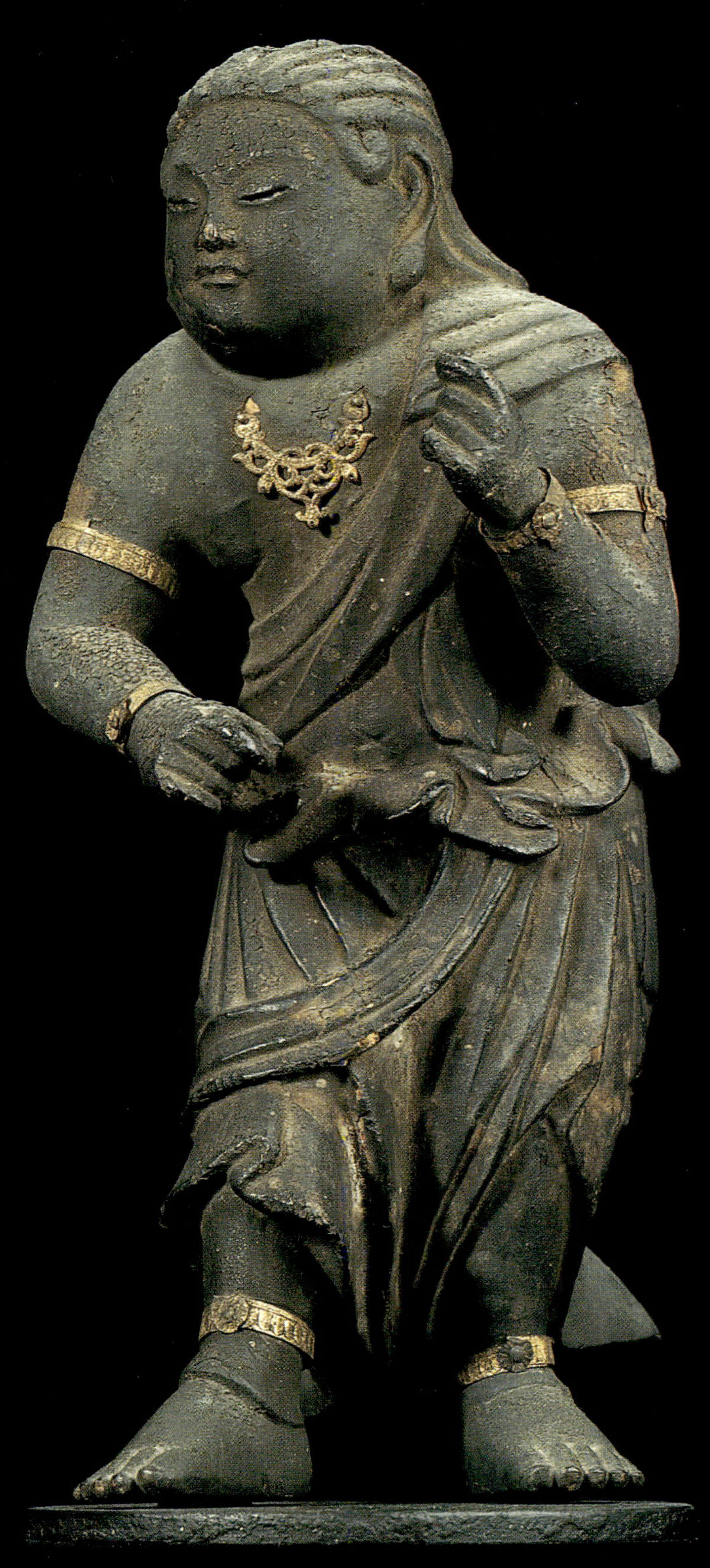

3

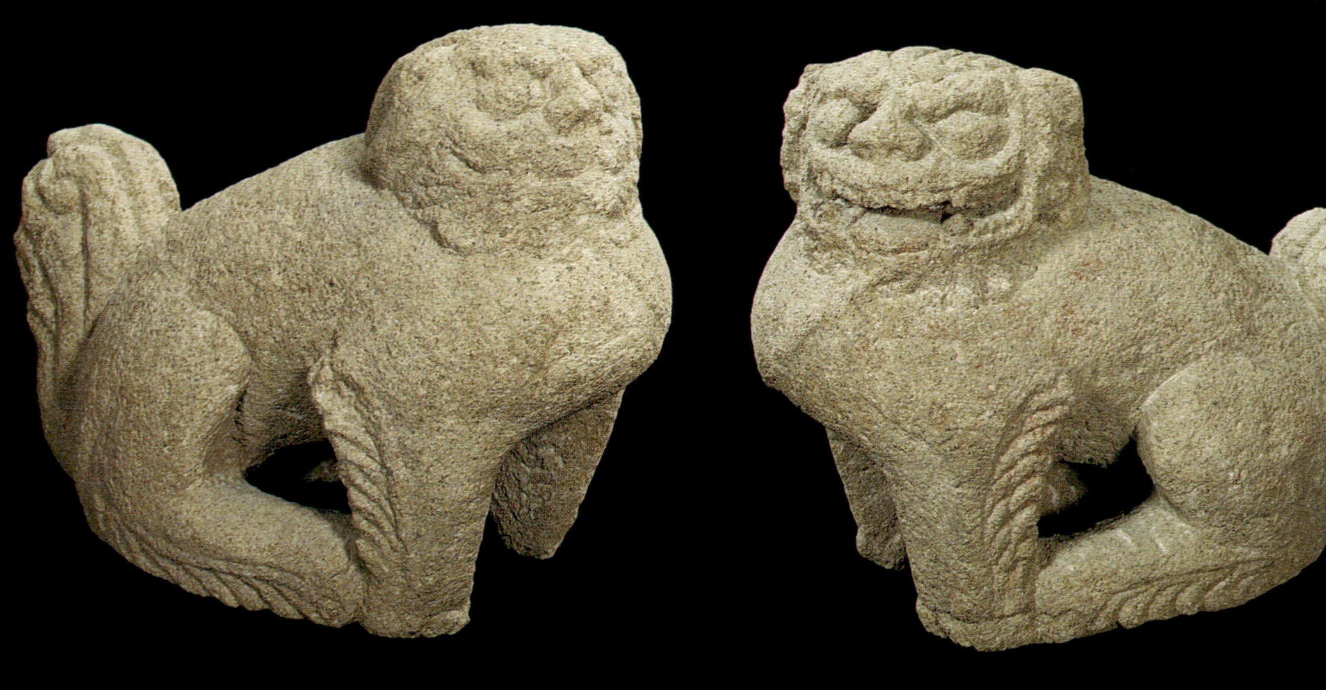

4

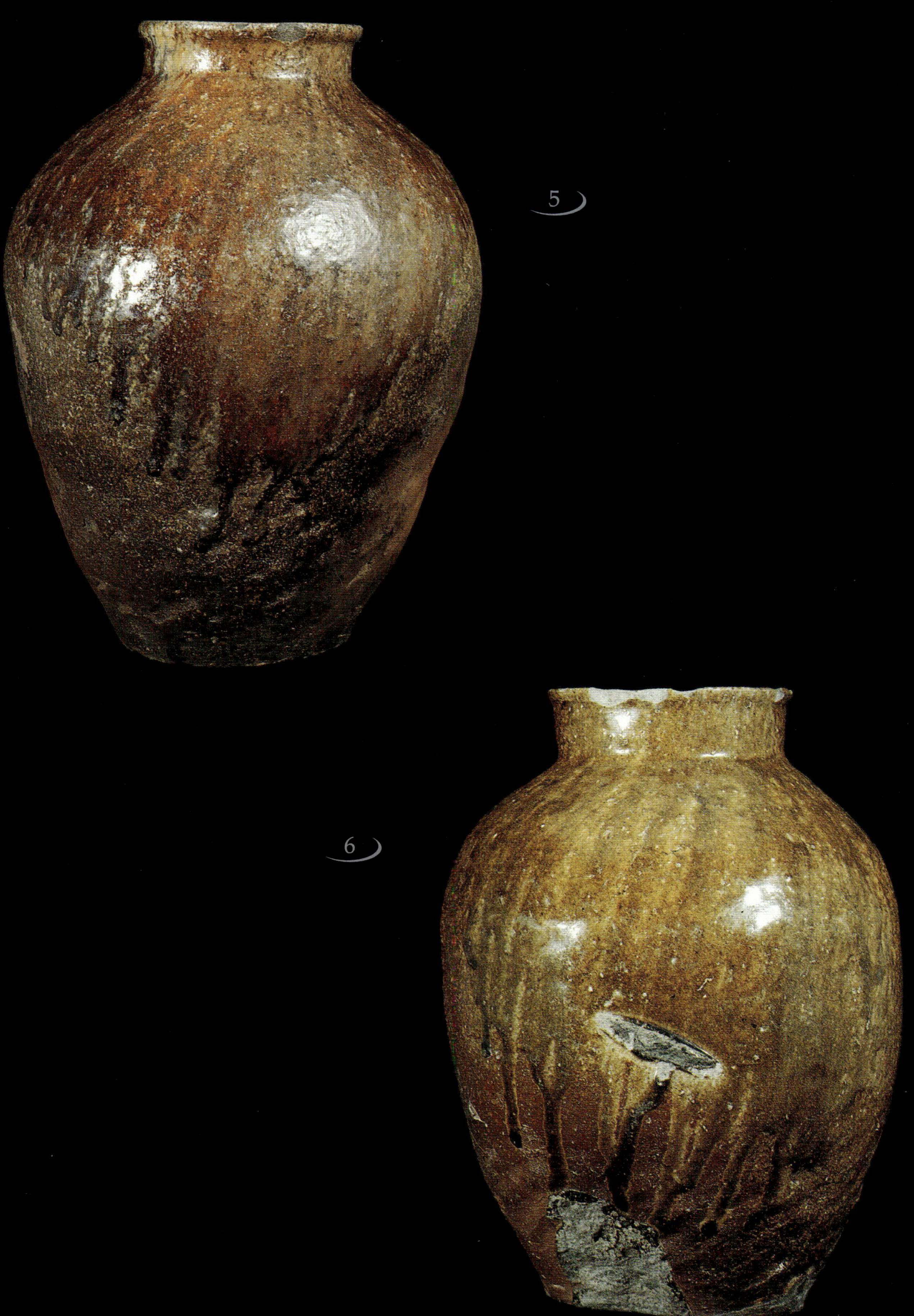

5

6

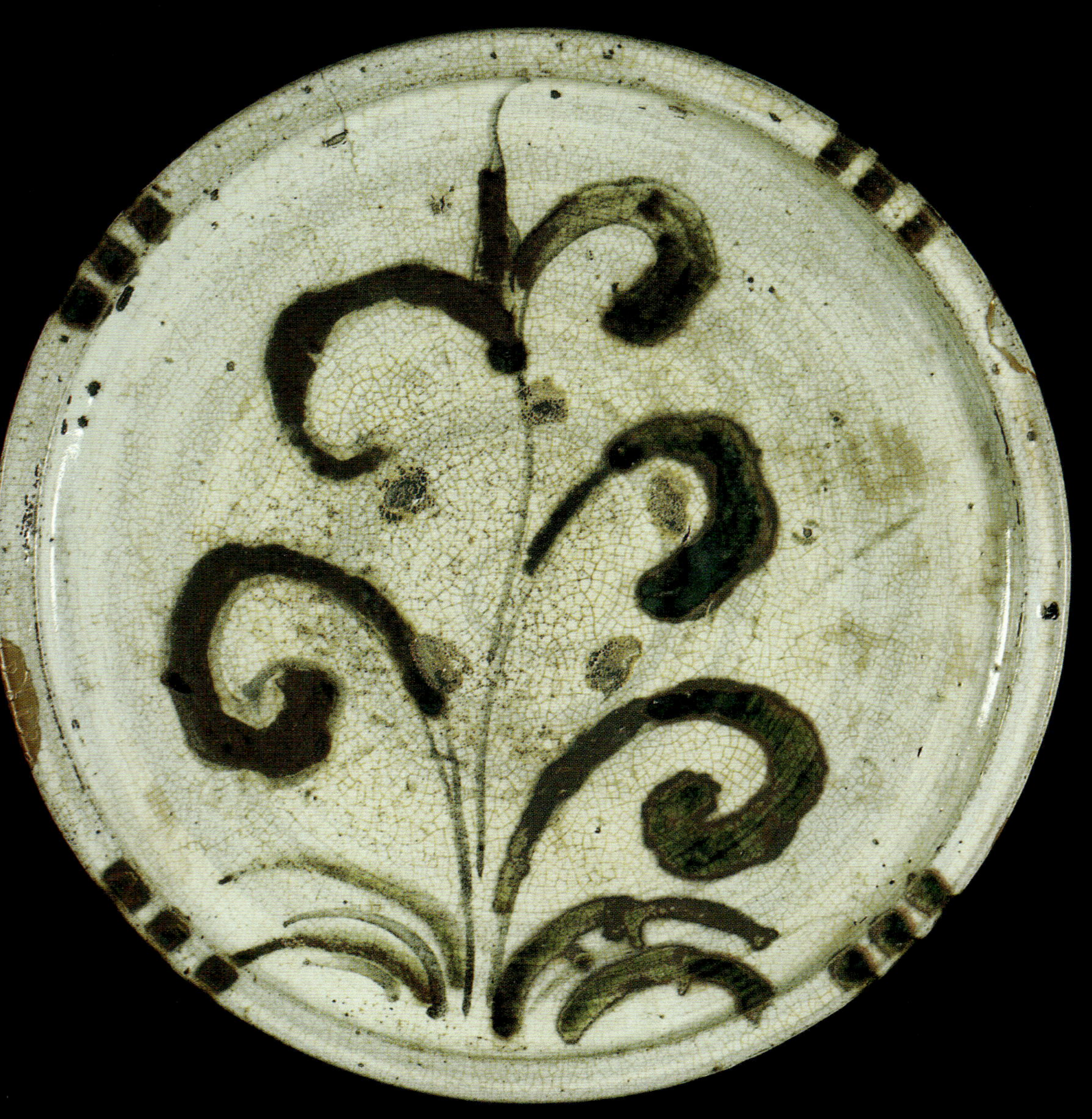

7

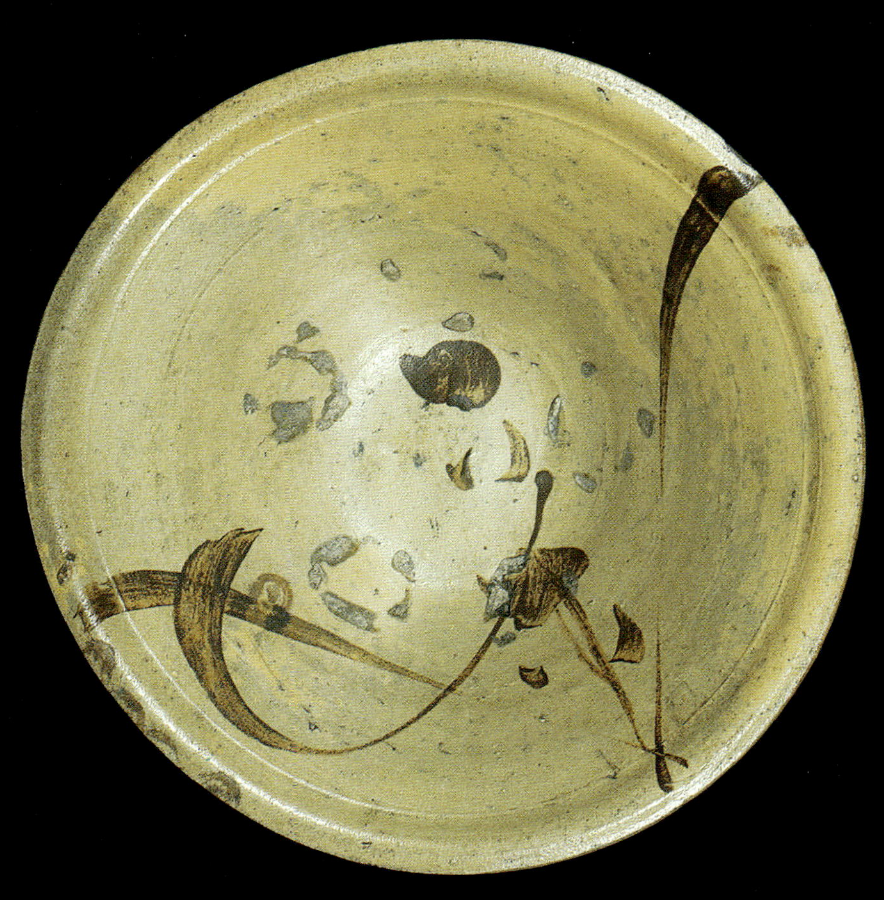
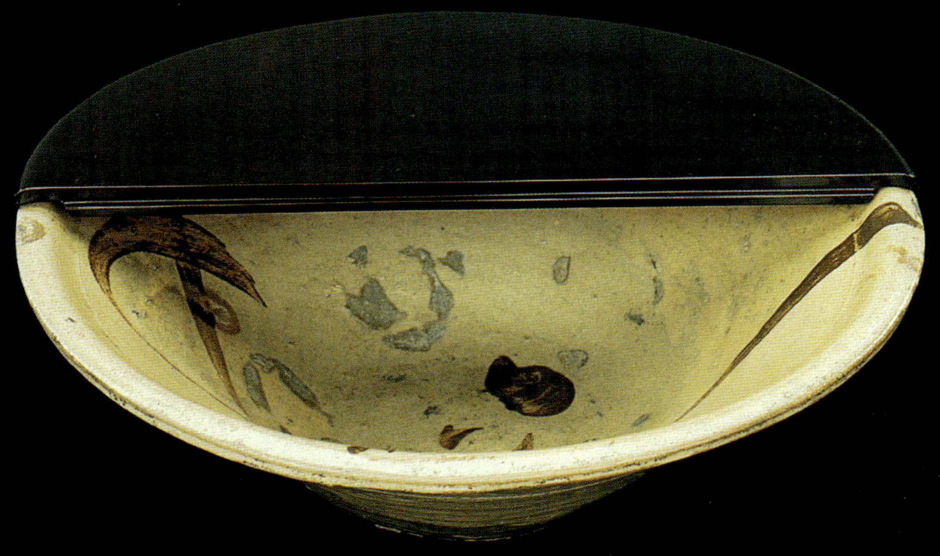

8

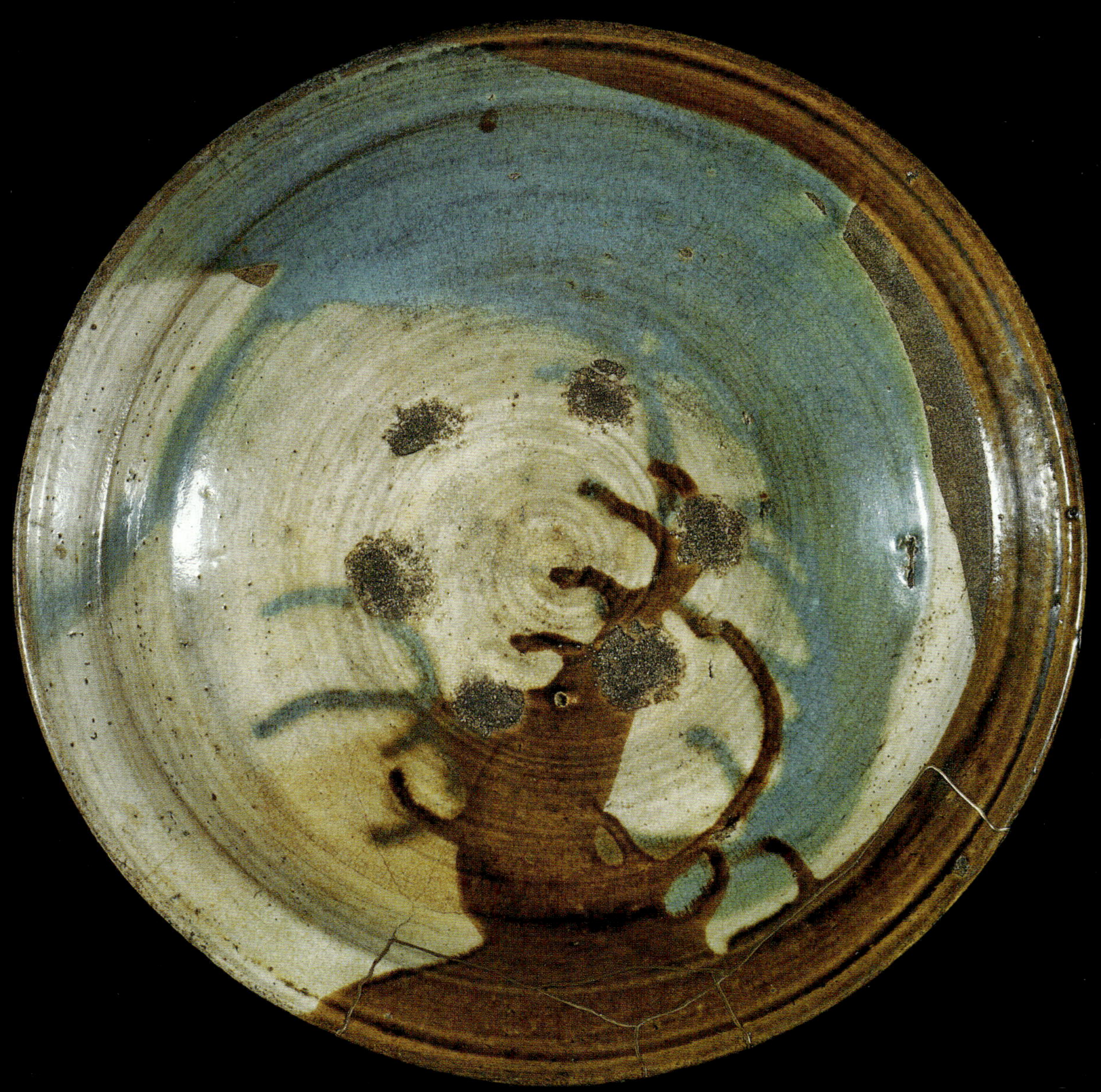

9

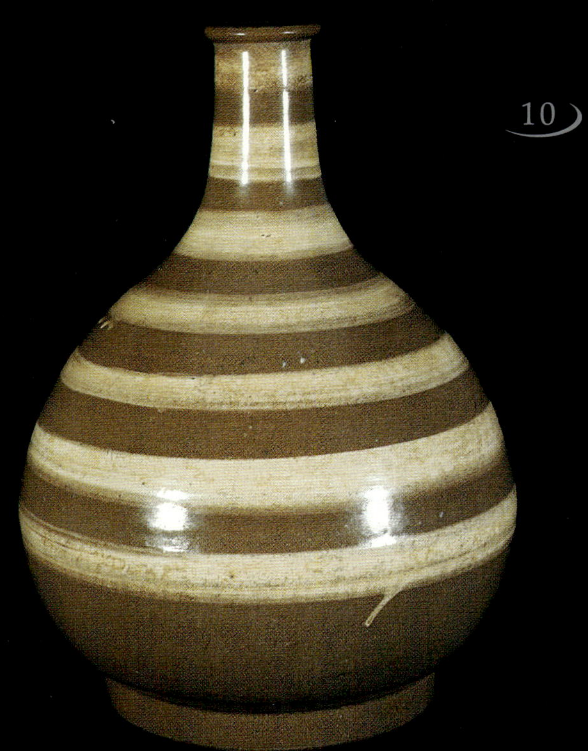

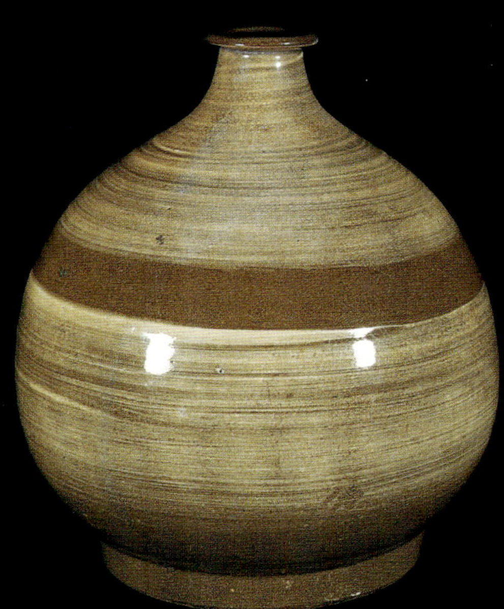

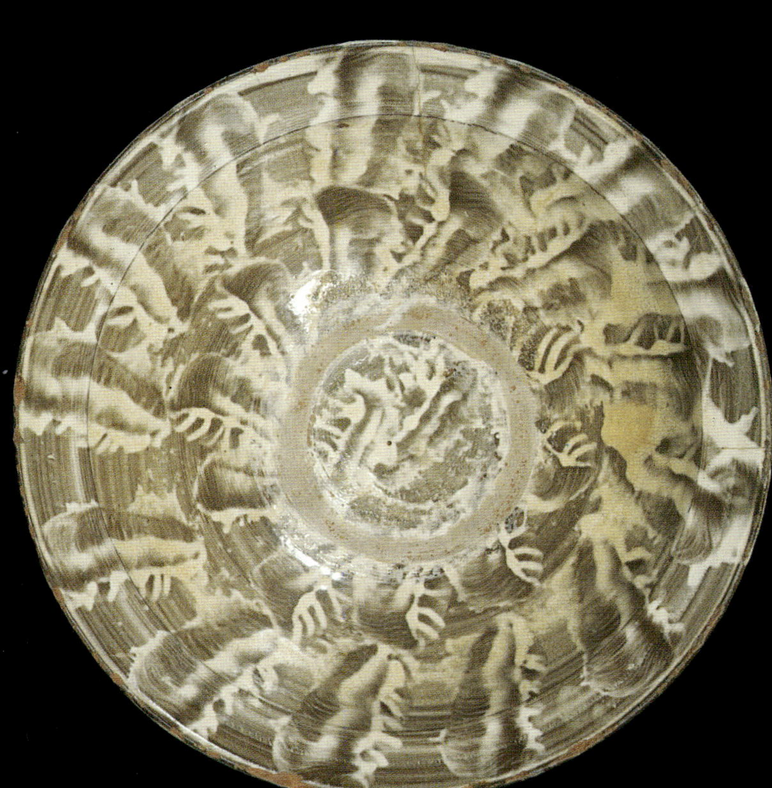

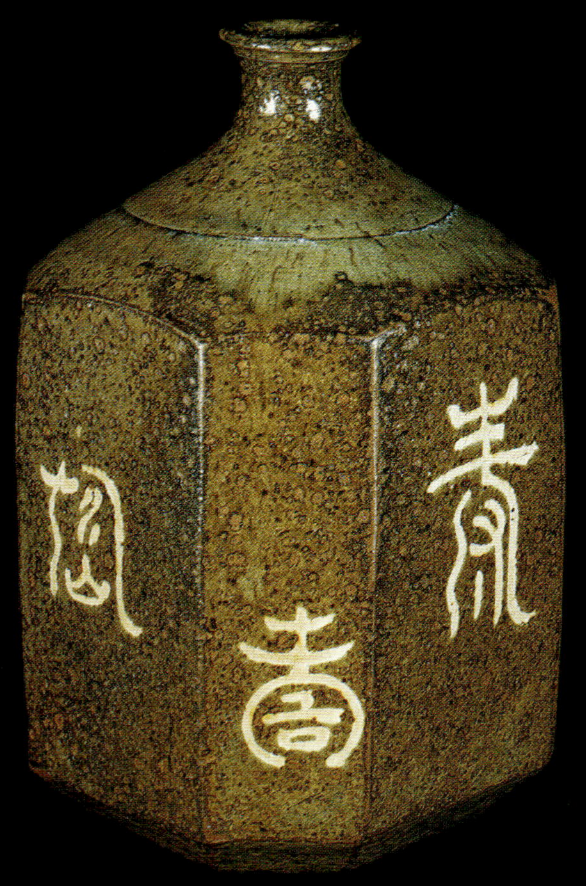

13

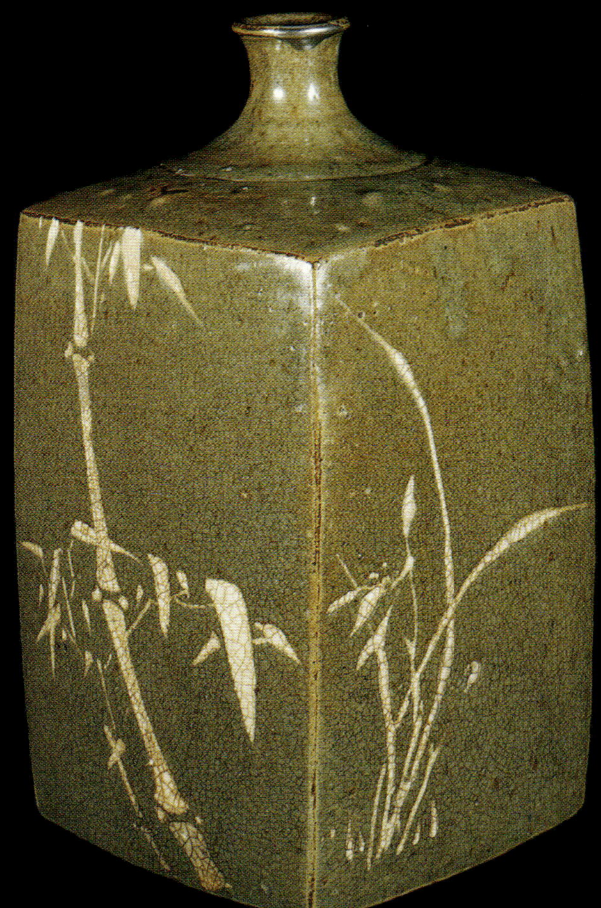

14

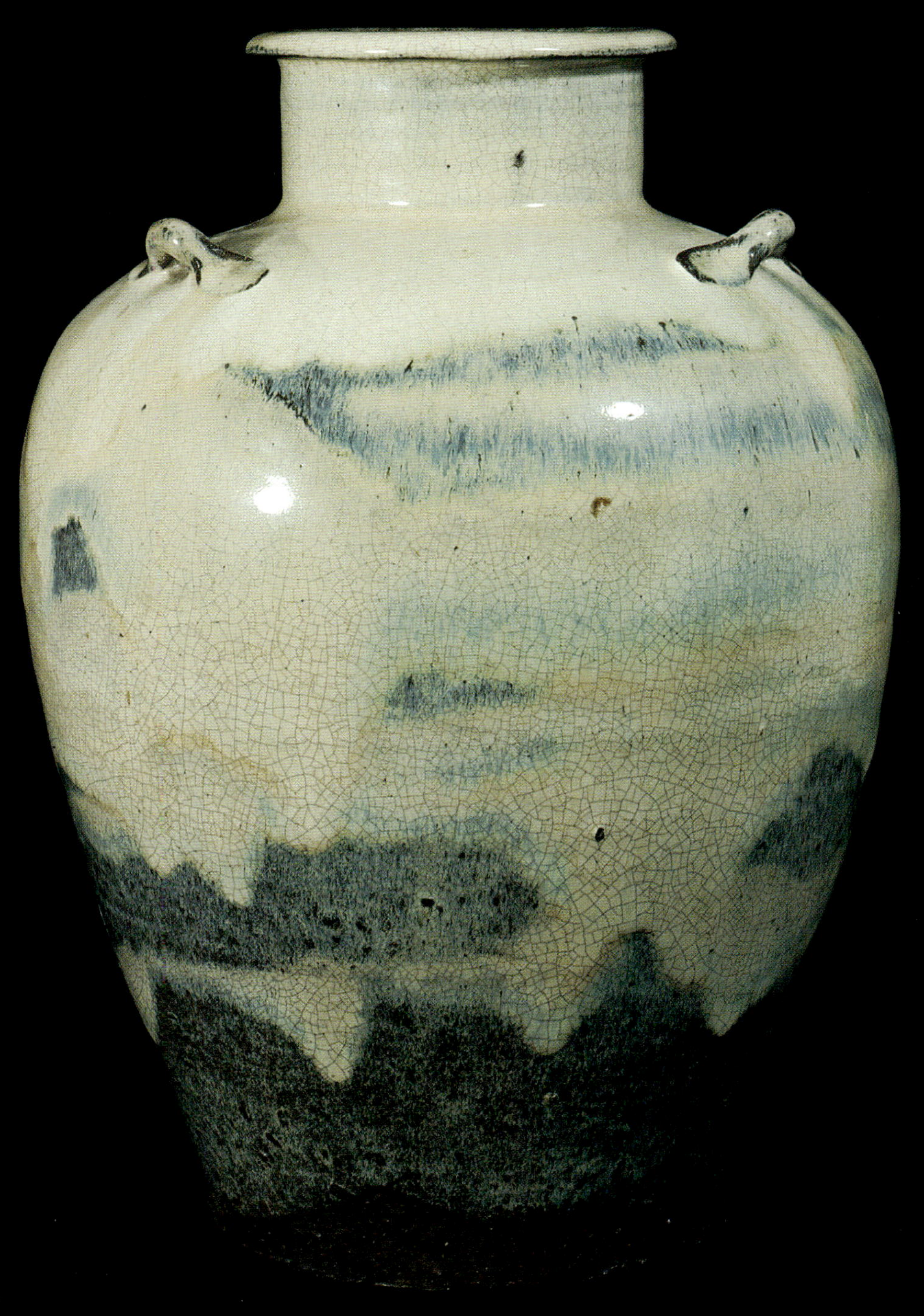

15

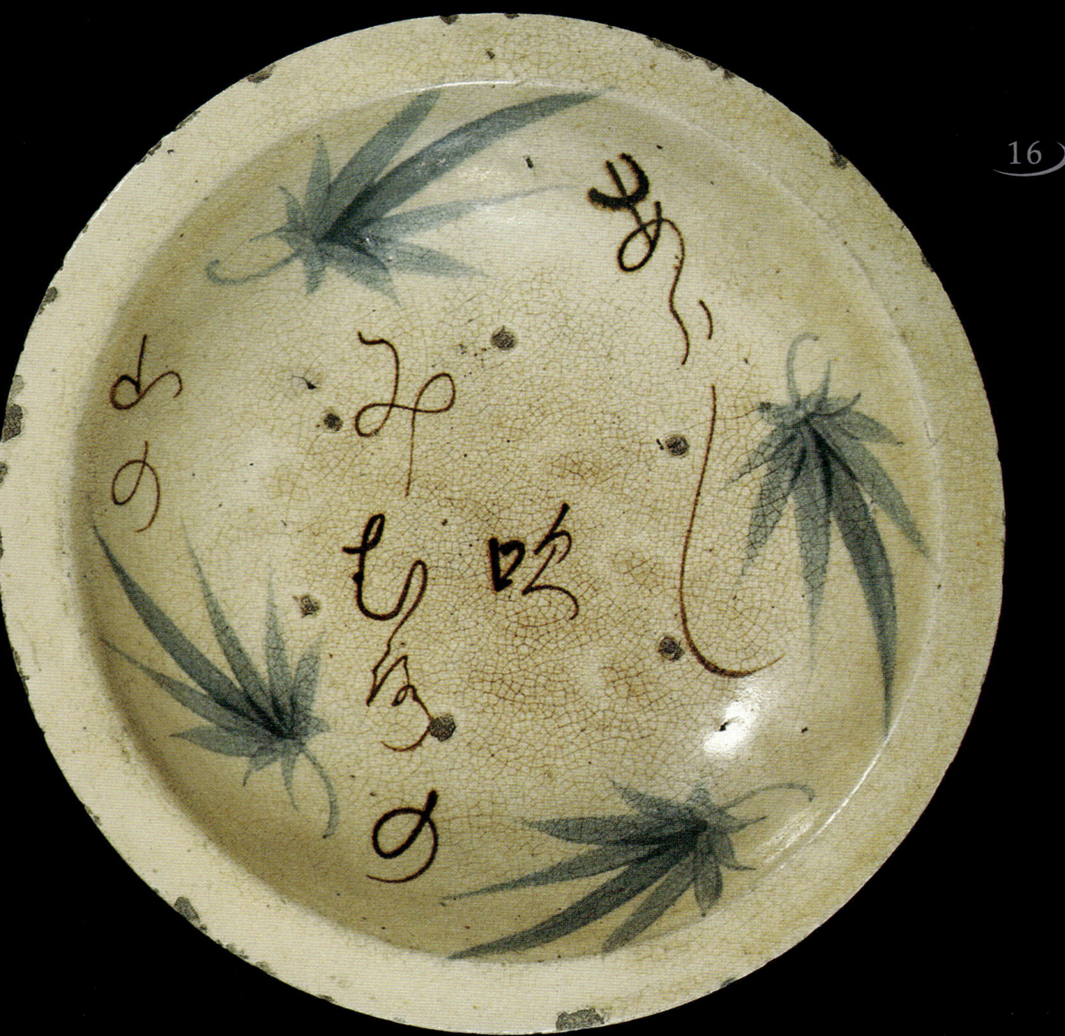

16

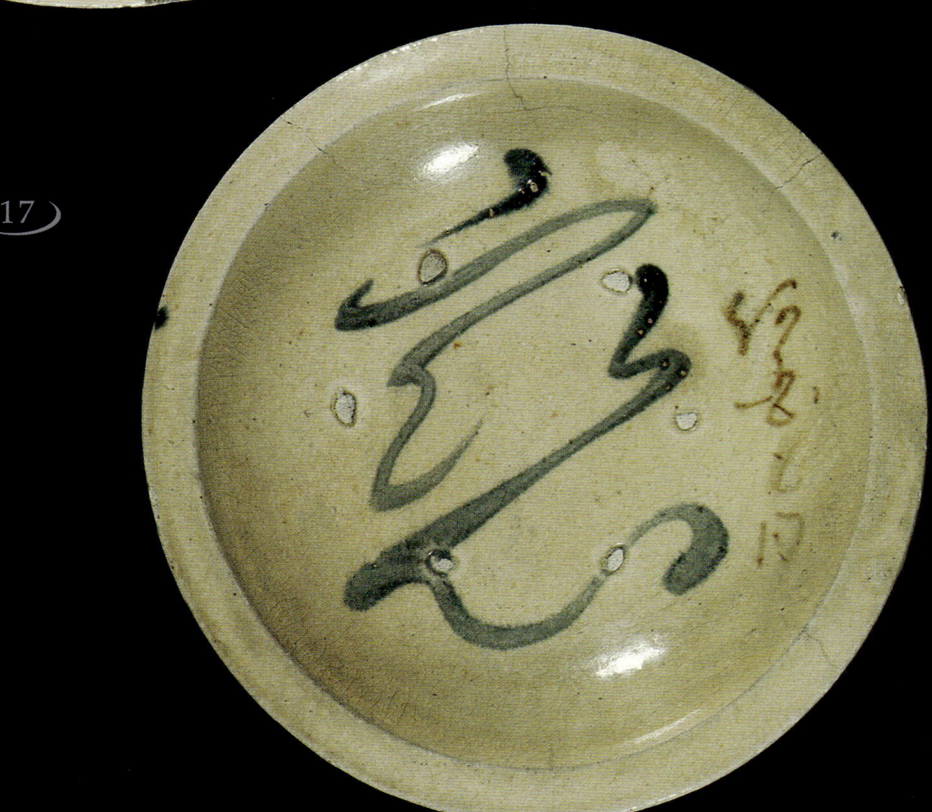

17

24

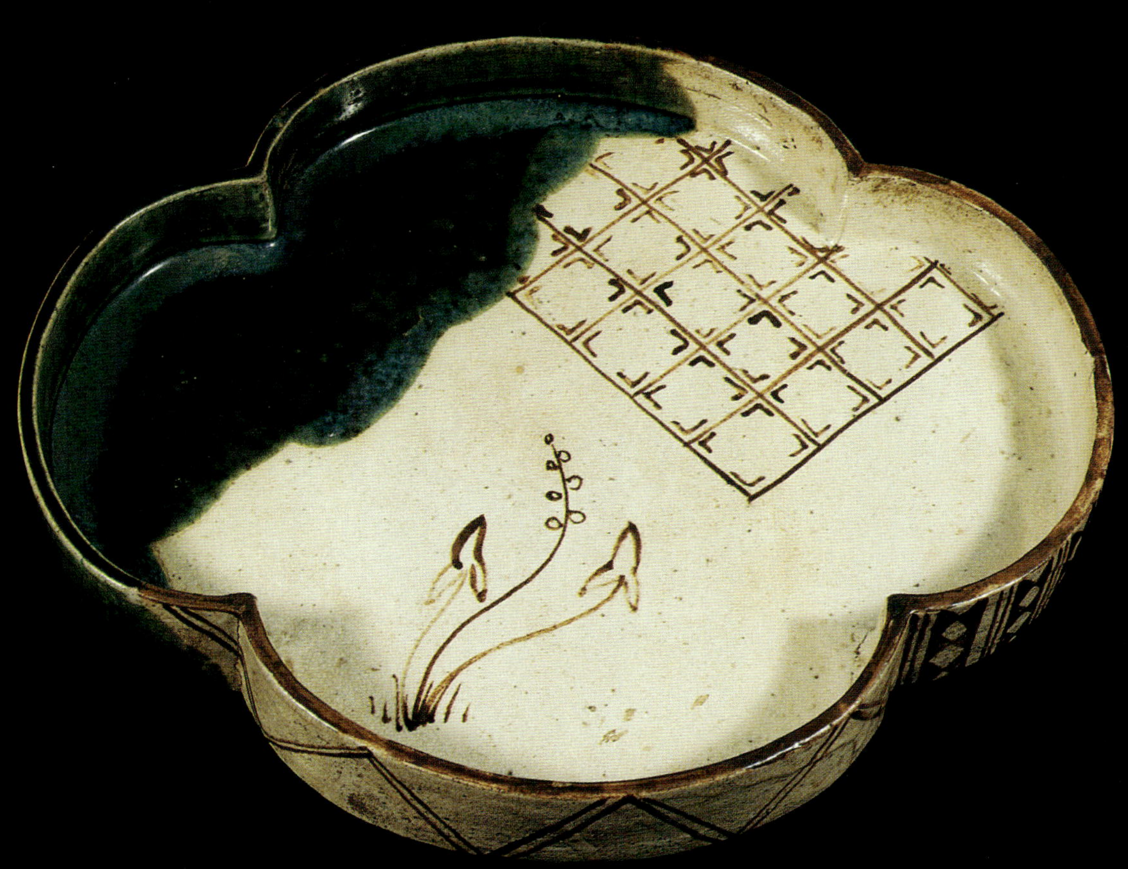

18

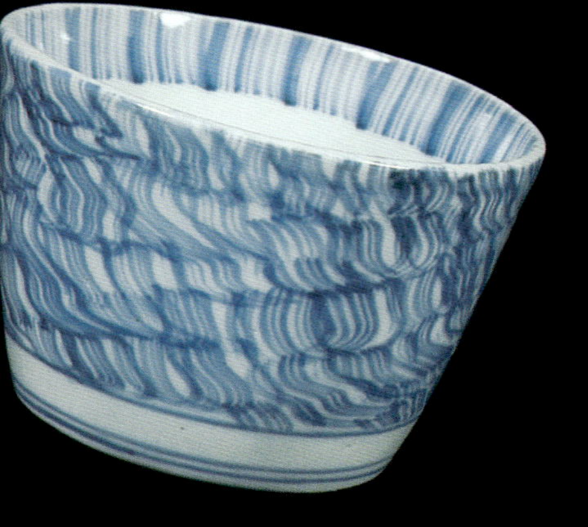
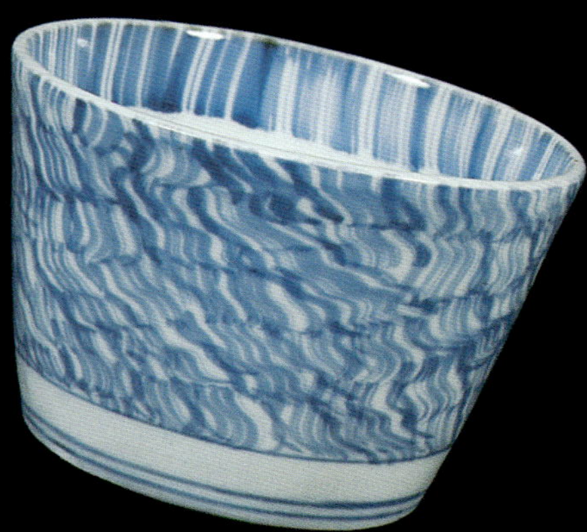
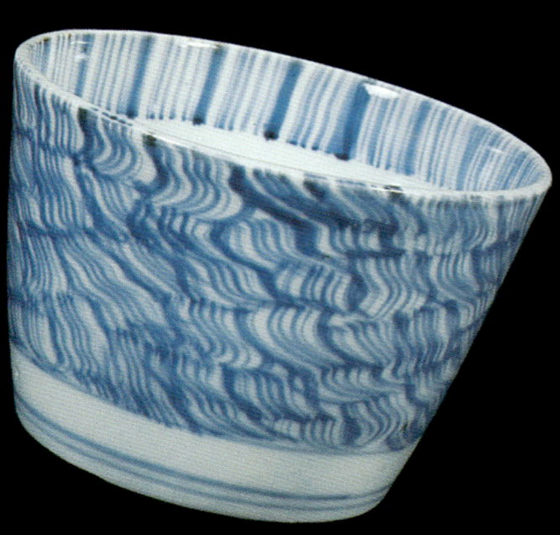
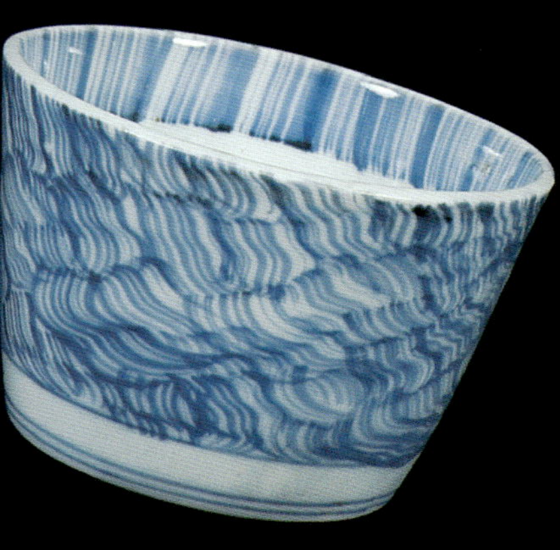
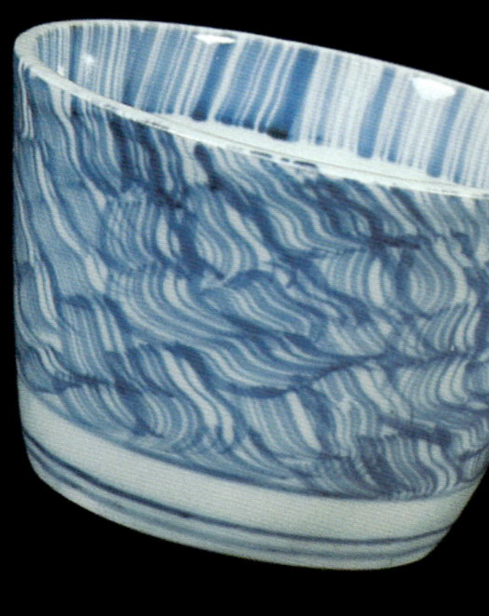

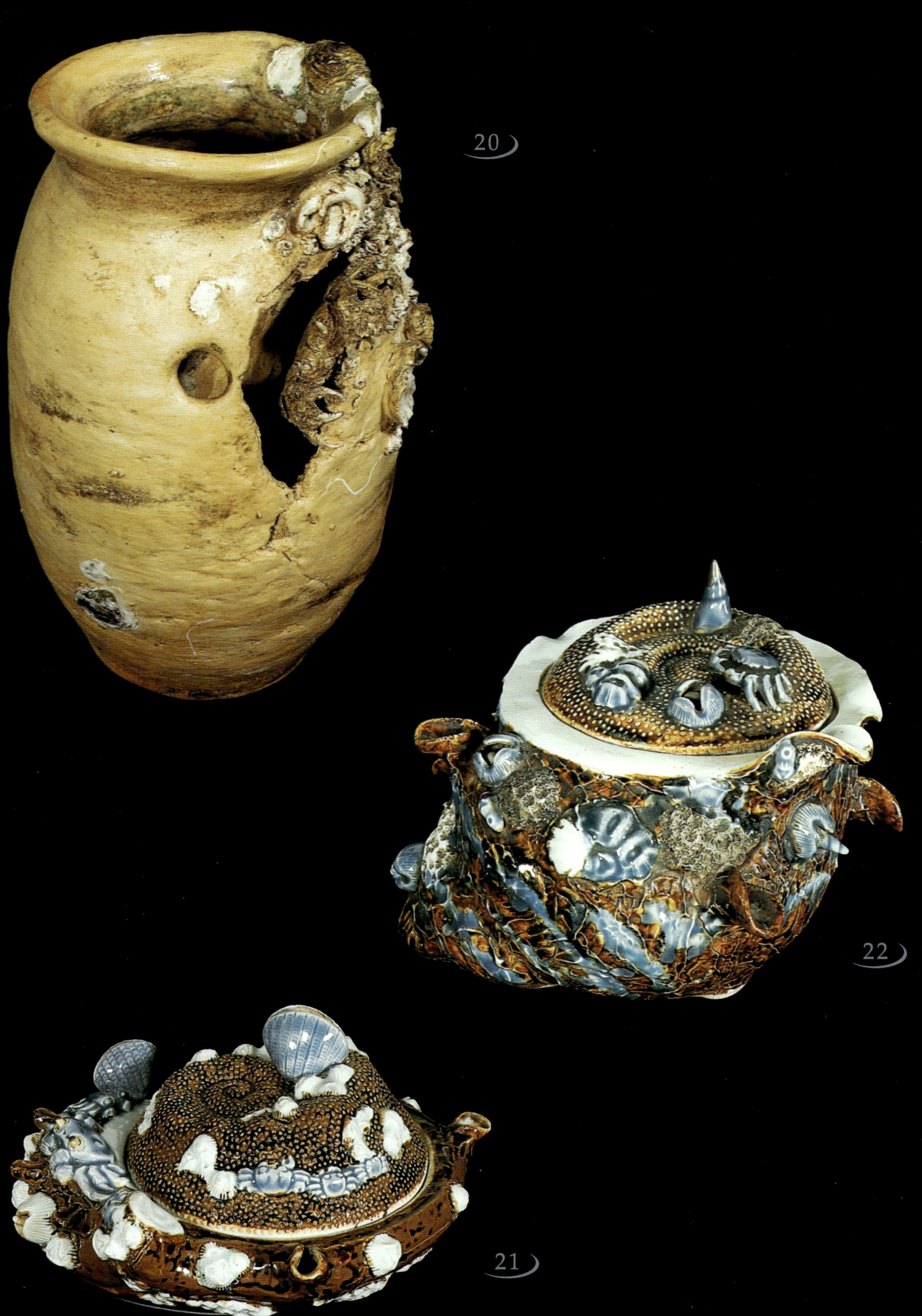

20

22

21

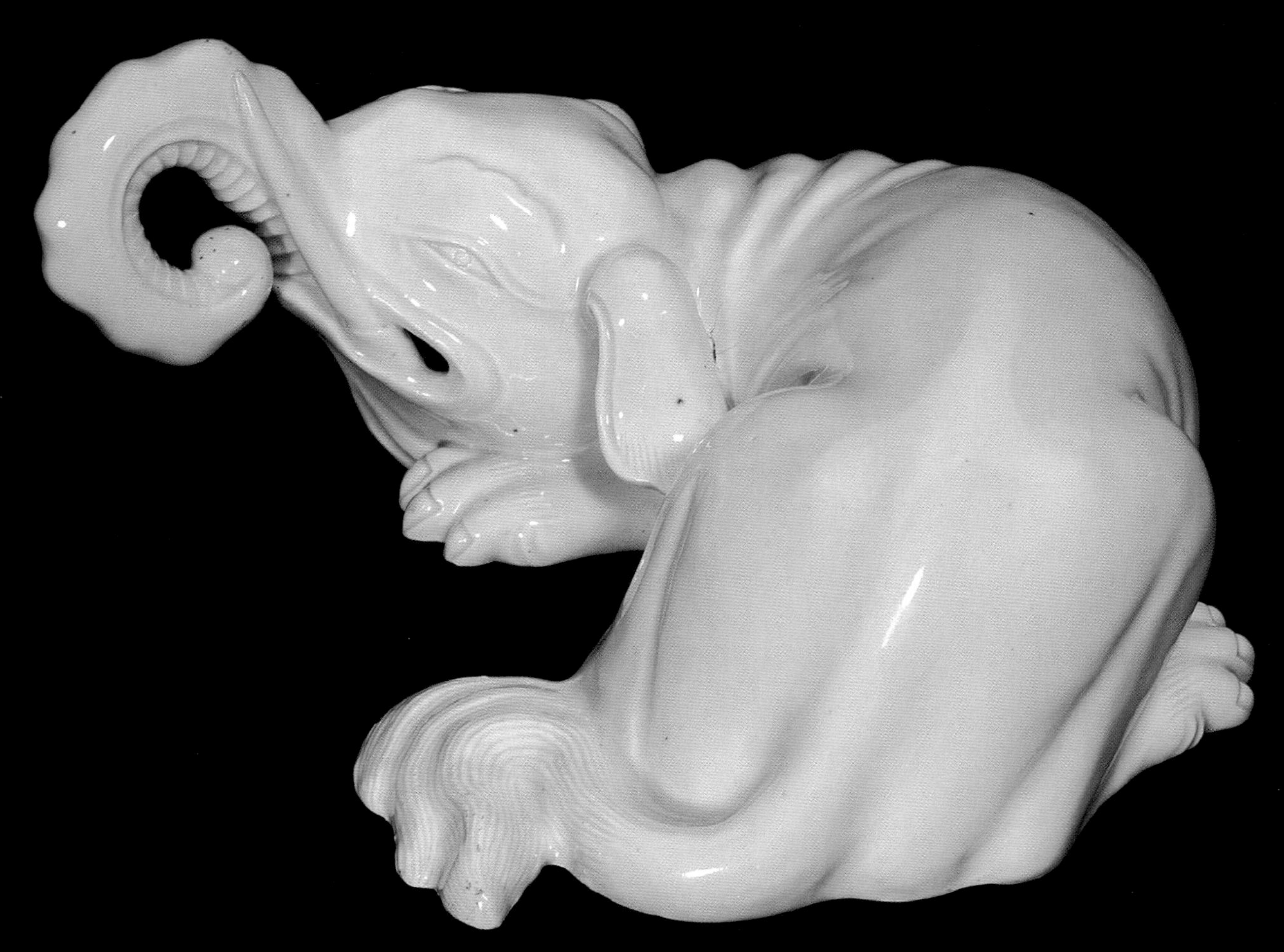

23

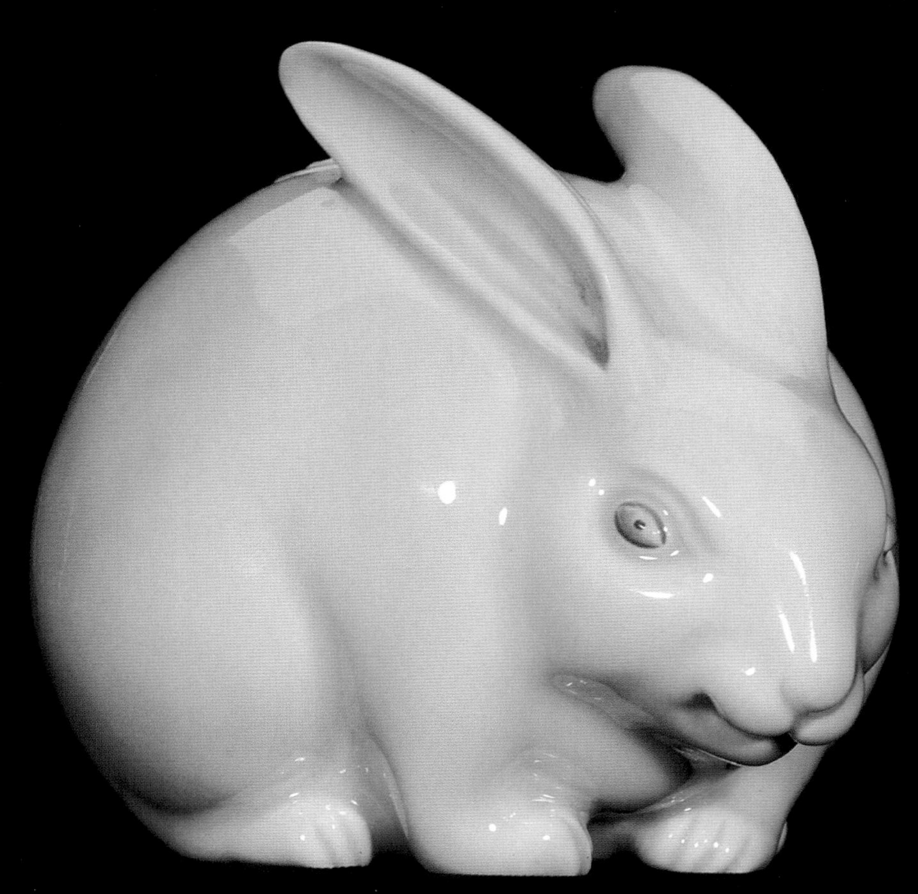

24

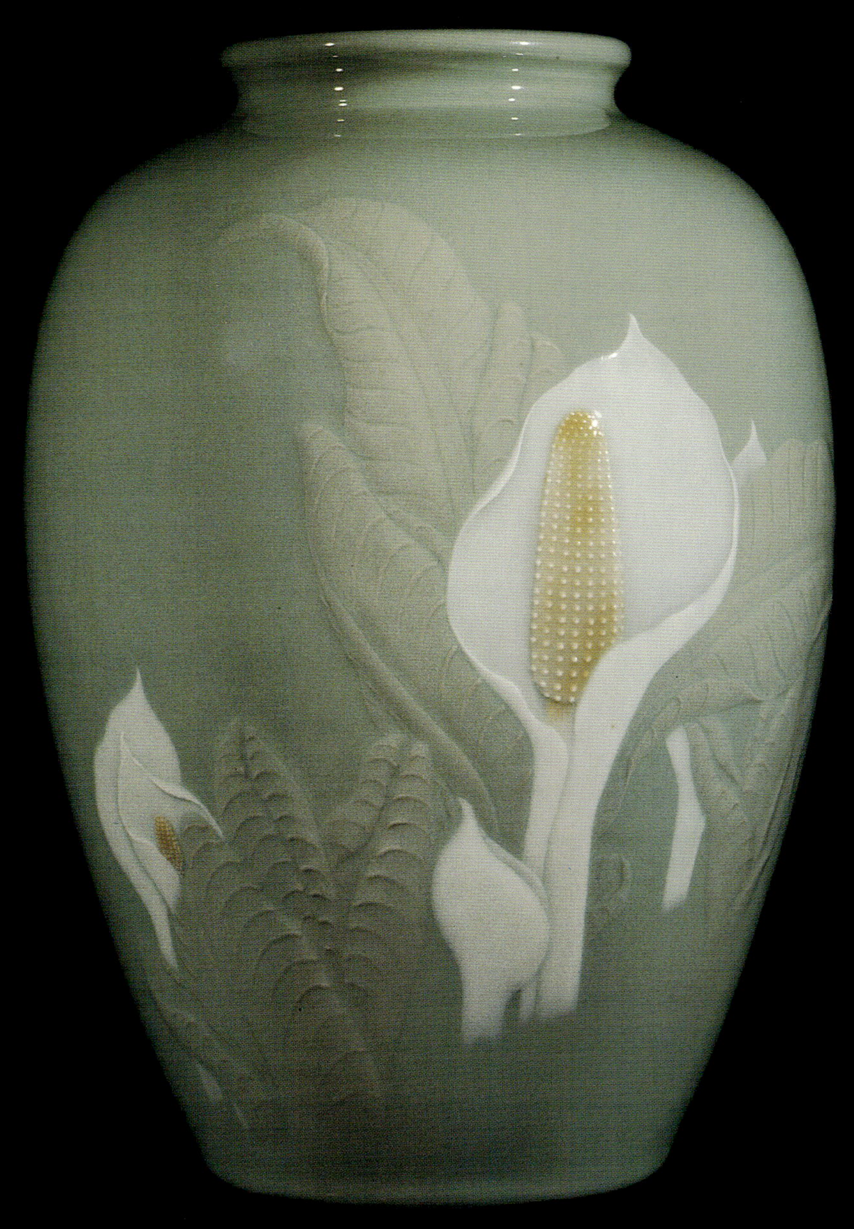

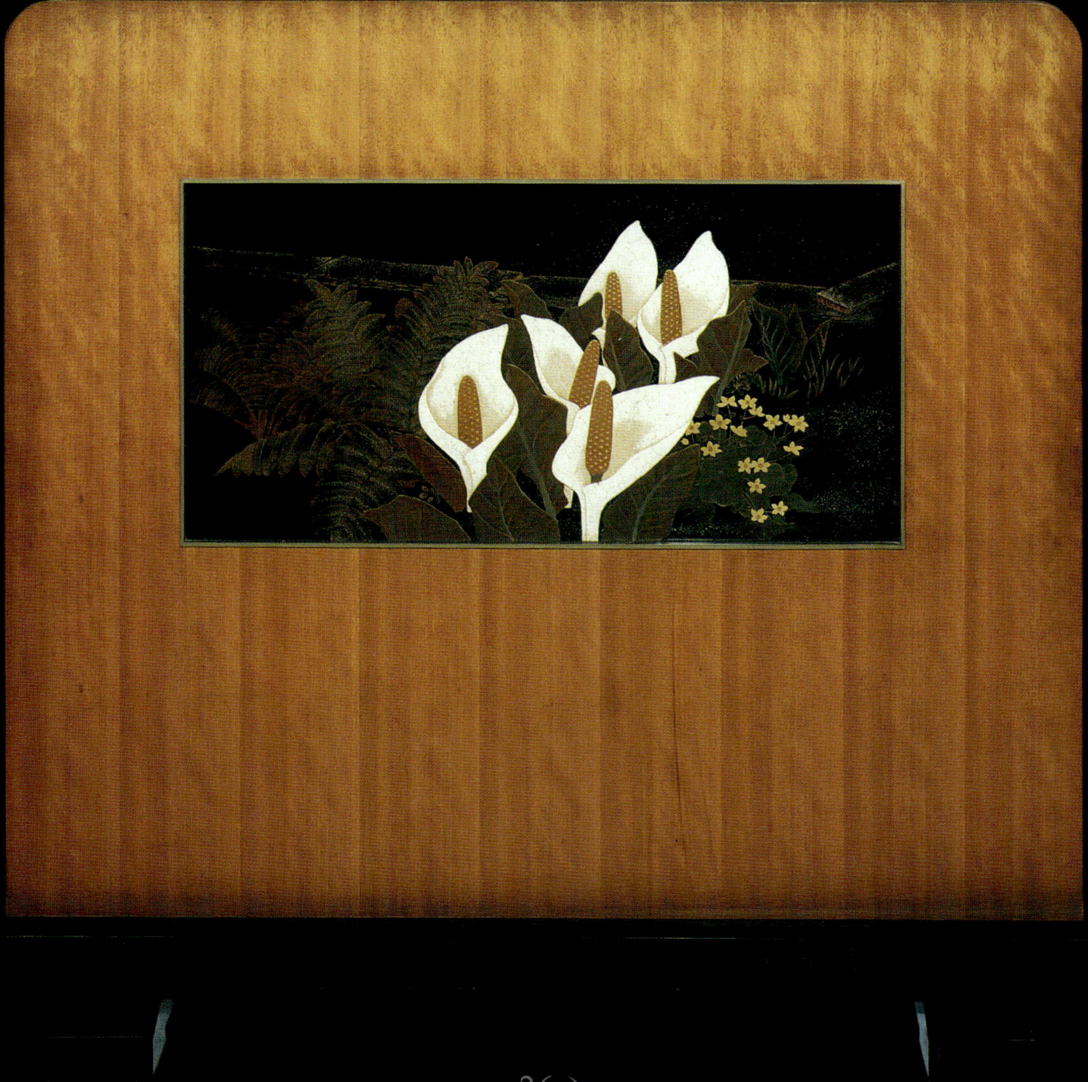

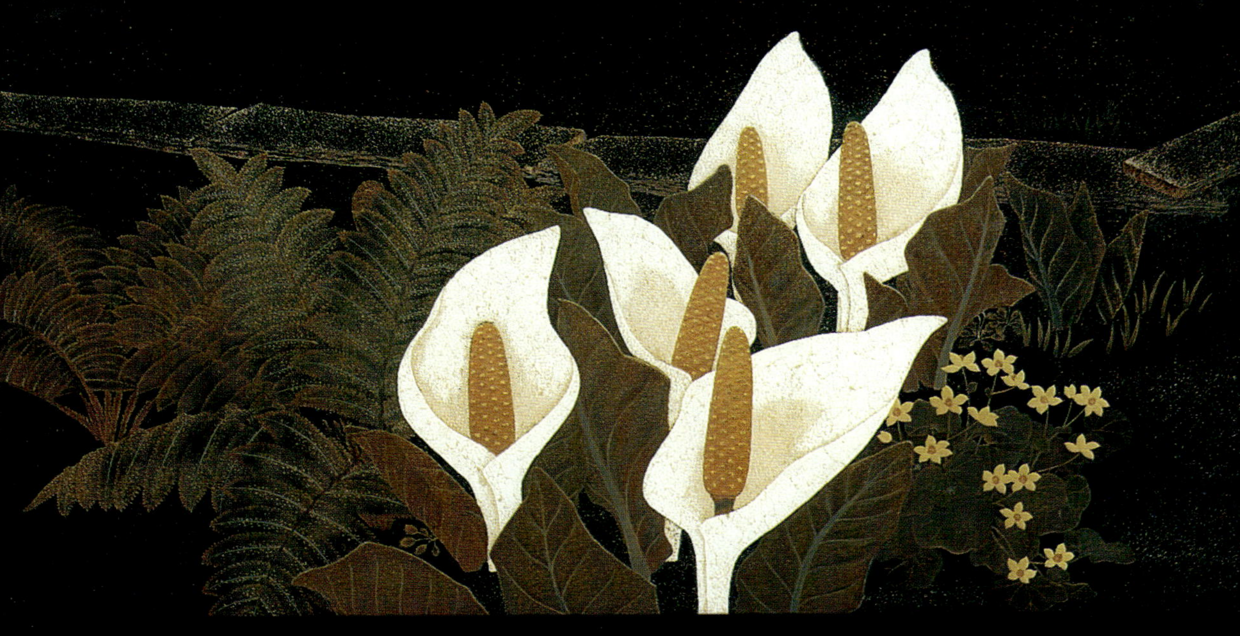

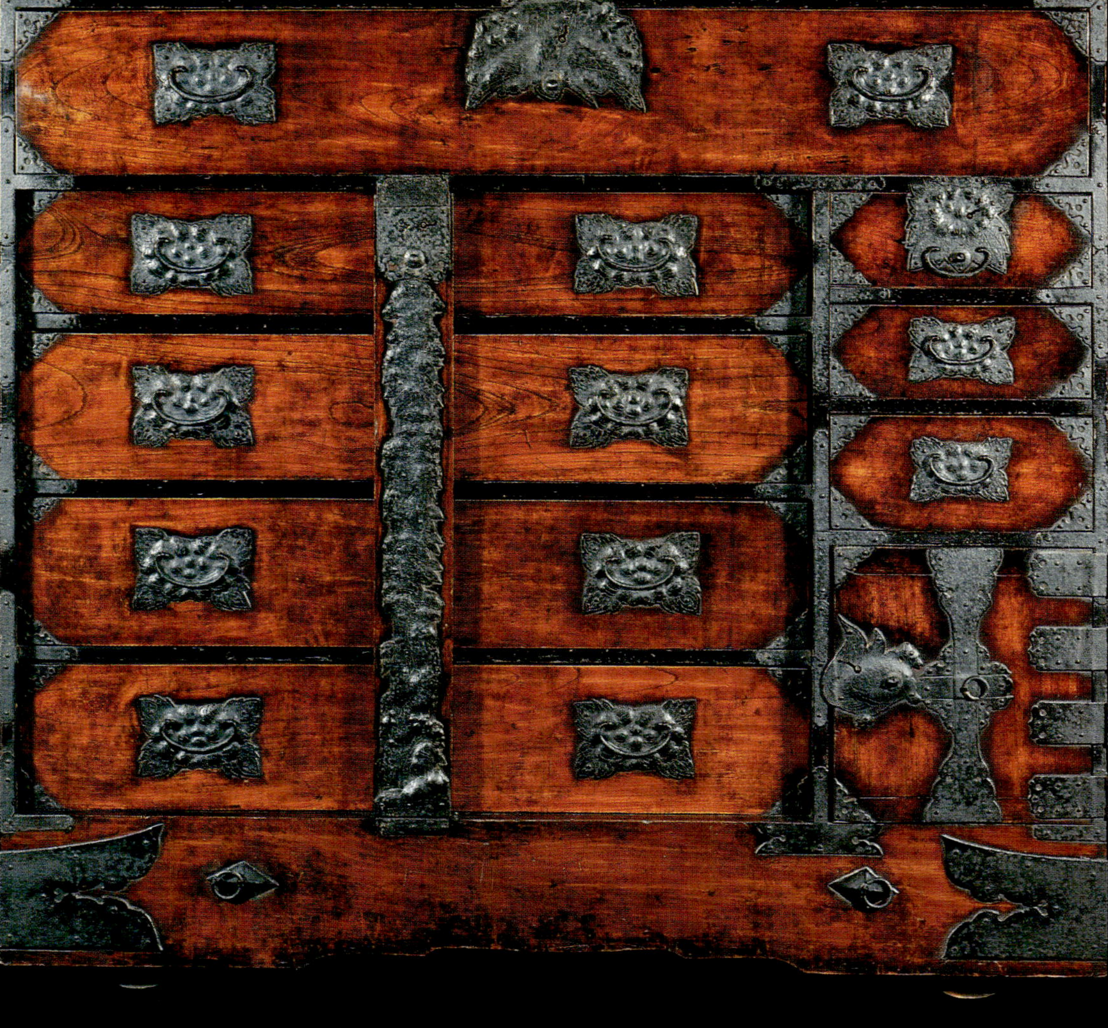

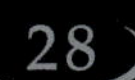

28

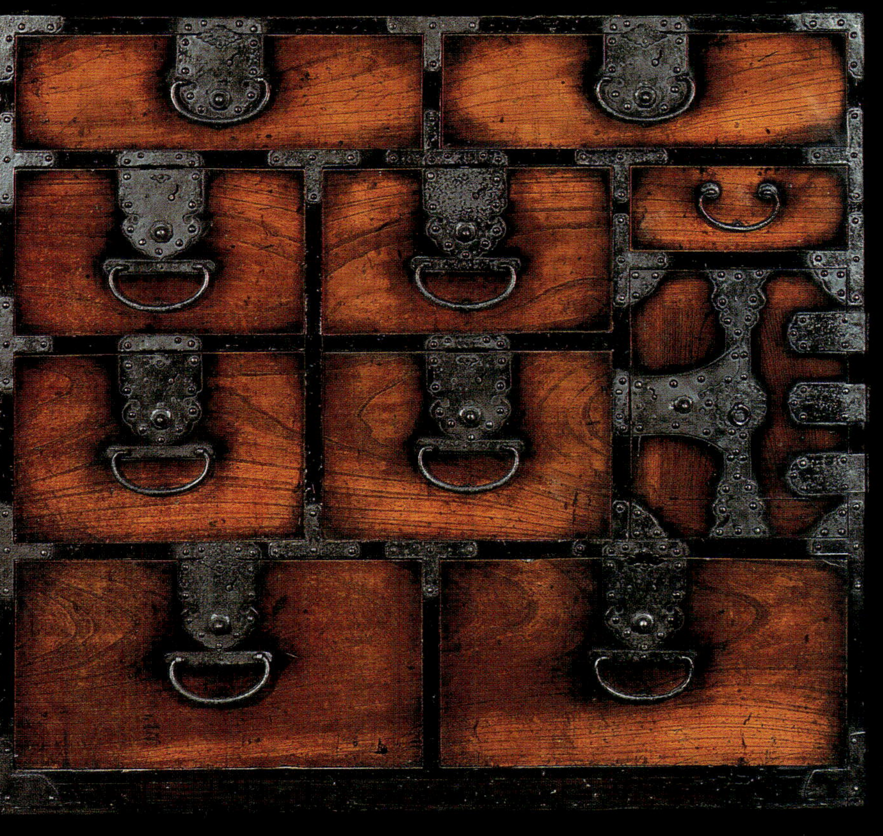

29

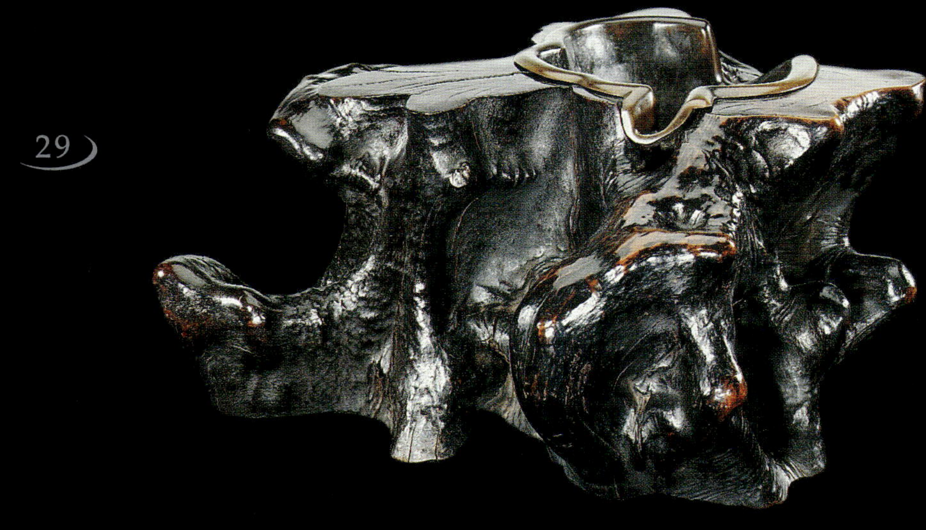

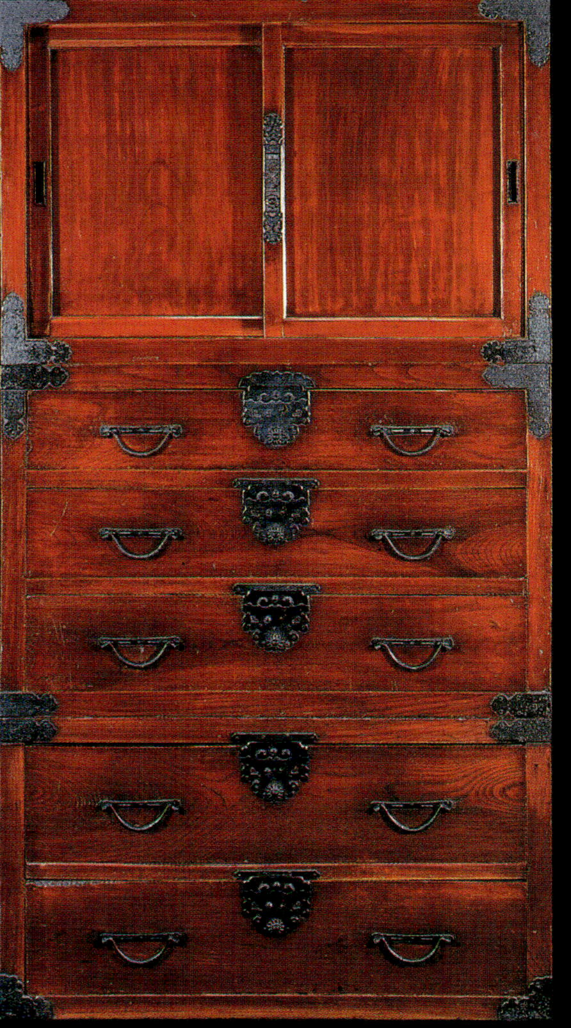

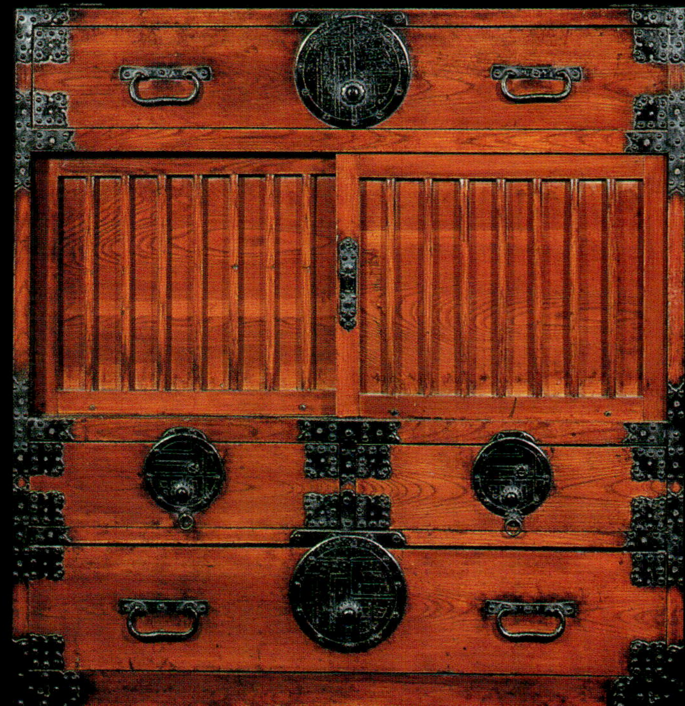

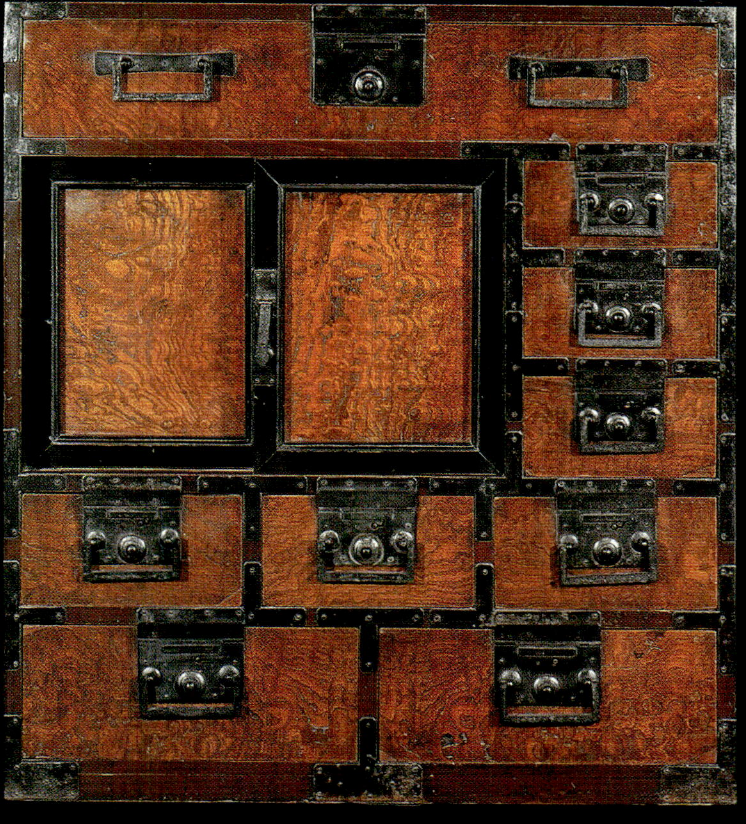

32

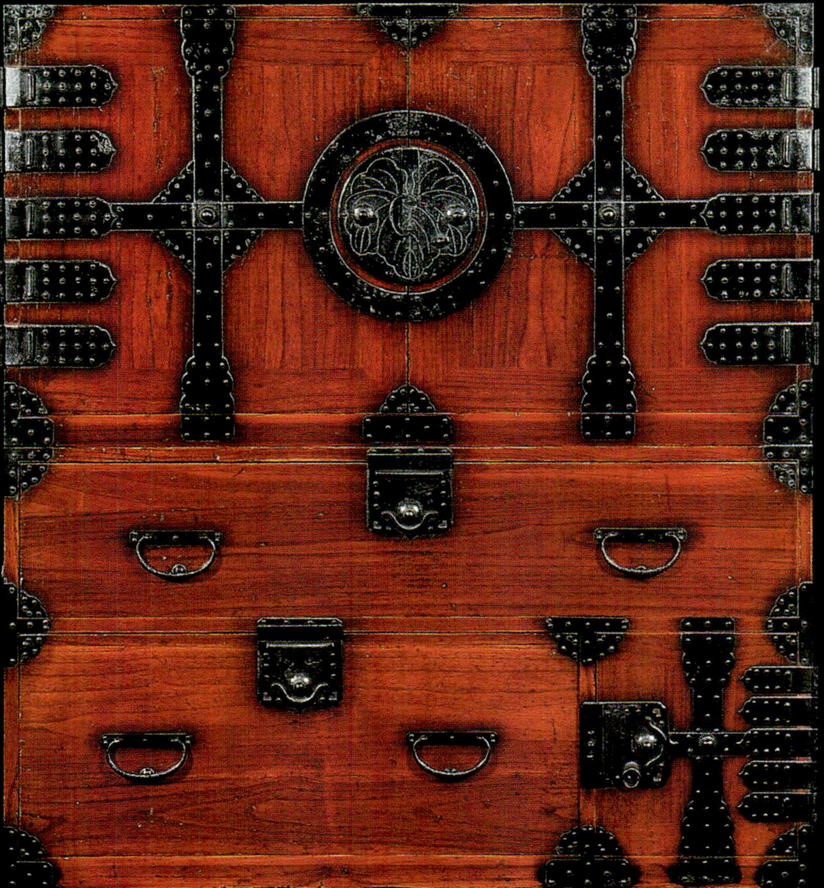

33

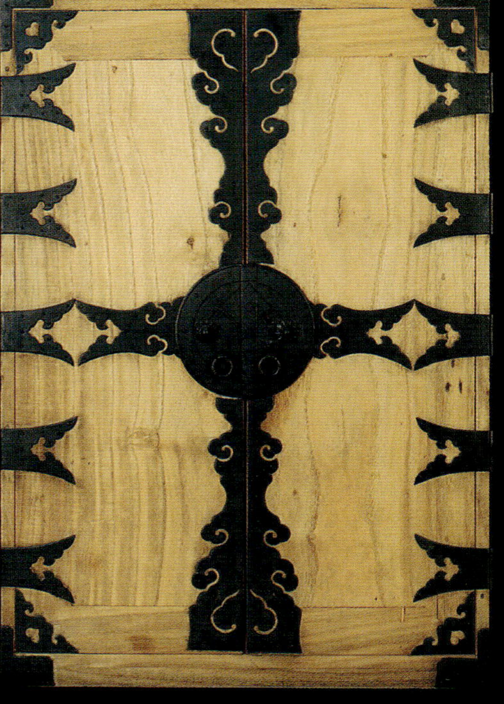

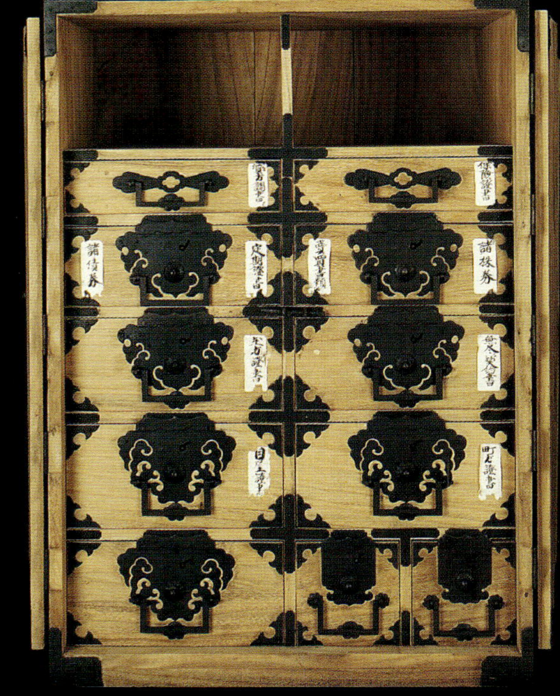

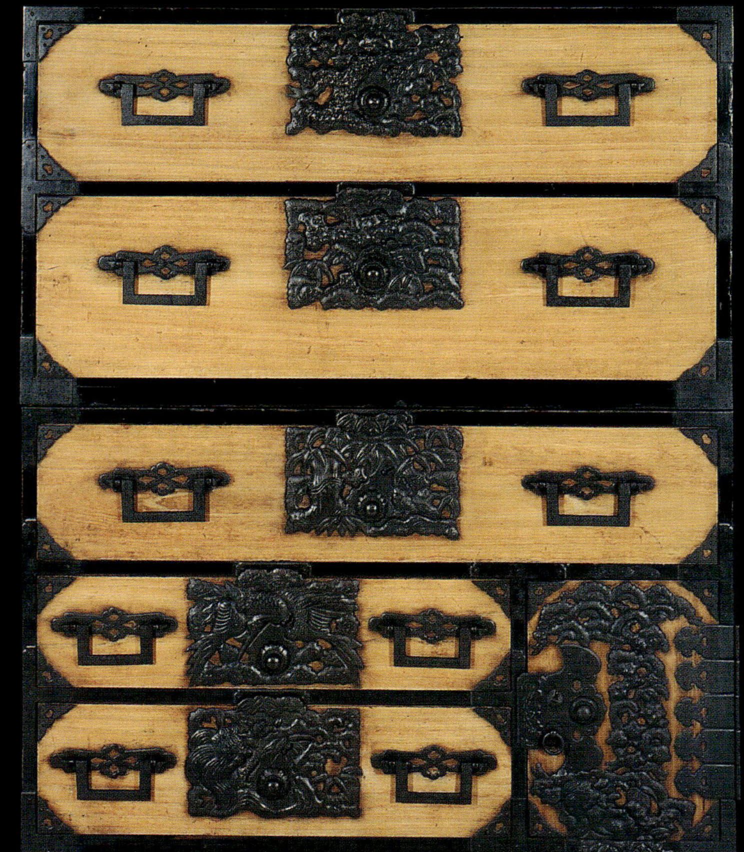

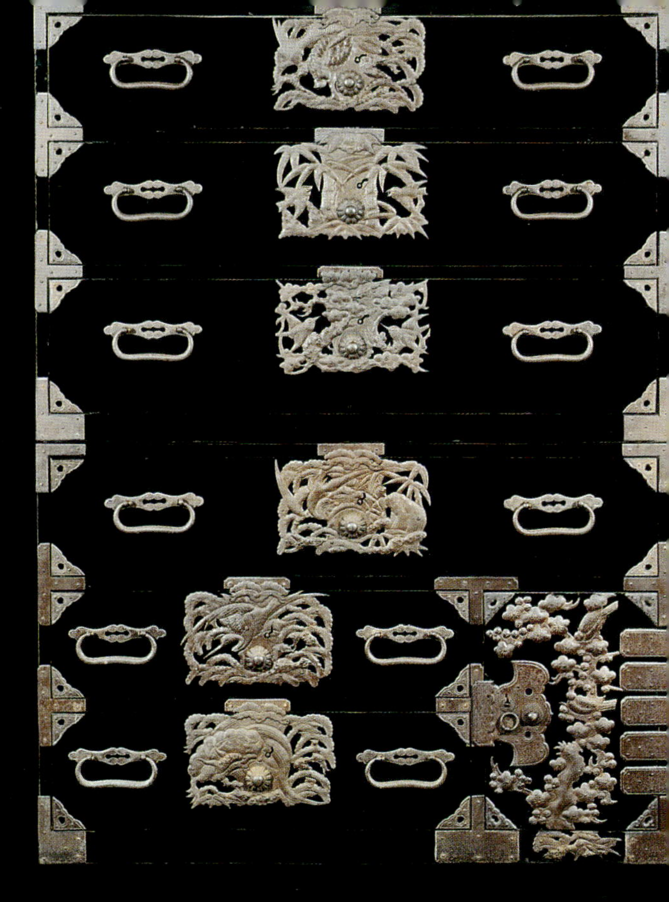

37

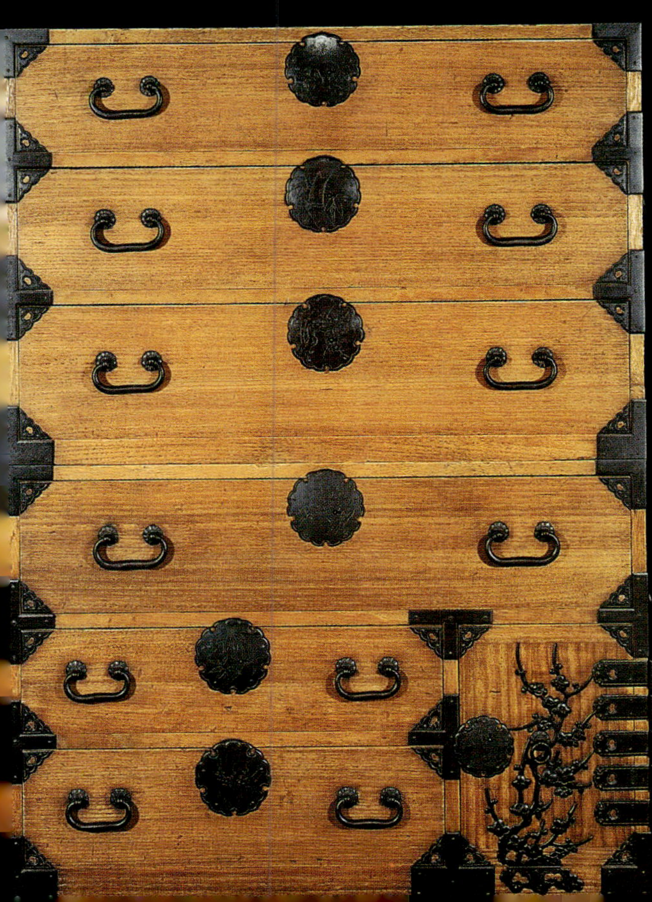

36

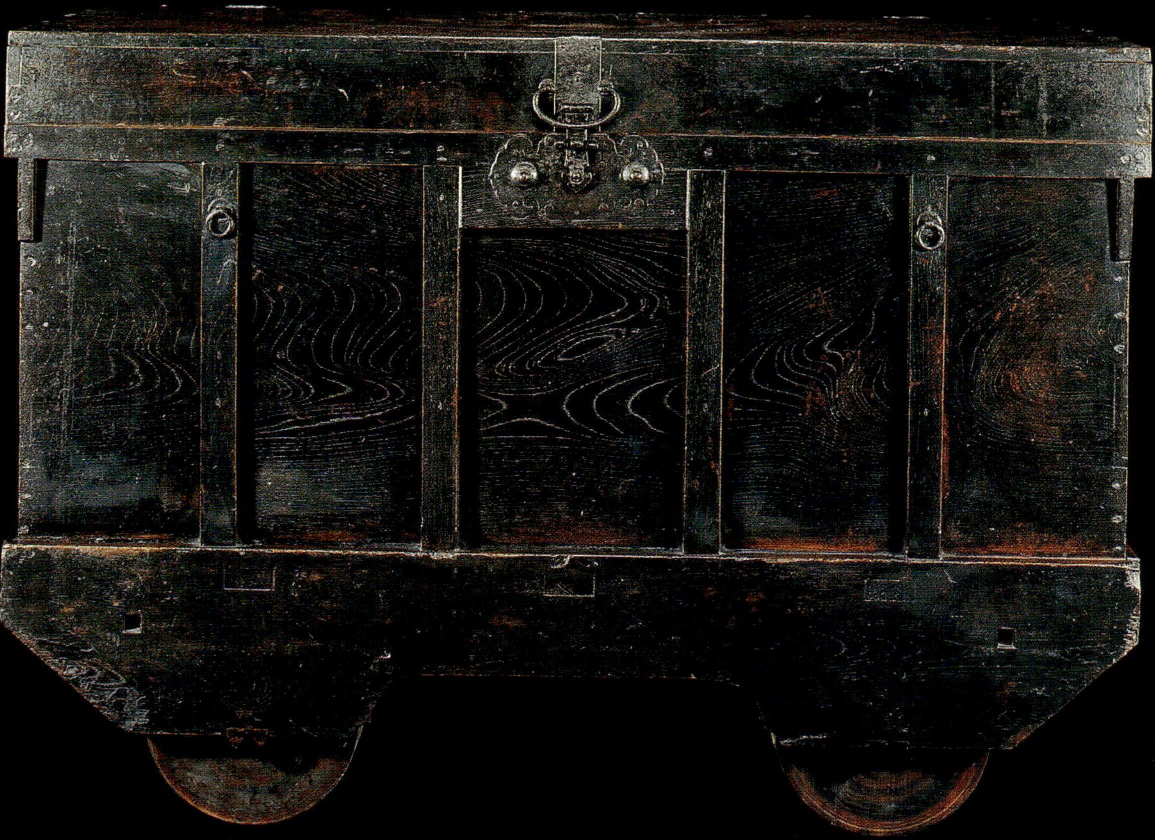

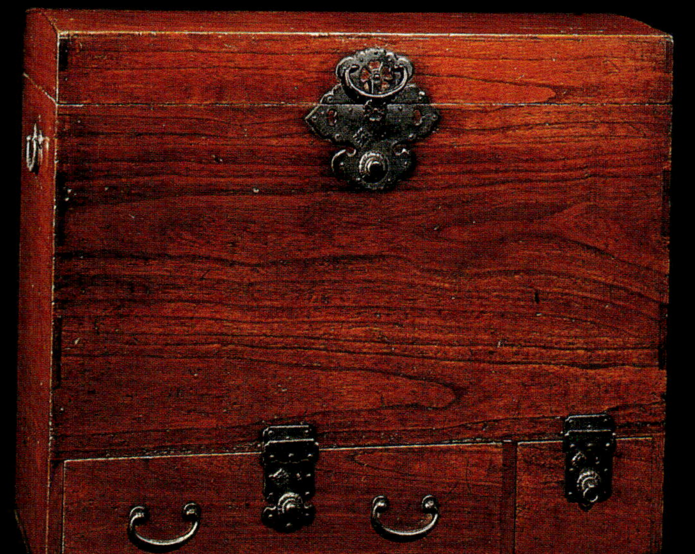

38

39

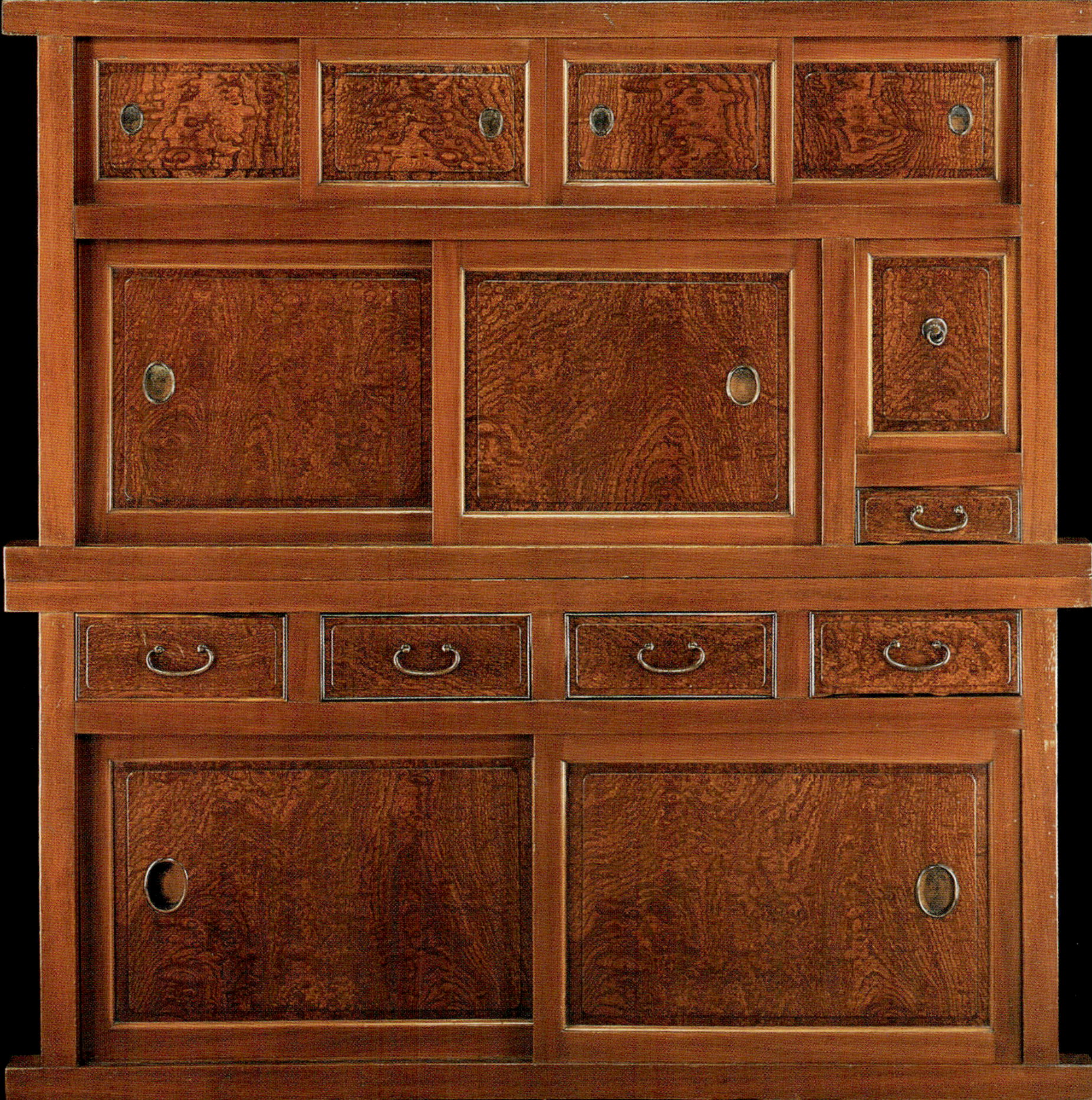

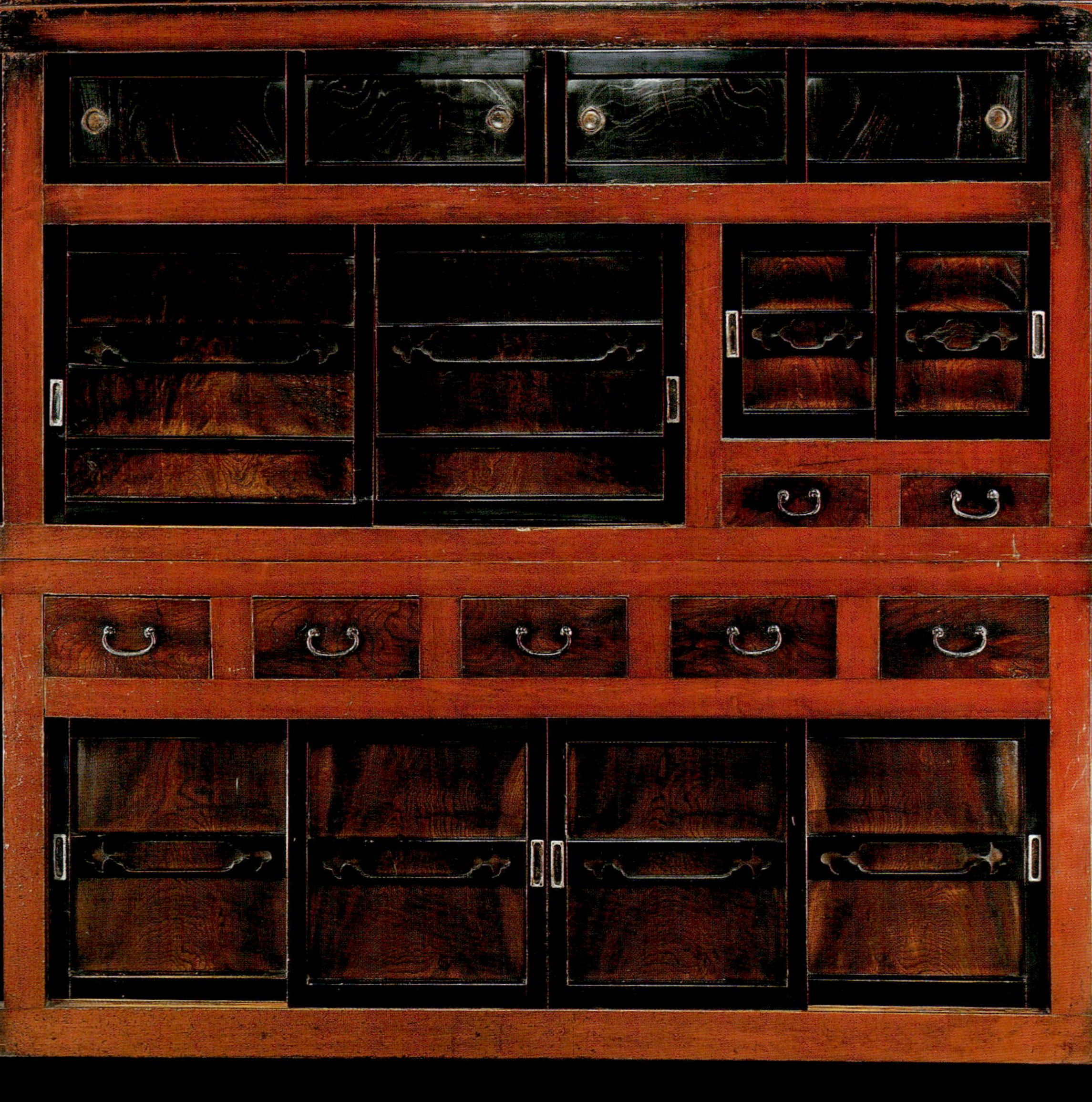

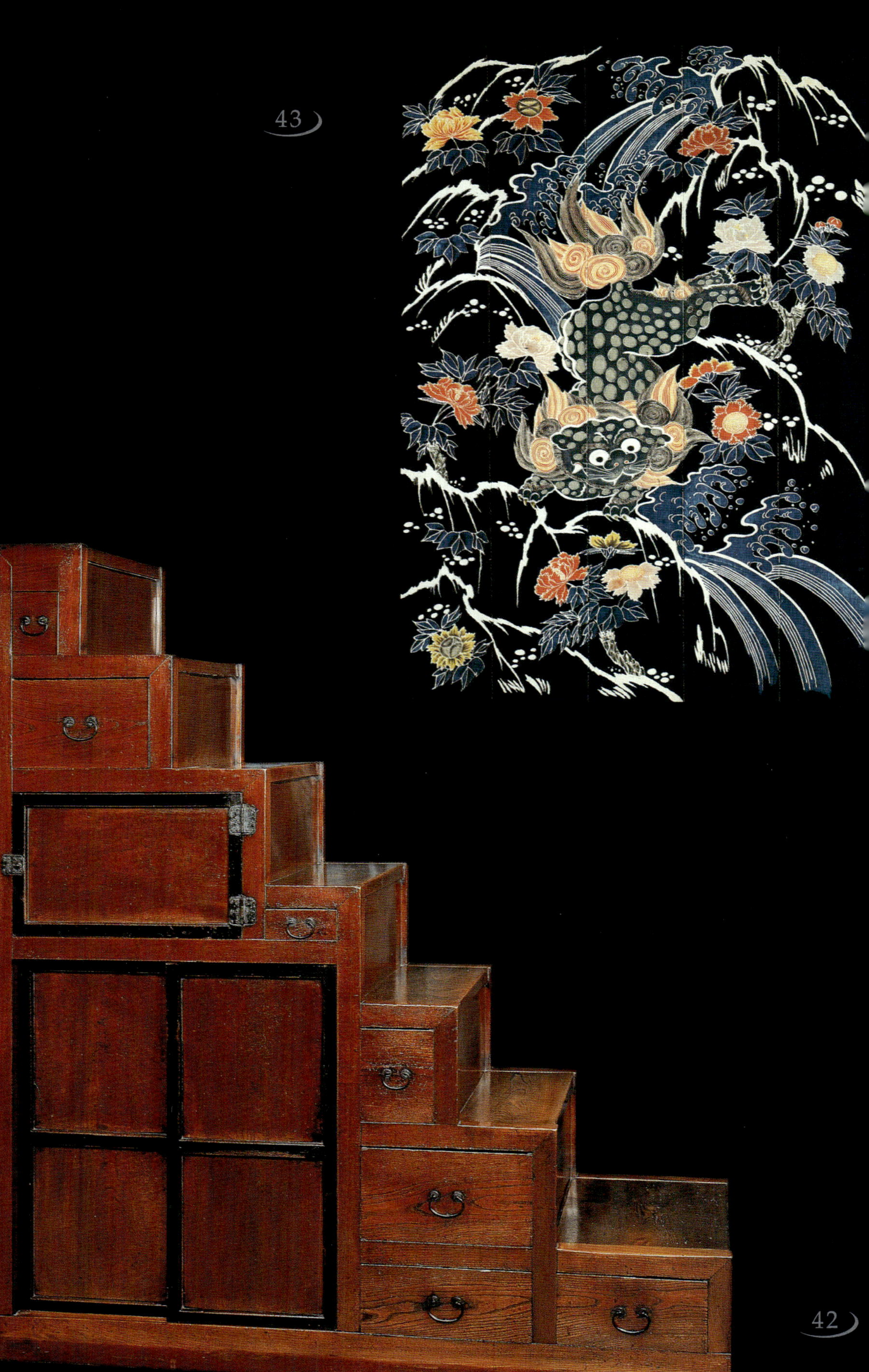

43

42

41

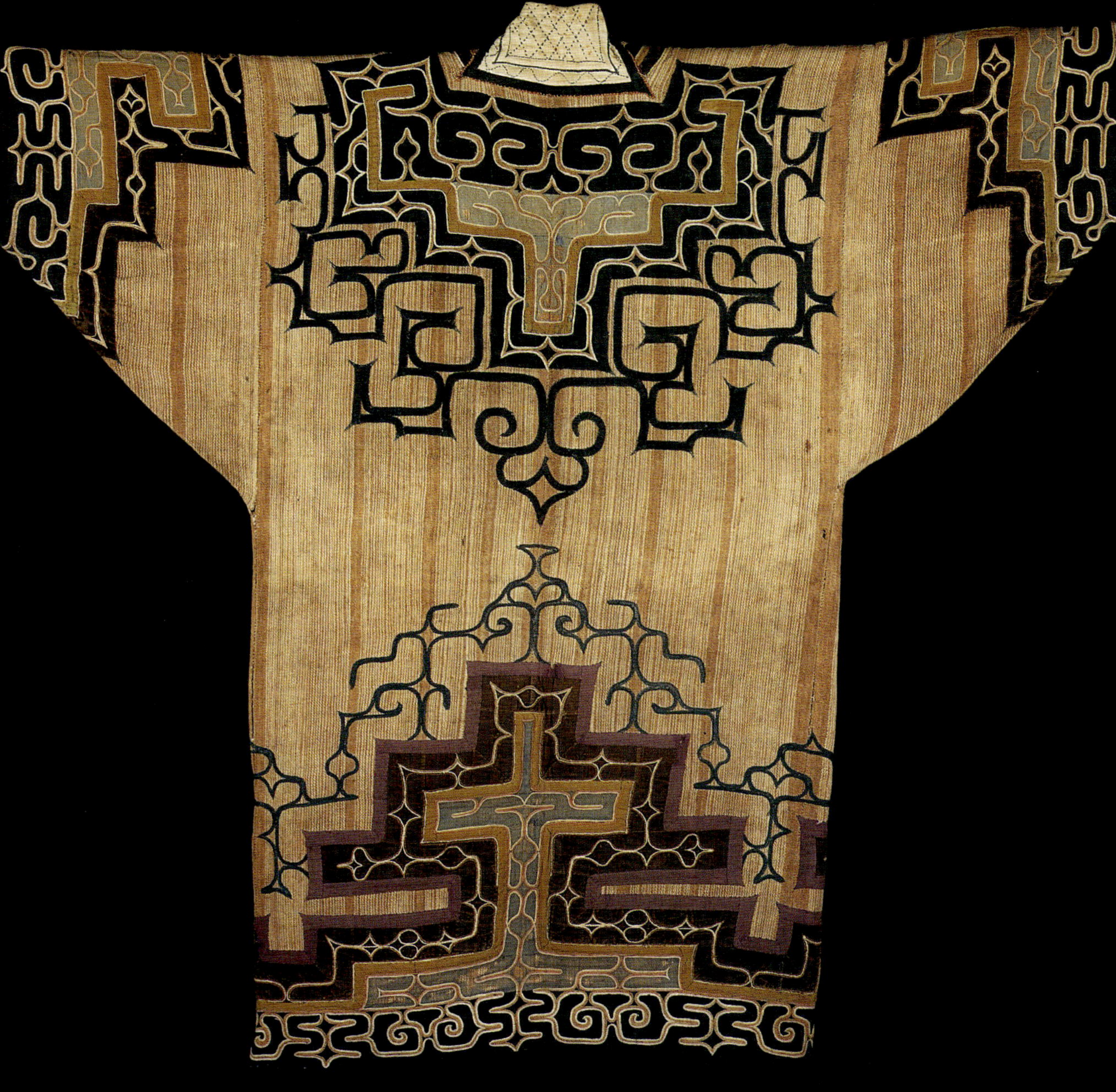

44

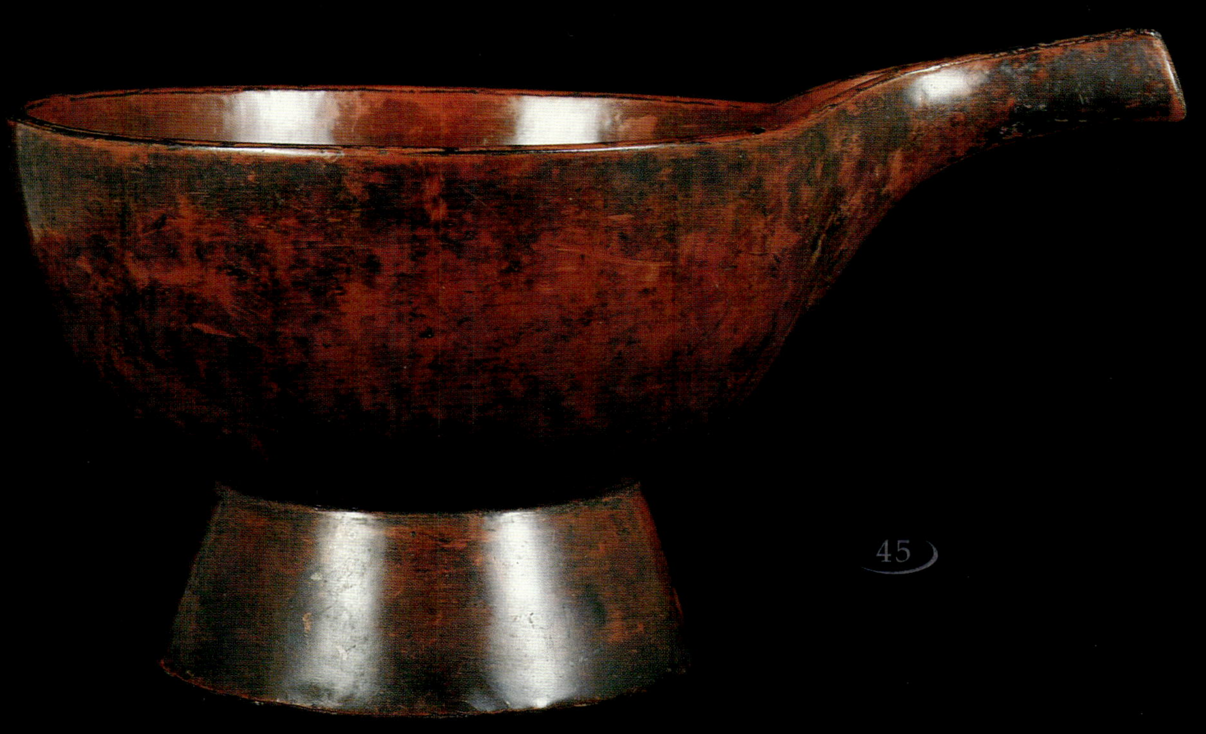

45

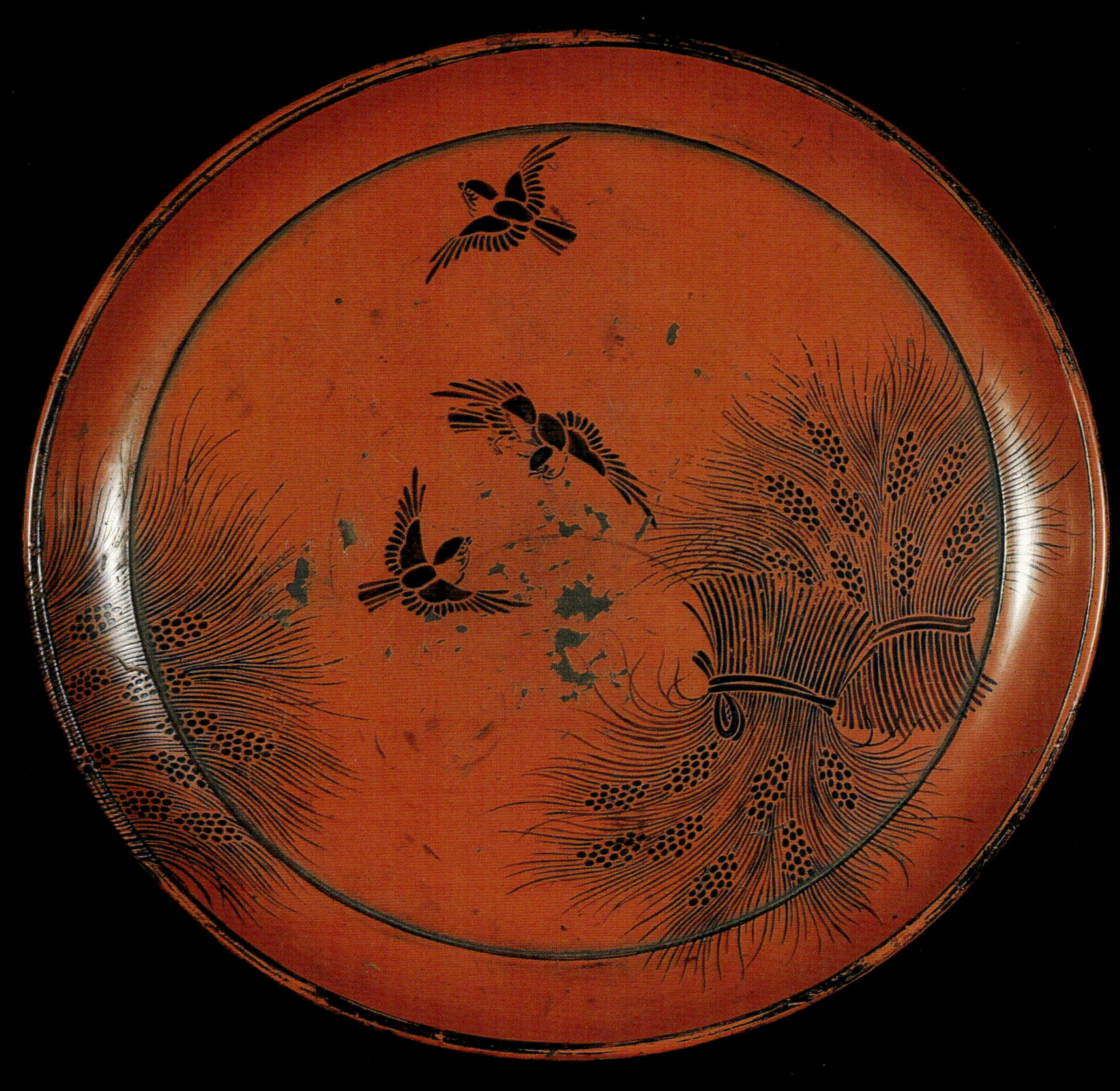

46

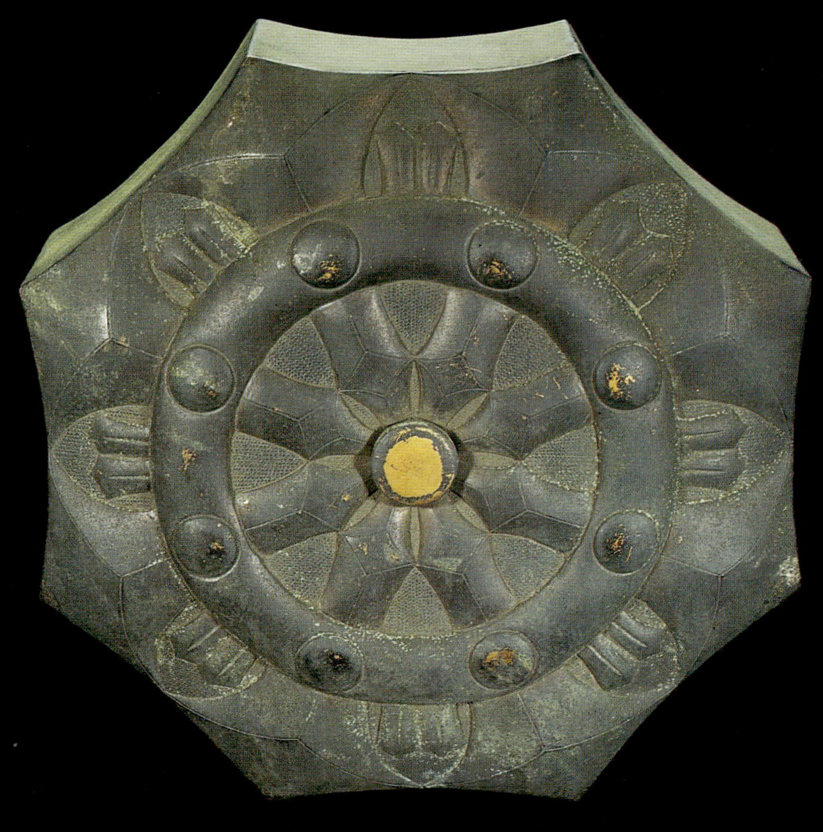

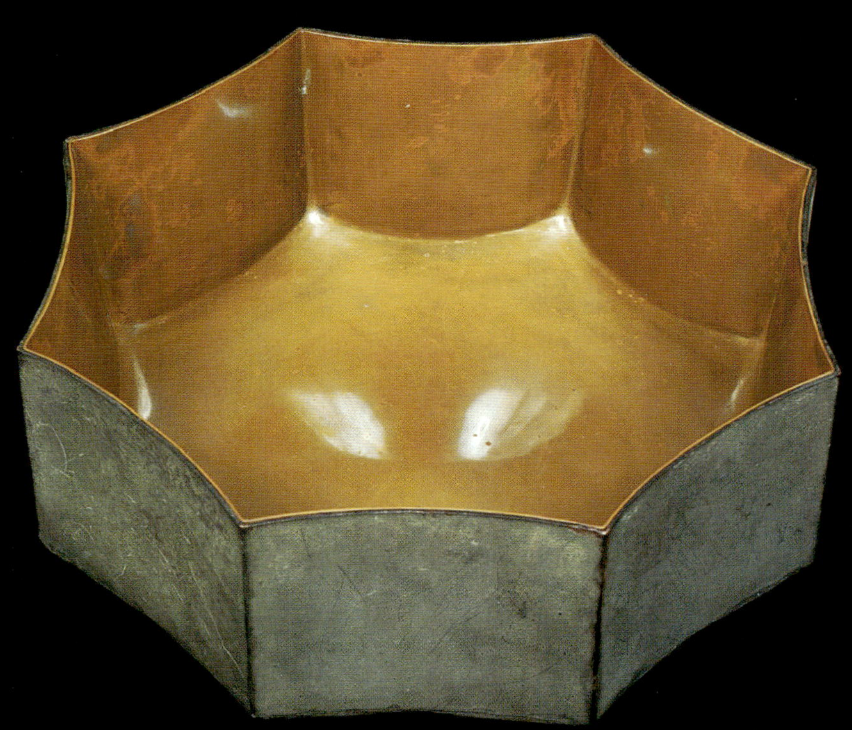

47

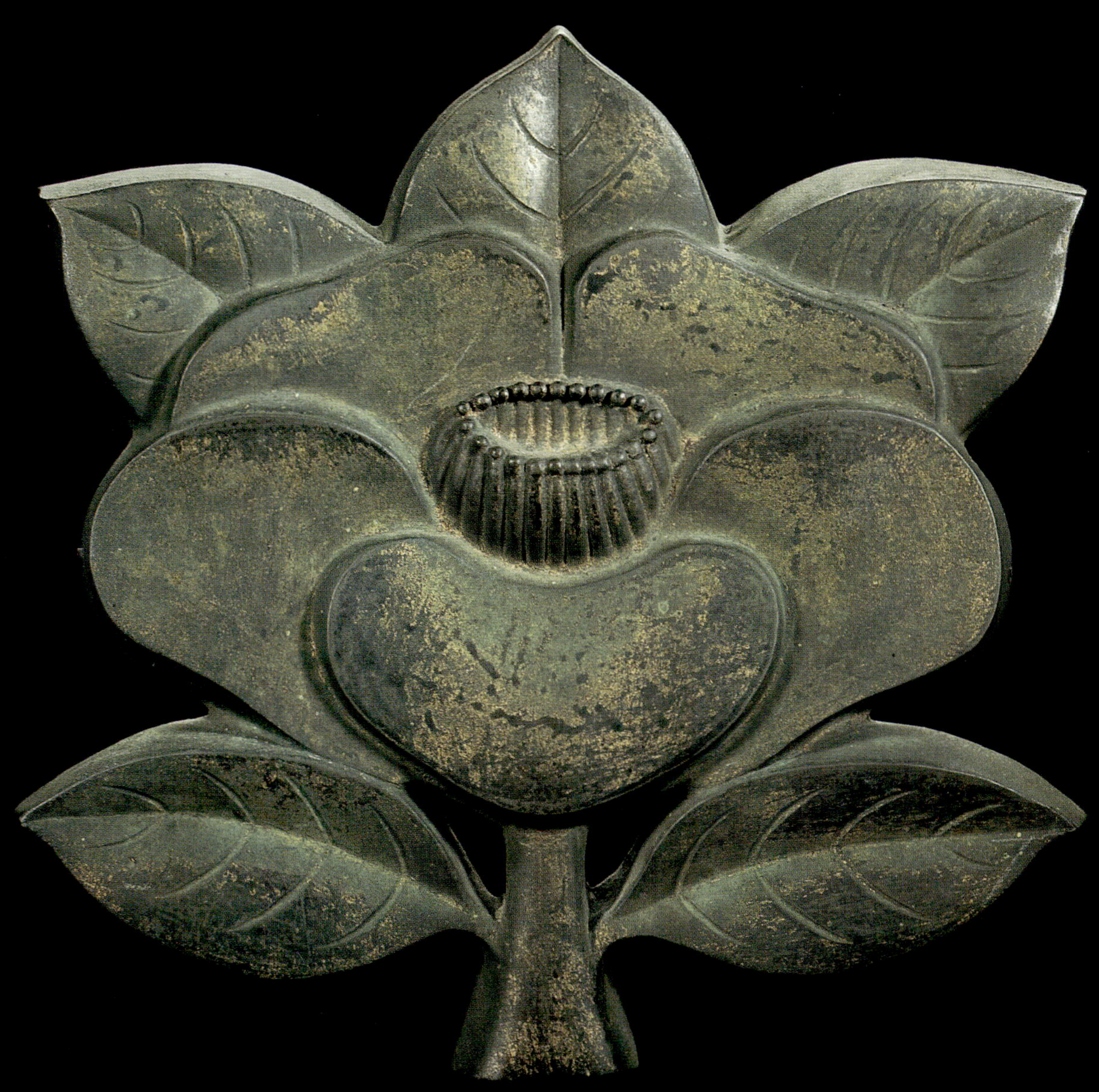

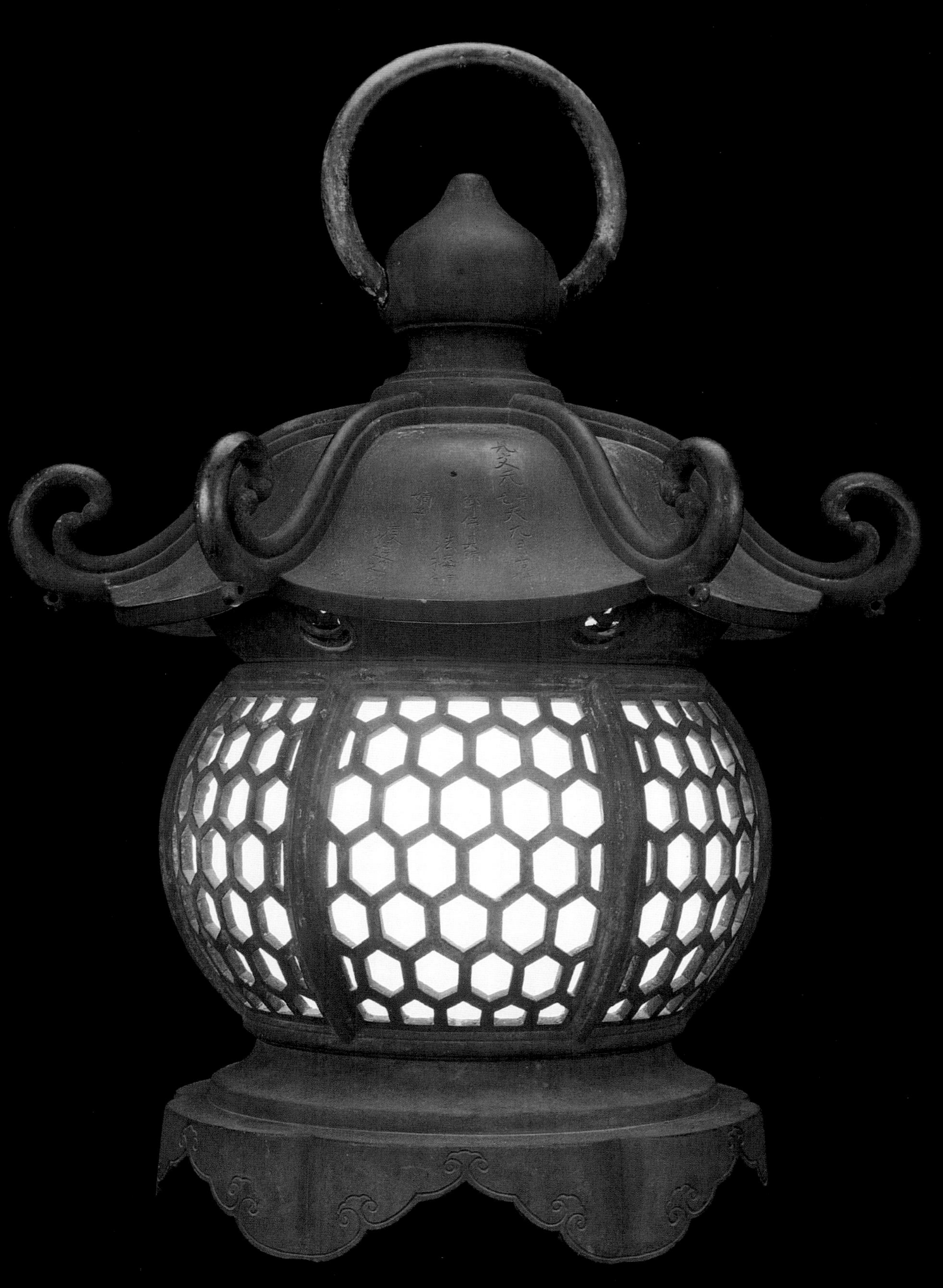

49

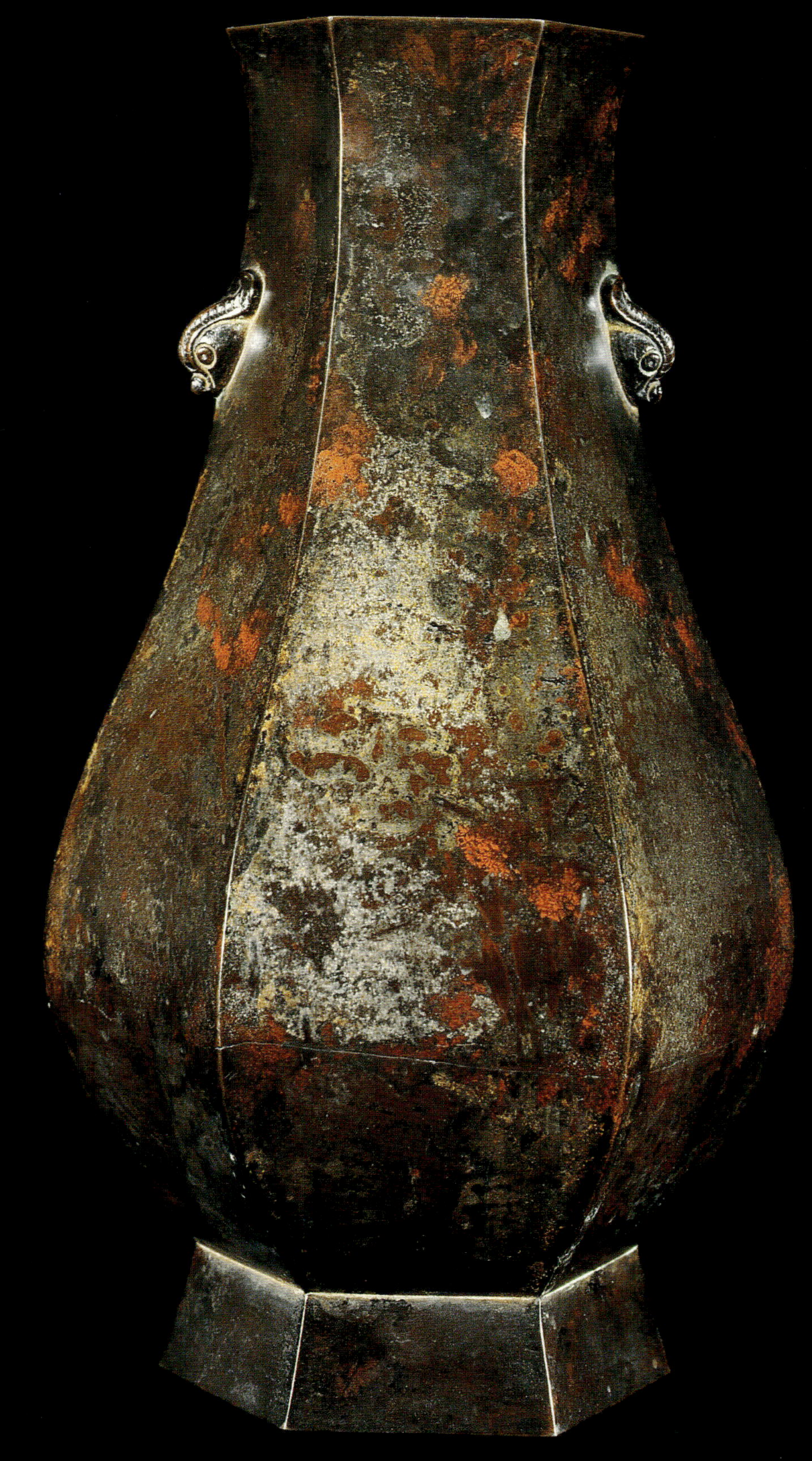

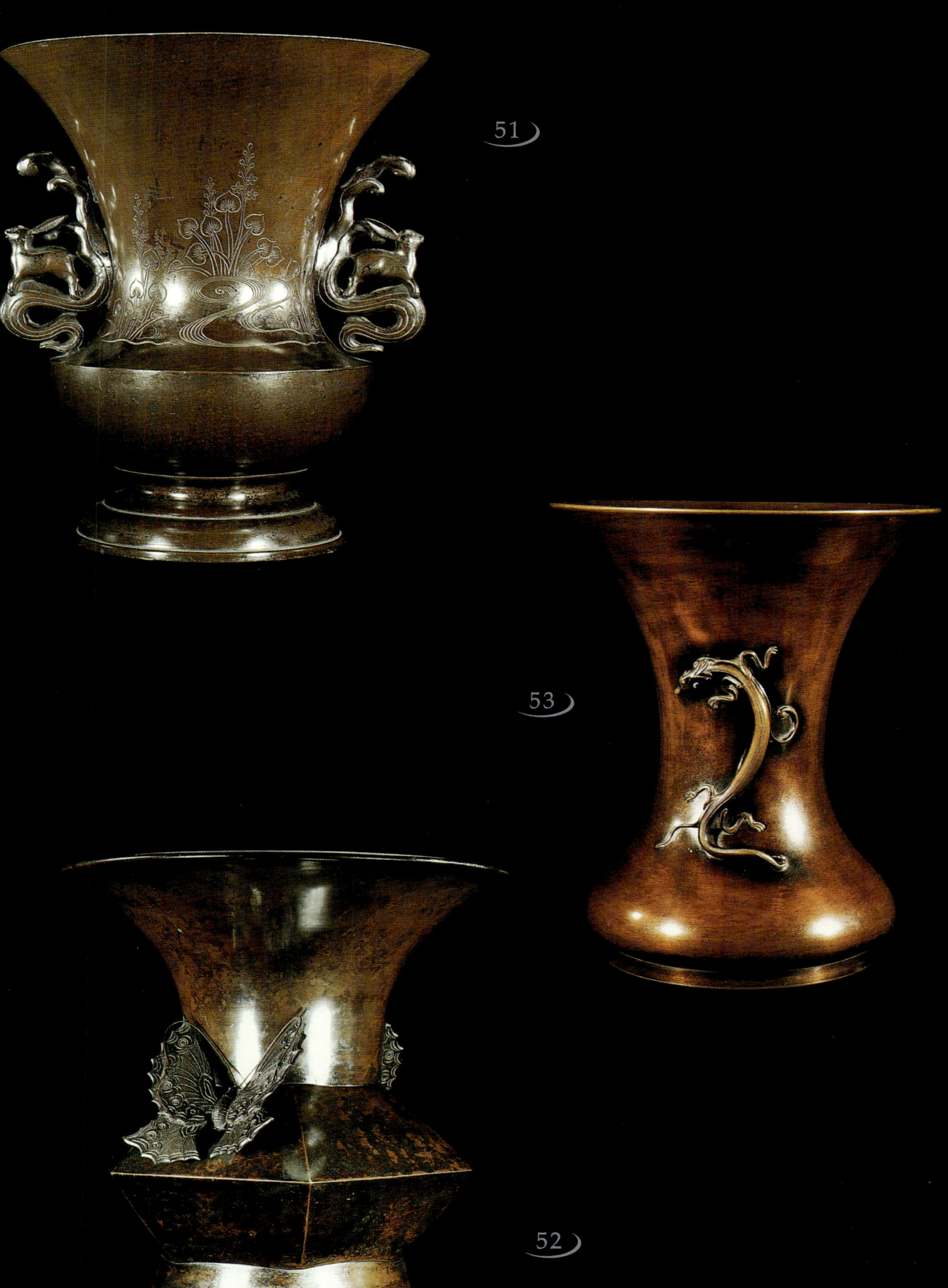

51

53

52

49

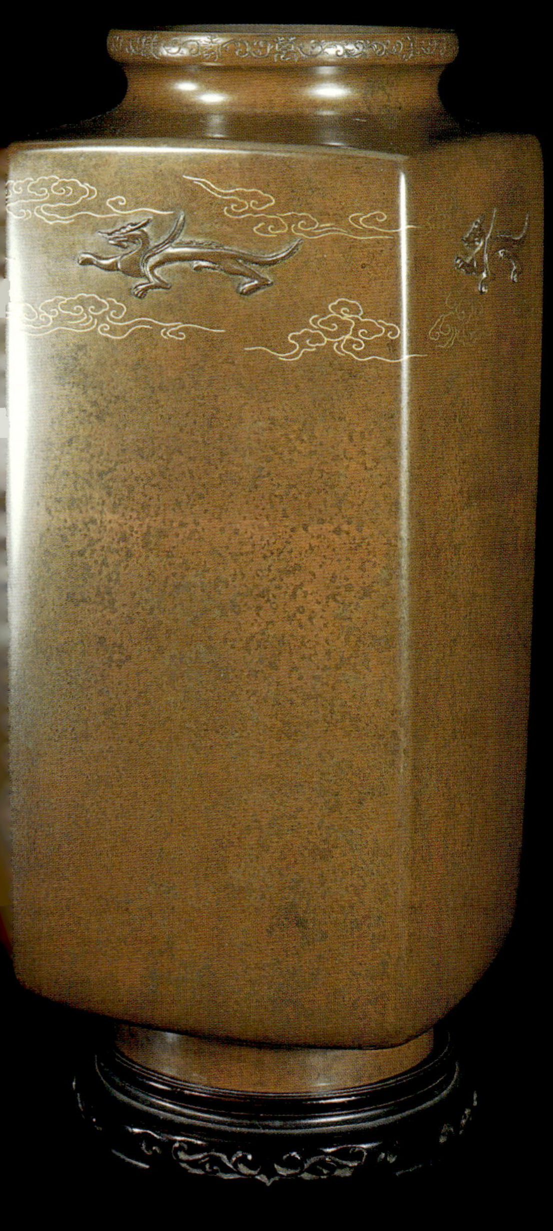
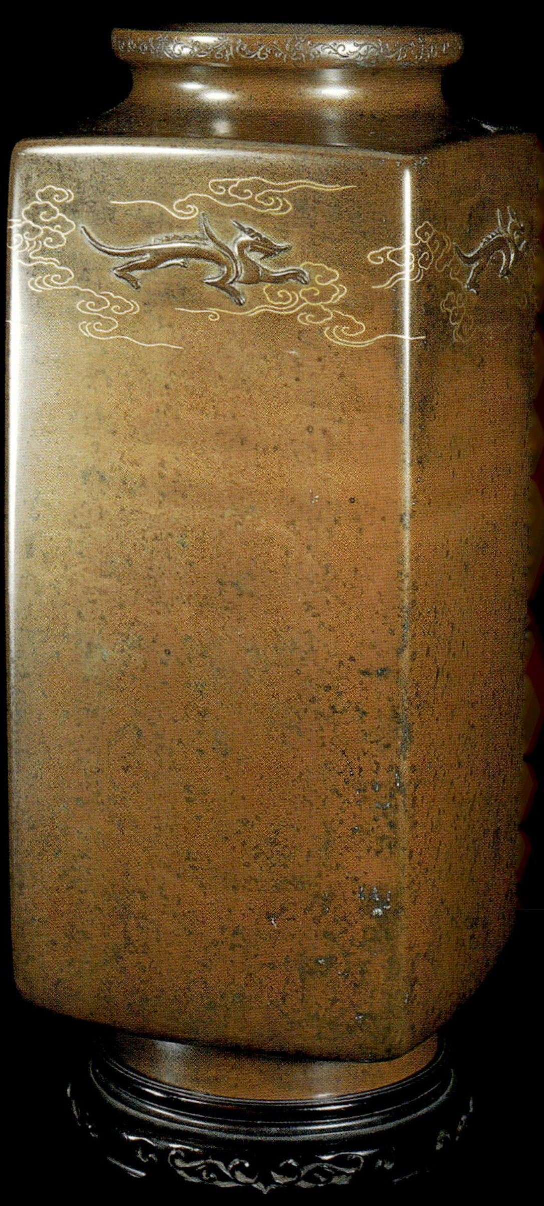

54

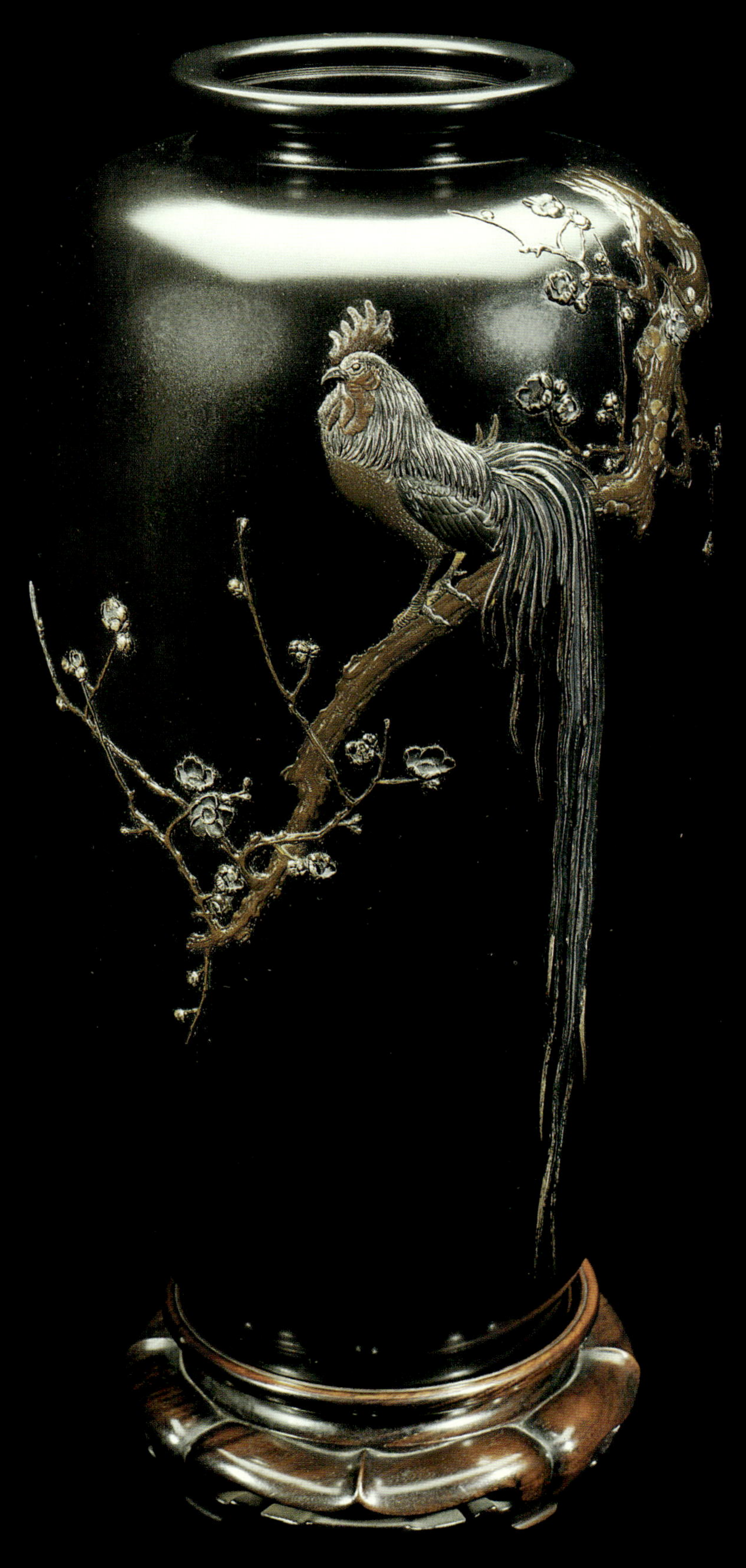

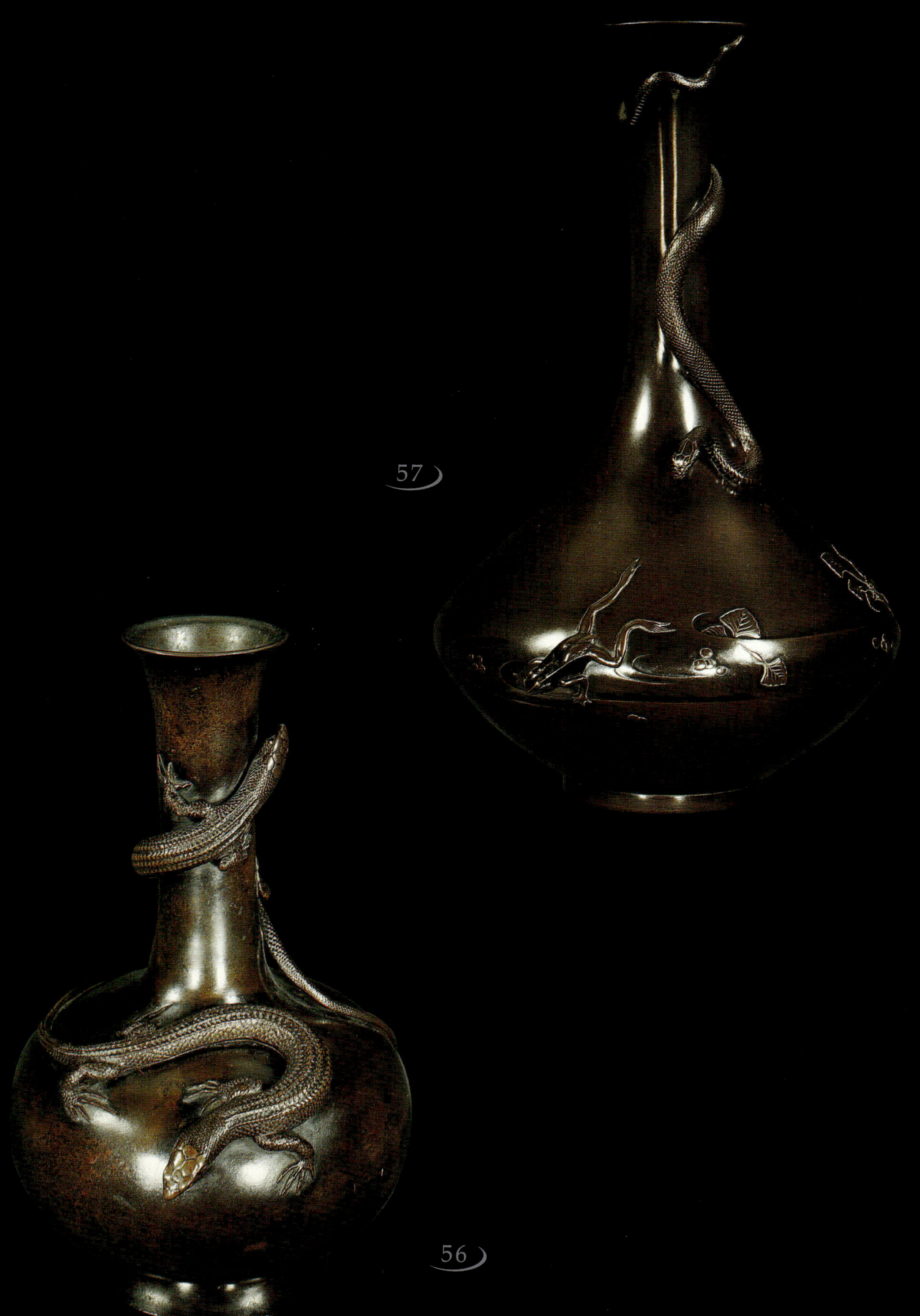

57
56

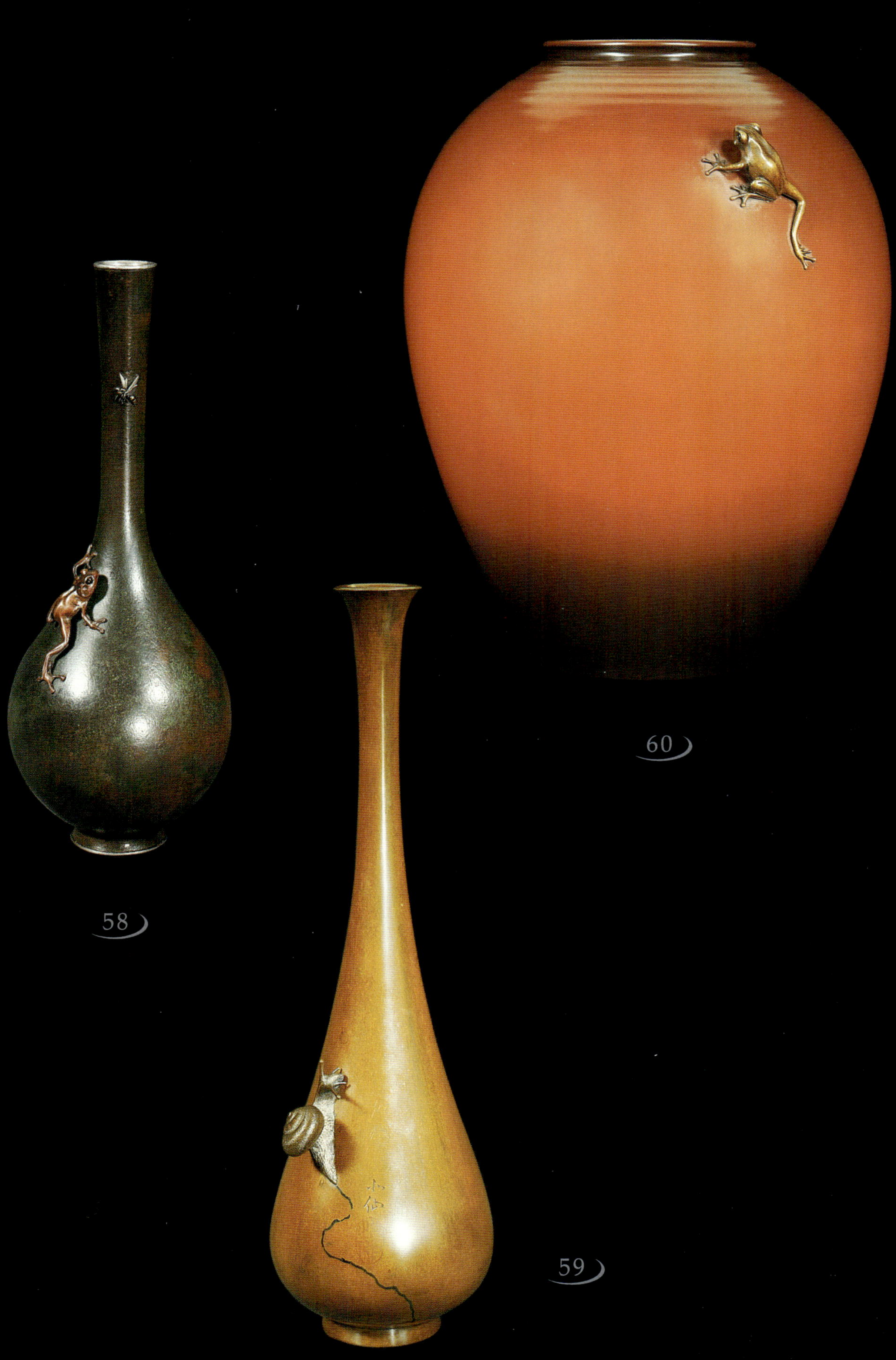

53

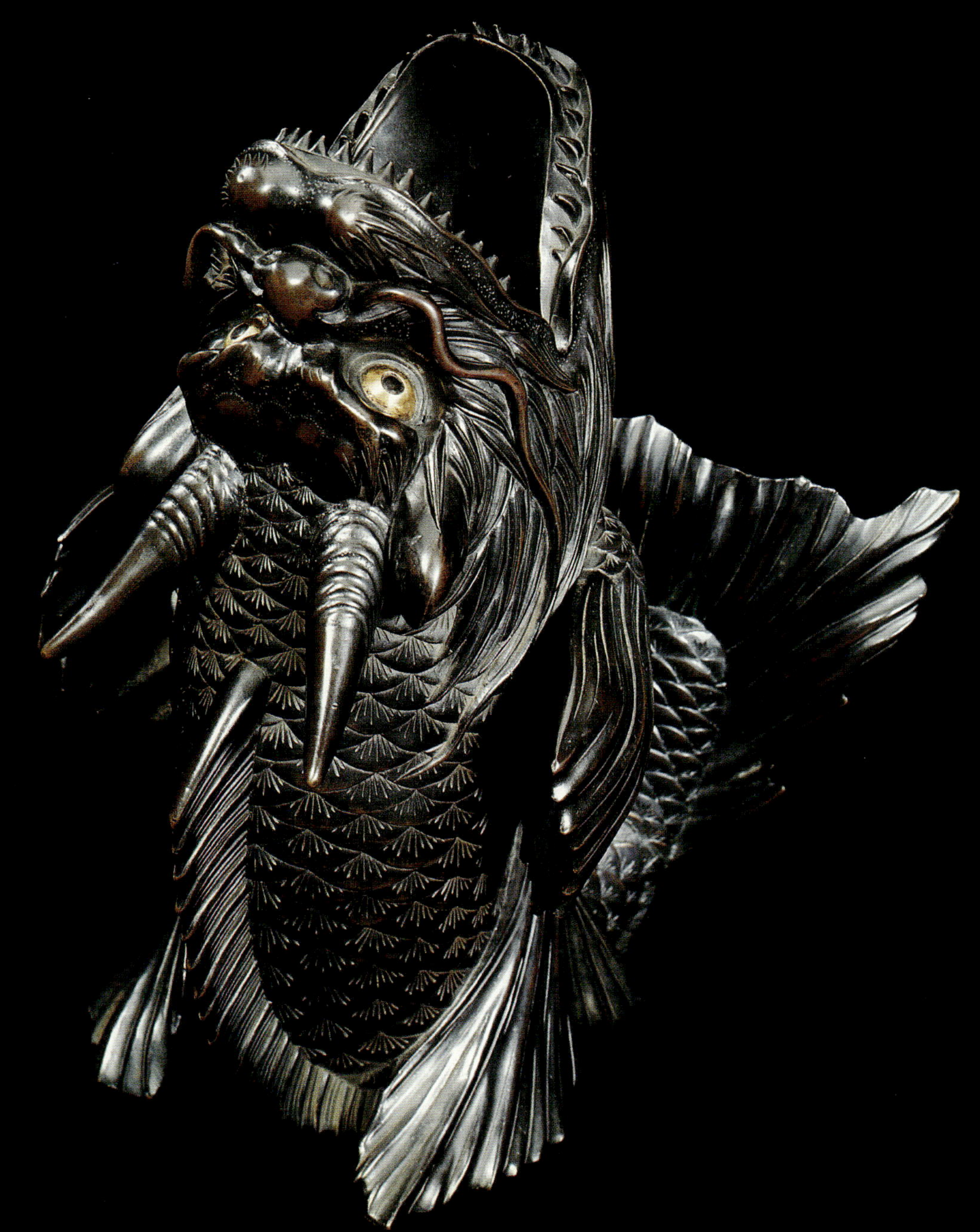

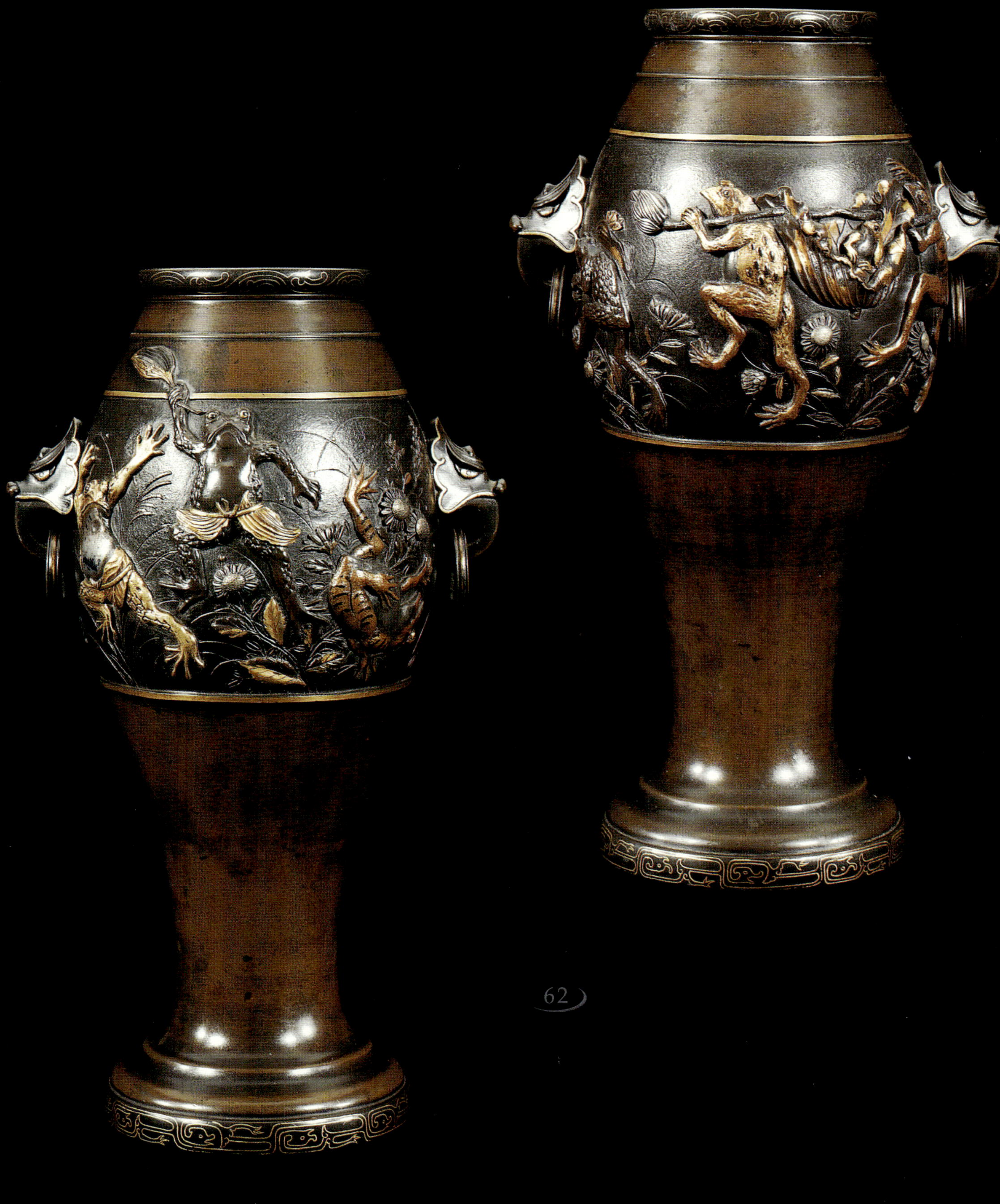

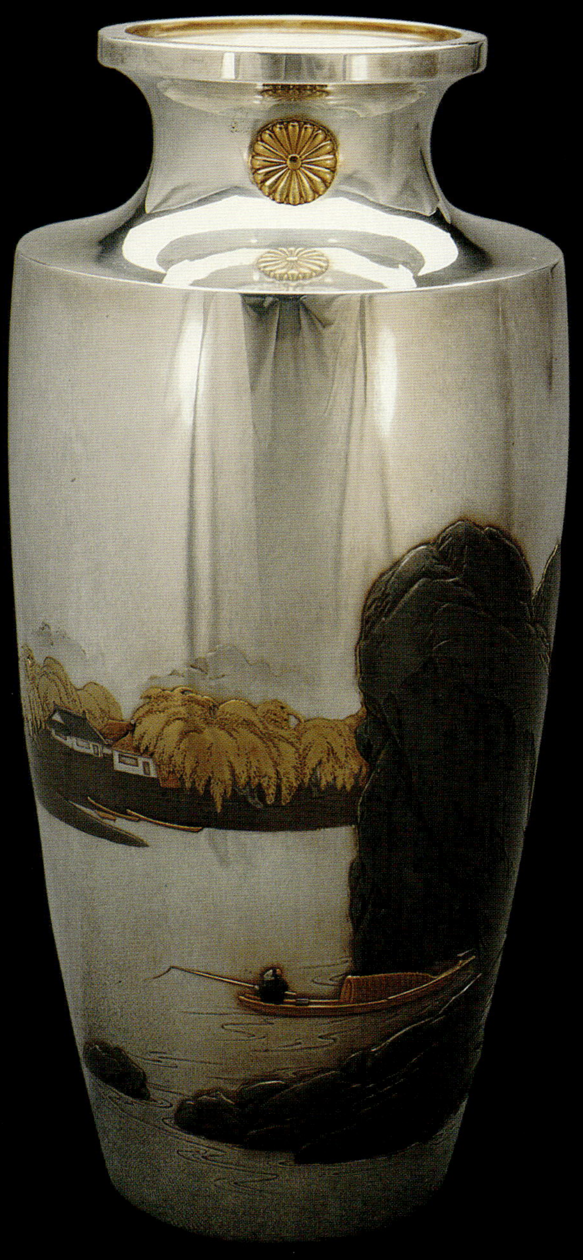
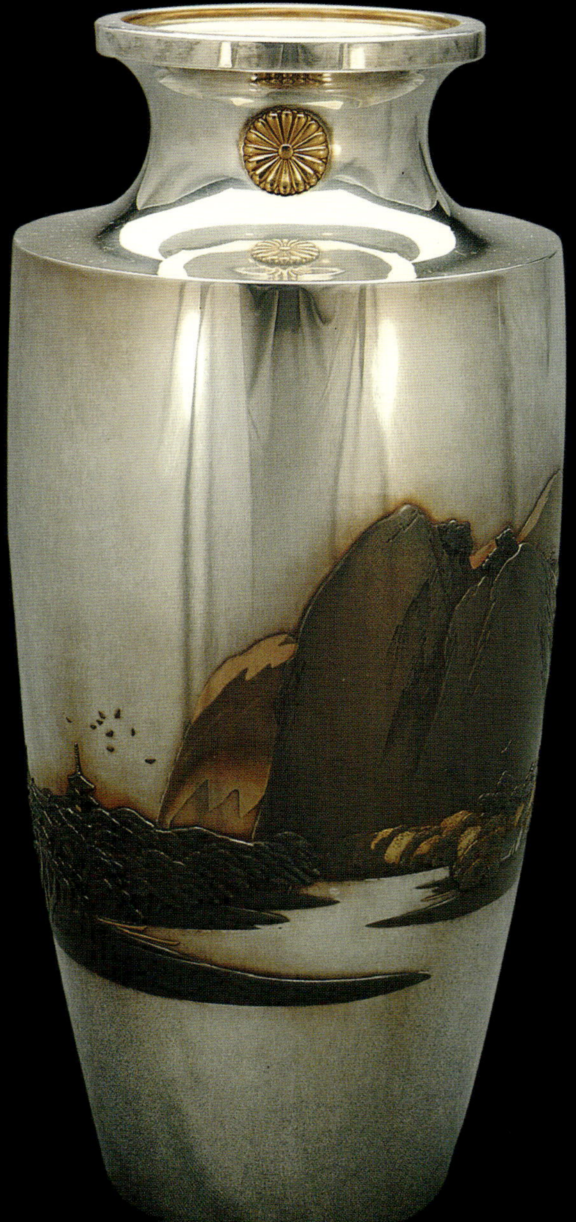

56

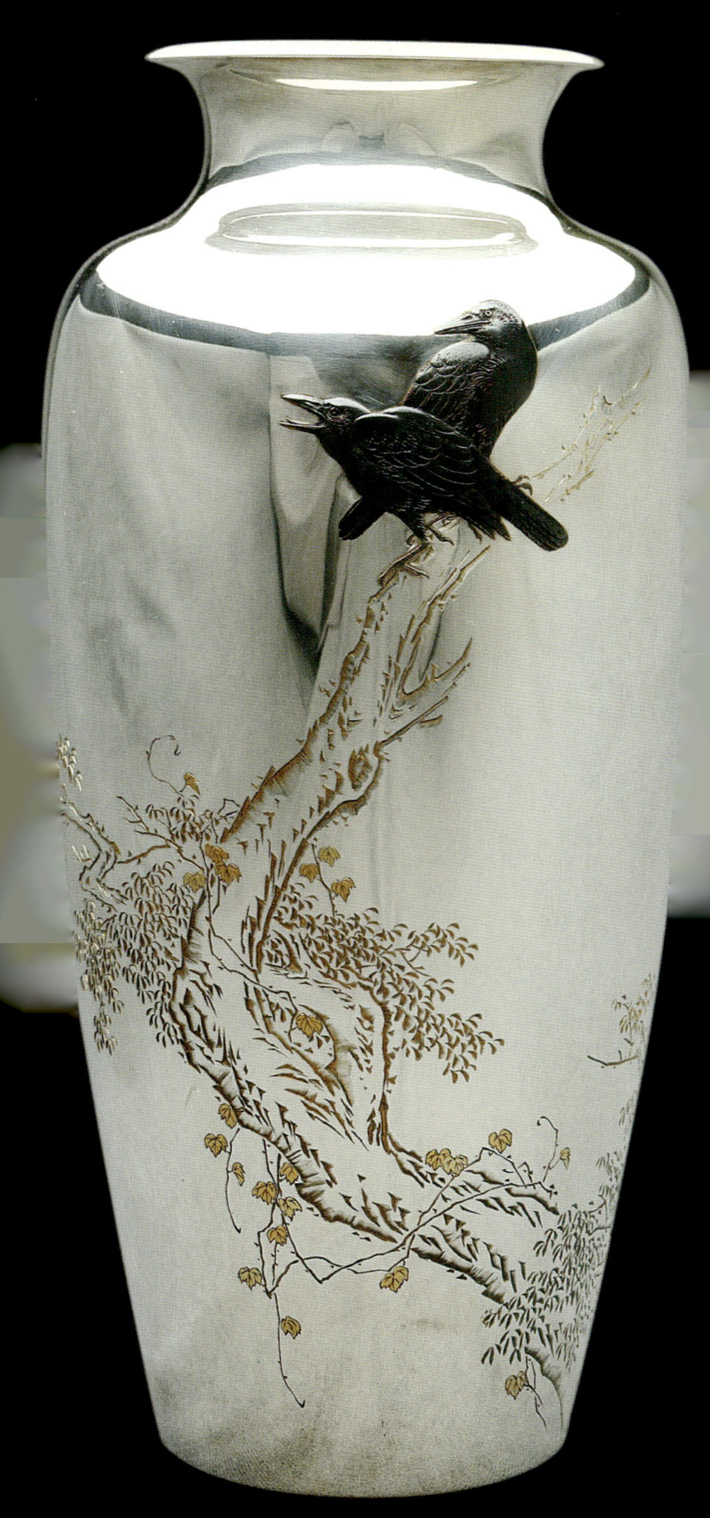

64

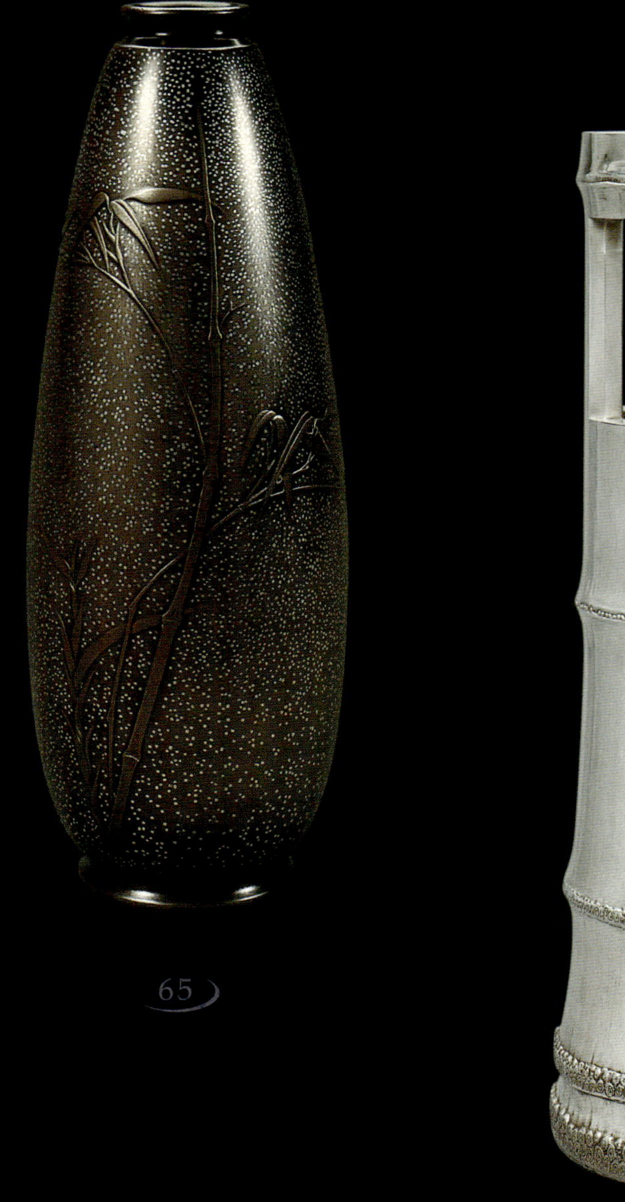

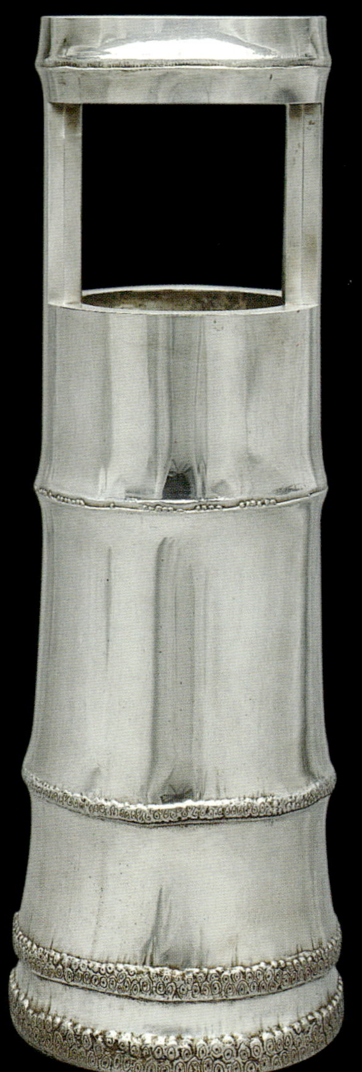

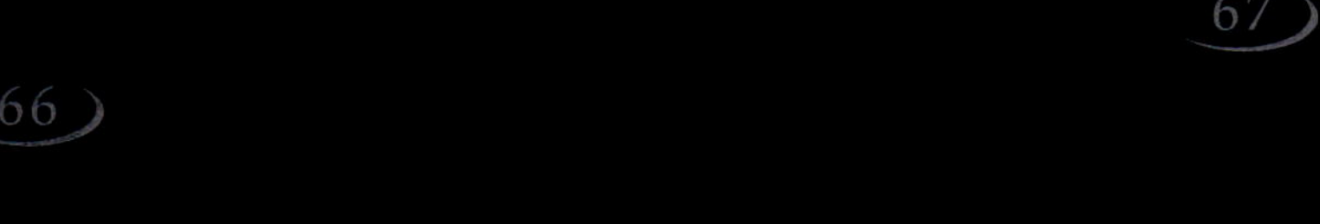

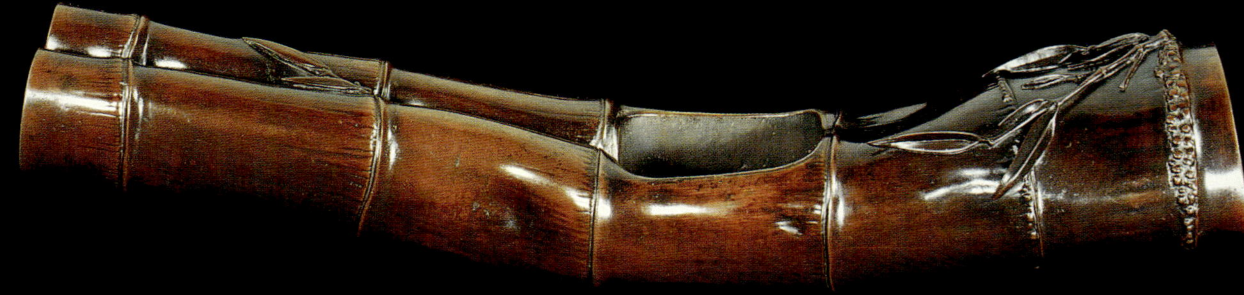

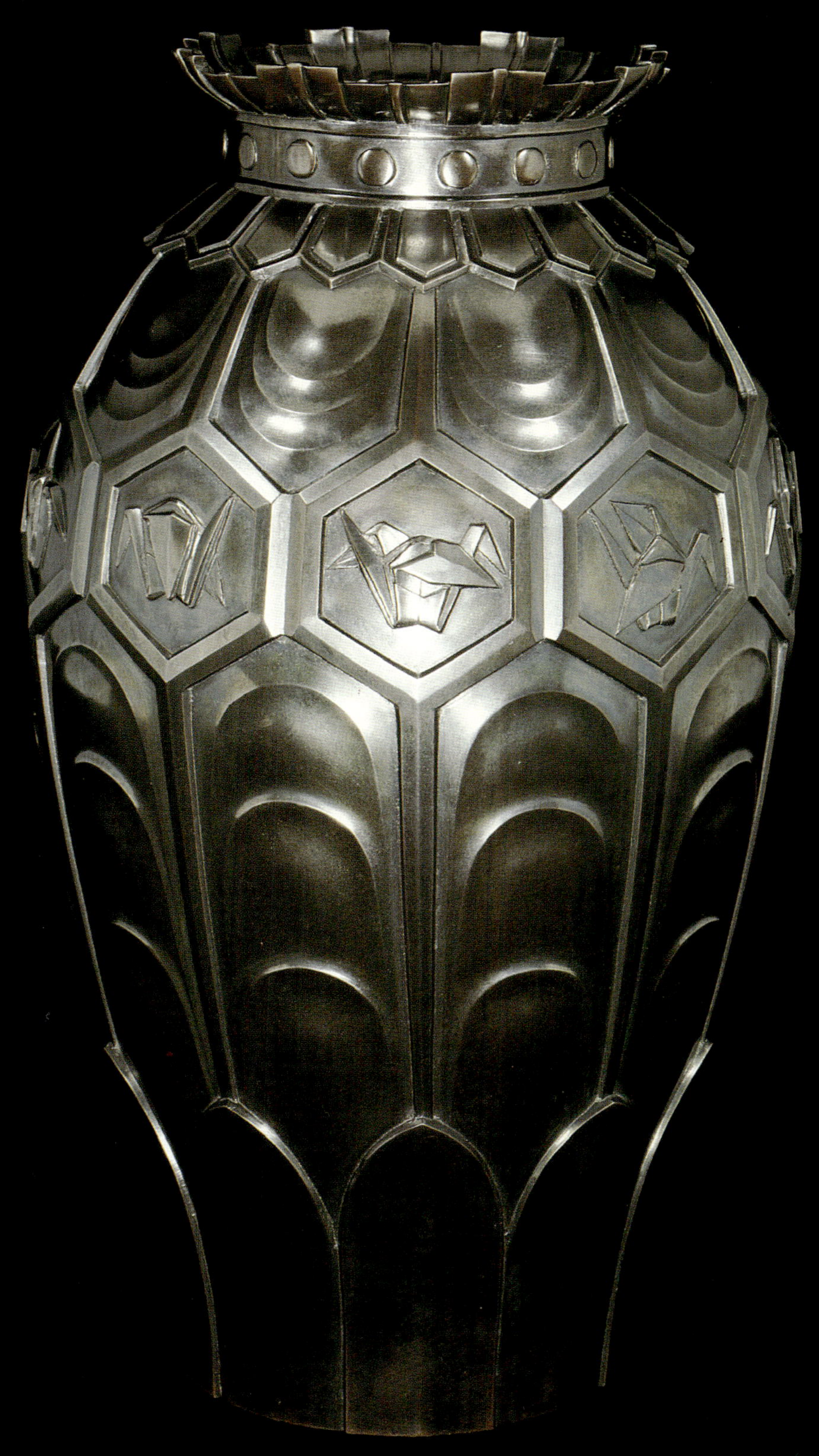

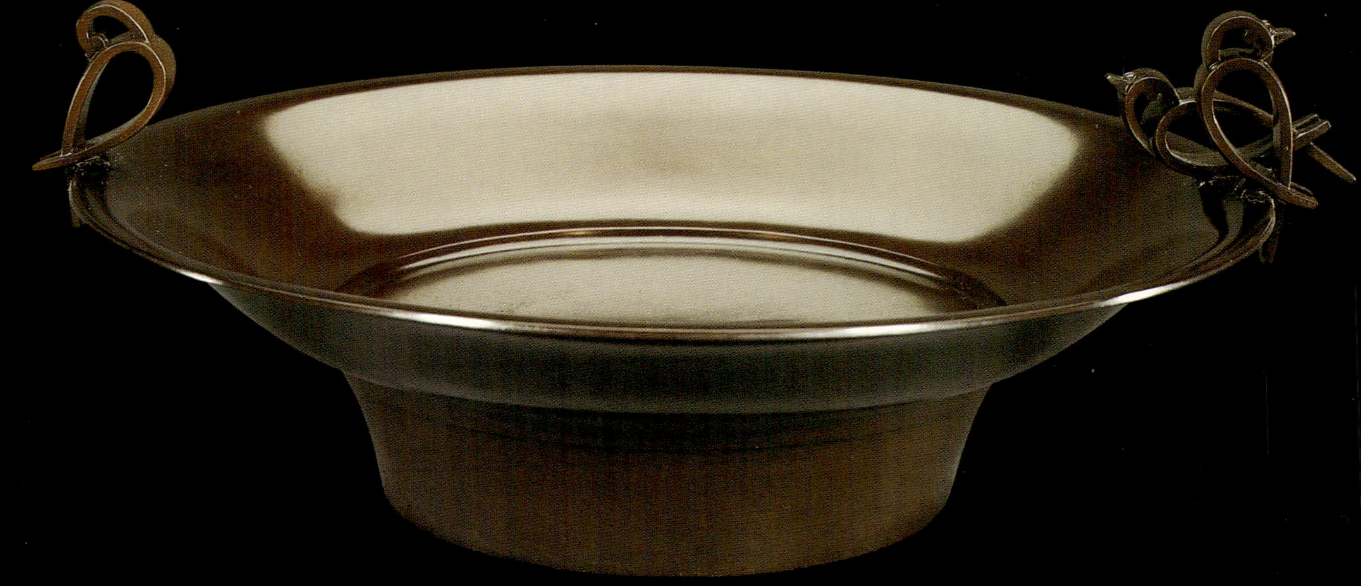

69

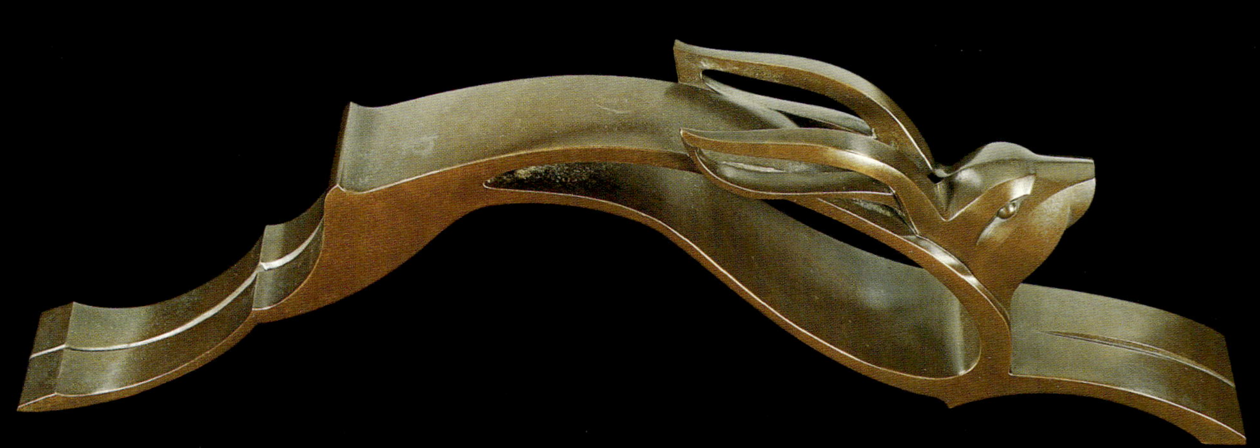

70

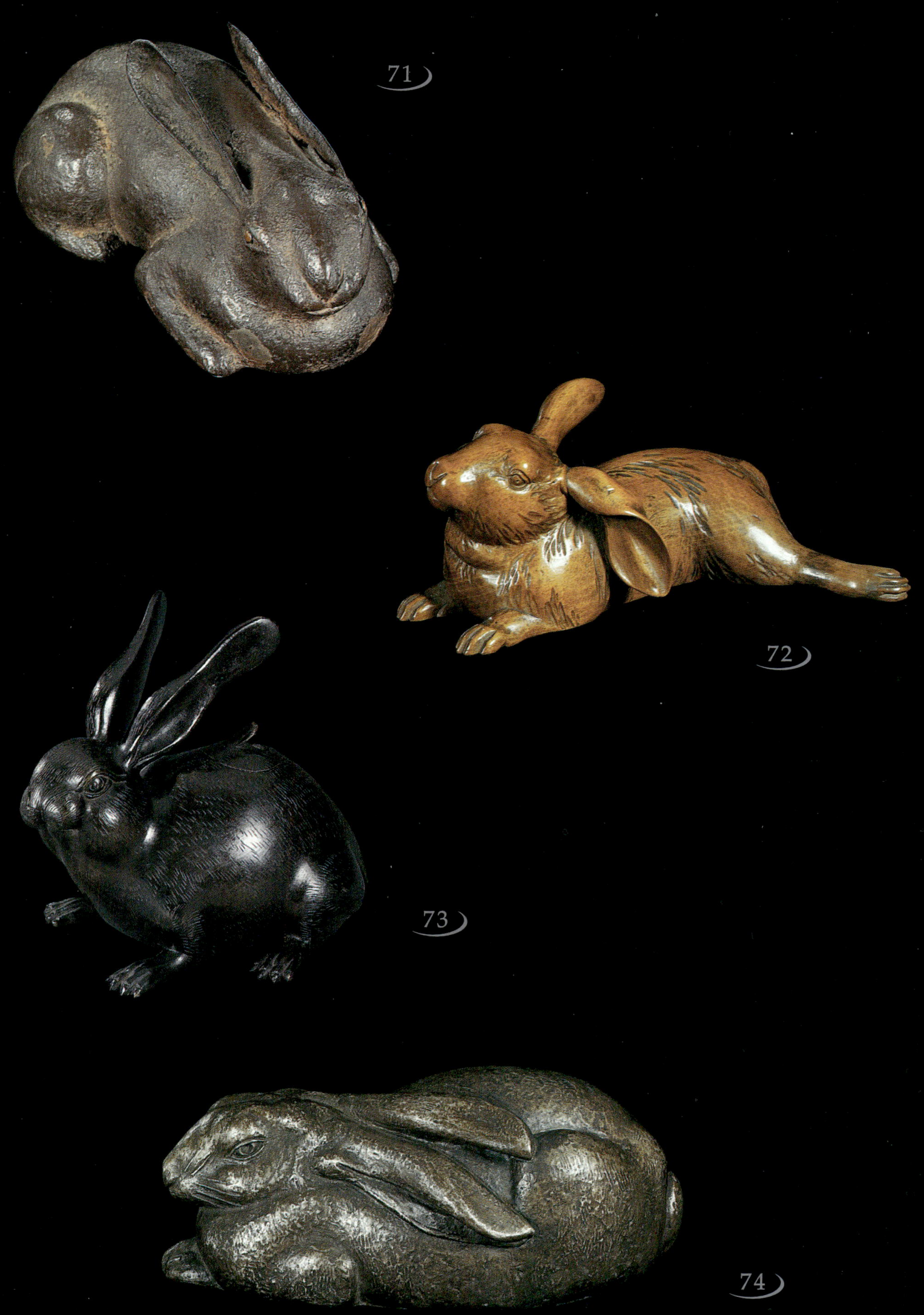

71
72
73
74

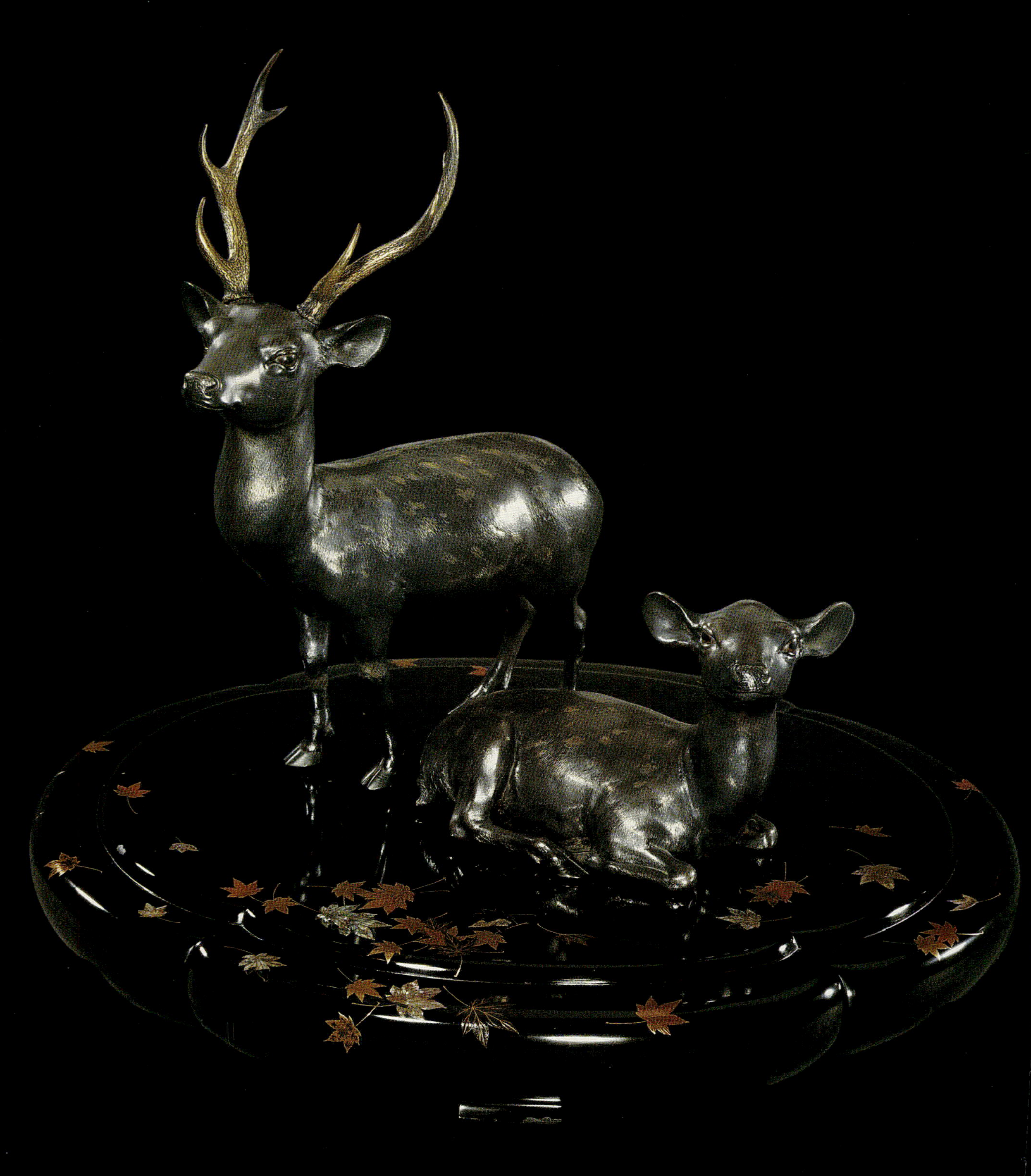

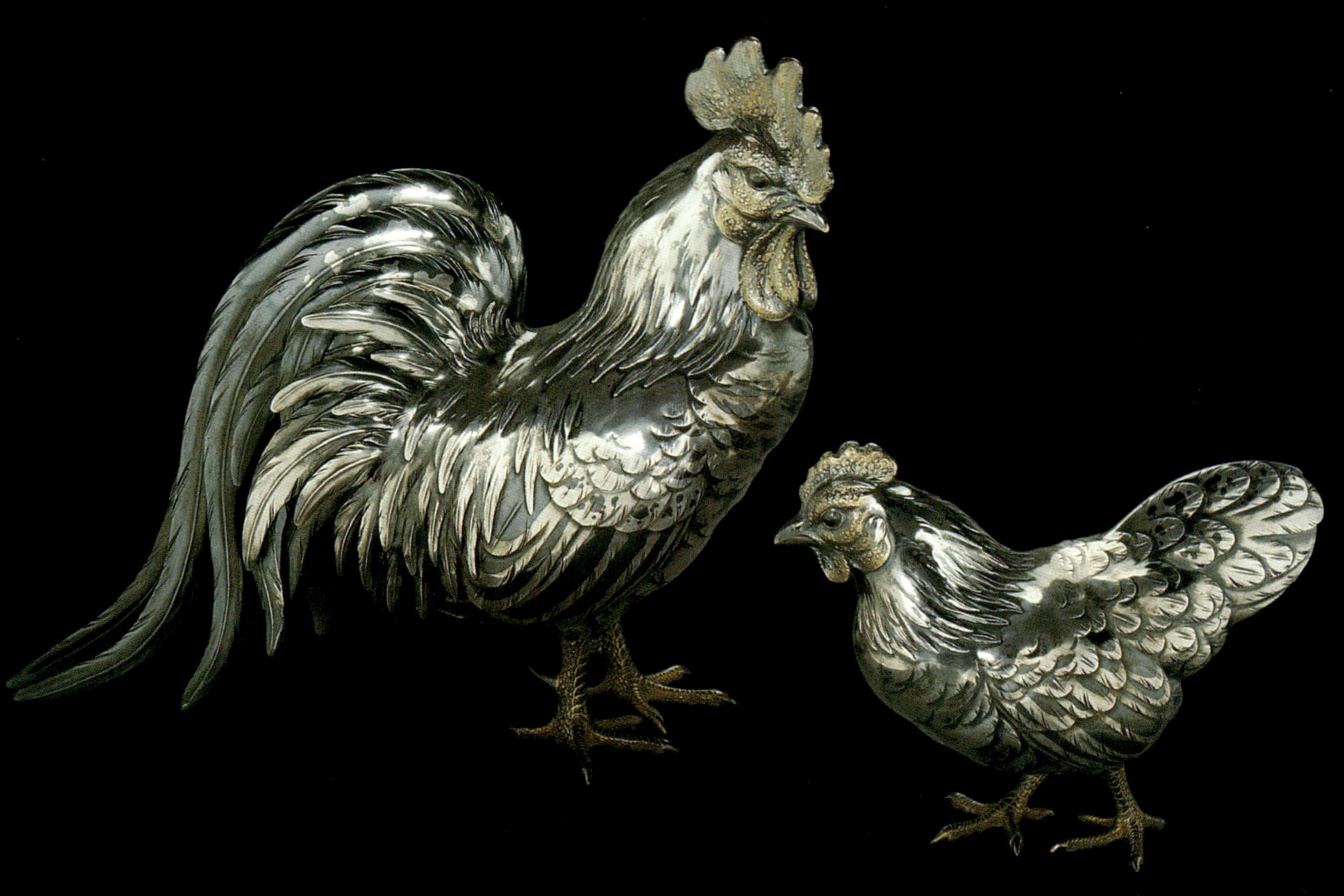

76

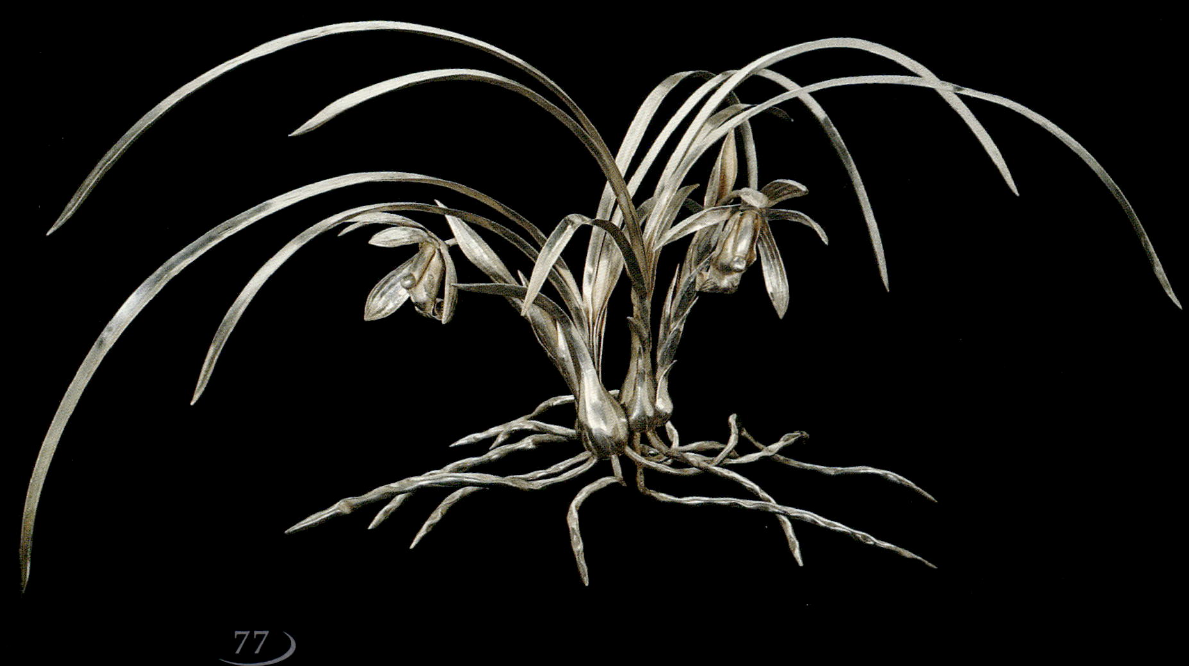

77

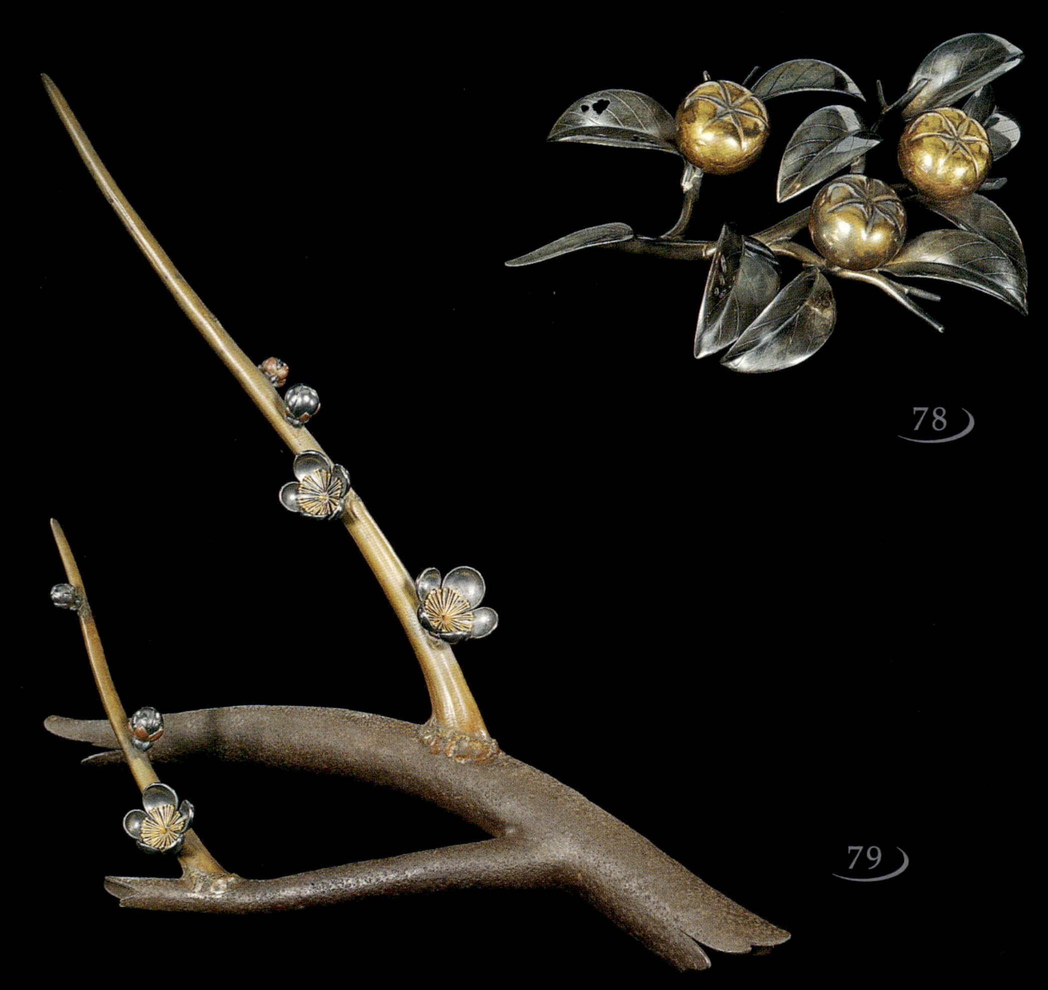

78

79

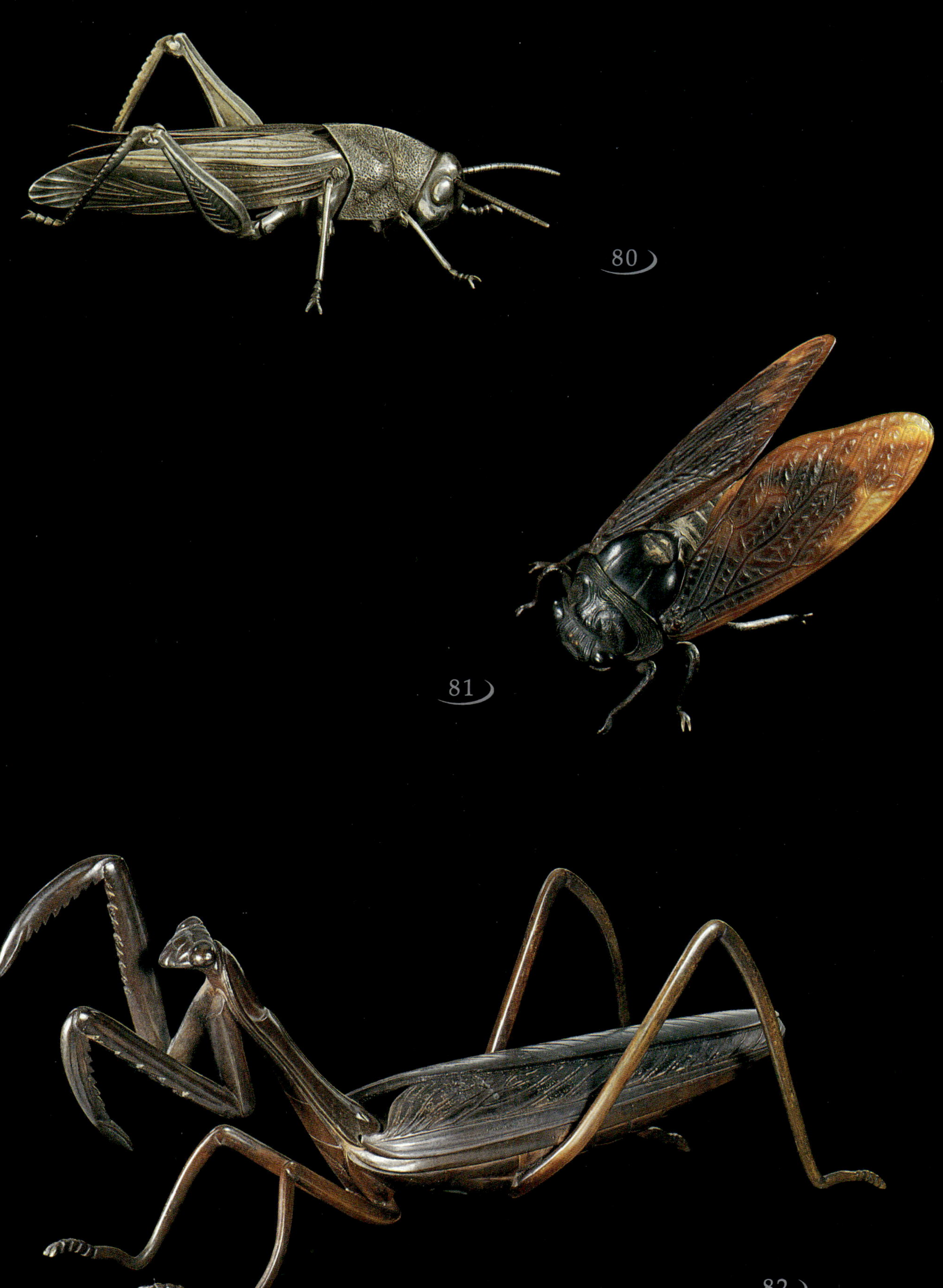

80
81
82

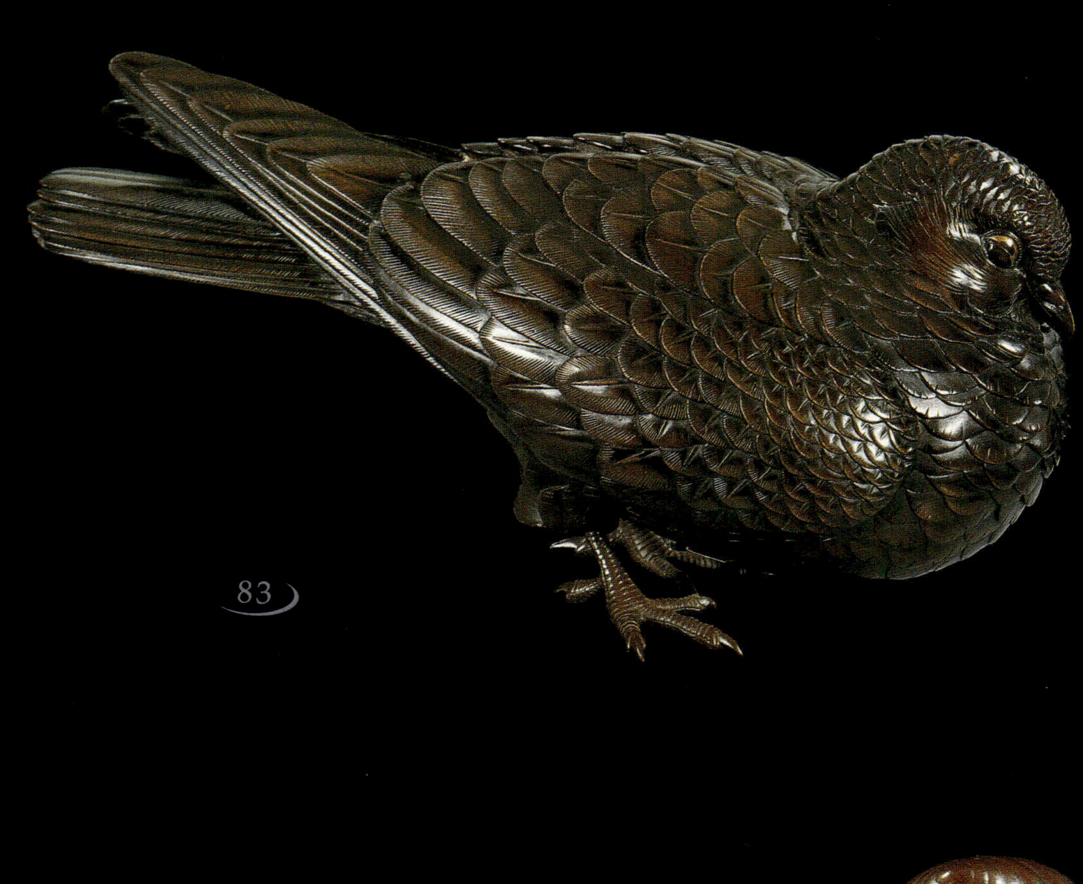

83

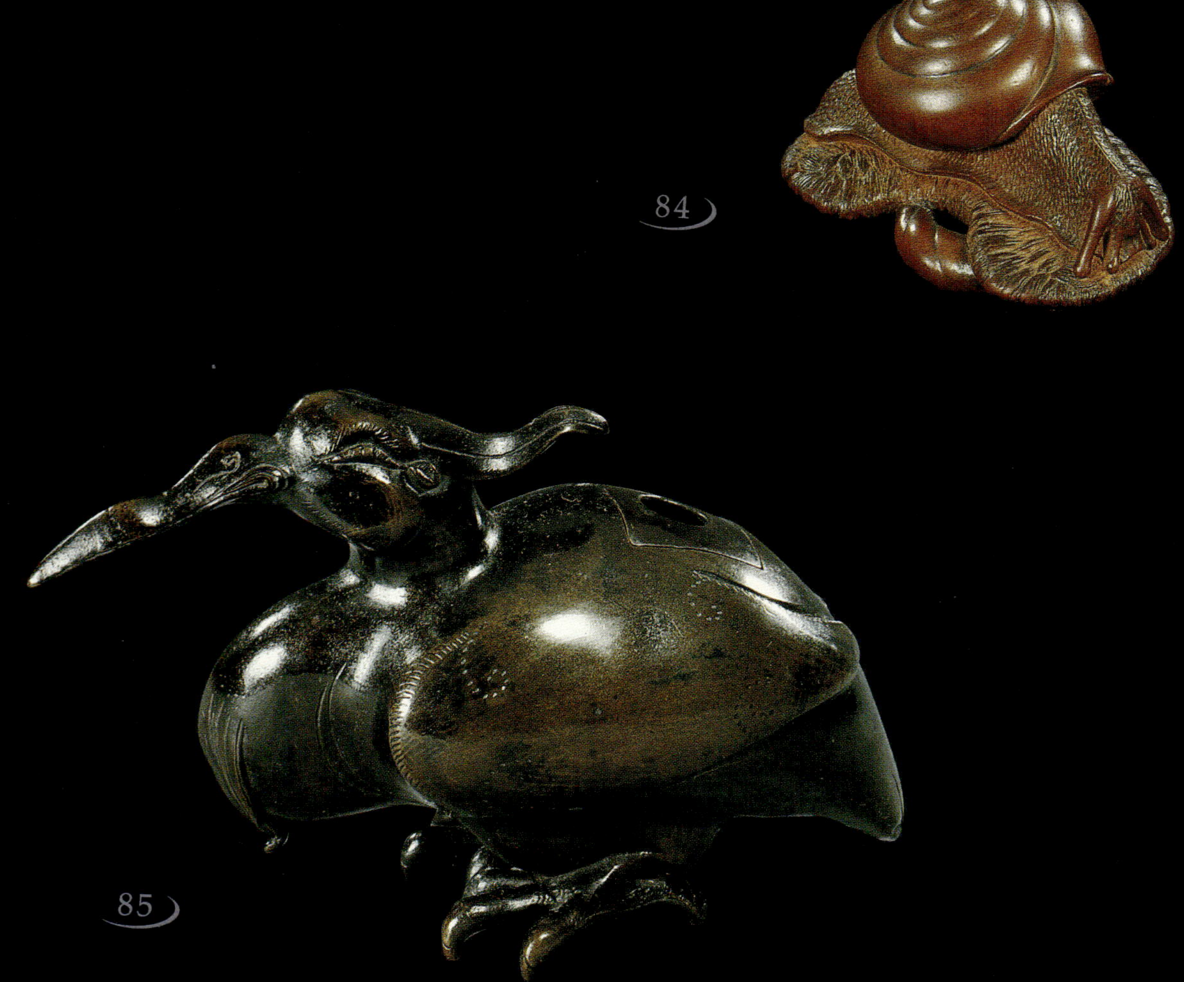

84

85

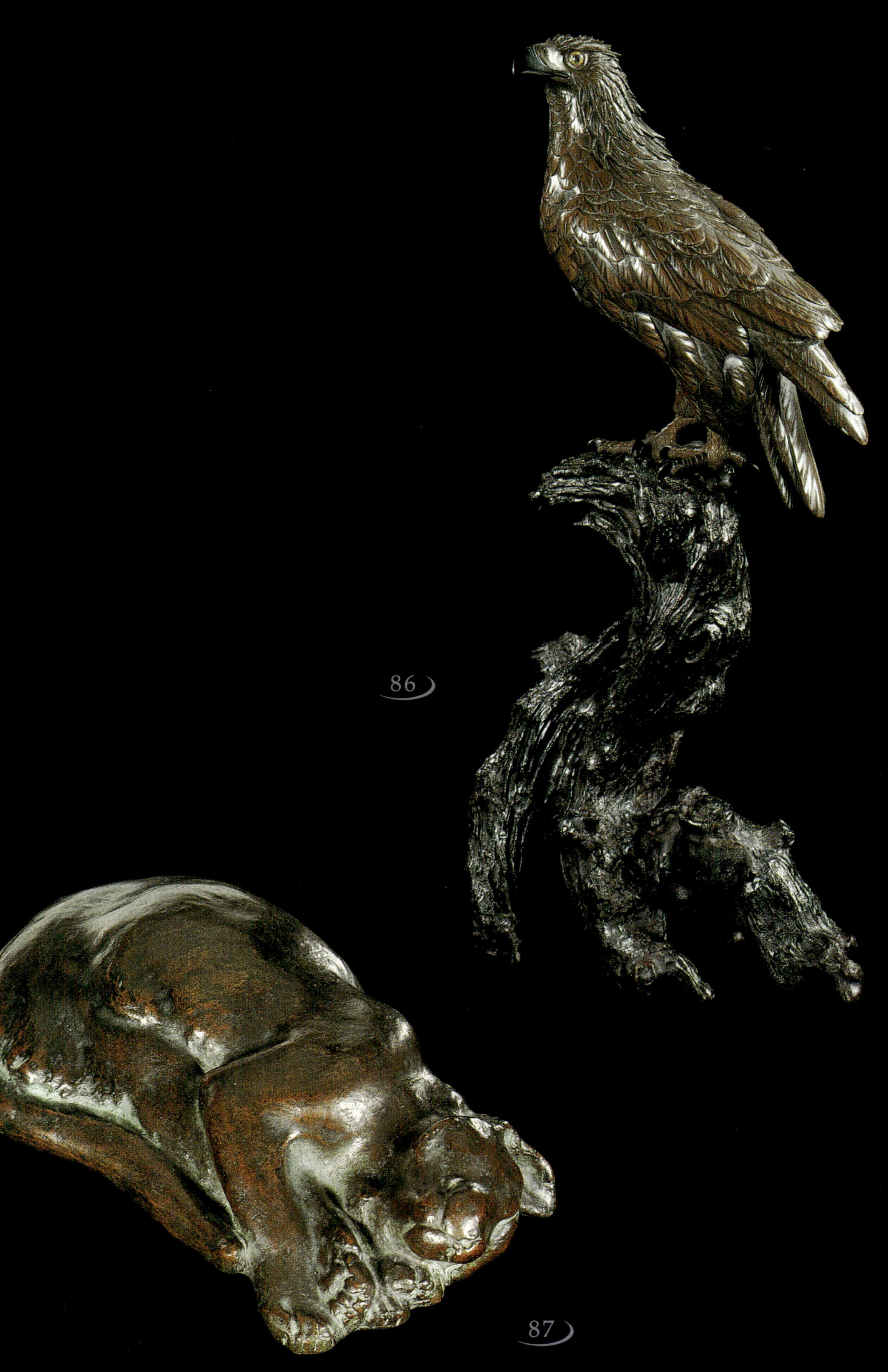

86

87

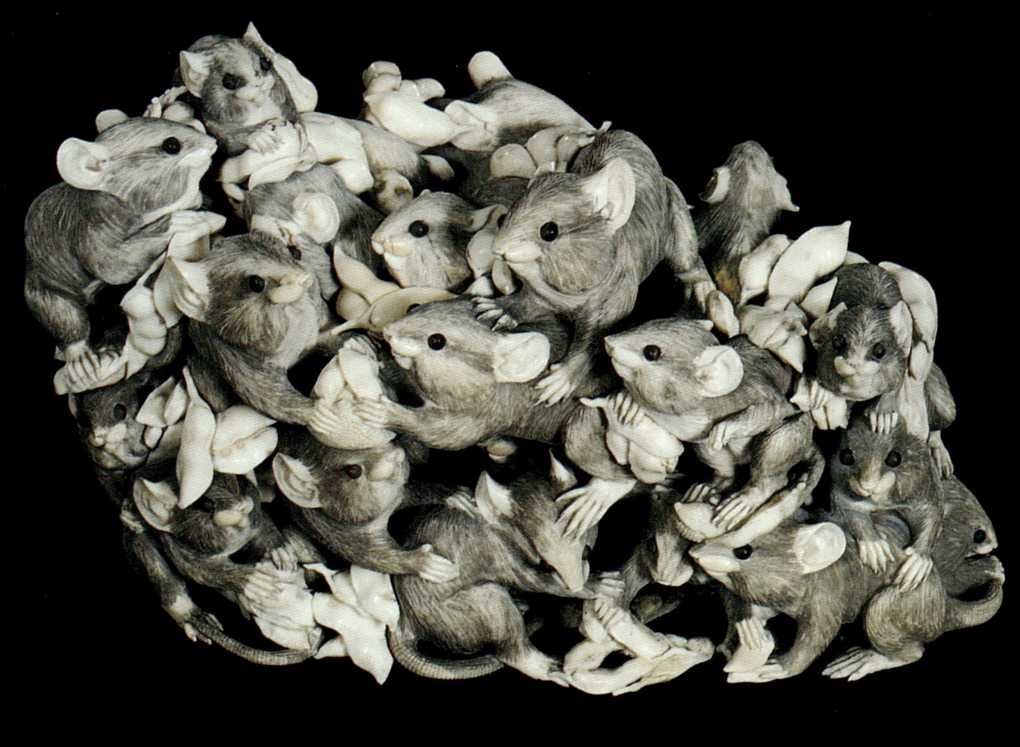

88

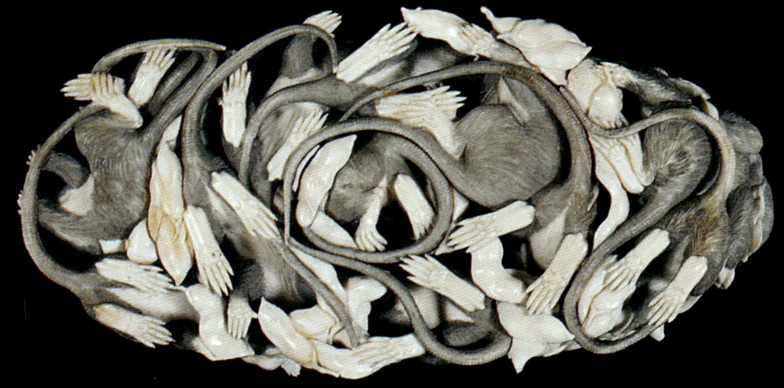

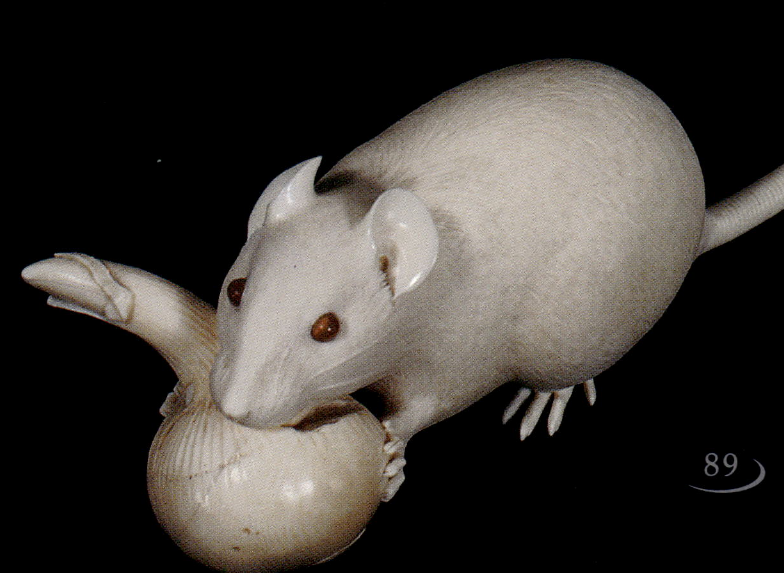

89

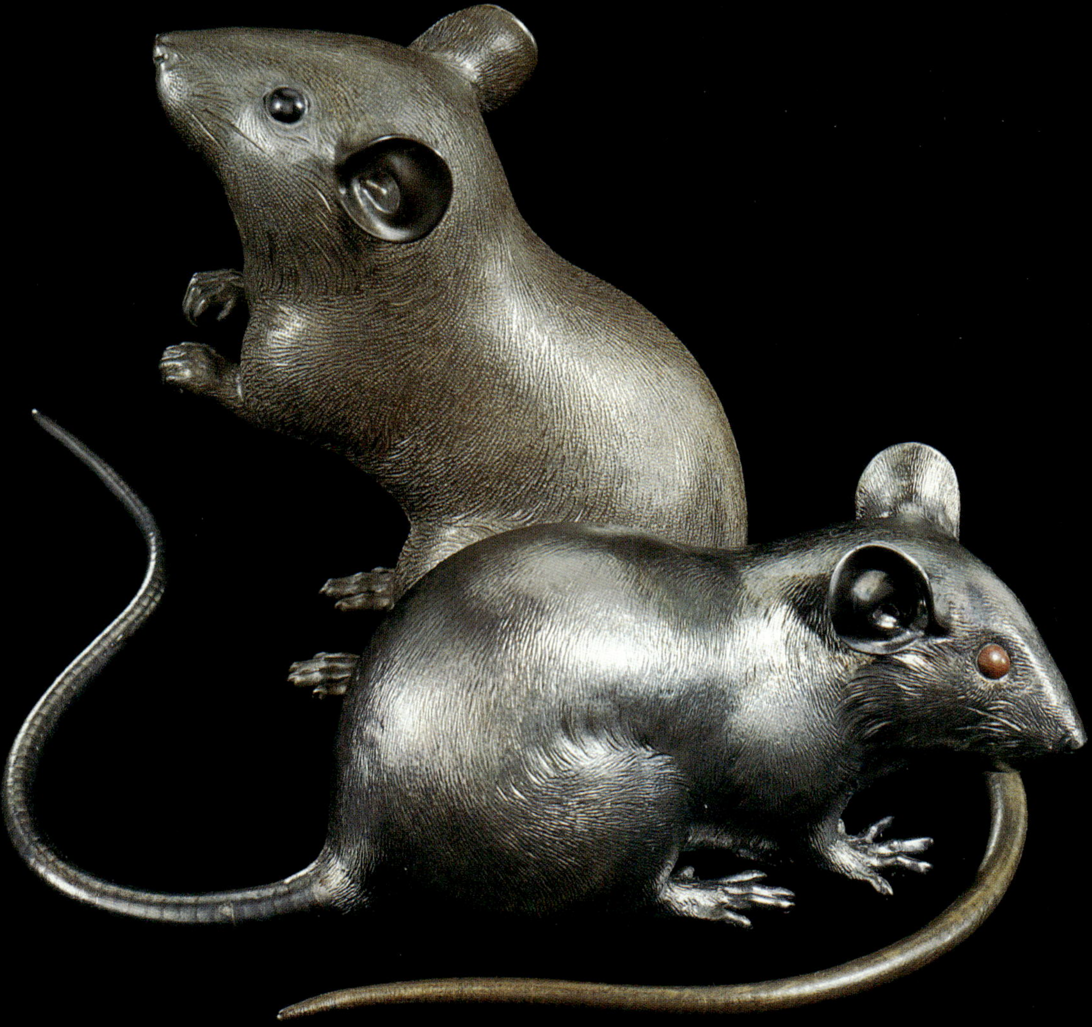

90

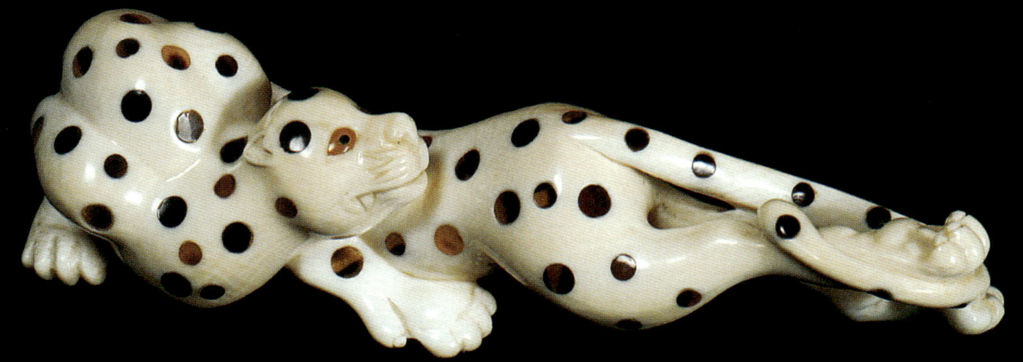

91

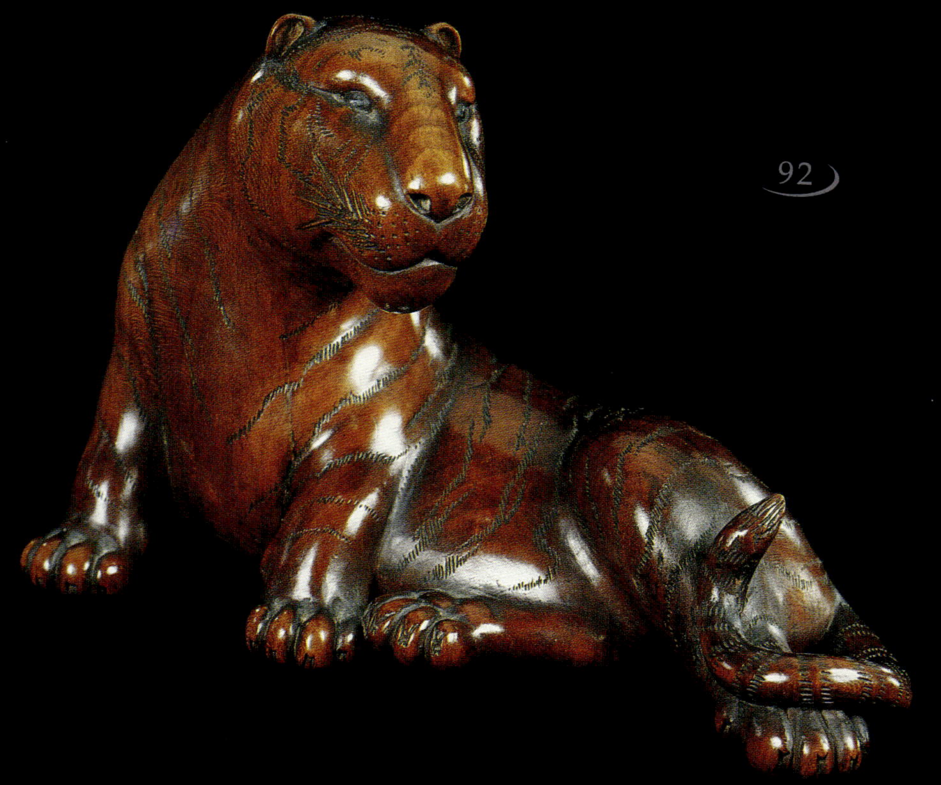

92

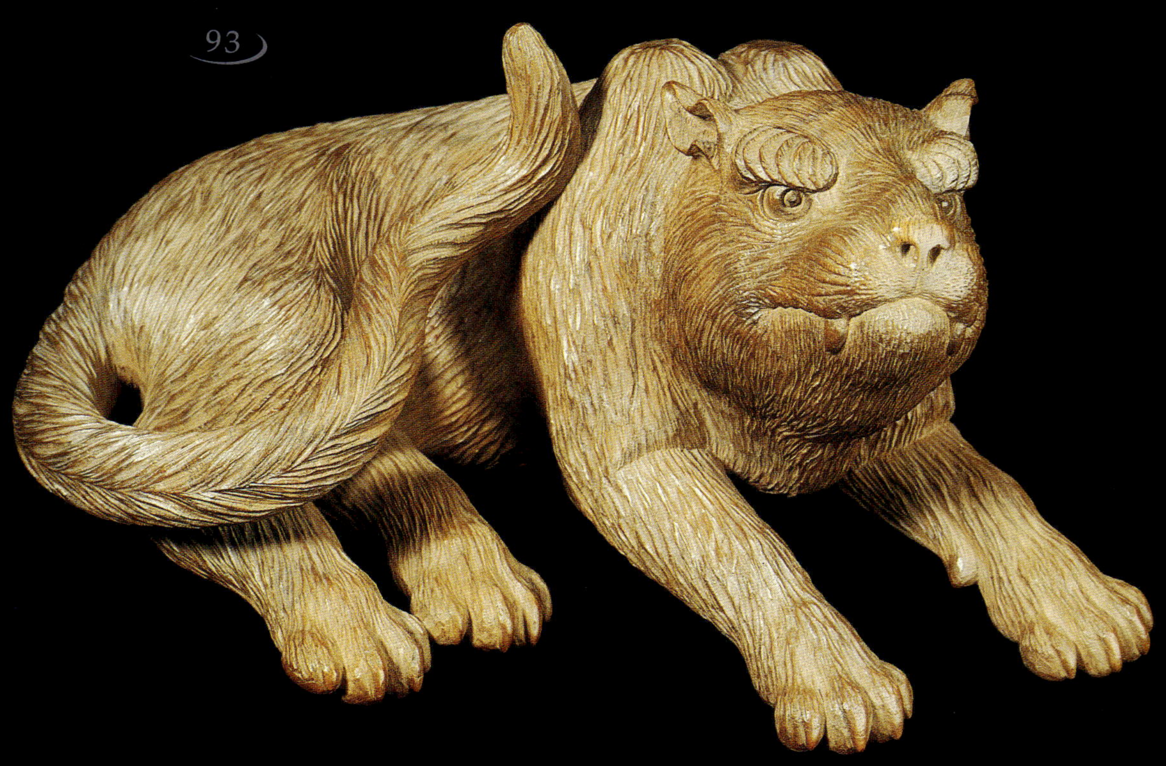

93

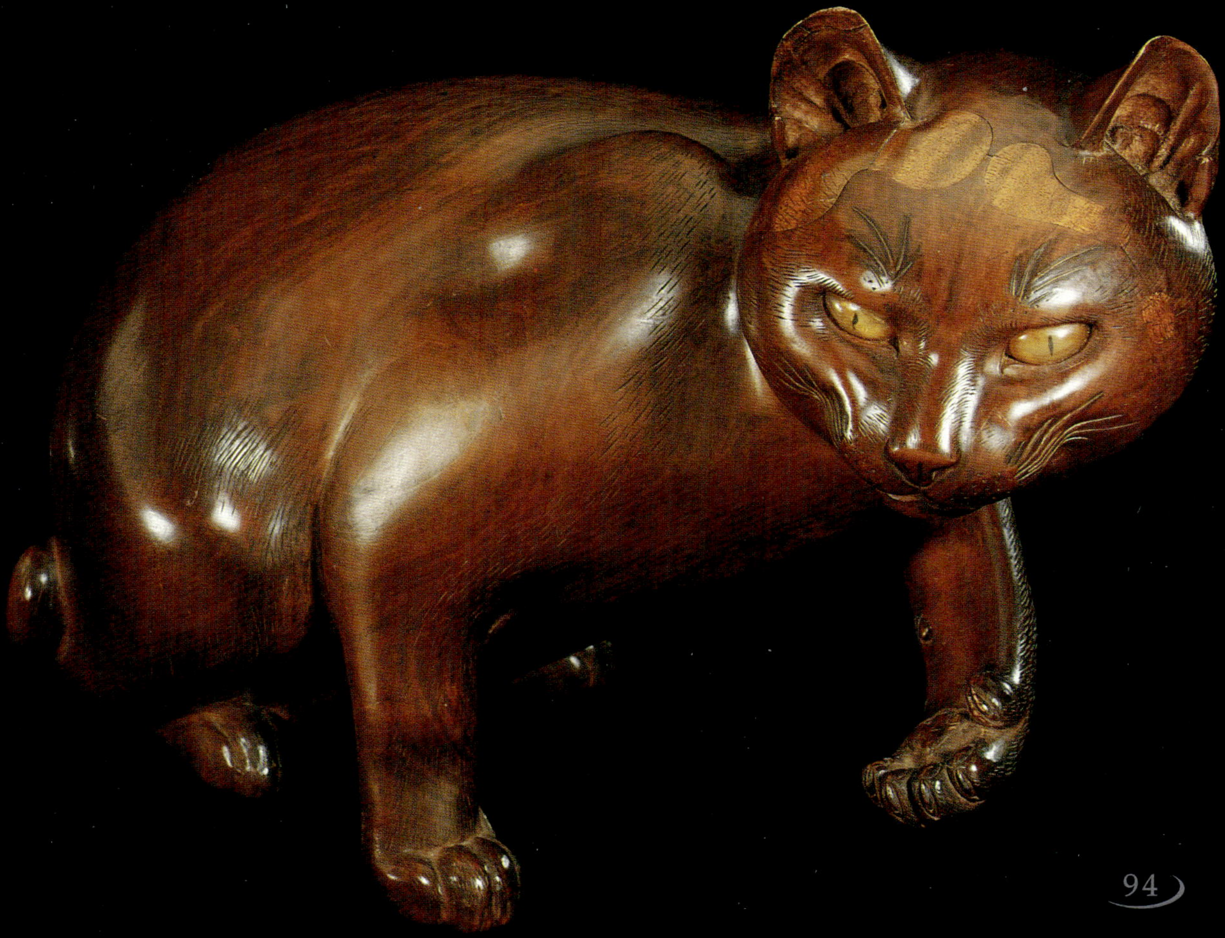

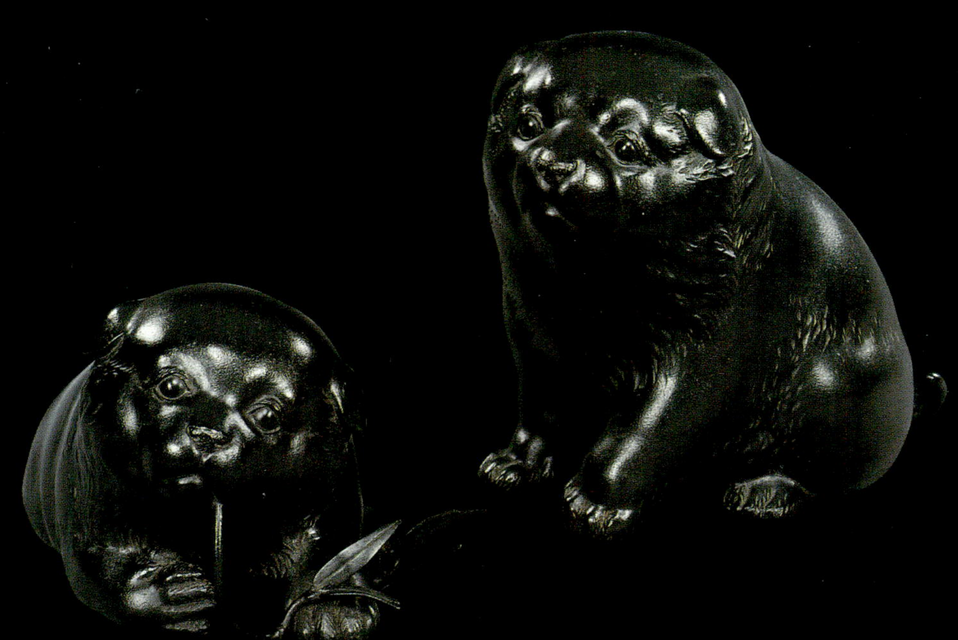

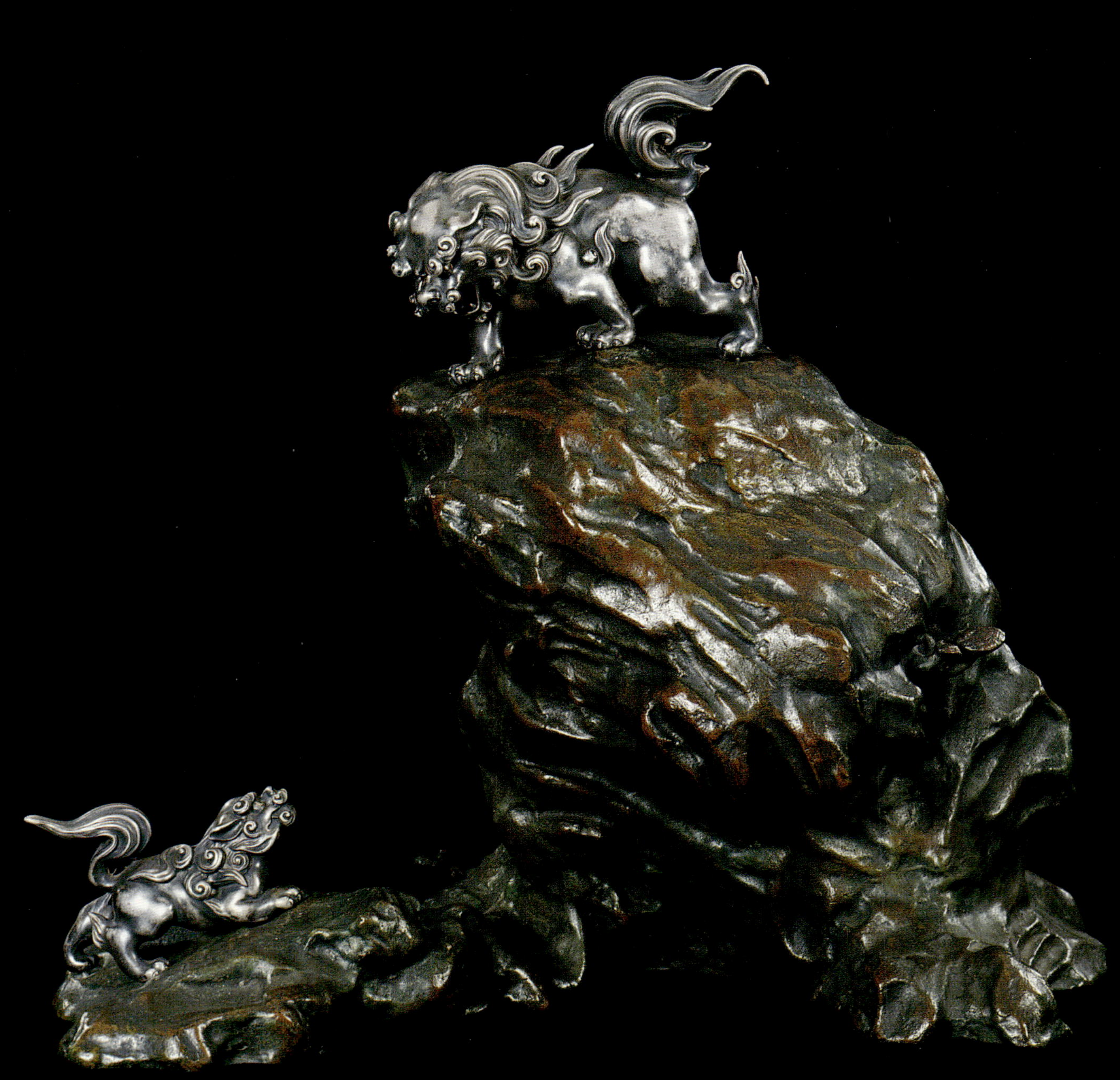

96

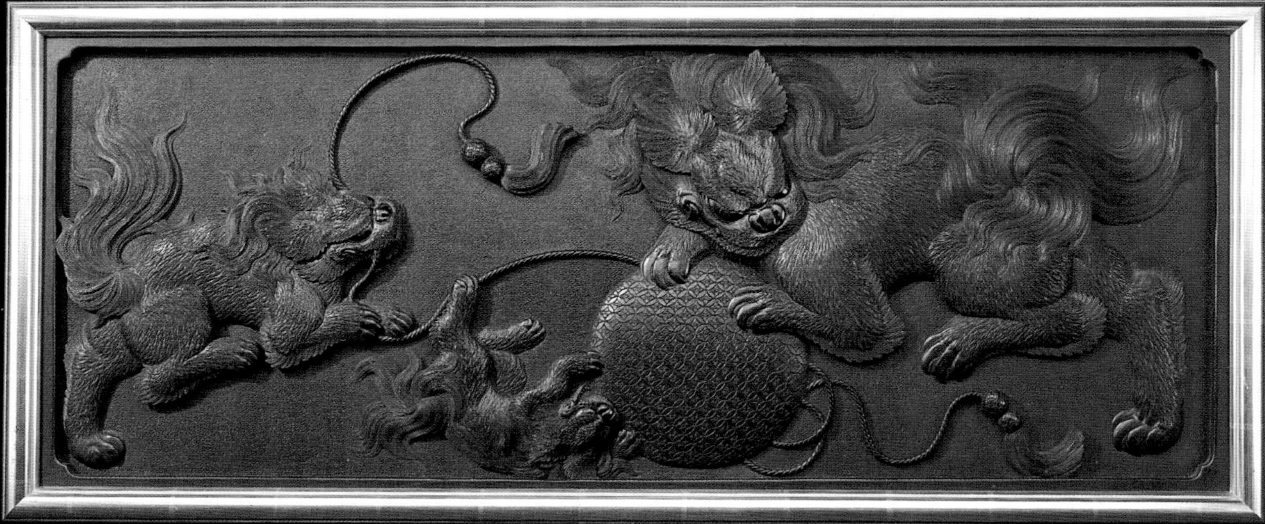

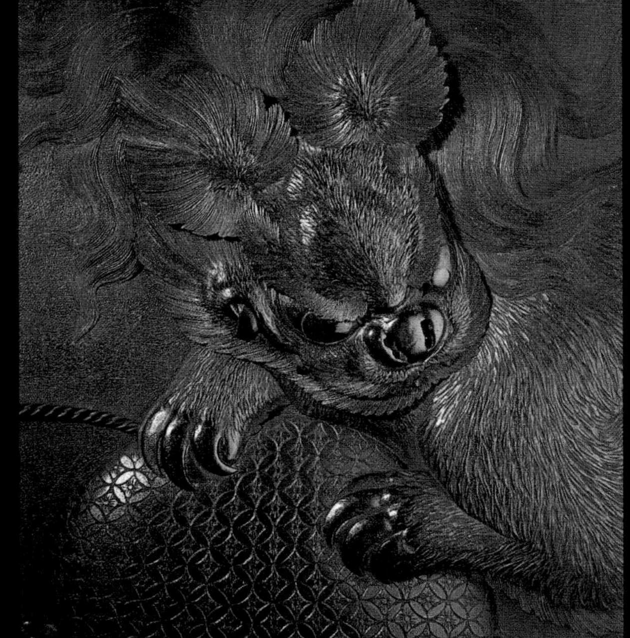

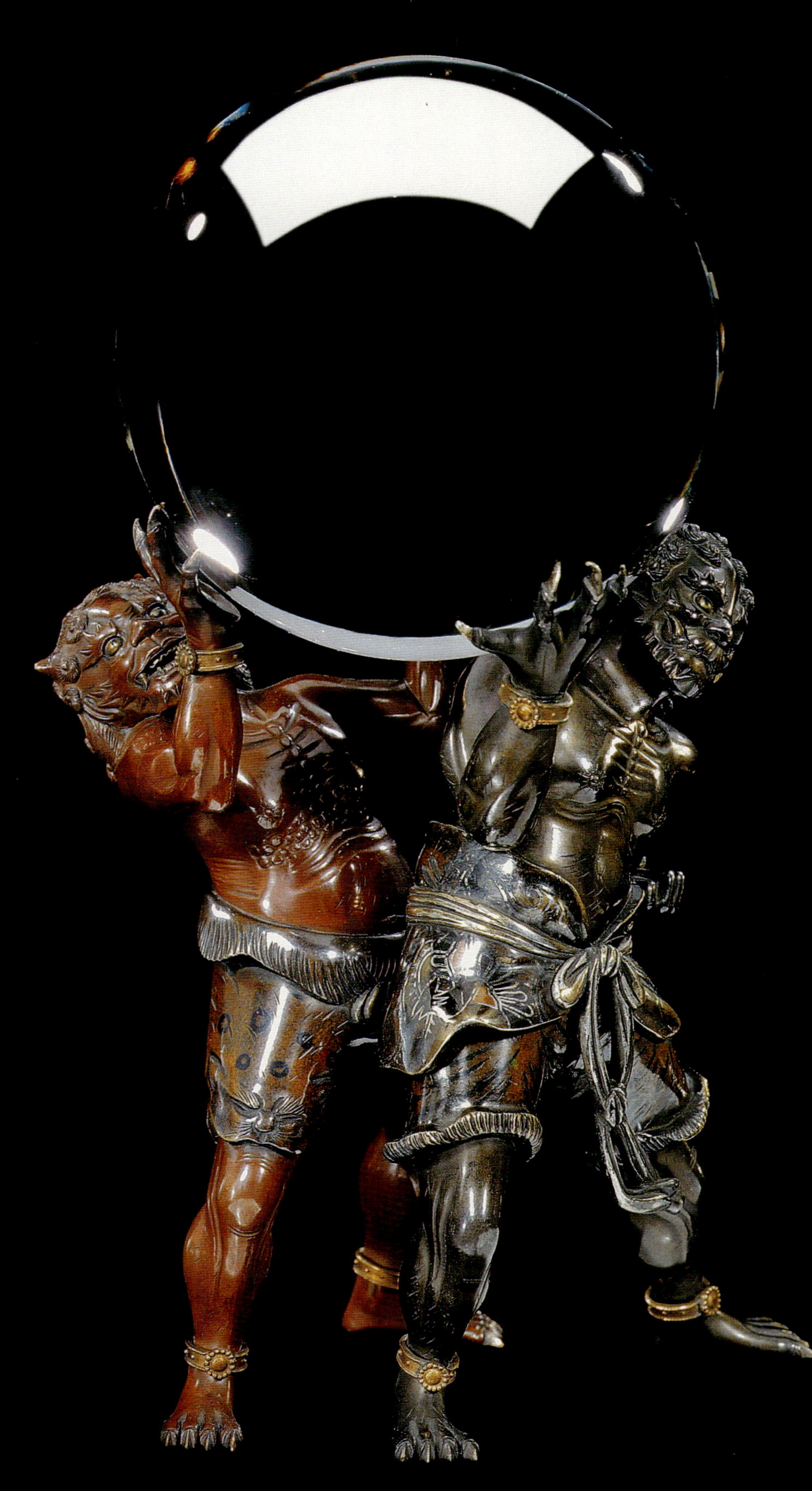

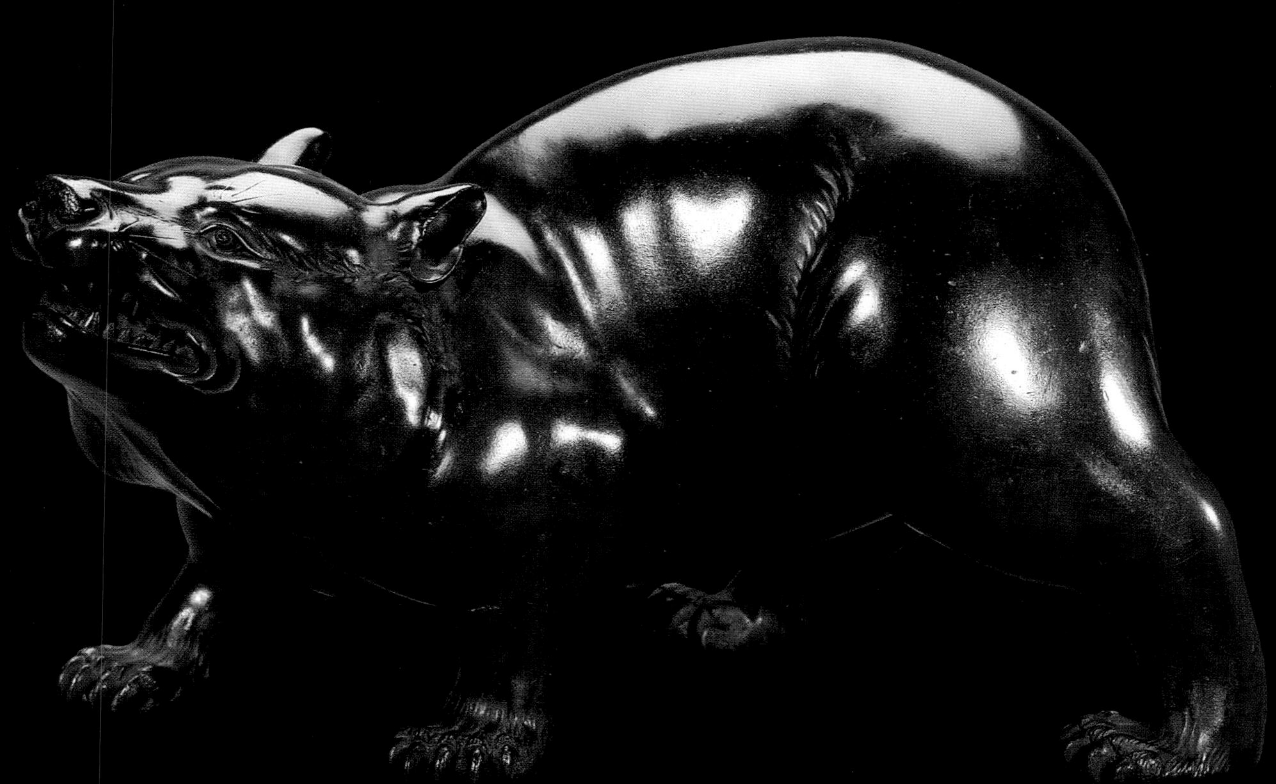

99

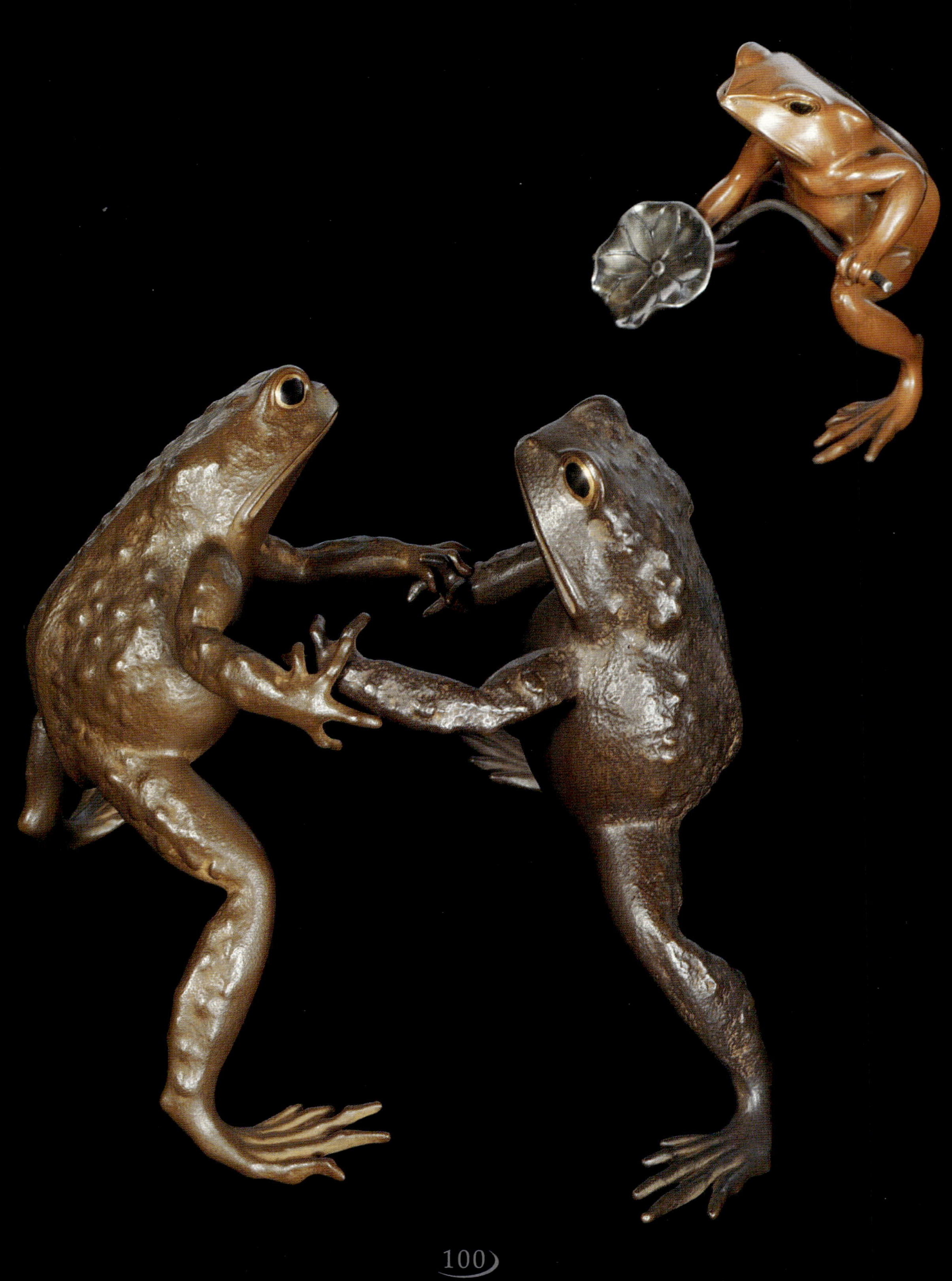

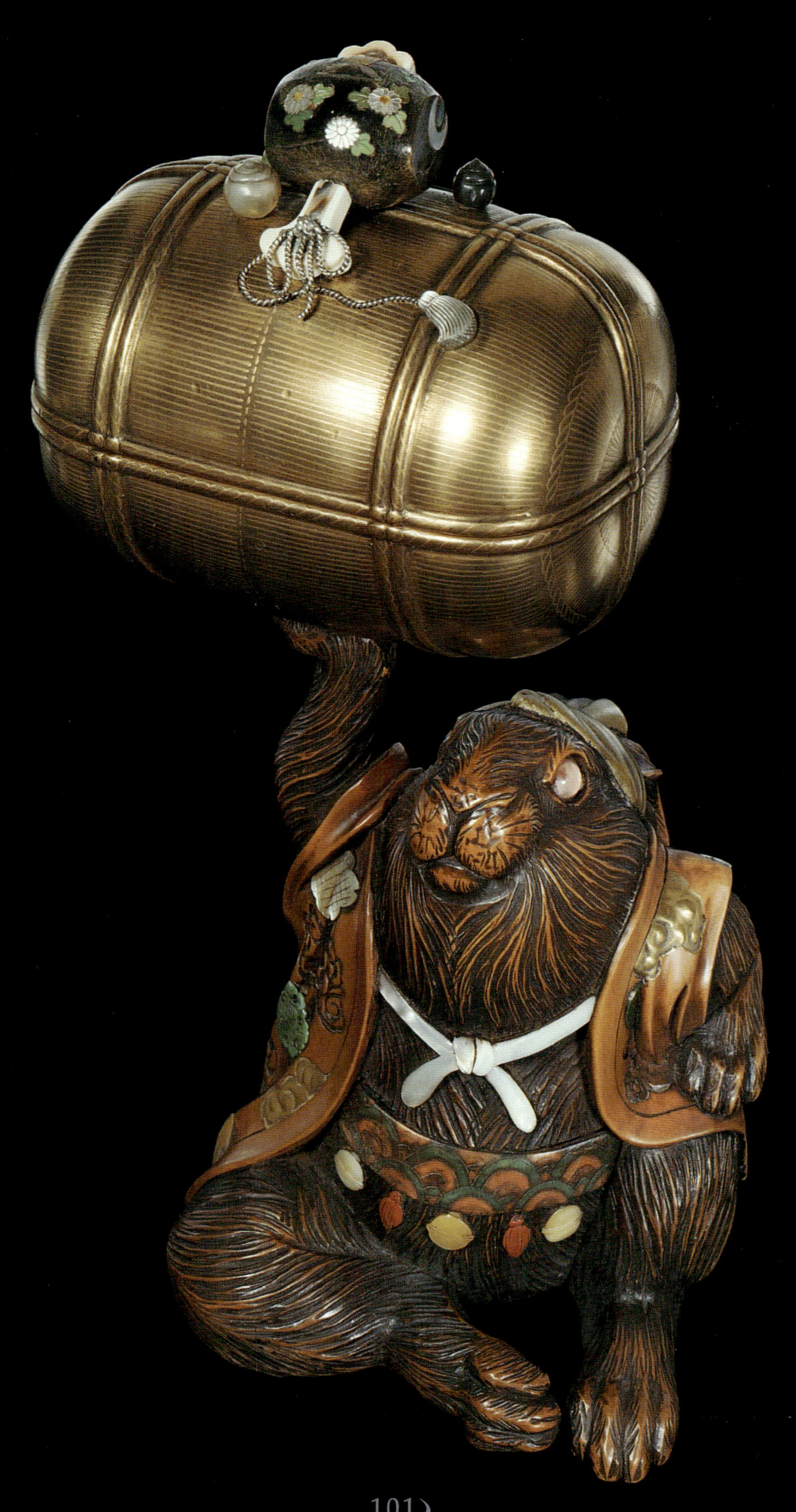

101

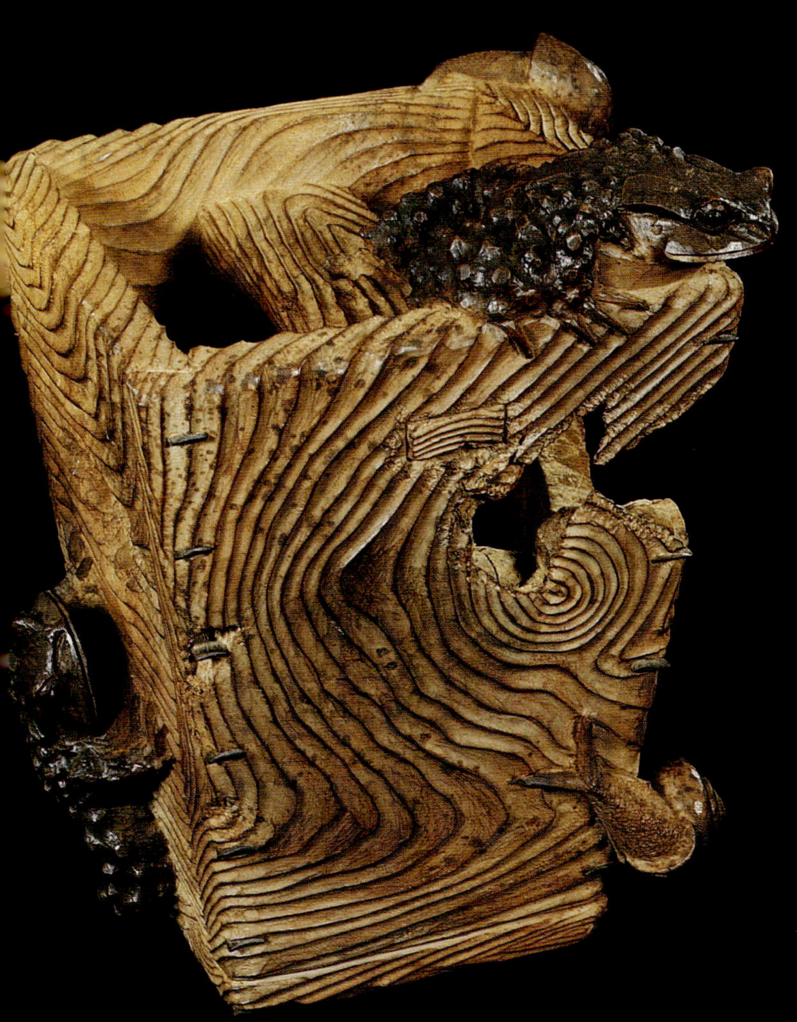

102

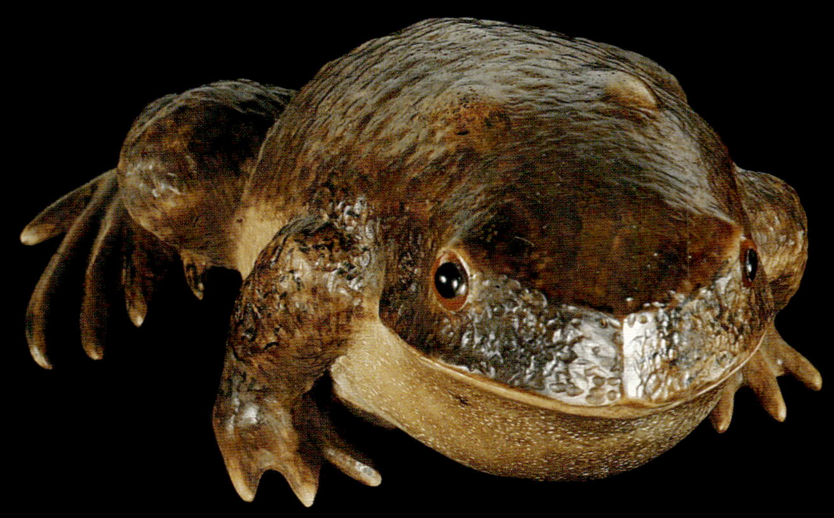

103

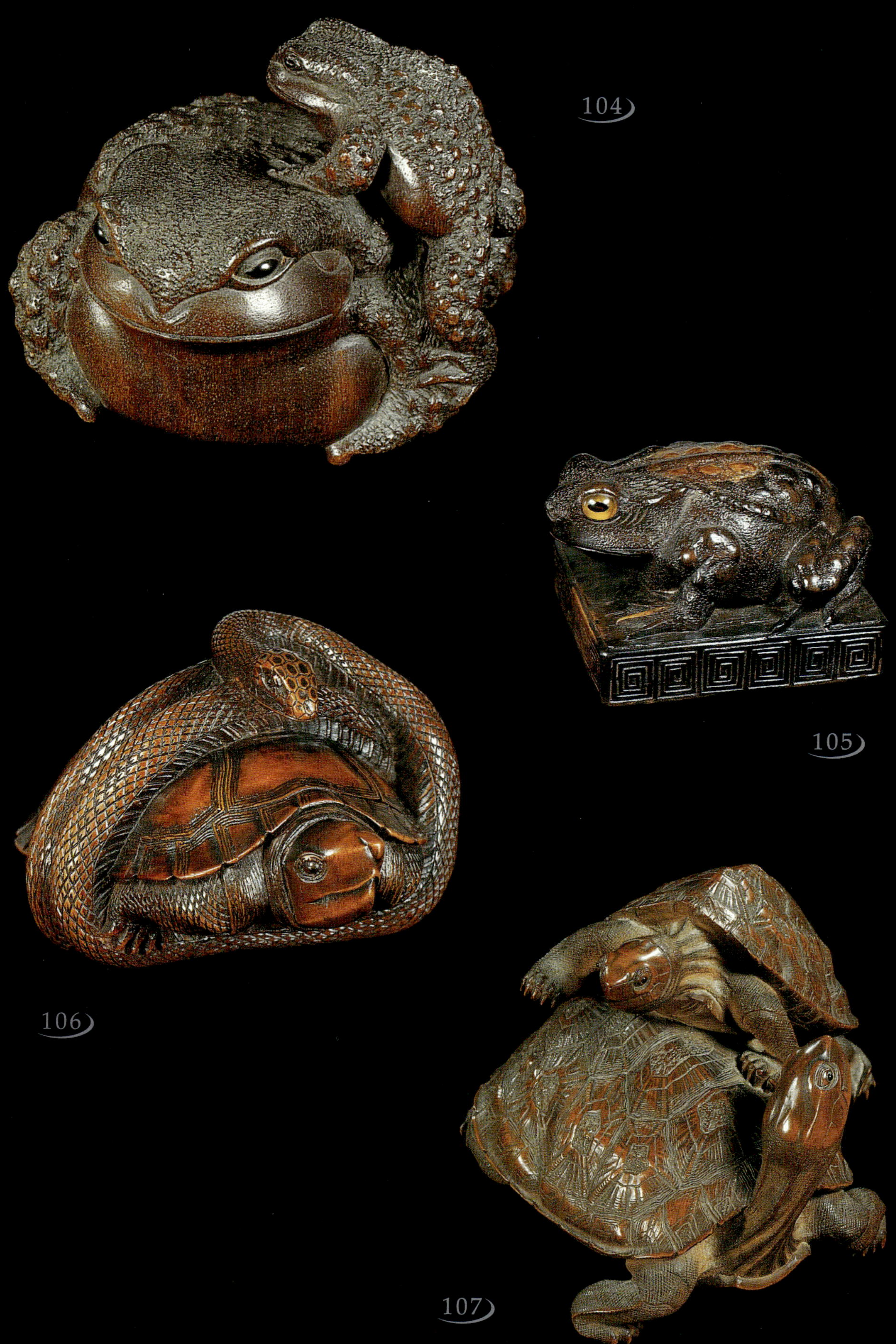
104
105
106
107

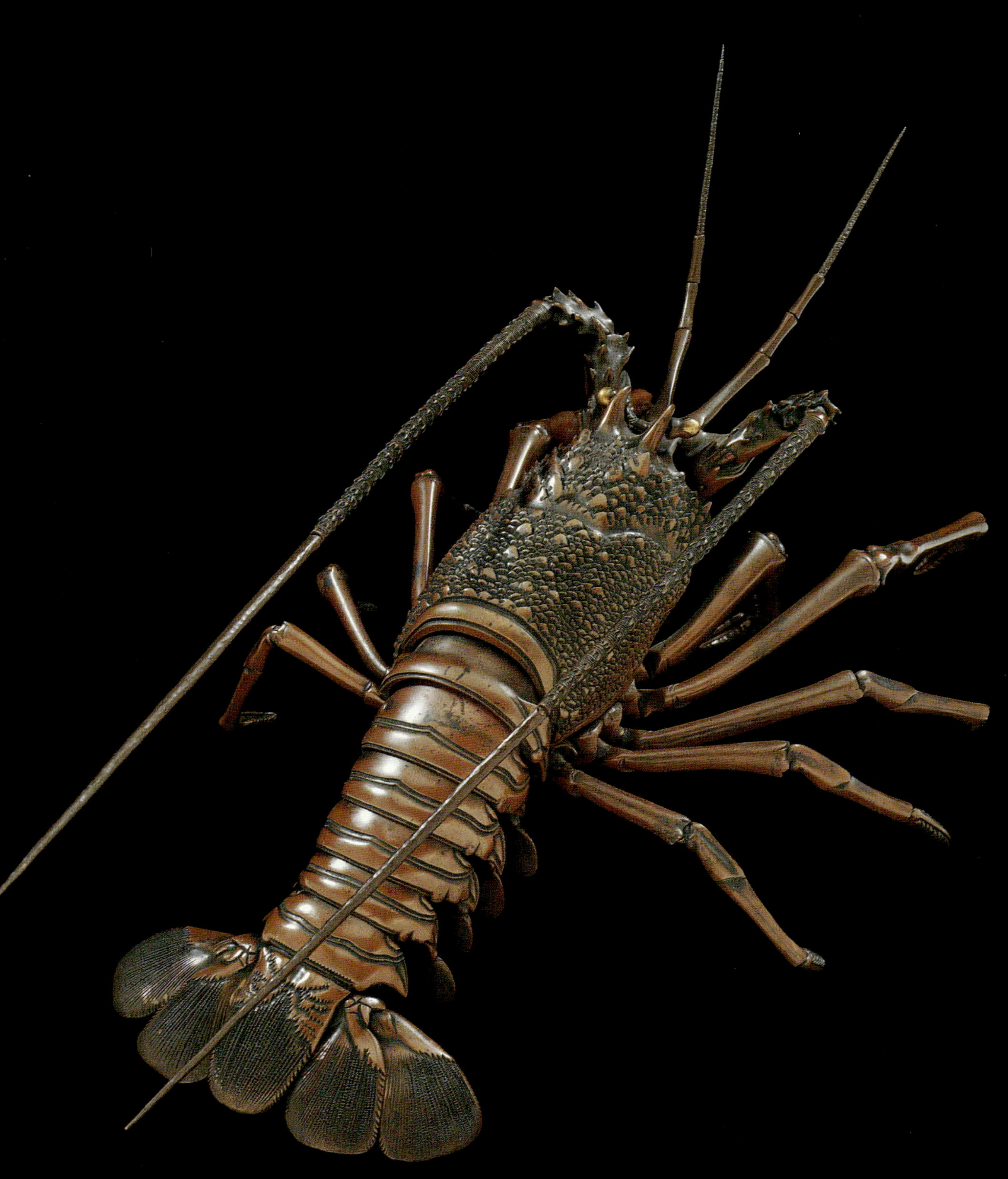

108

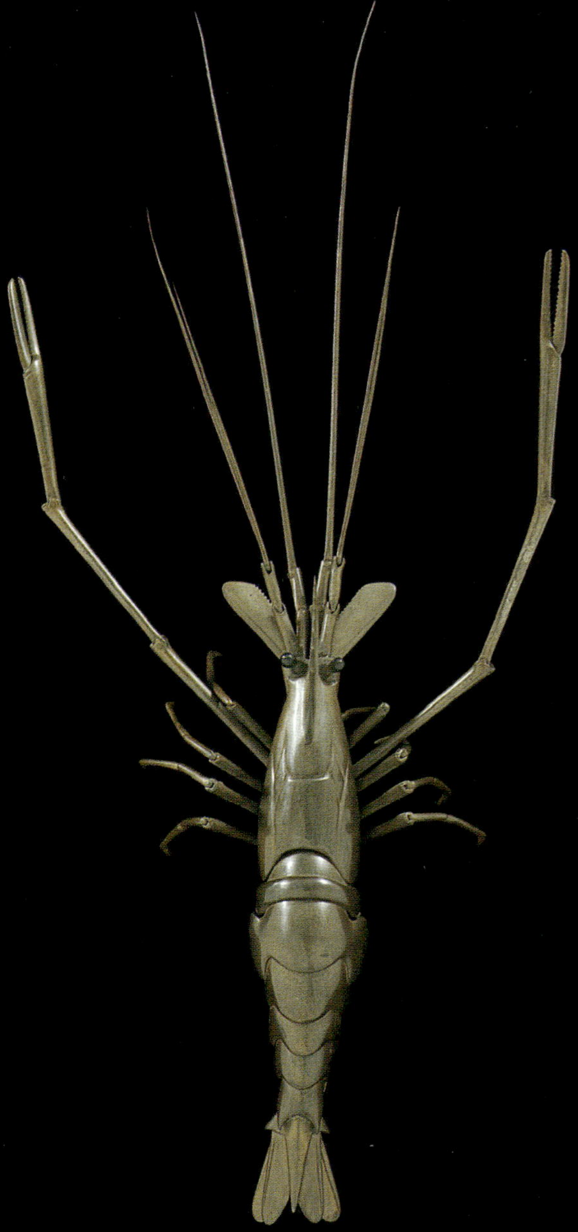

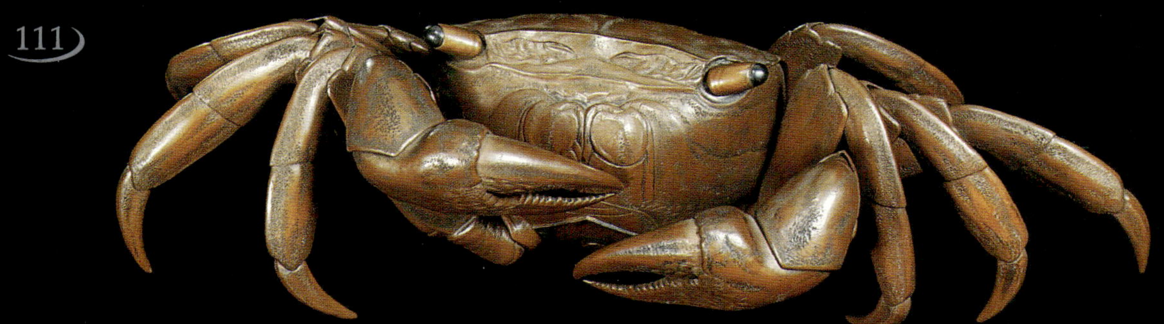

109

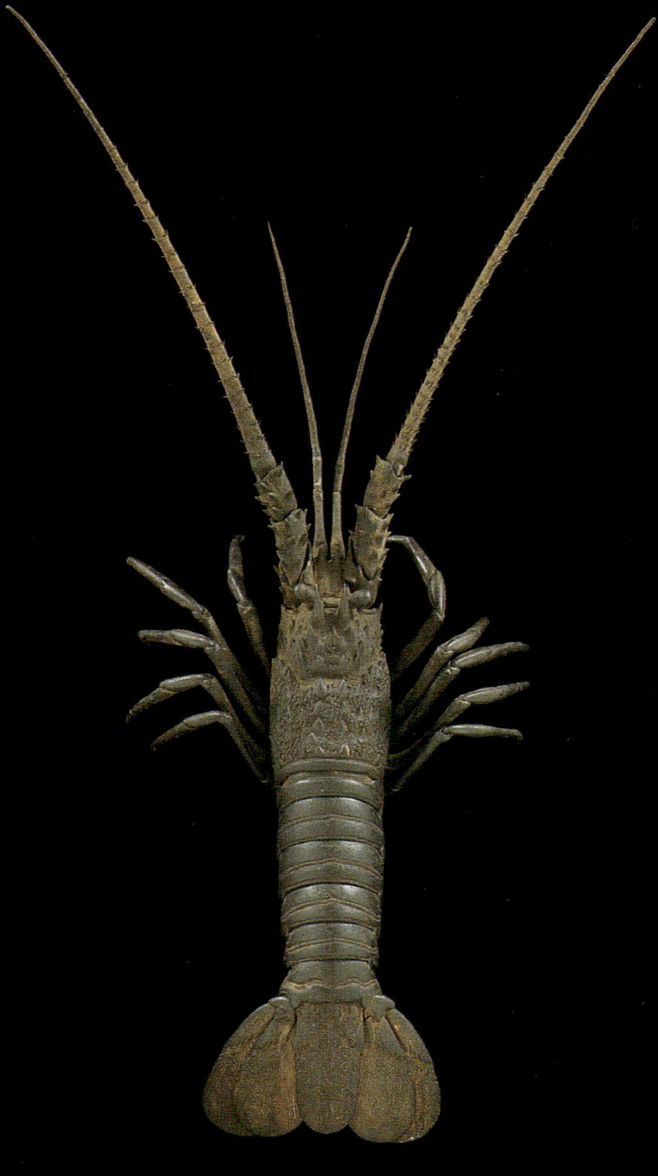

110

111

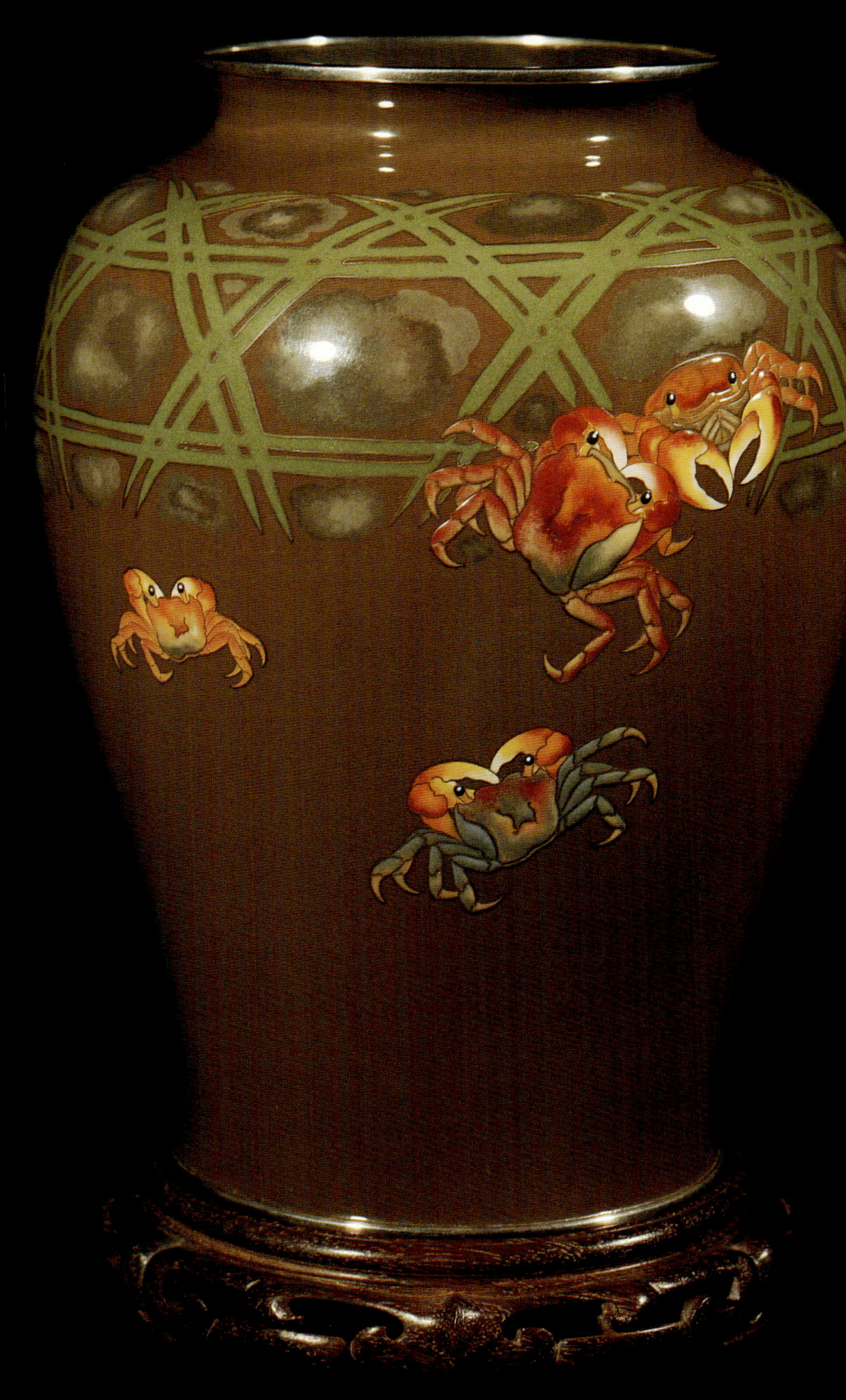

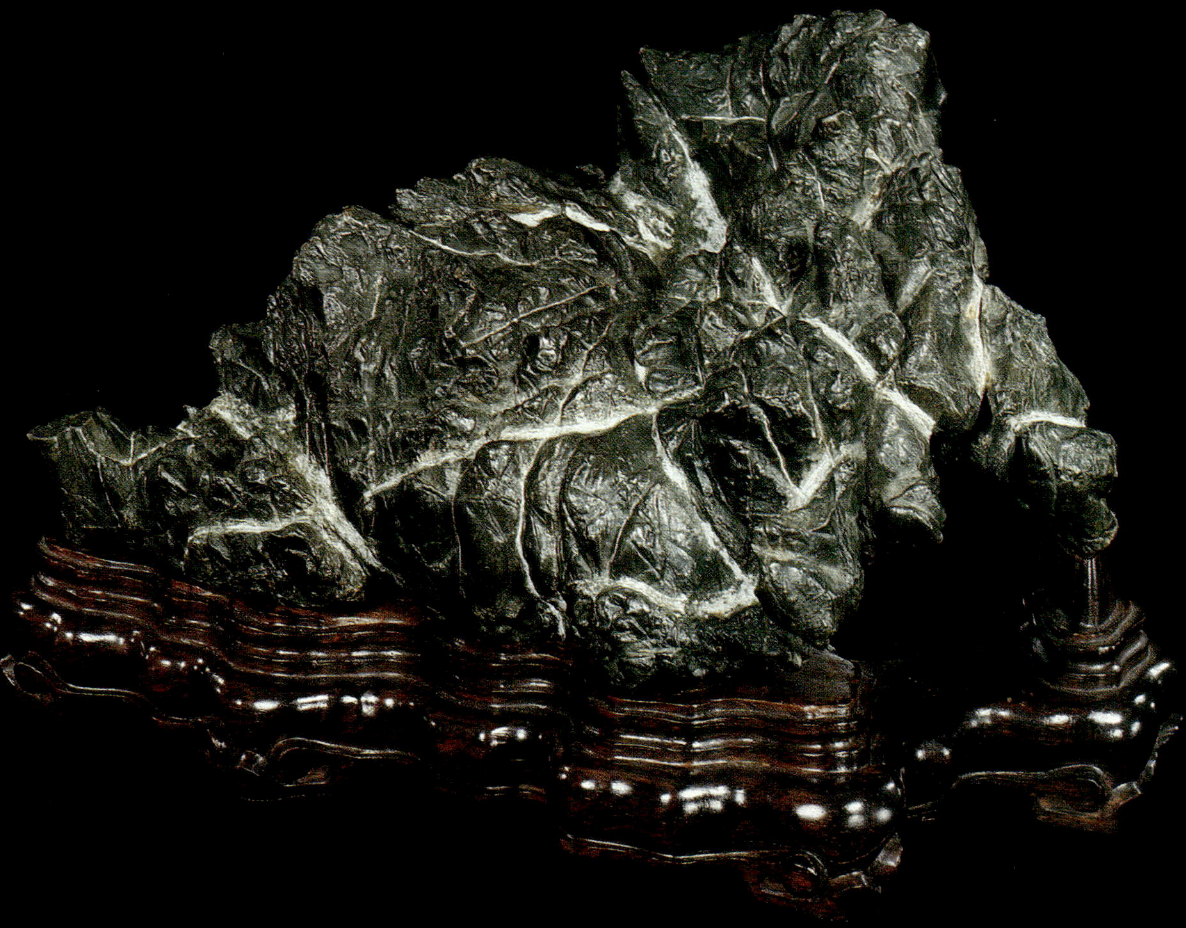

113

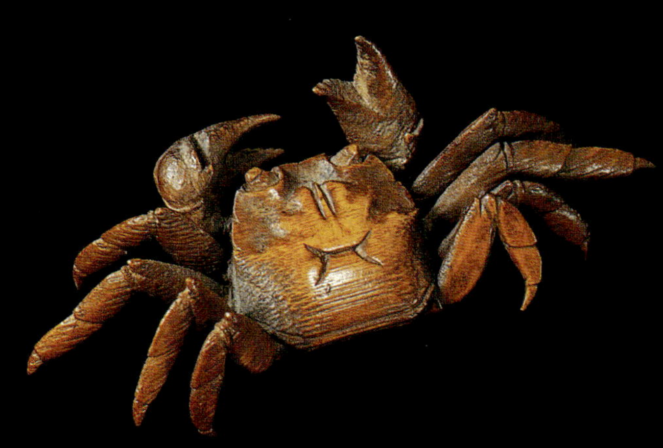

114

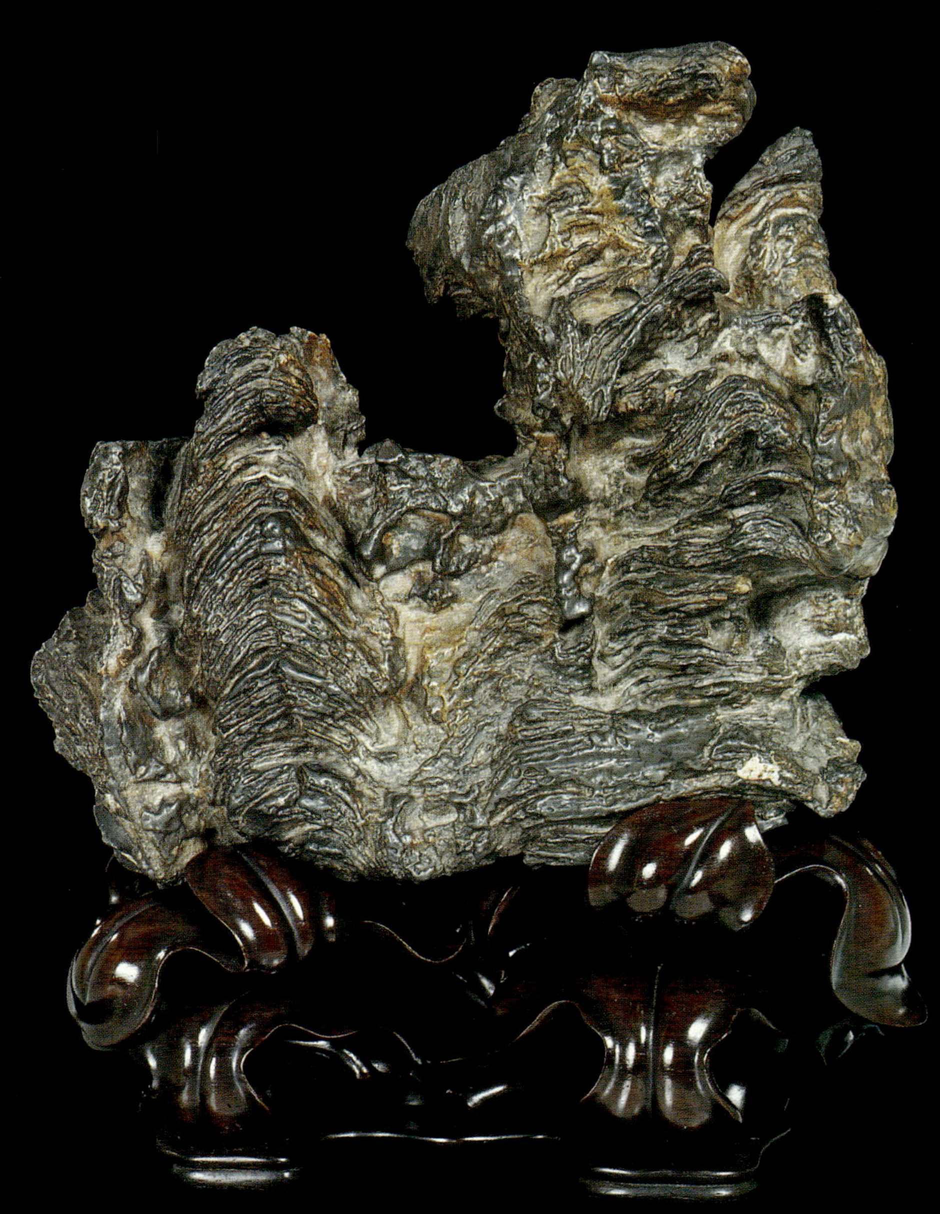

115

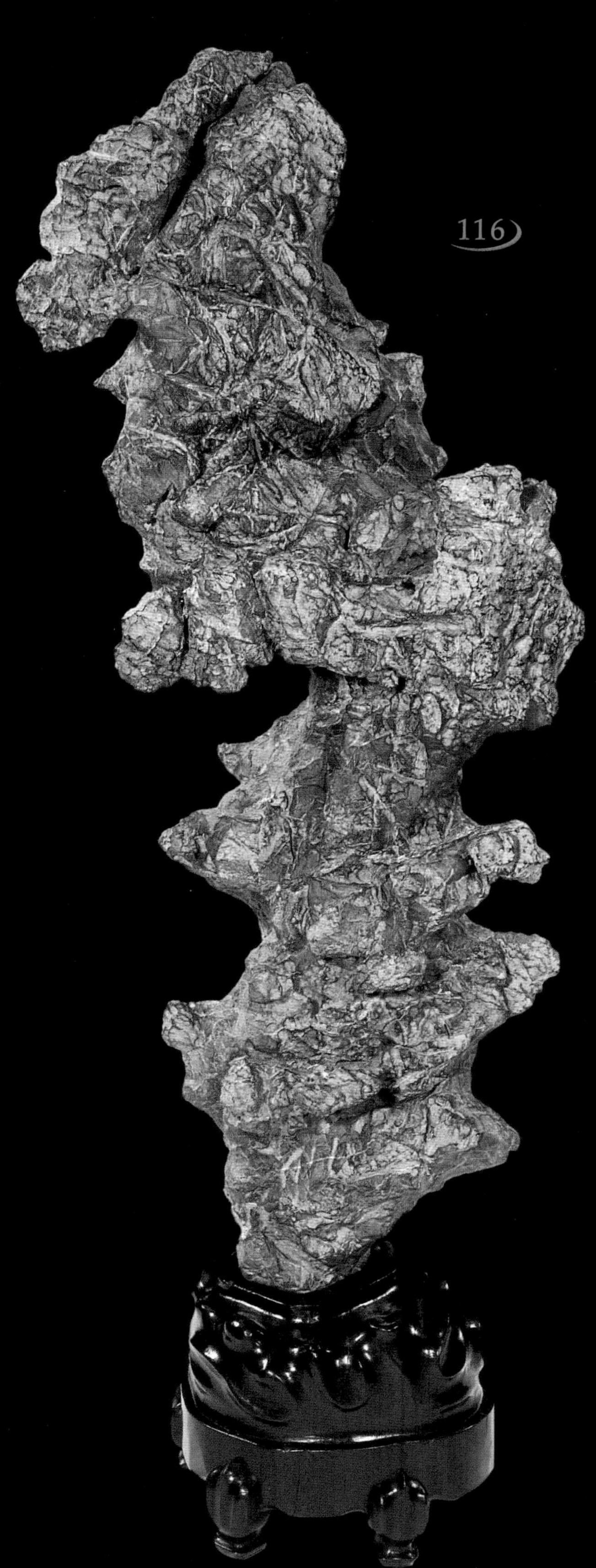

116

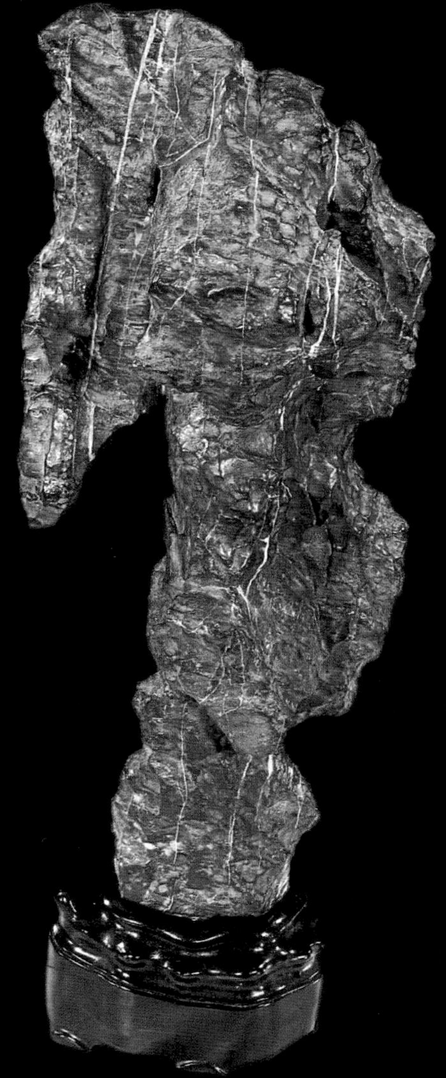

117

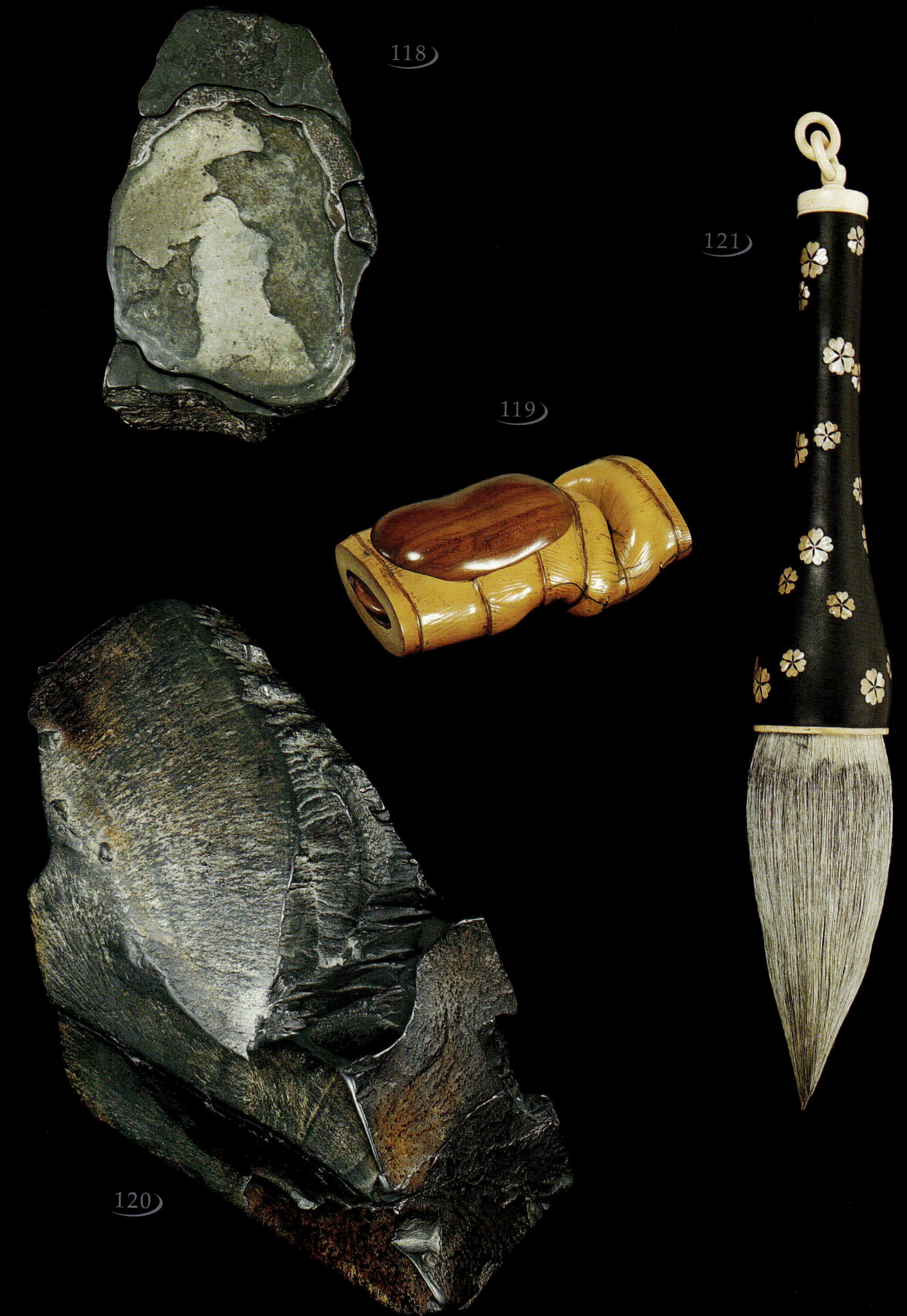

118
119
120
121

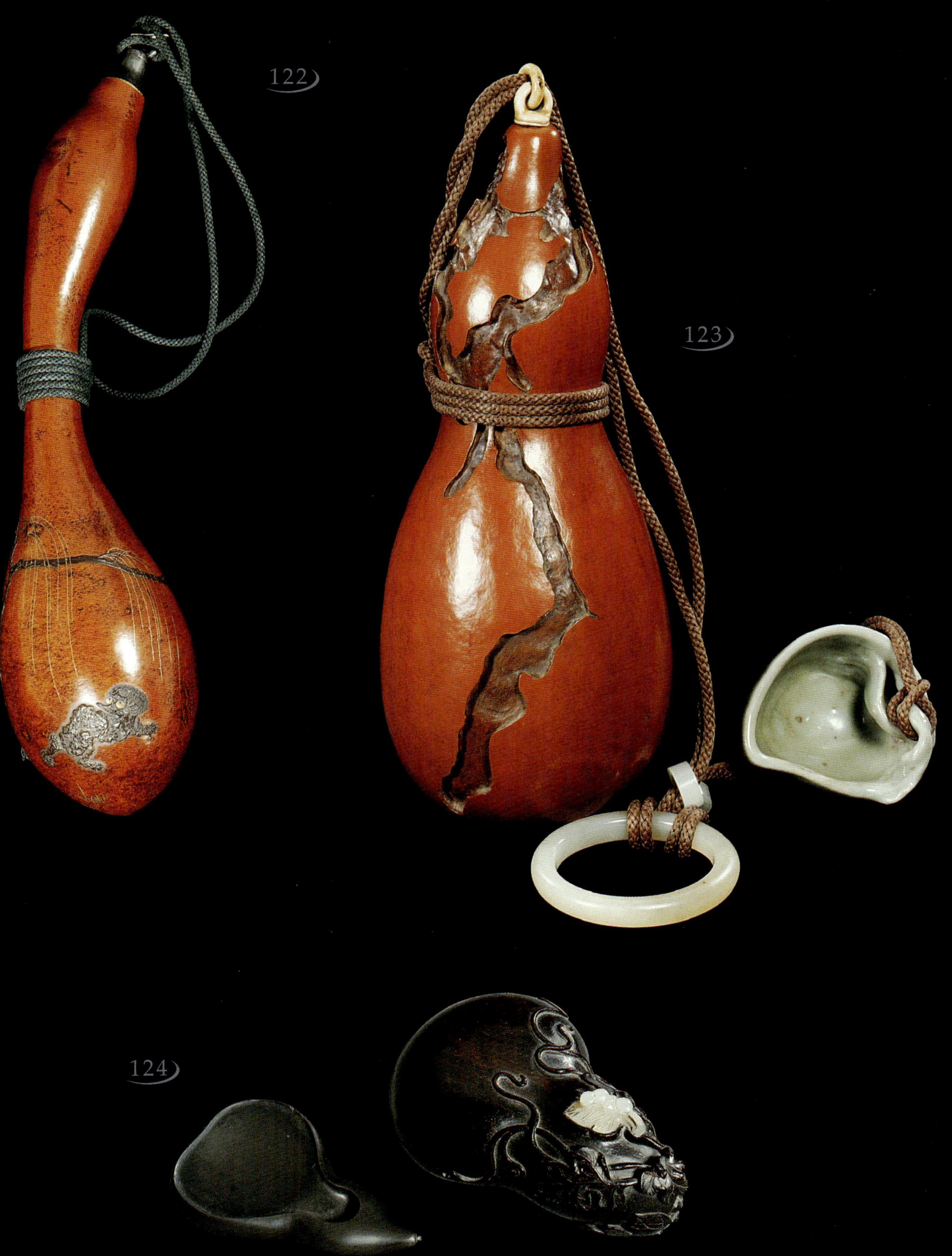

122
123
124

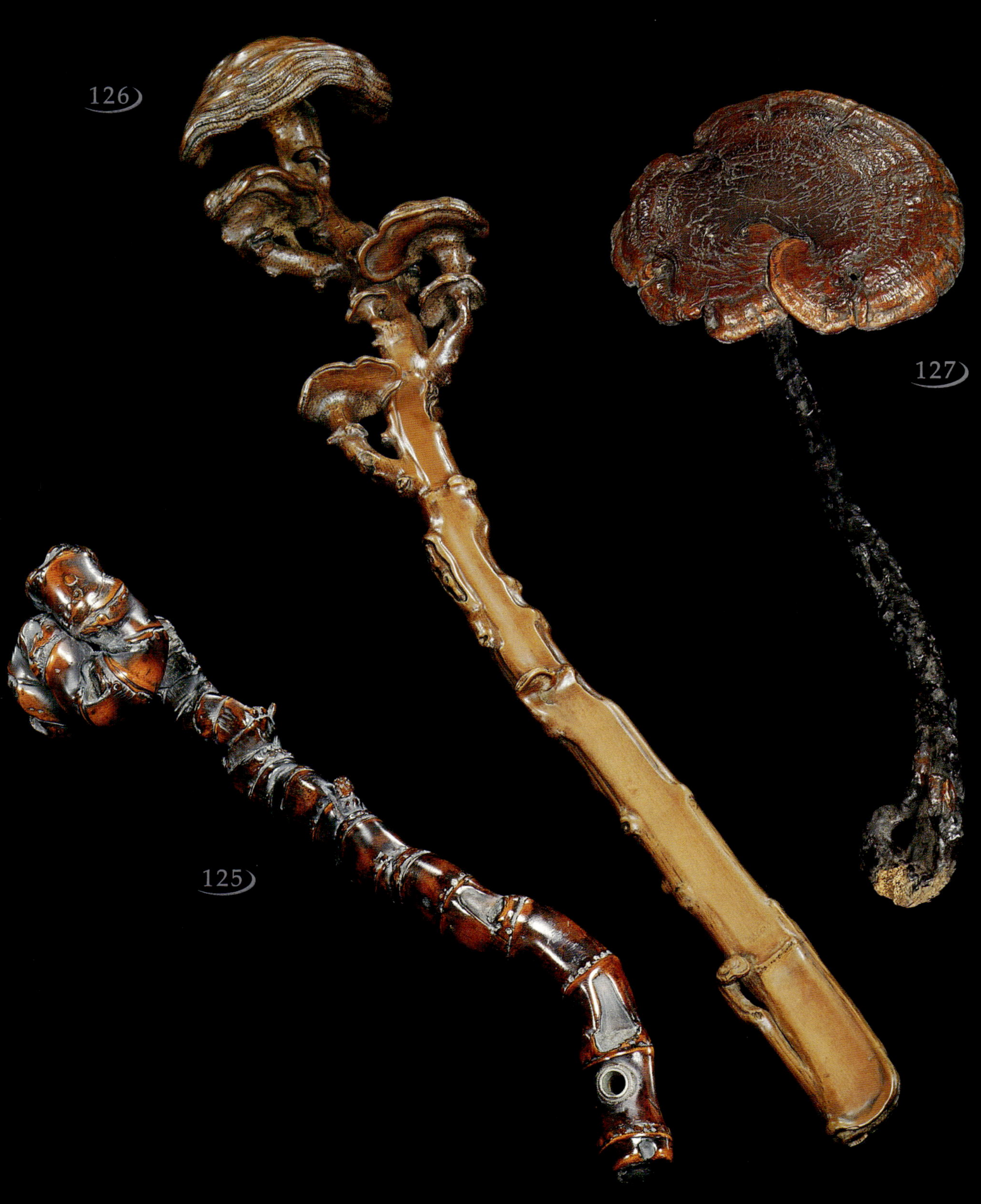

126
127
125

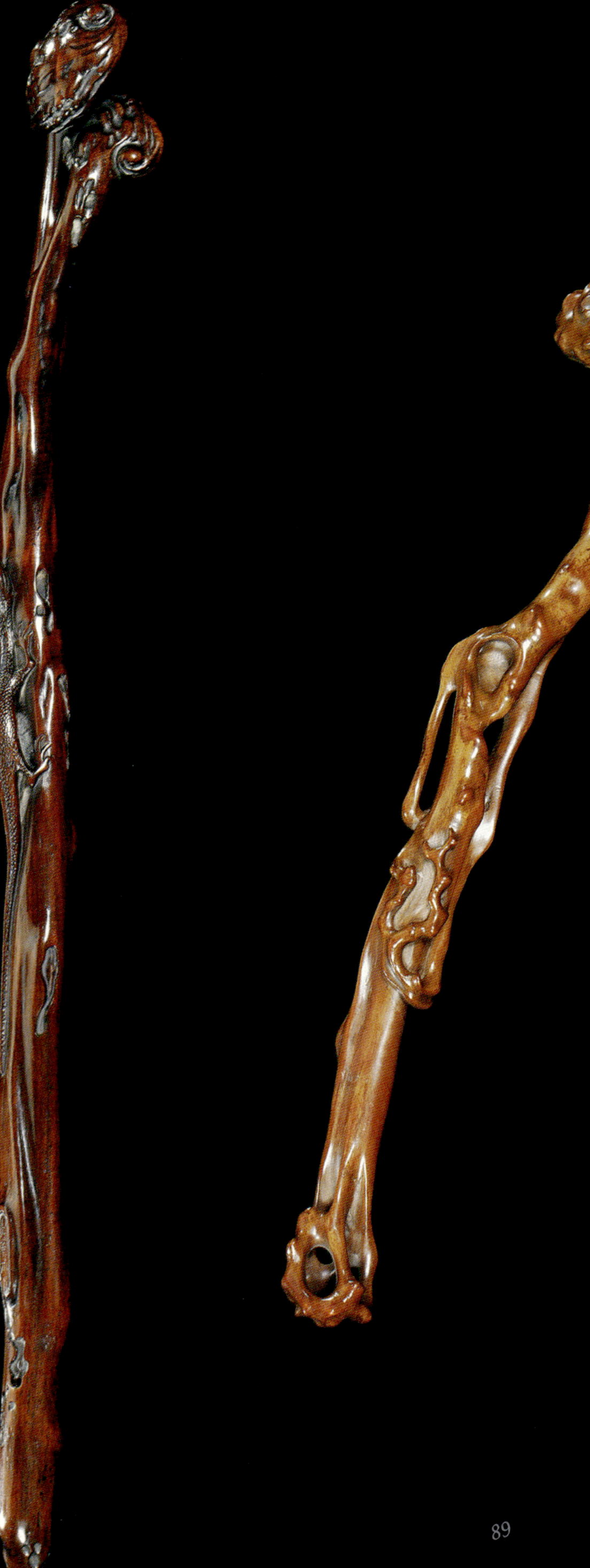

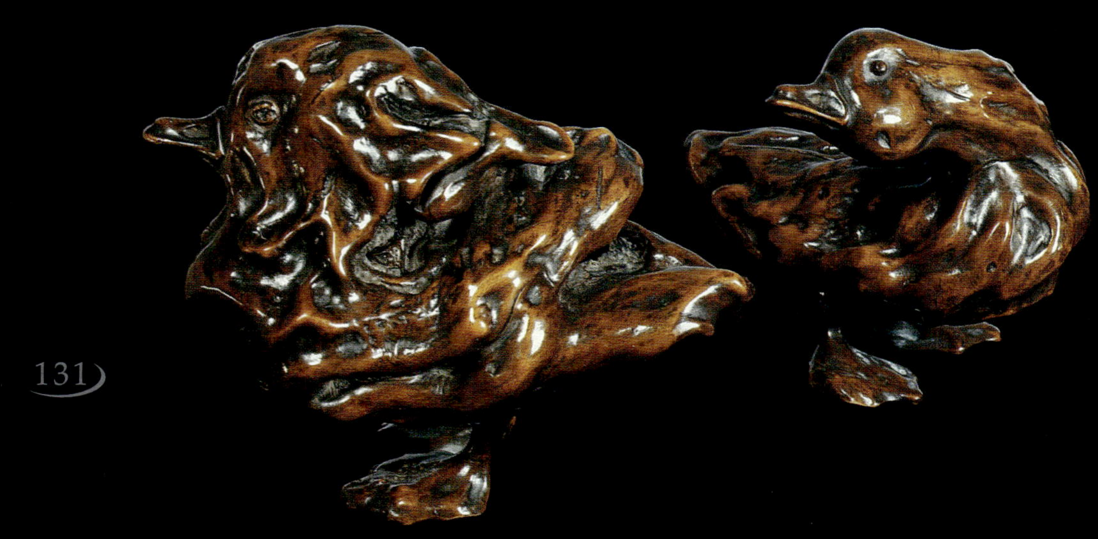

130

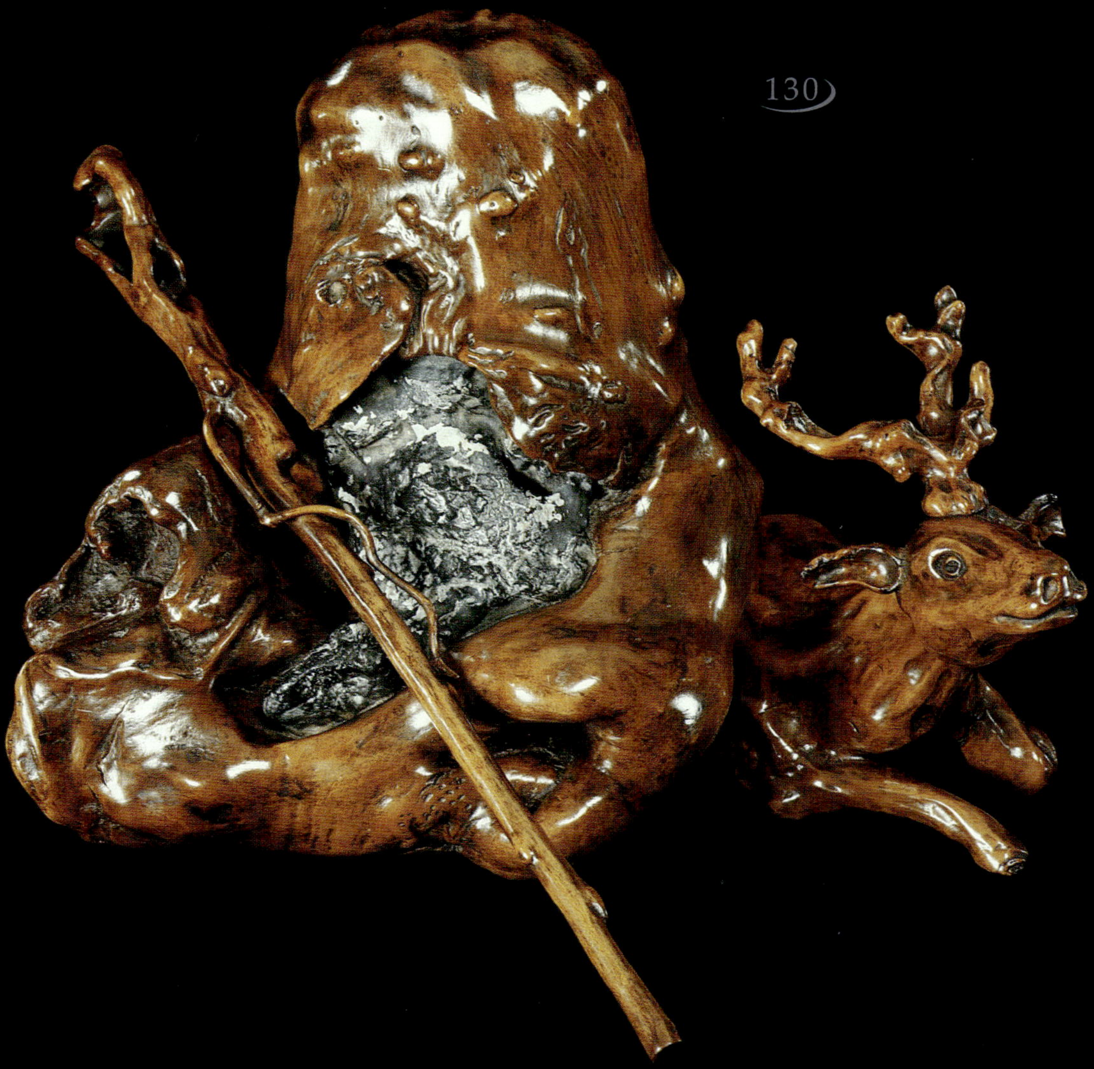

131

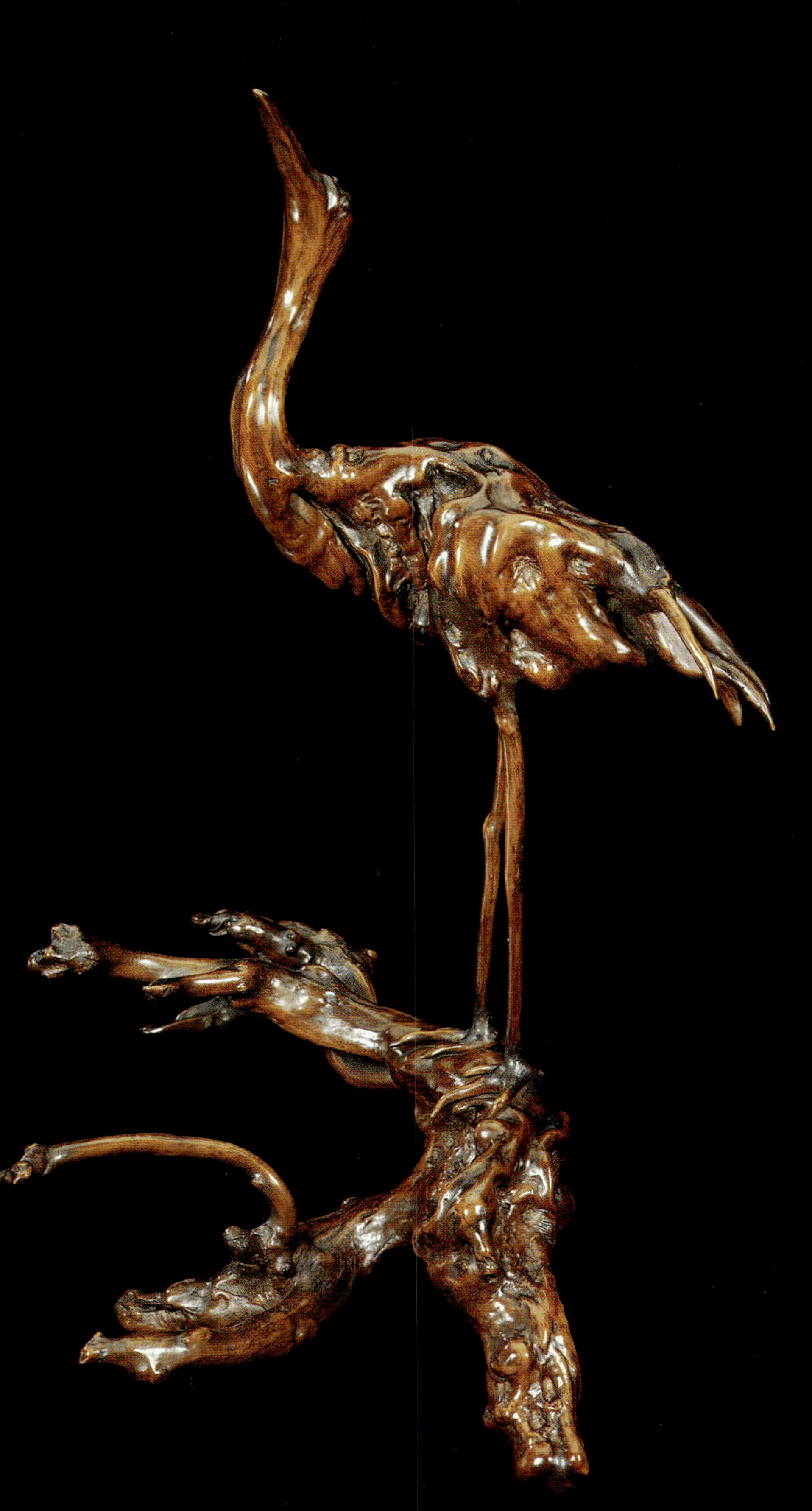

132

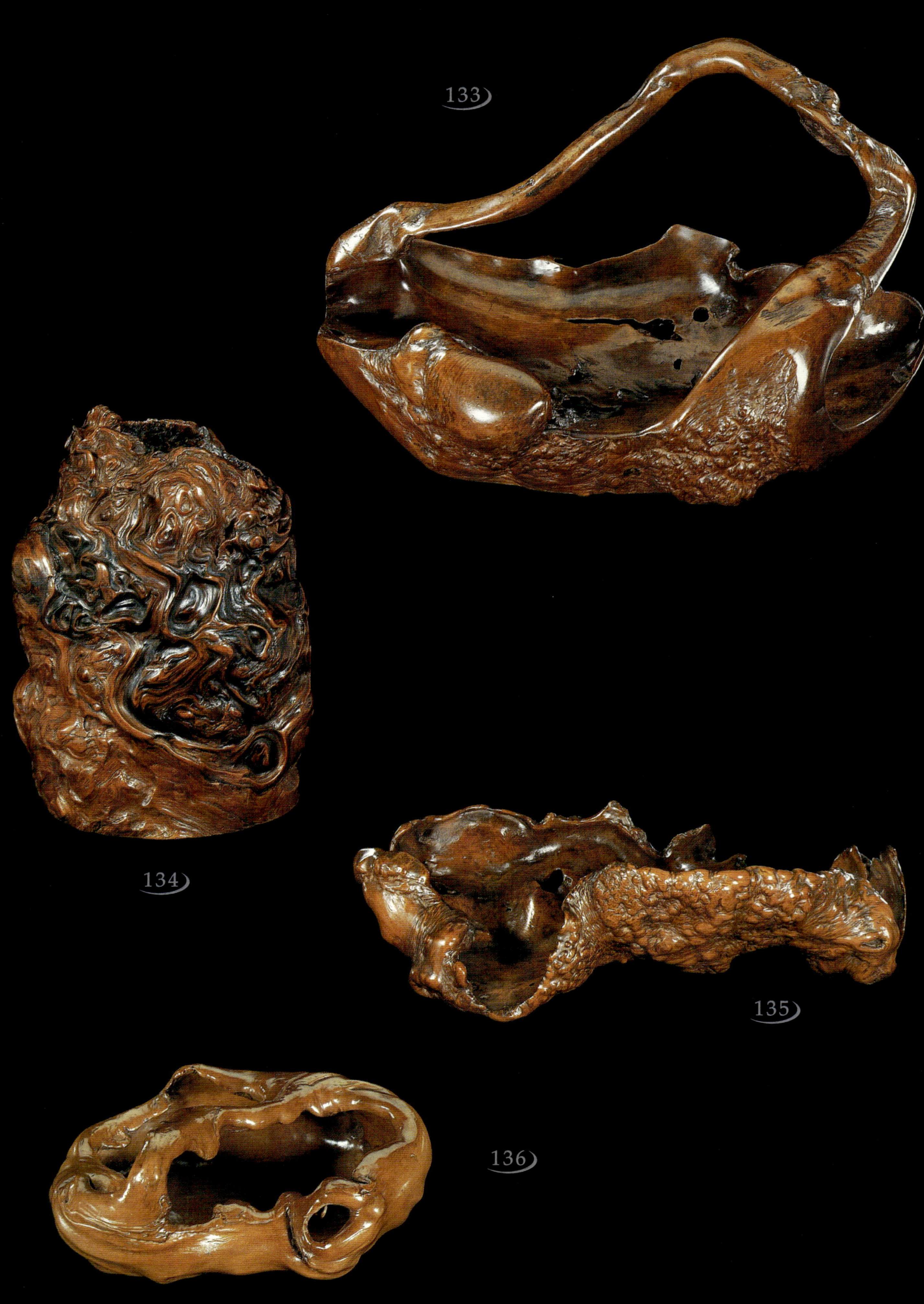

133
134
135
136

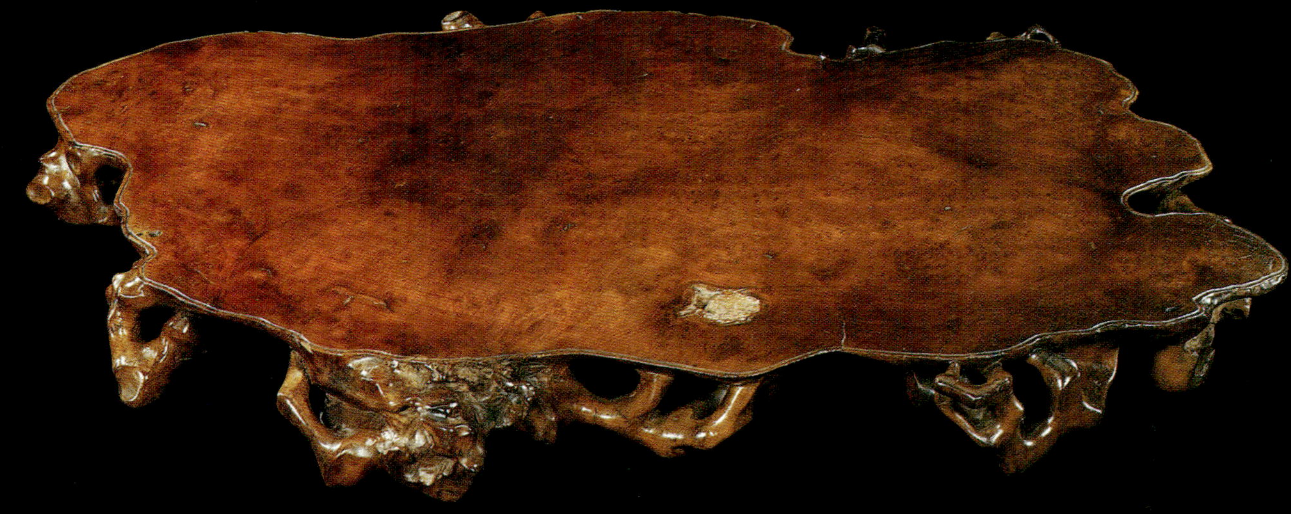

137

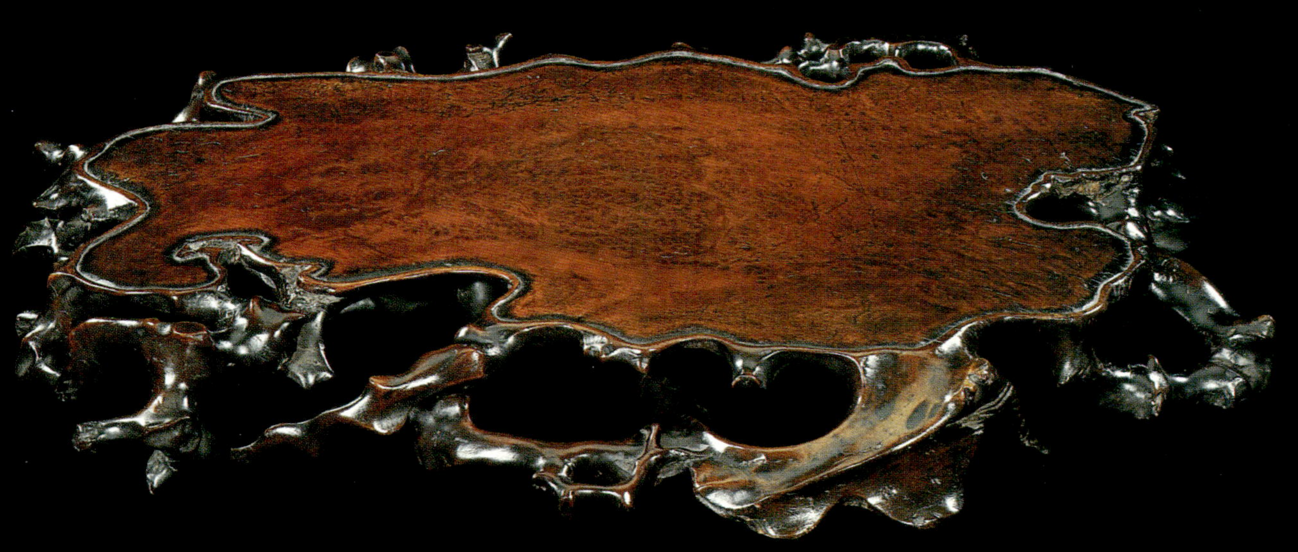

138

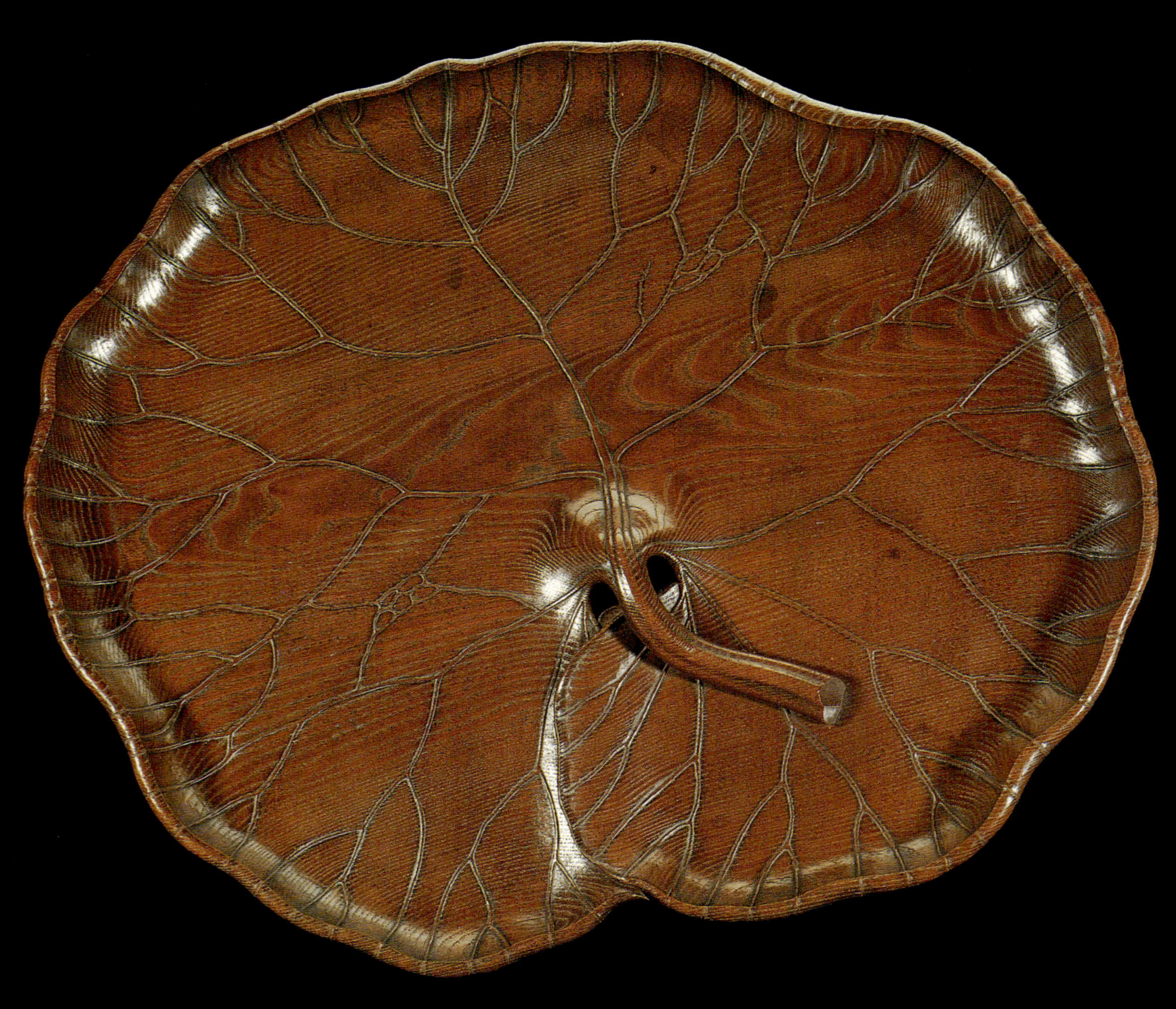

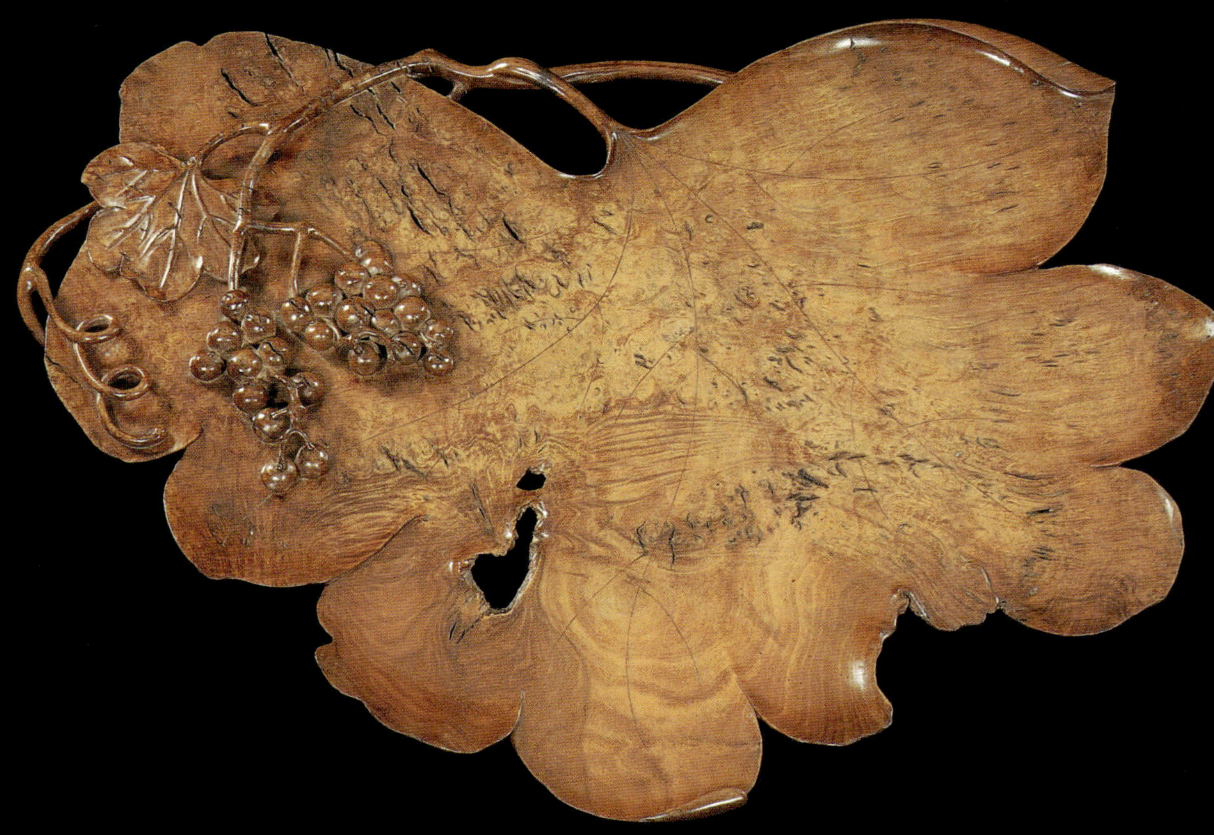

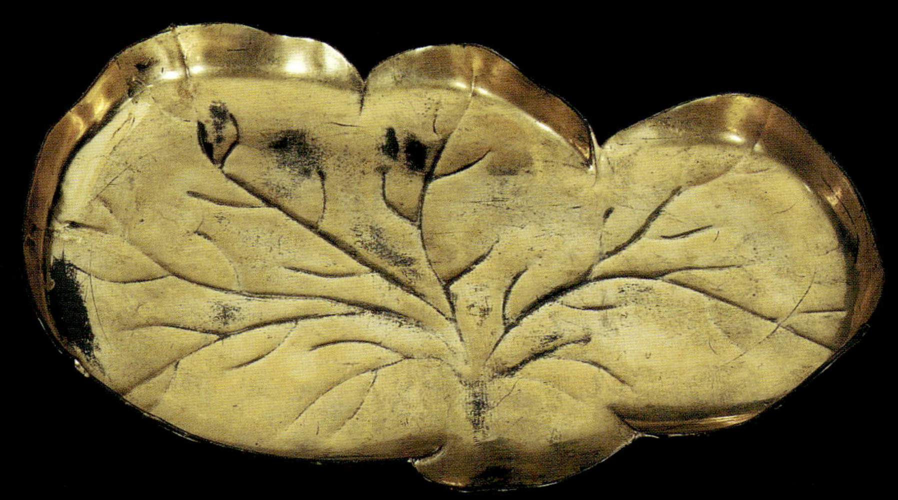

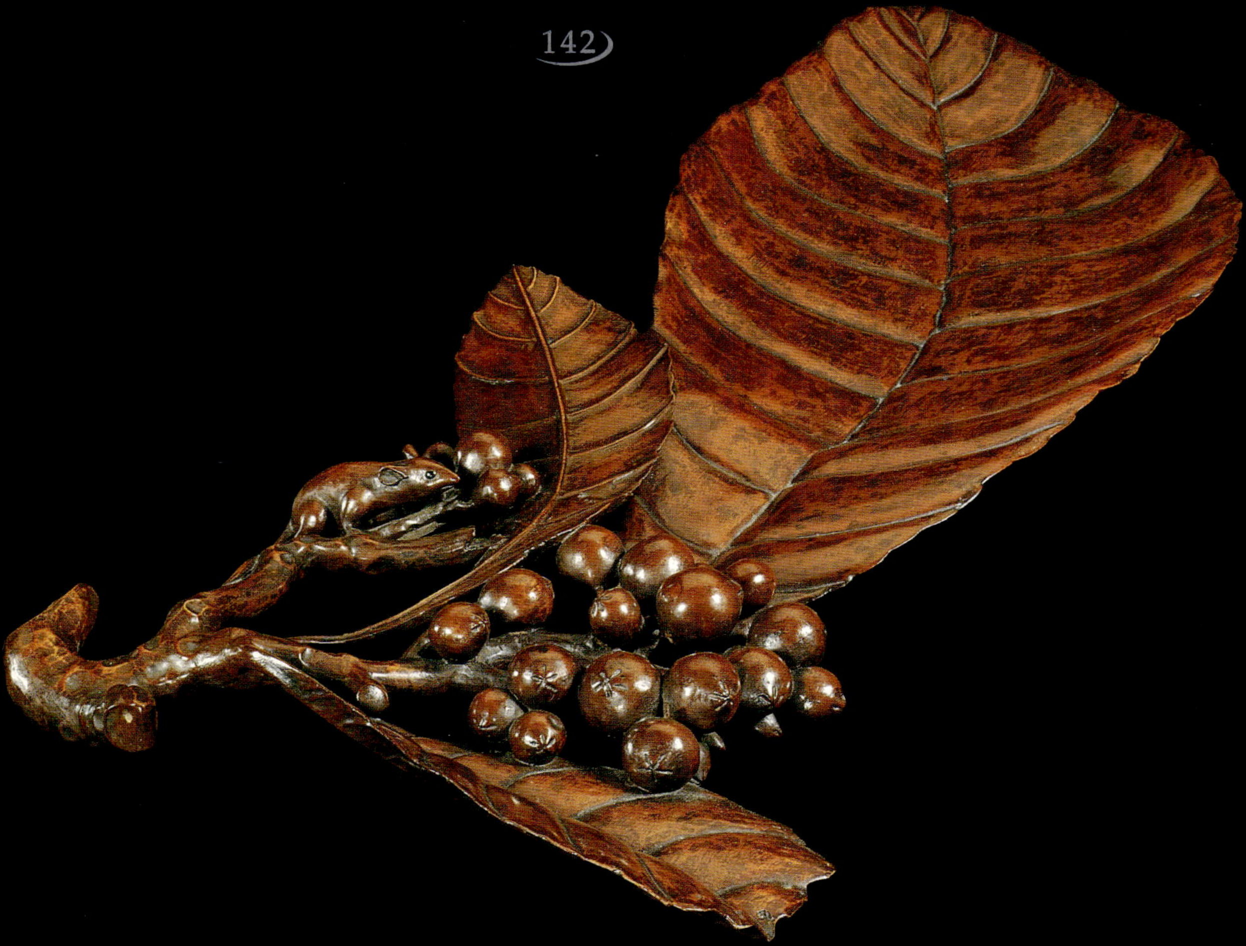

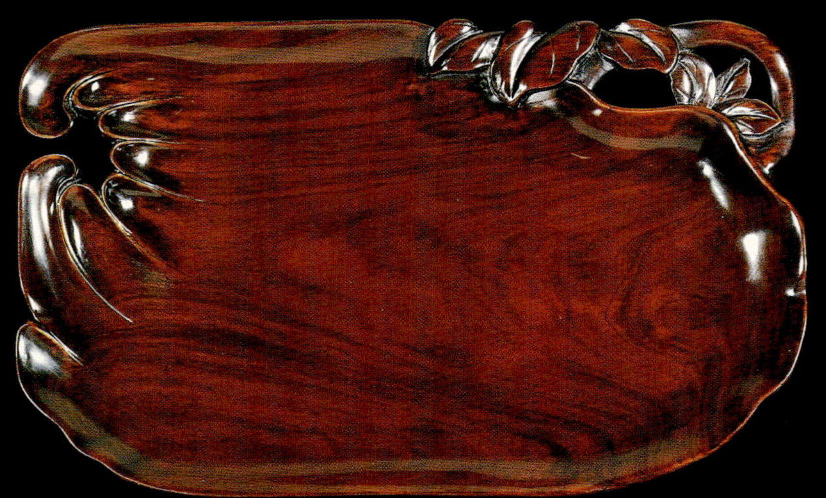

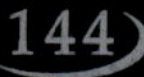

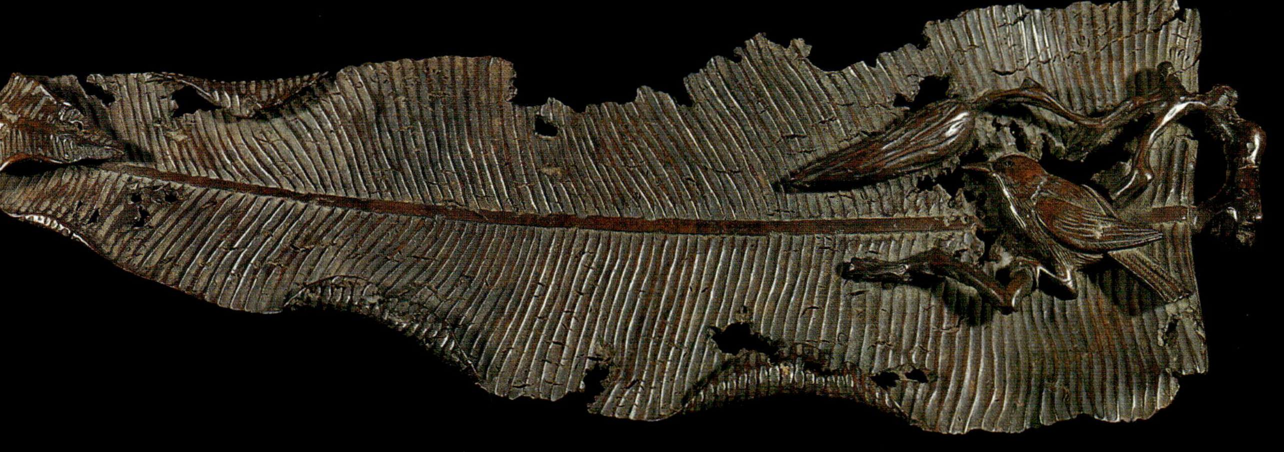

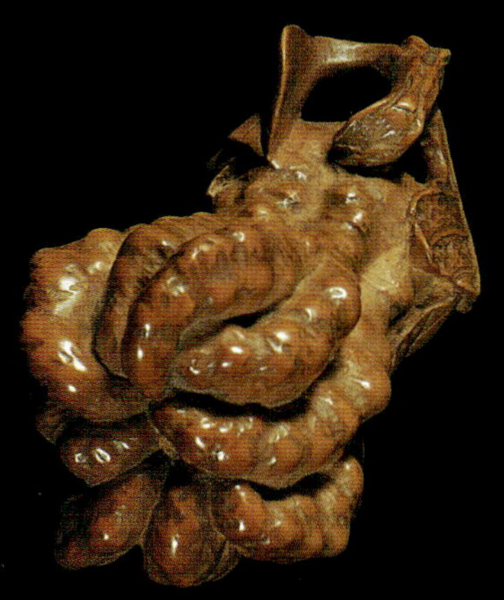

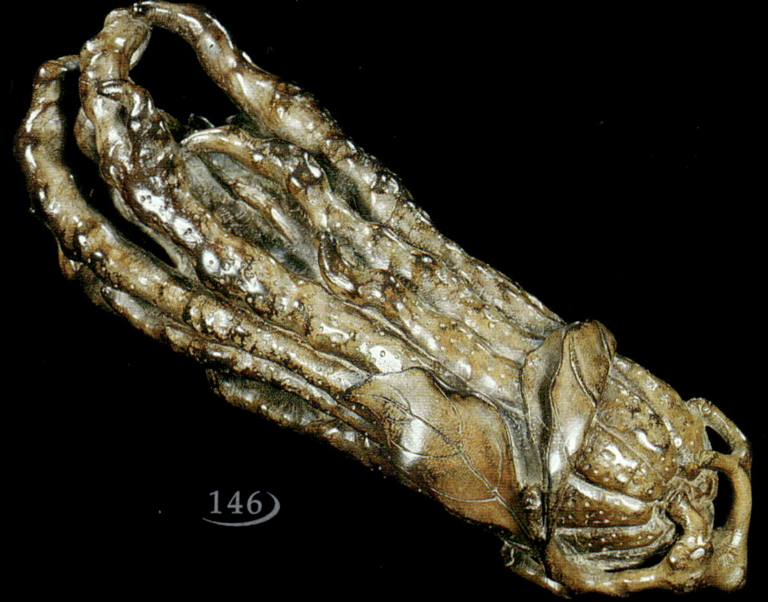

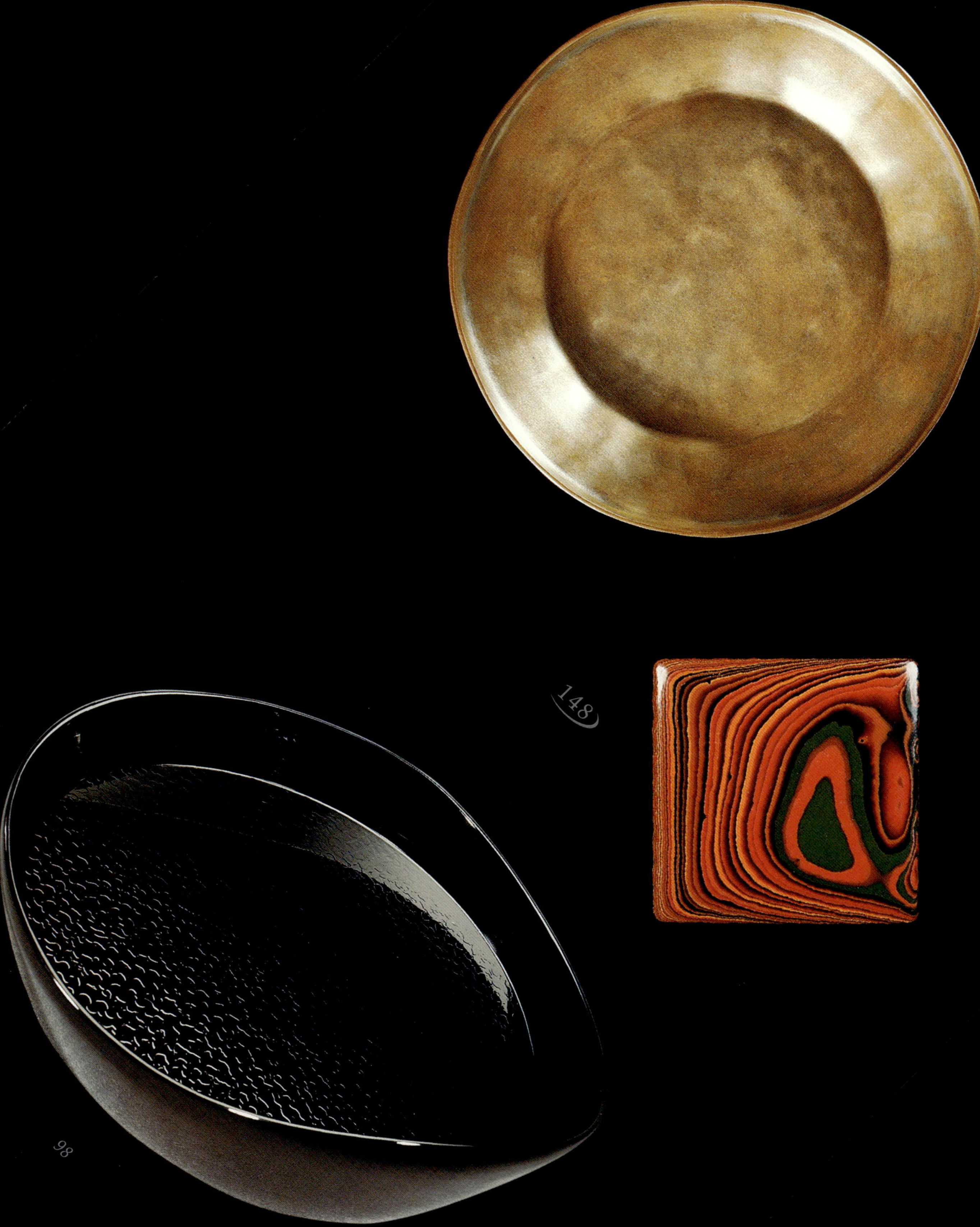
148
98

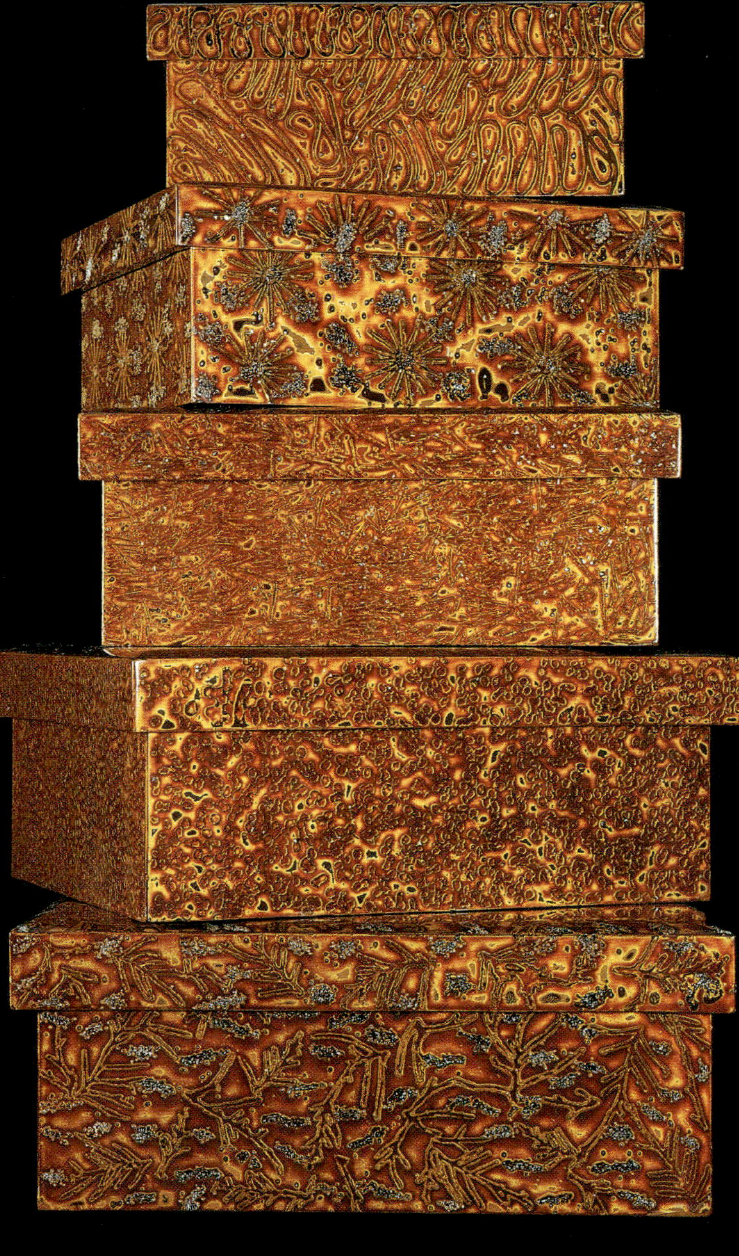

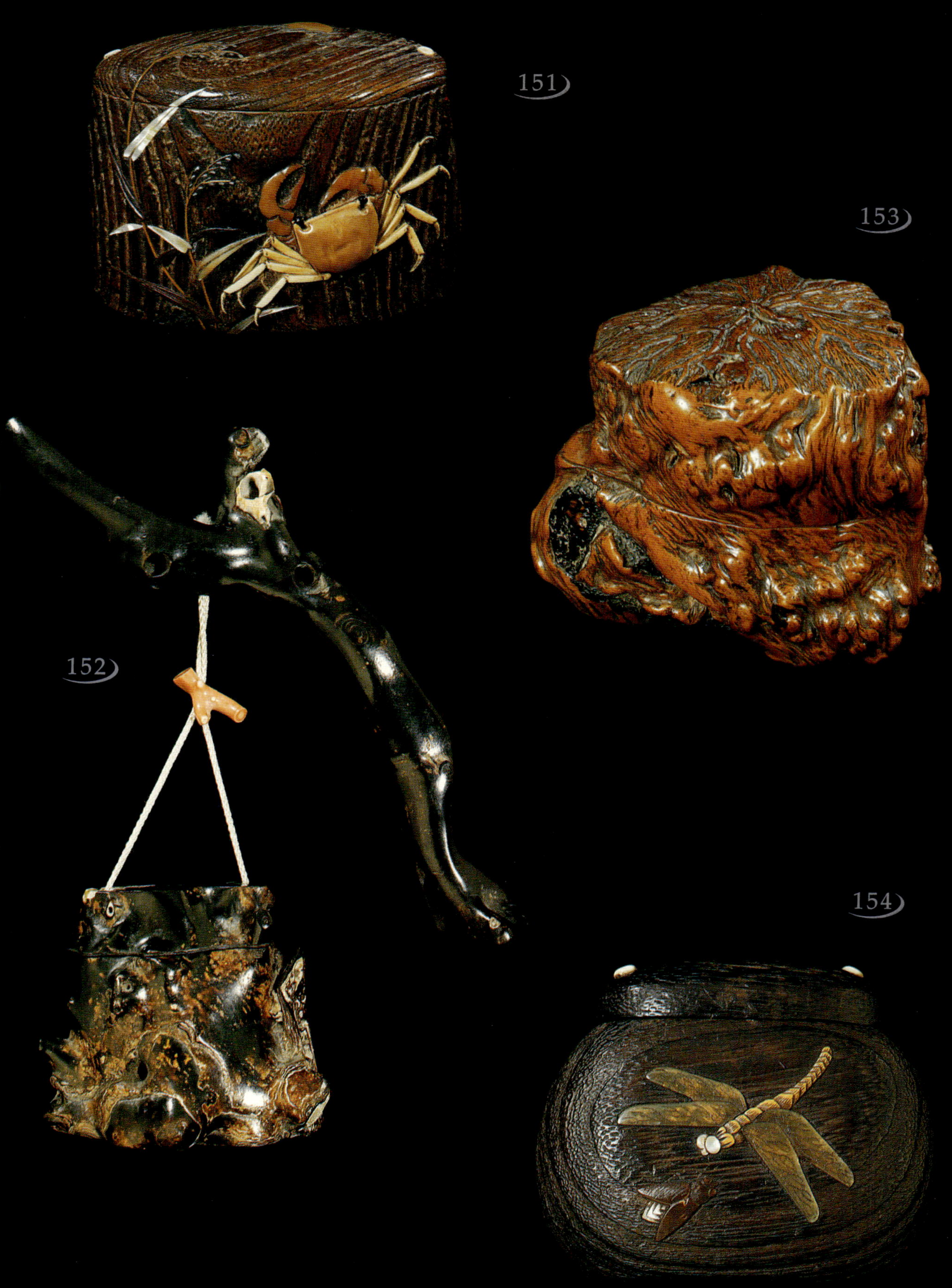
151
153
152
154

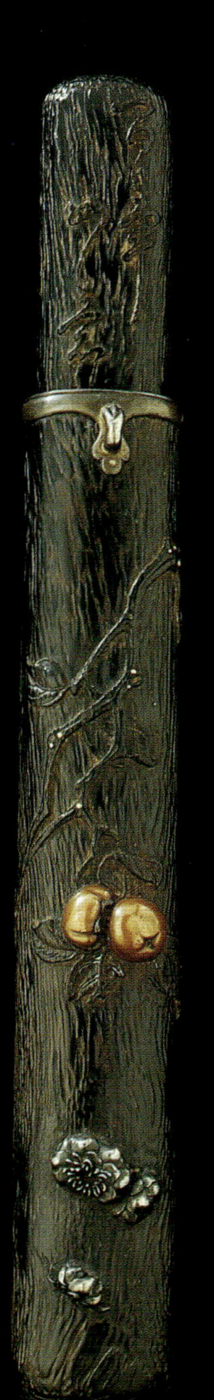

155
156
157

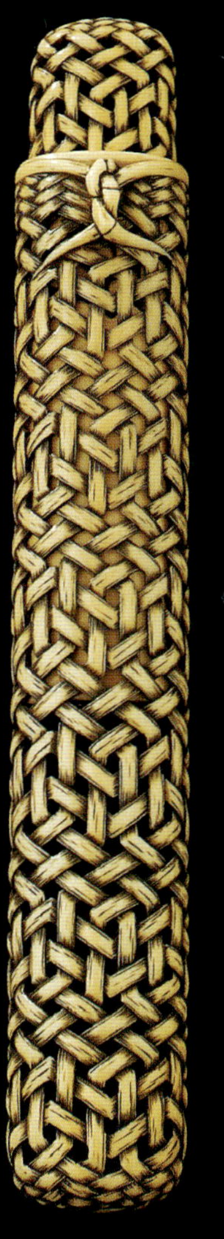

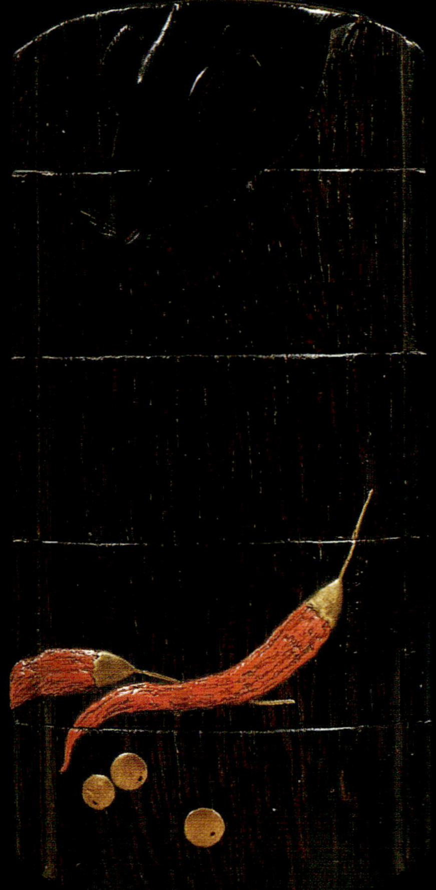
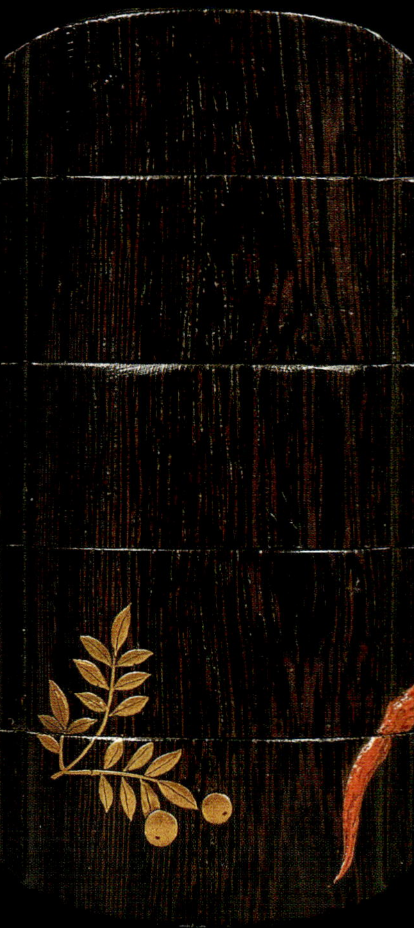

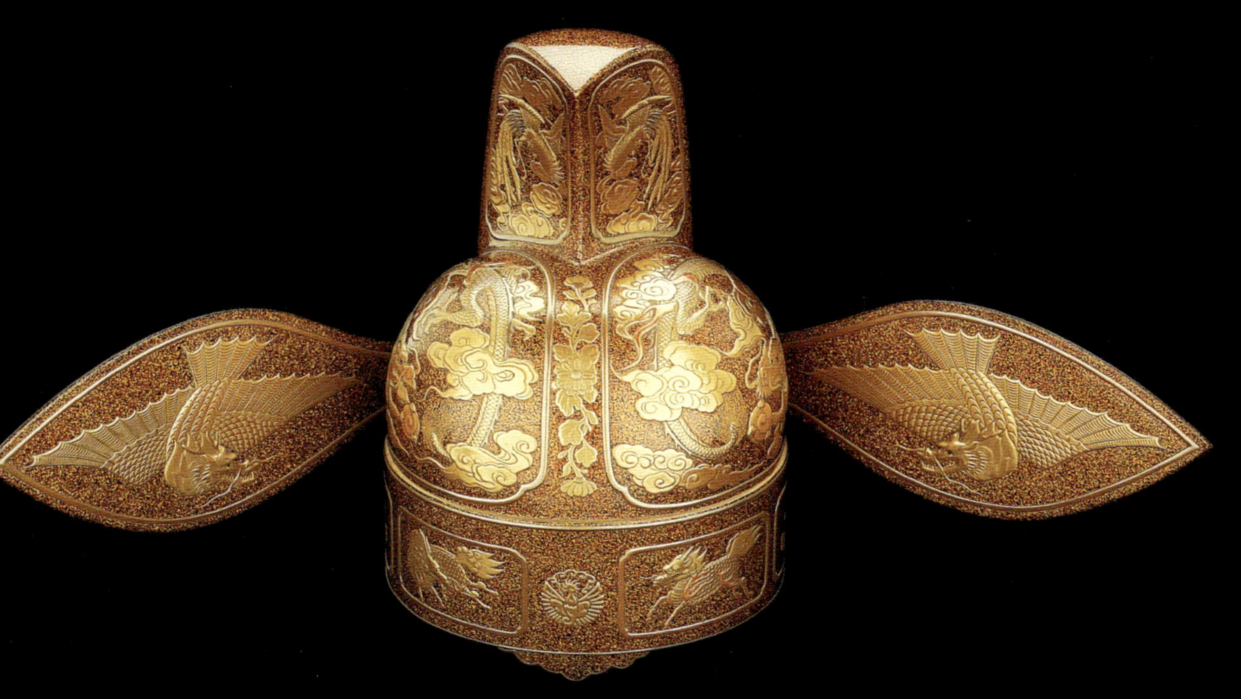

159

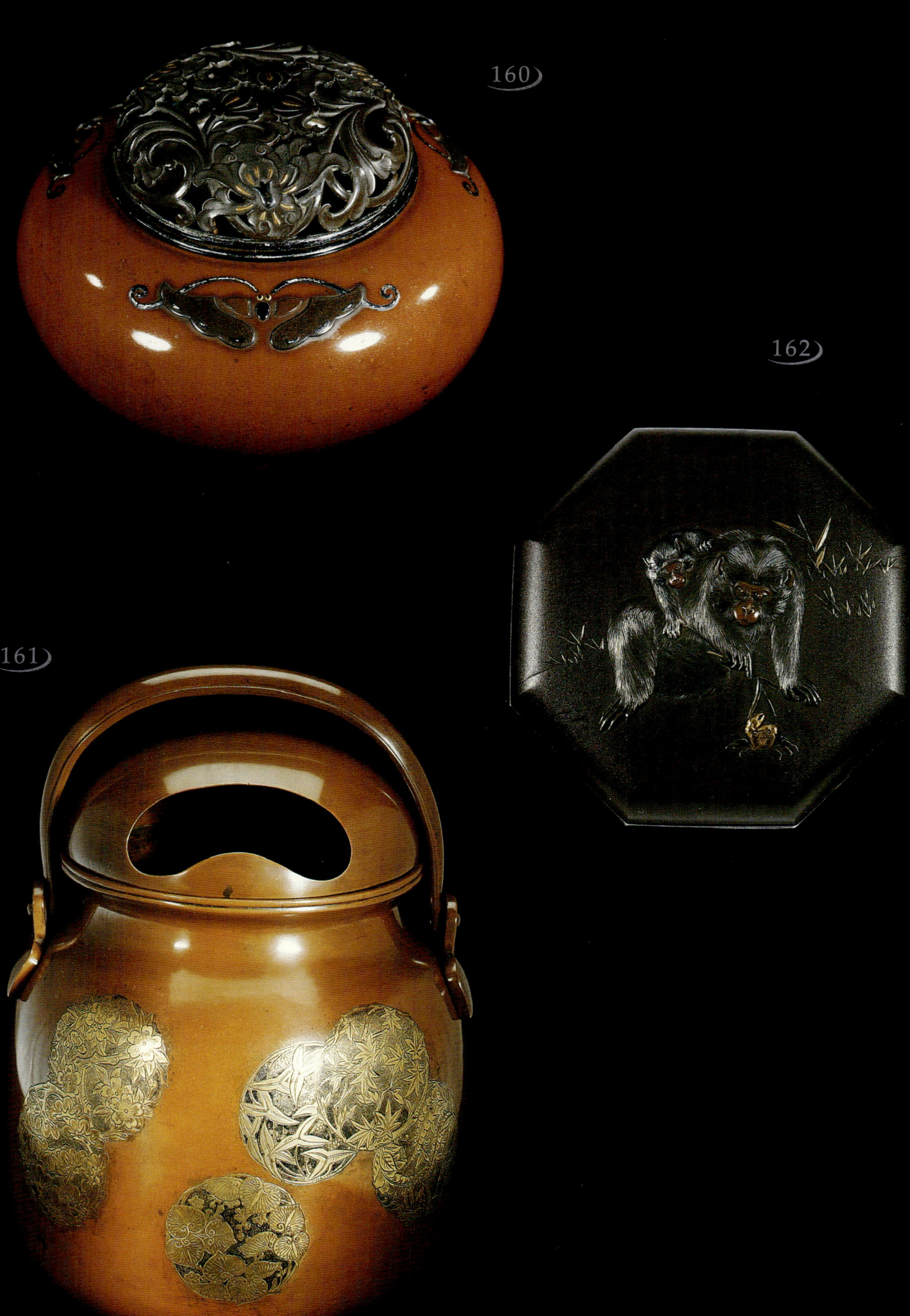

160
162
161

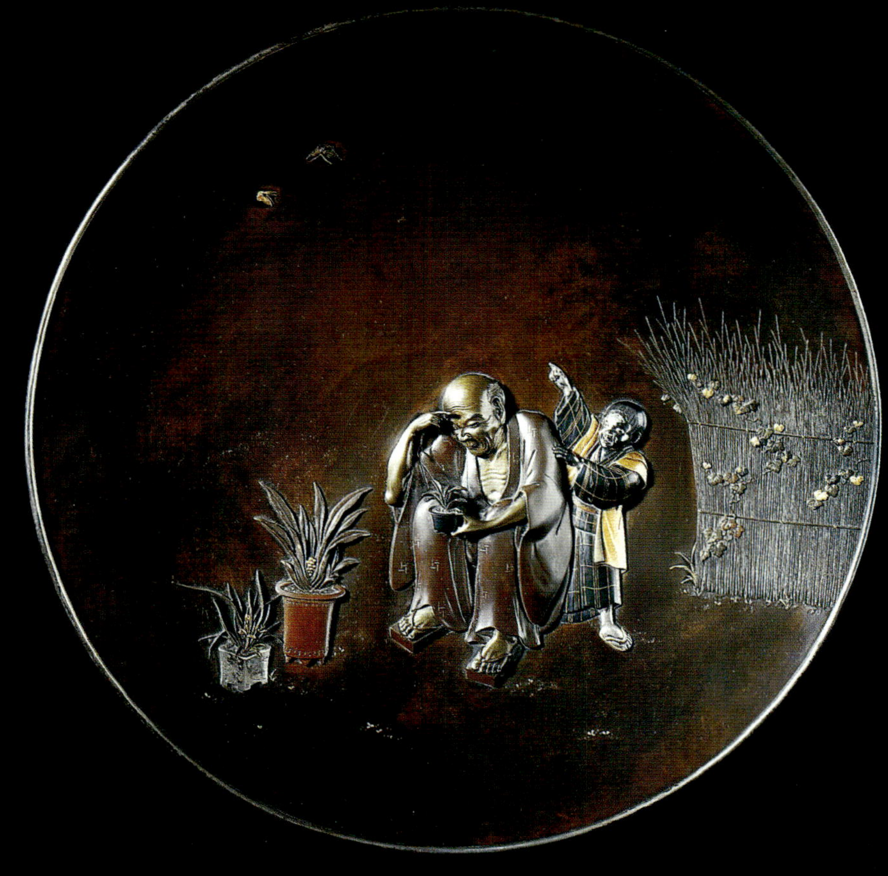

163

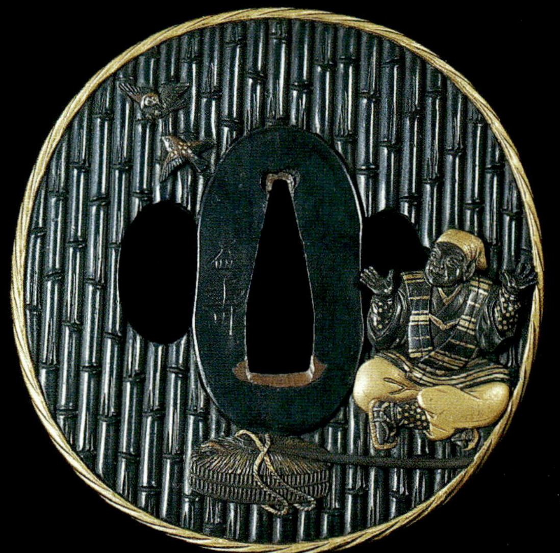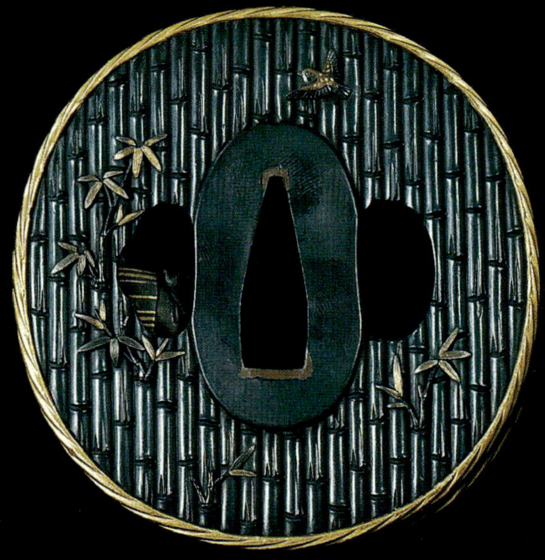

164

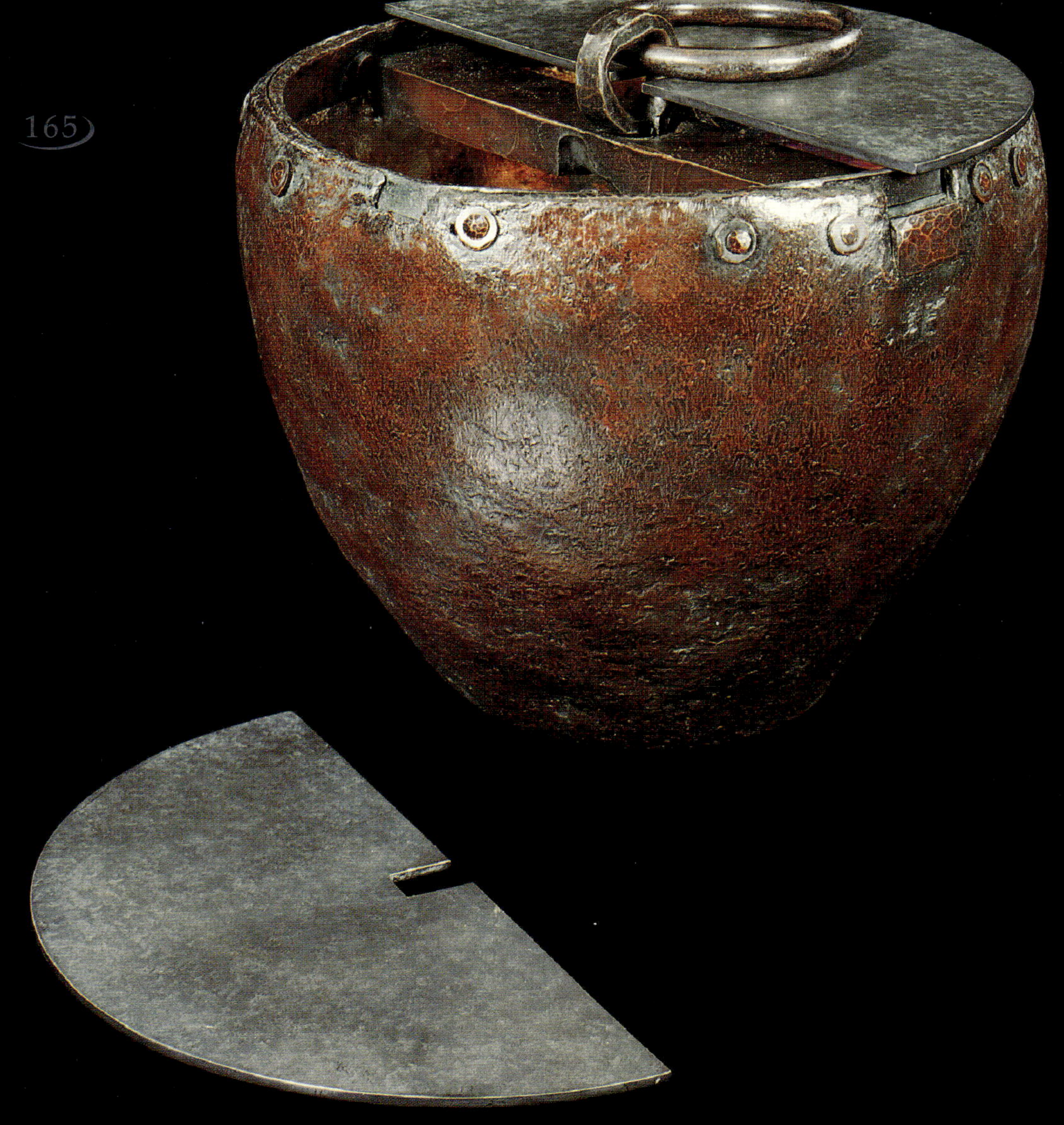

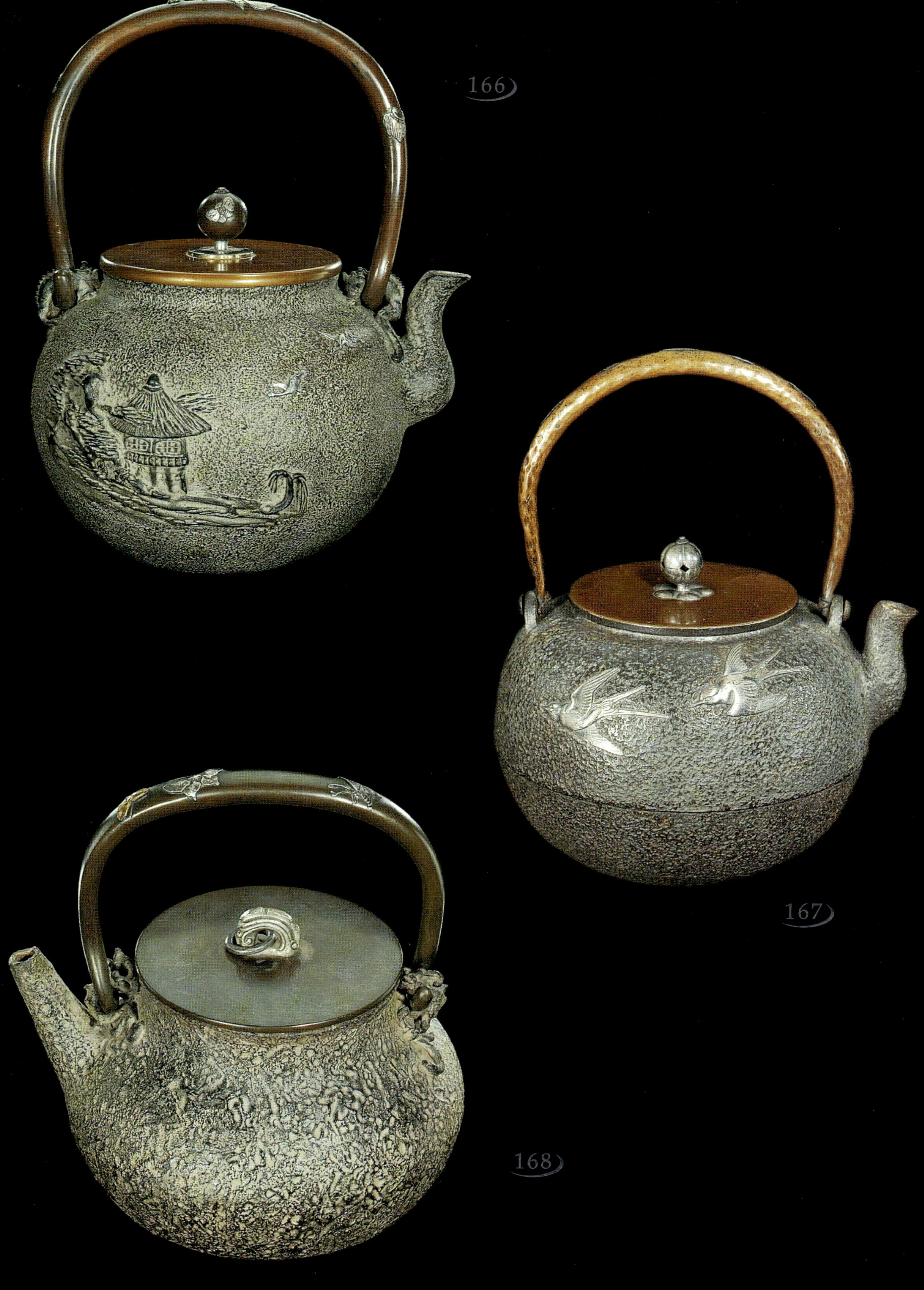
166
167
168

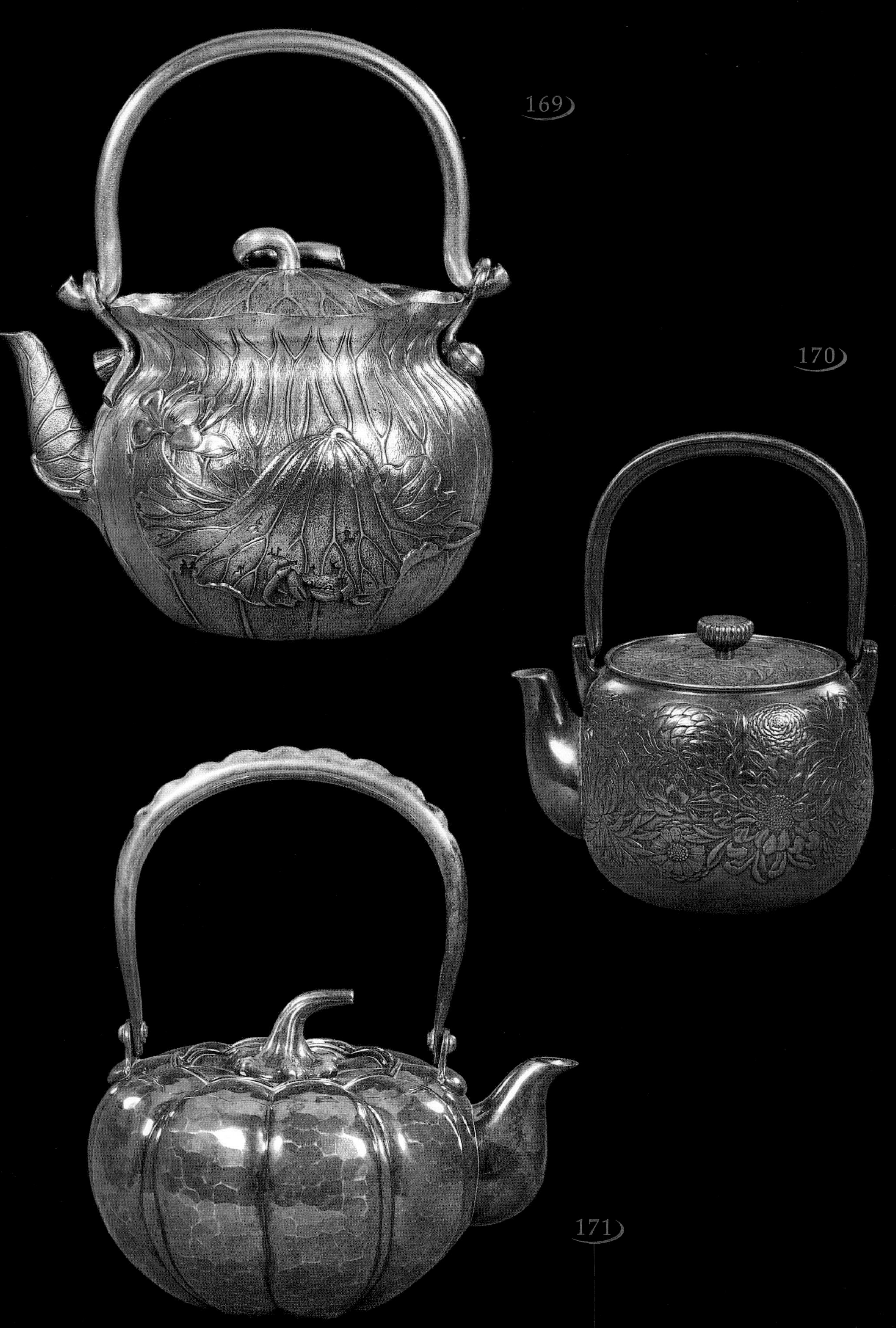

169

170

171

172
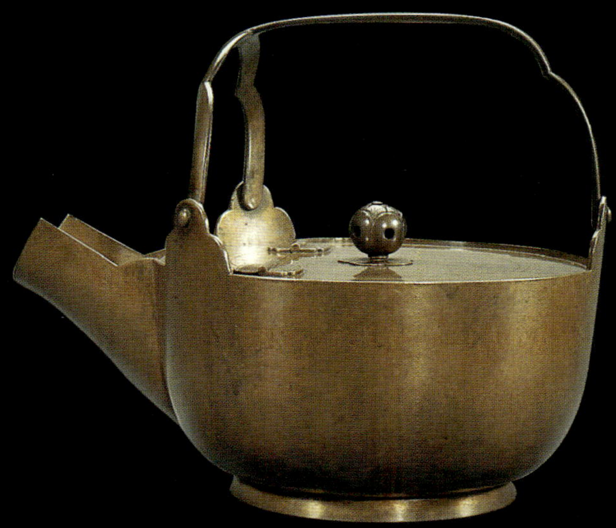
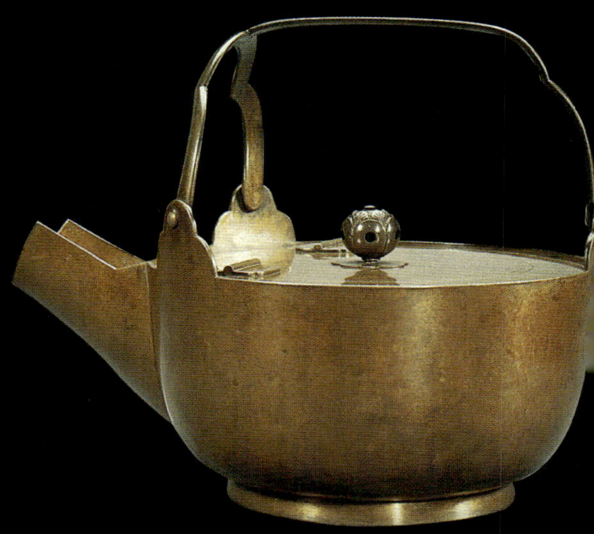

173
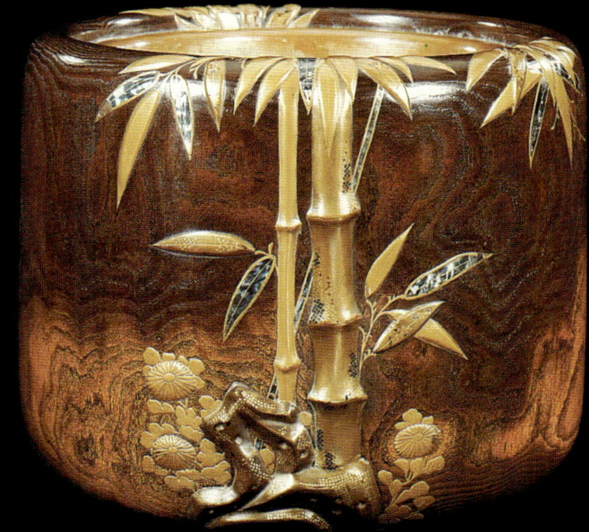
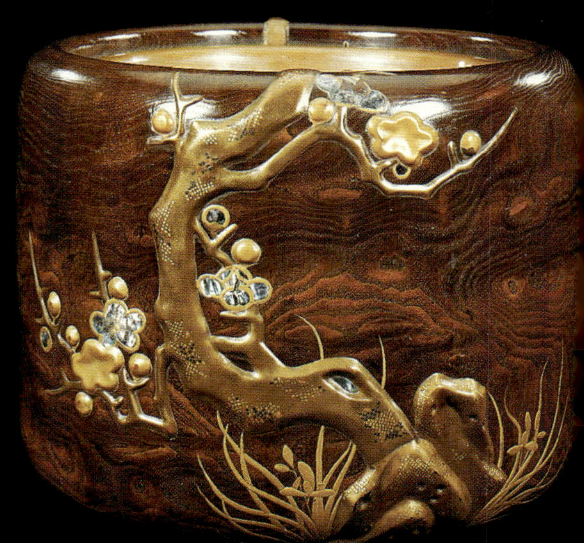

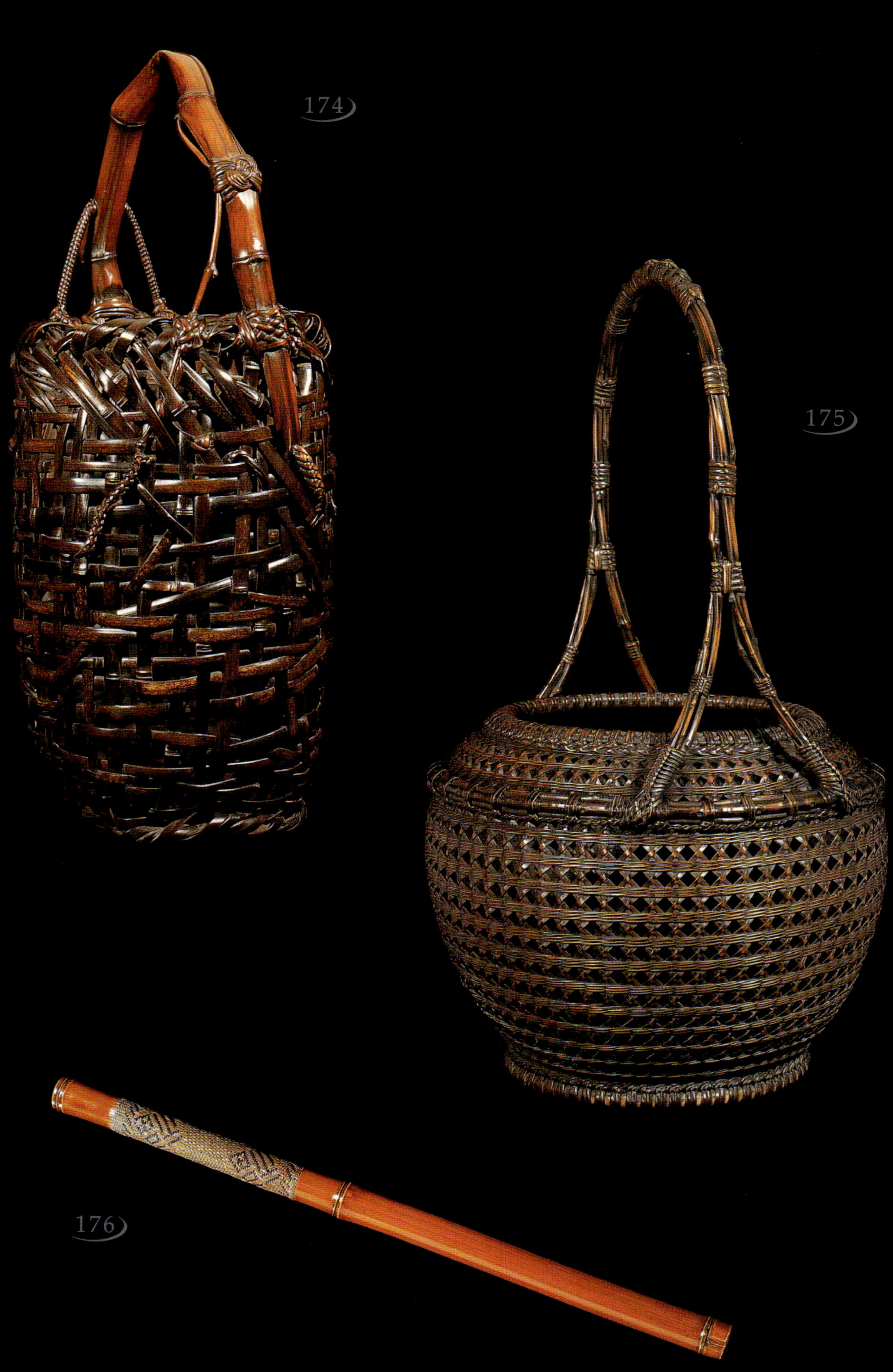

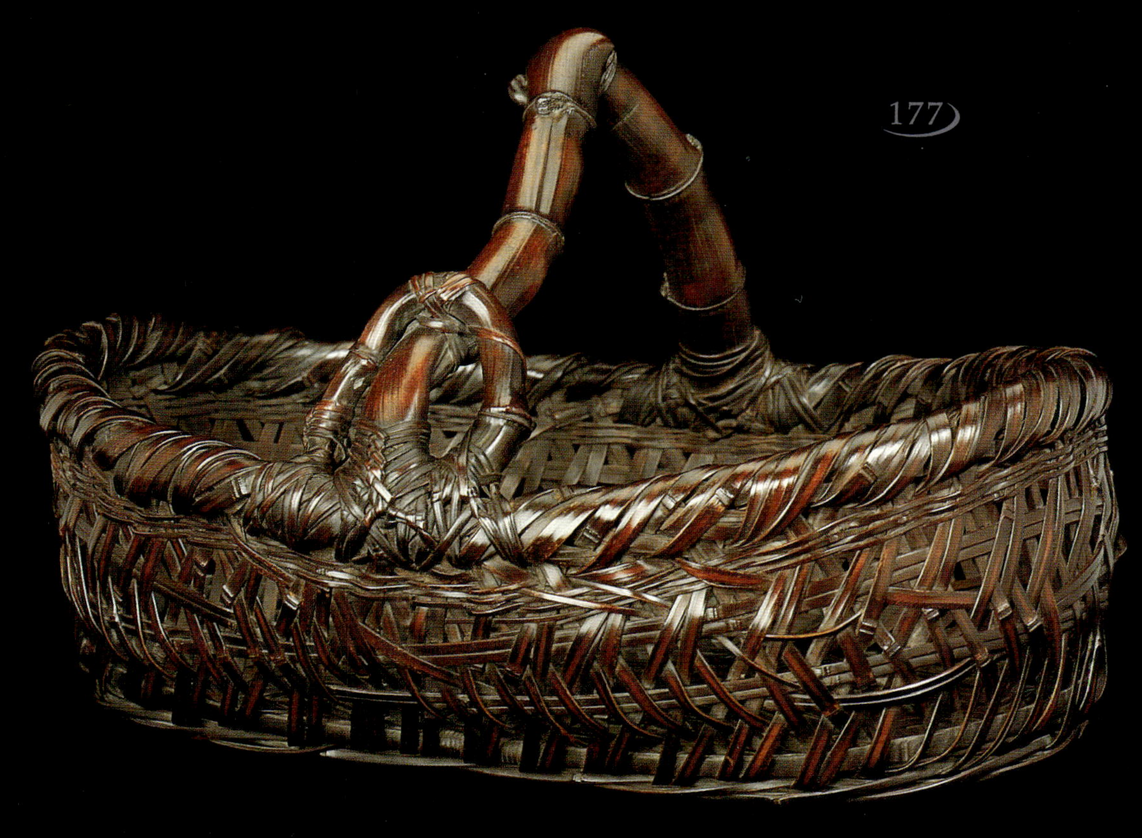

177

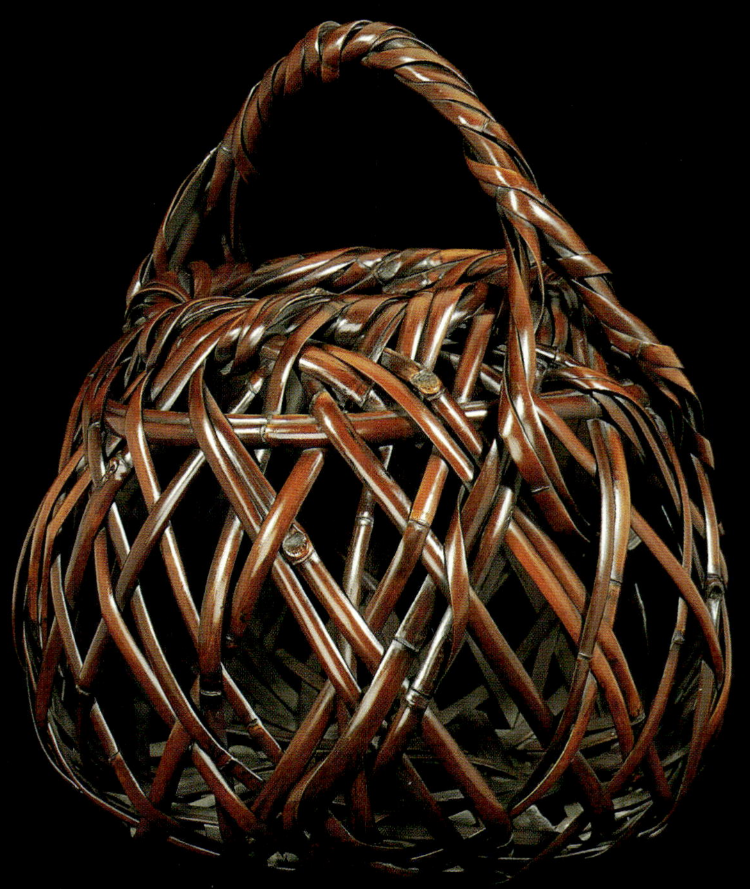

178

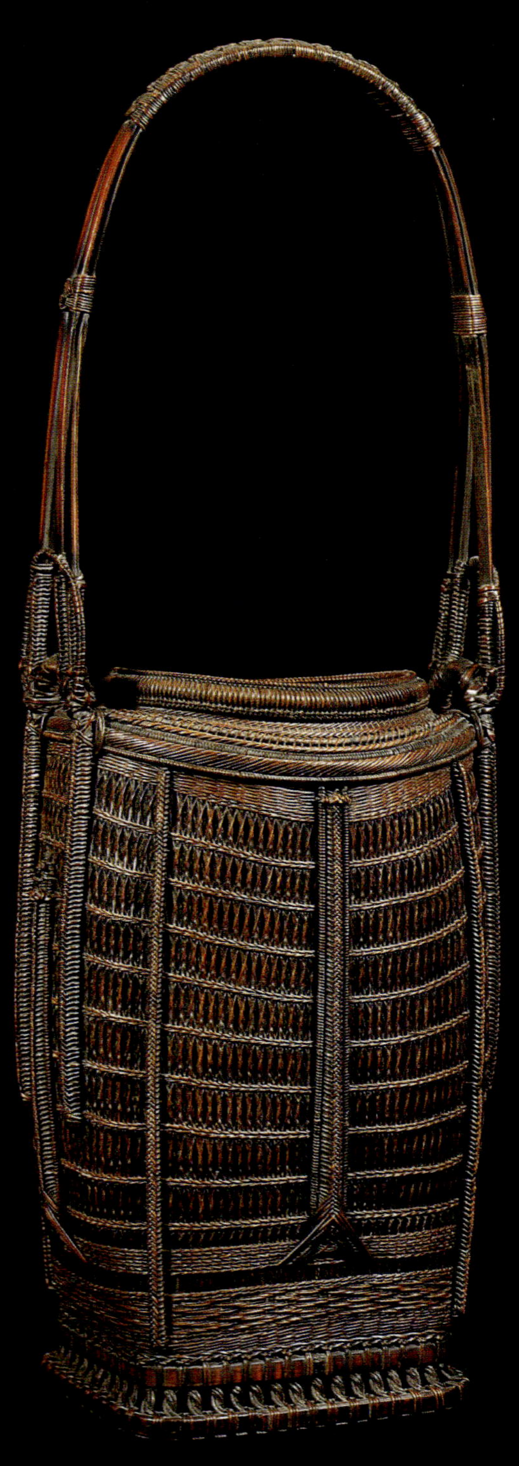
179

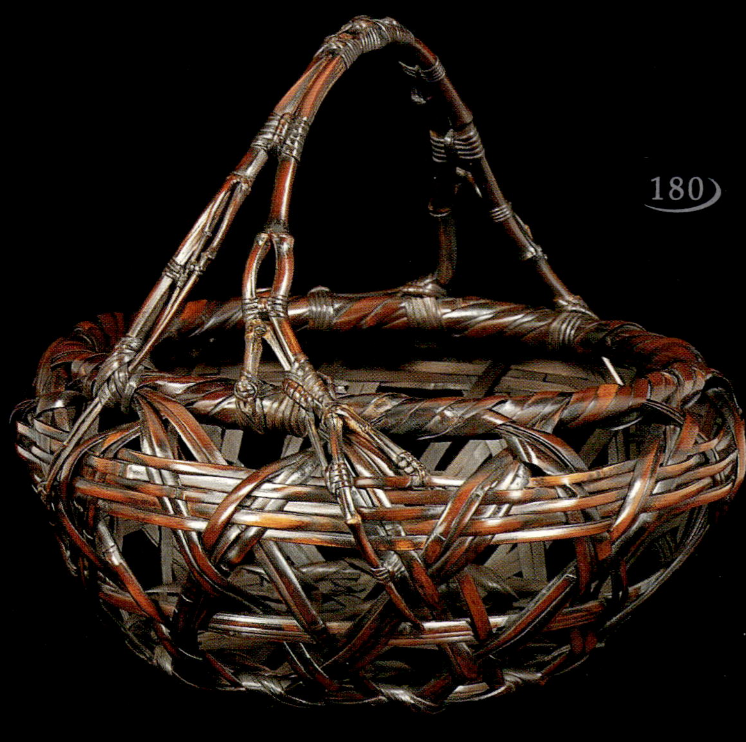
180

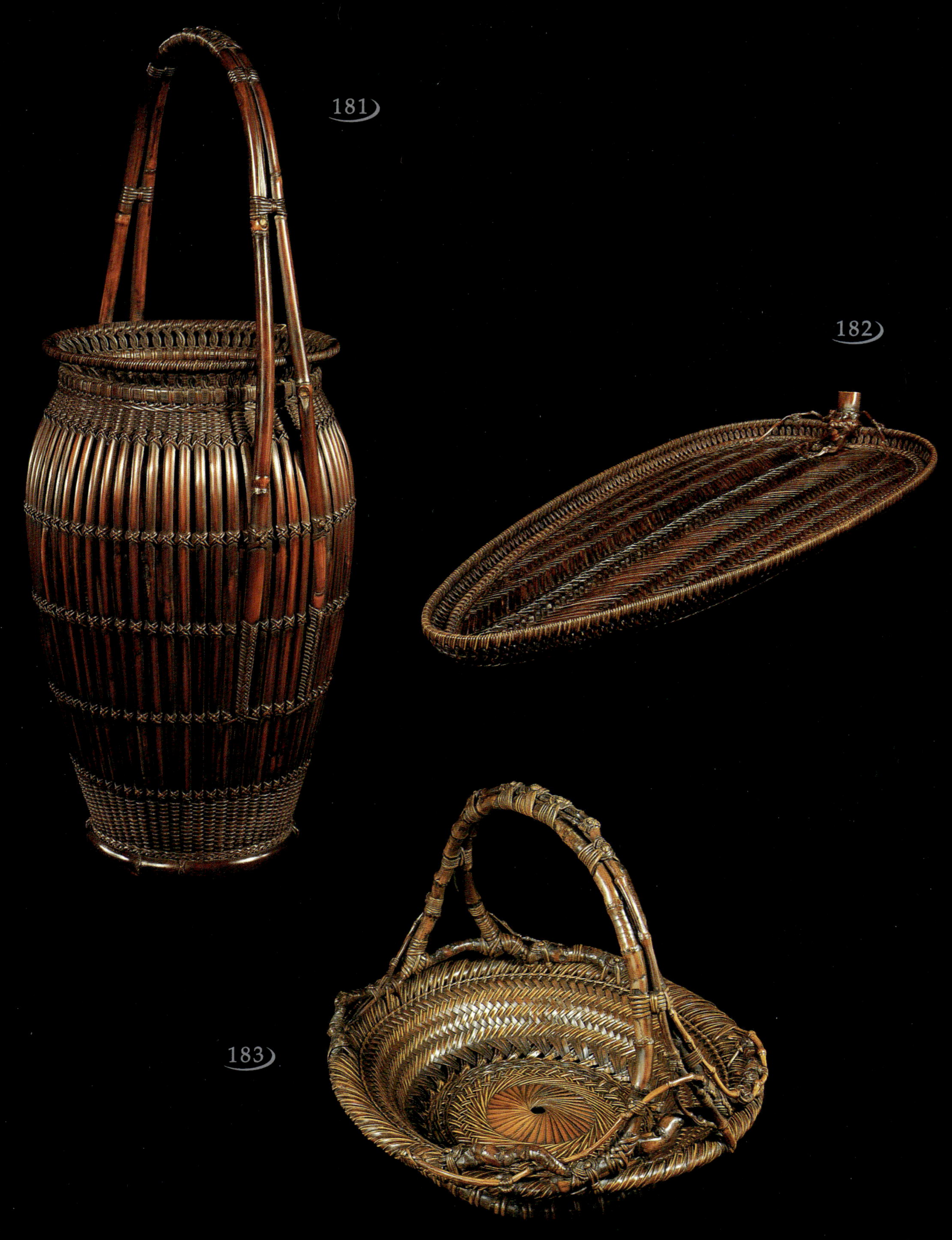

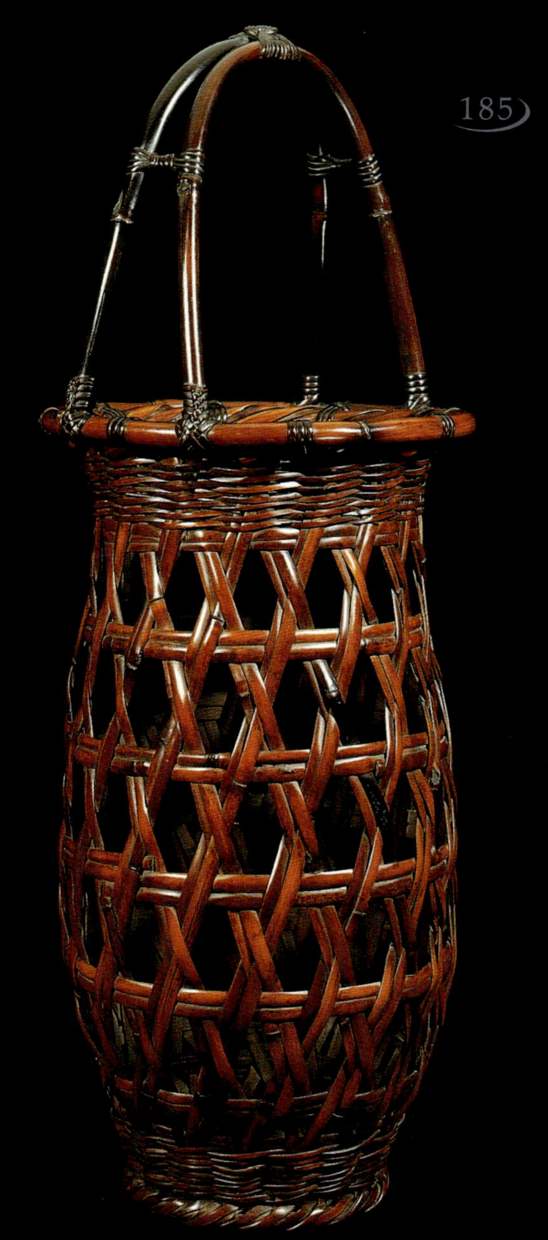

185

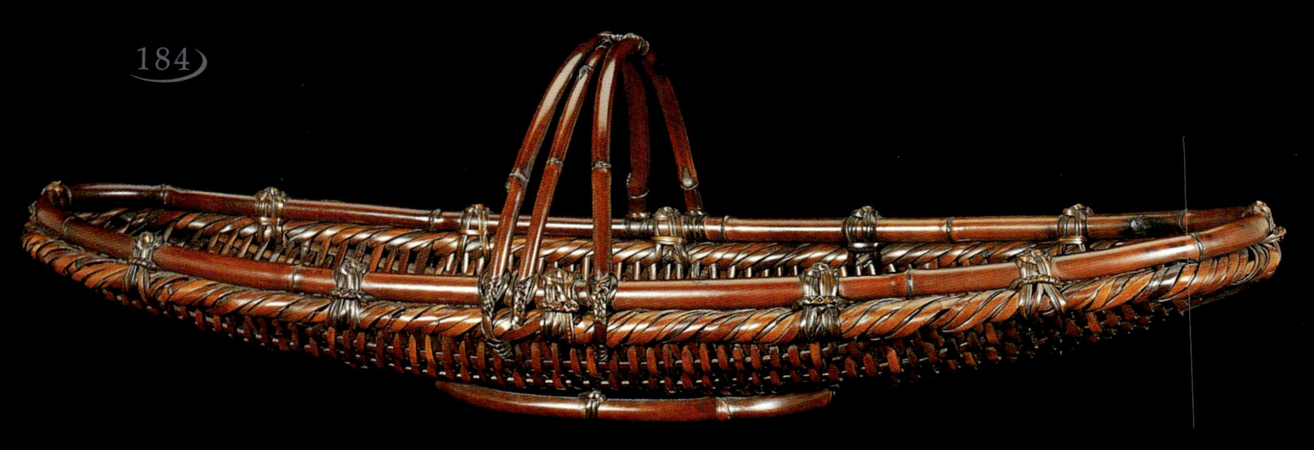

184

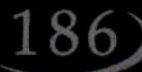

186

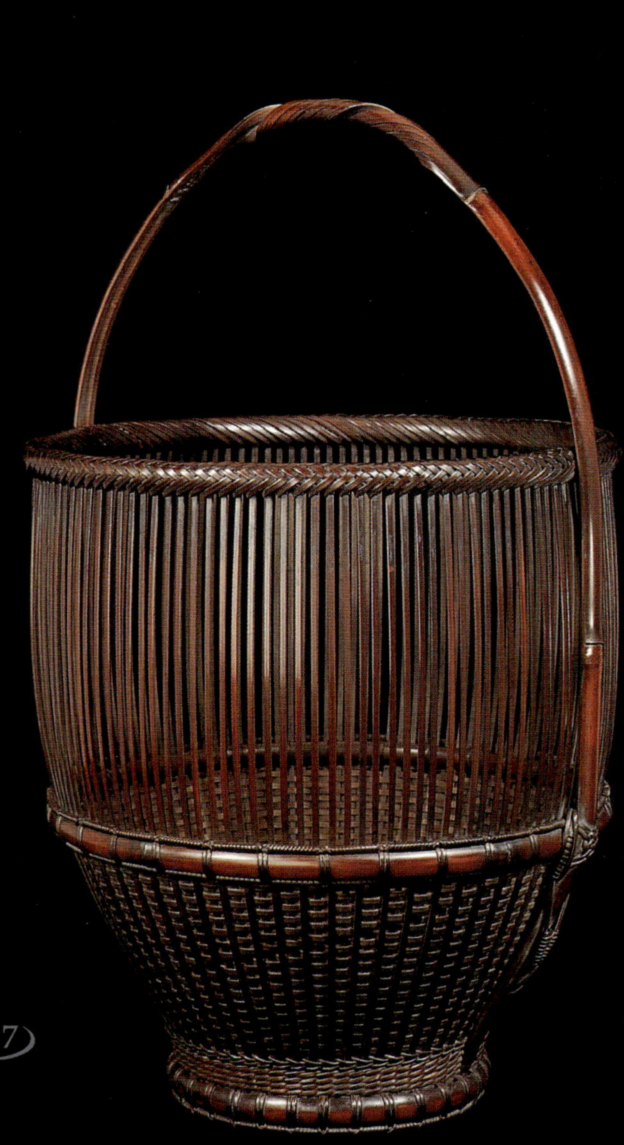

187

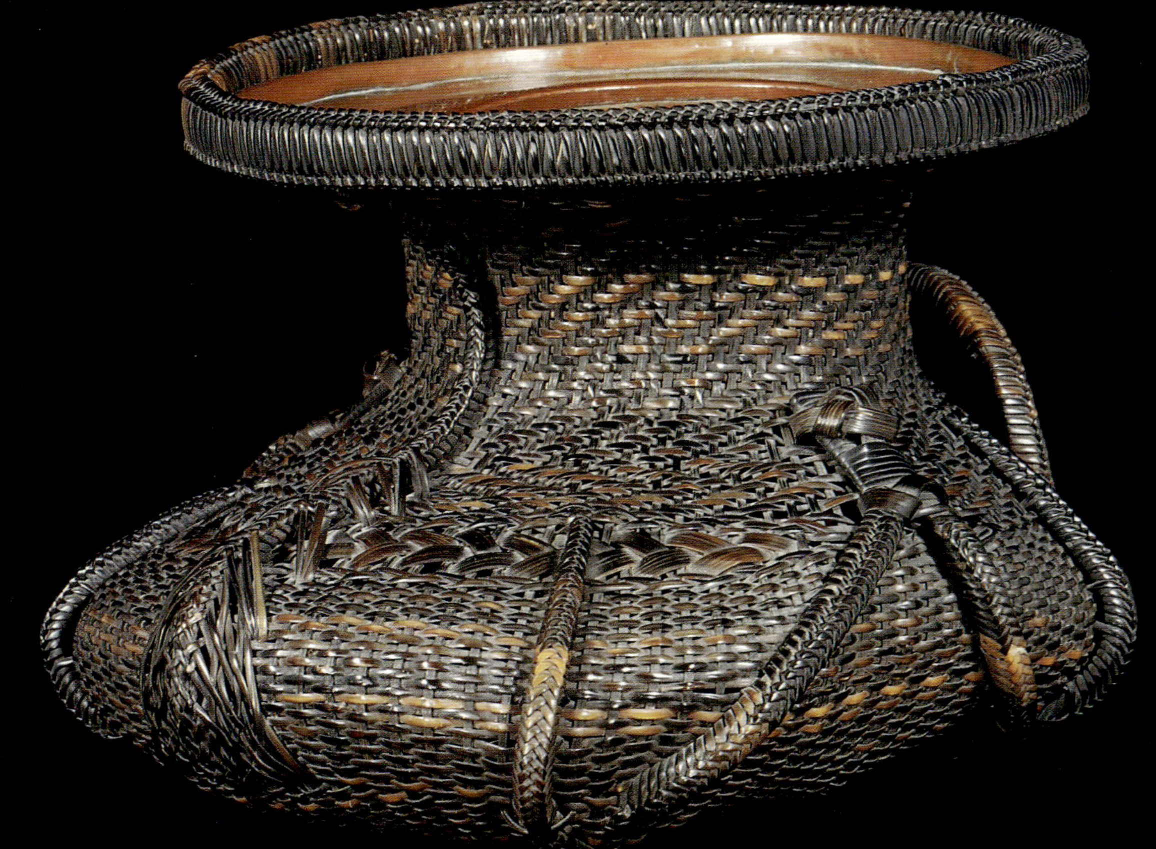

188

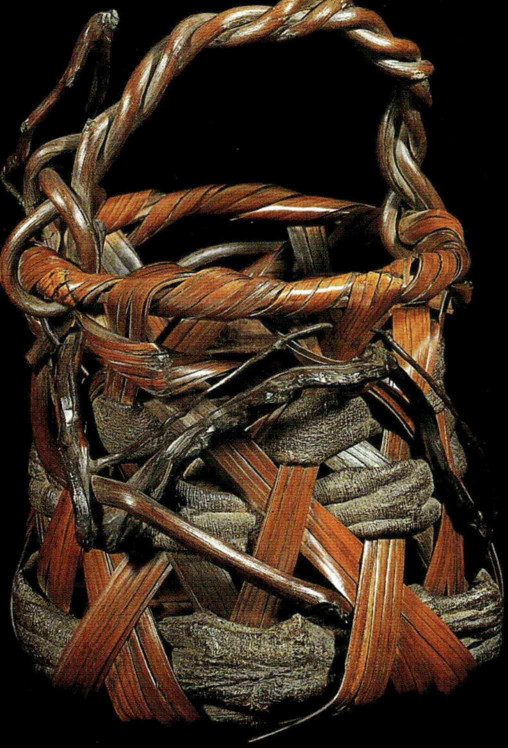

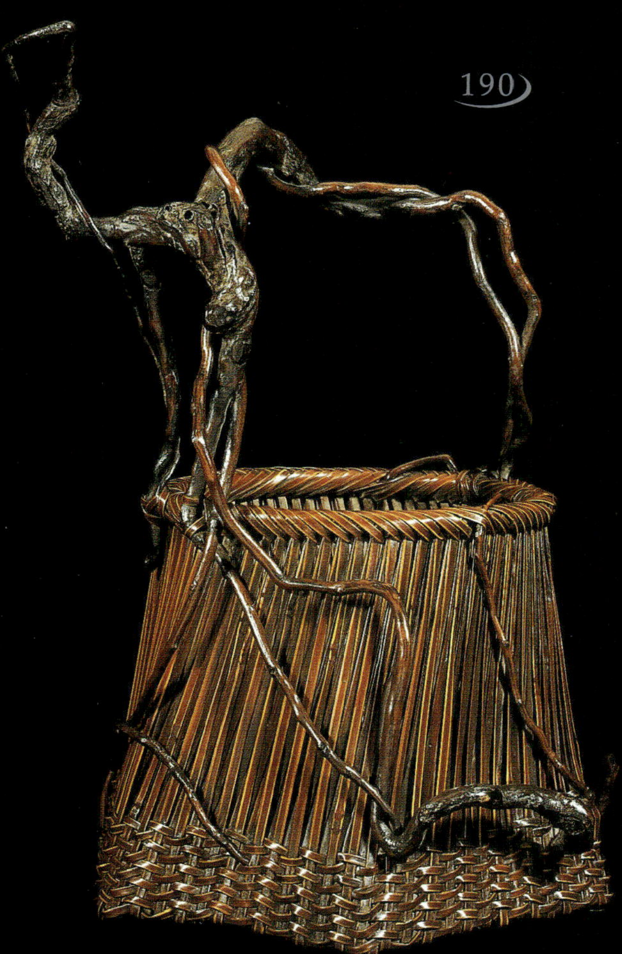

189

190

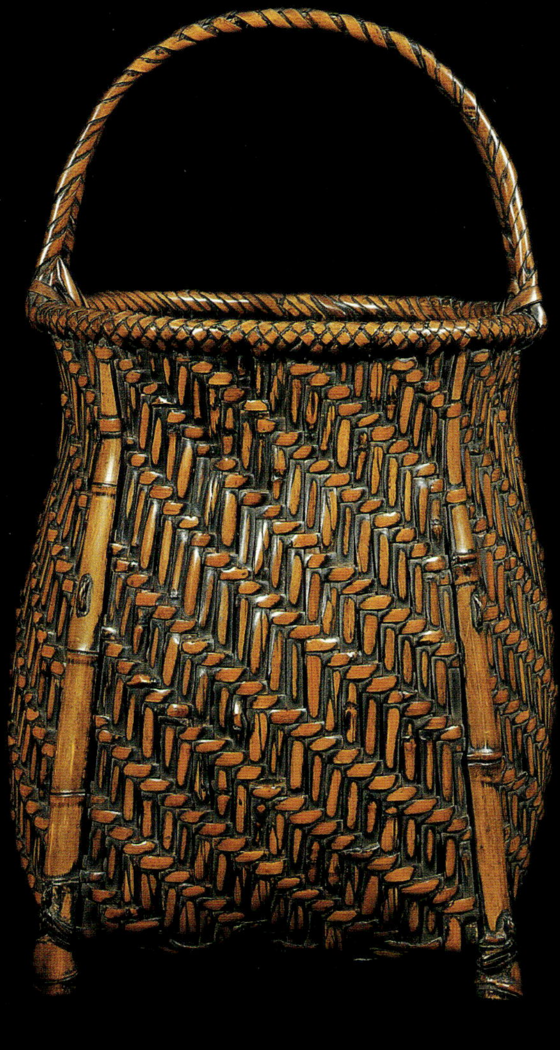

191

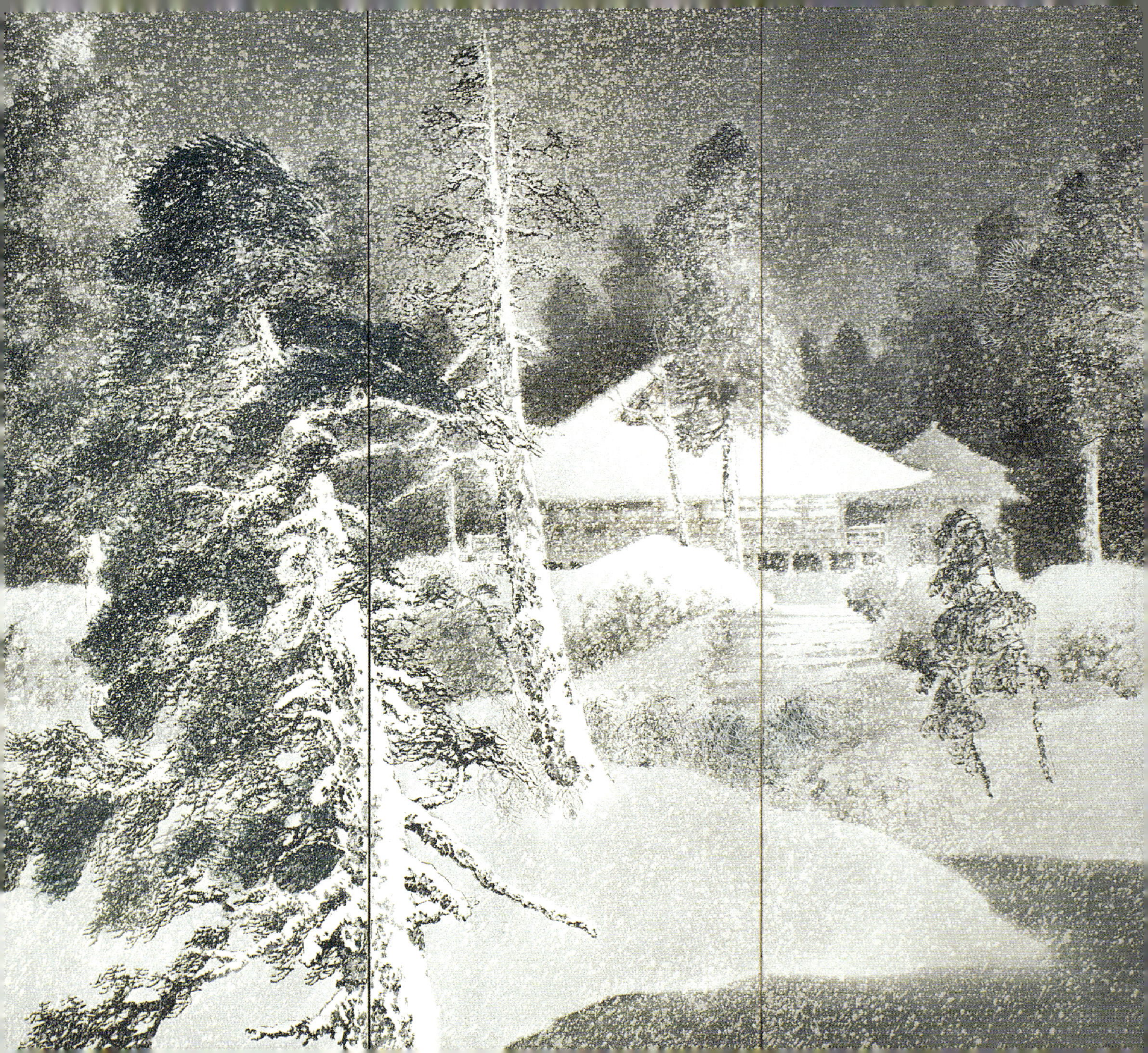

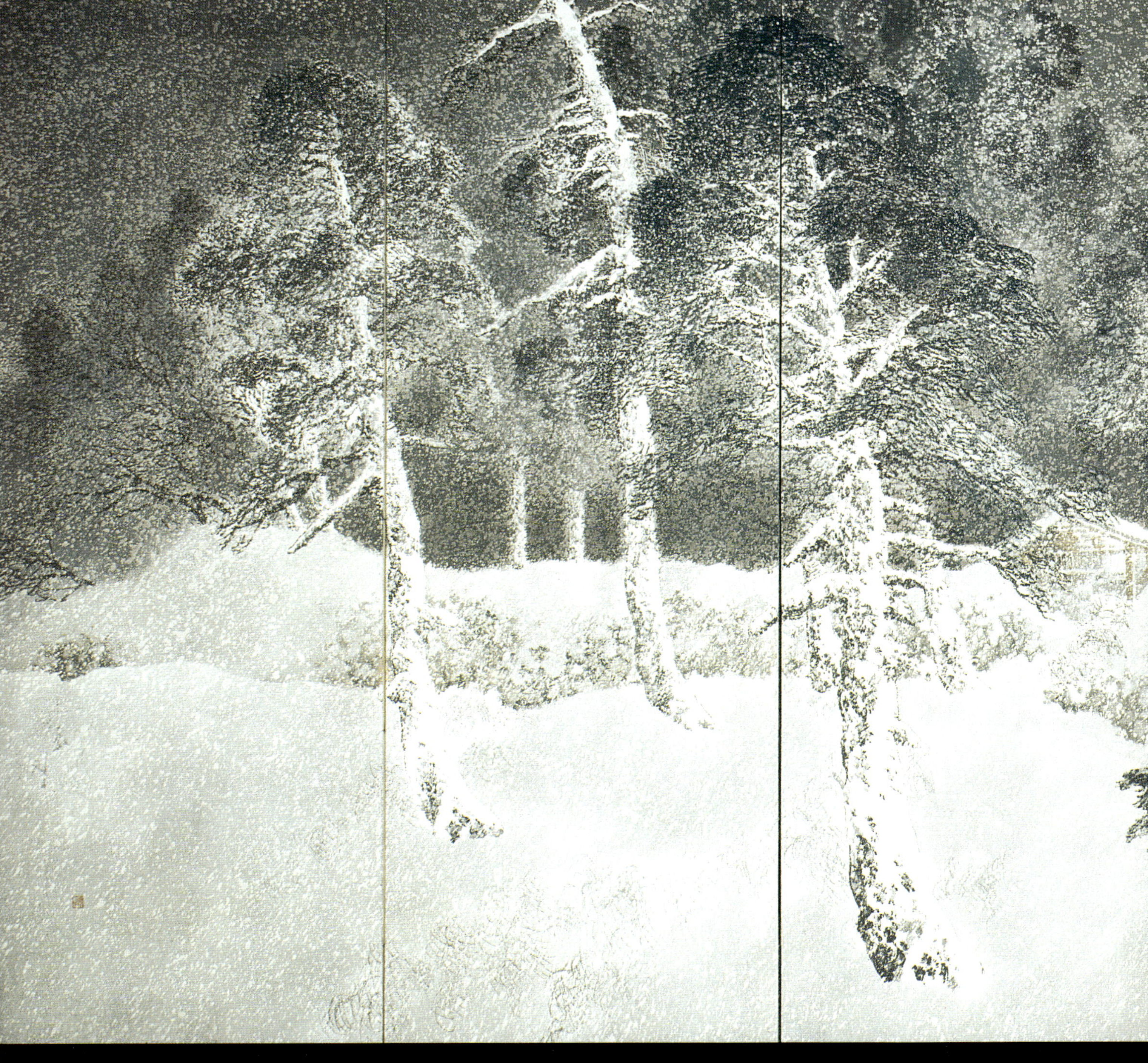

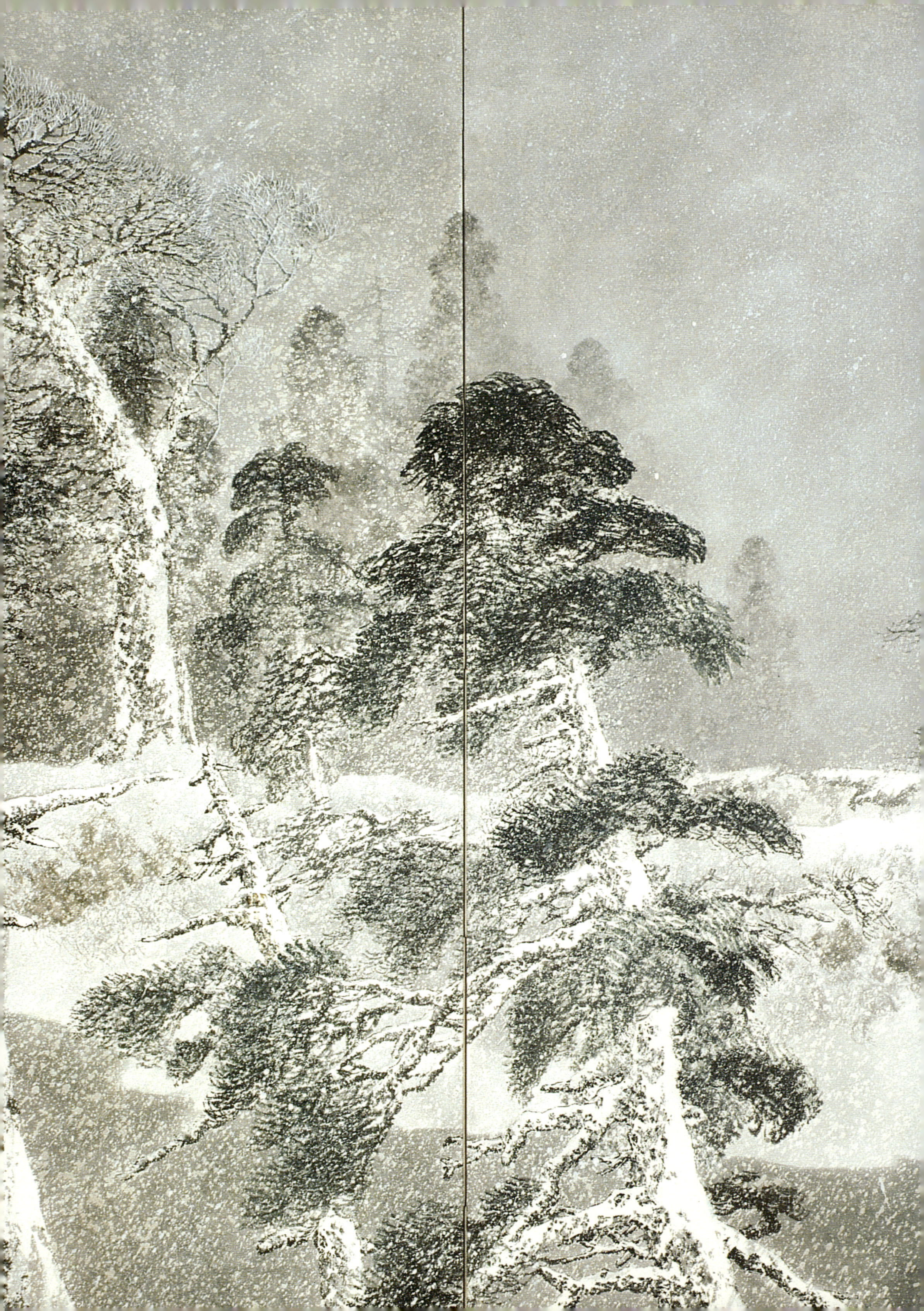

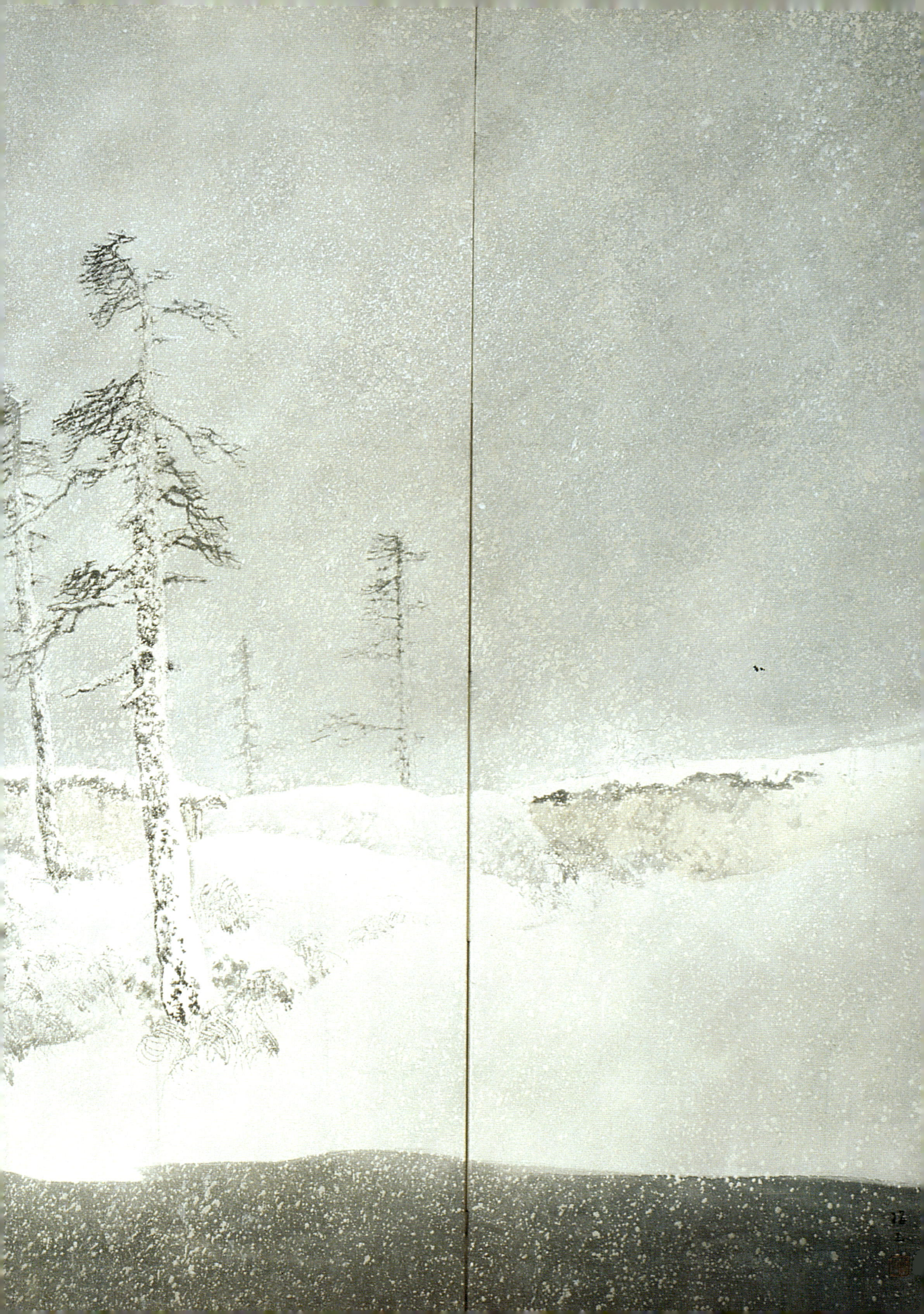

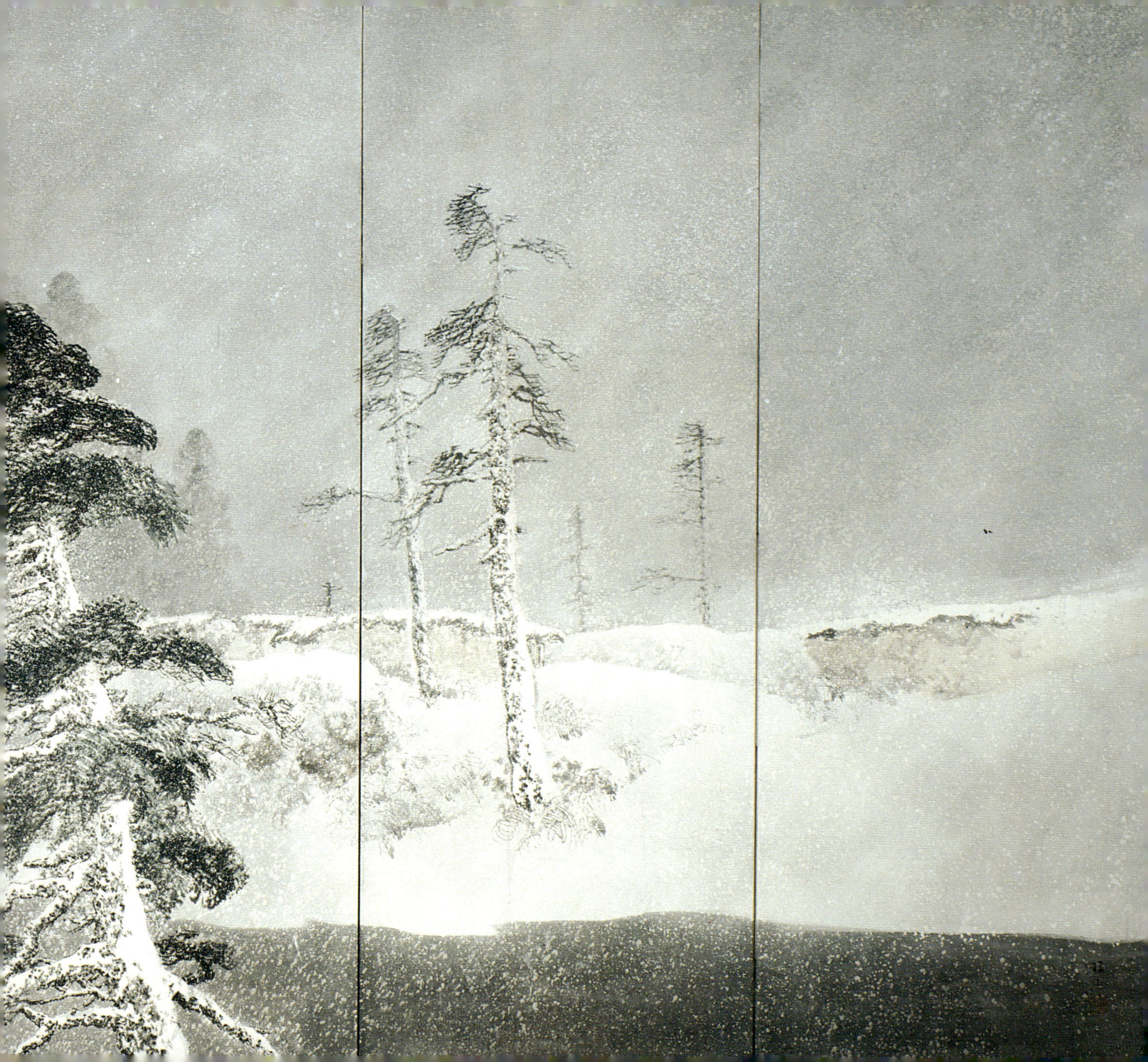

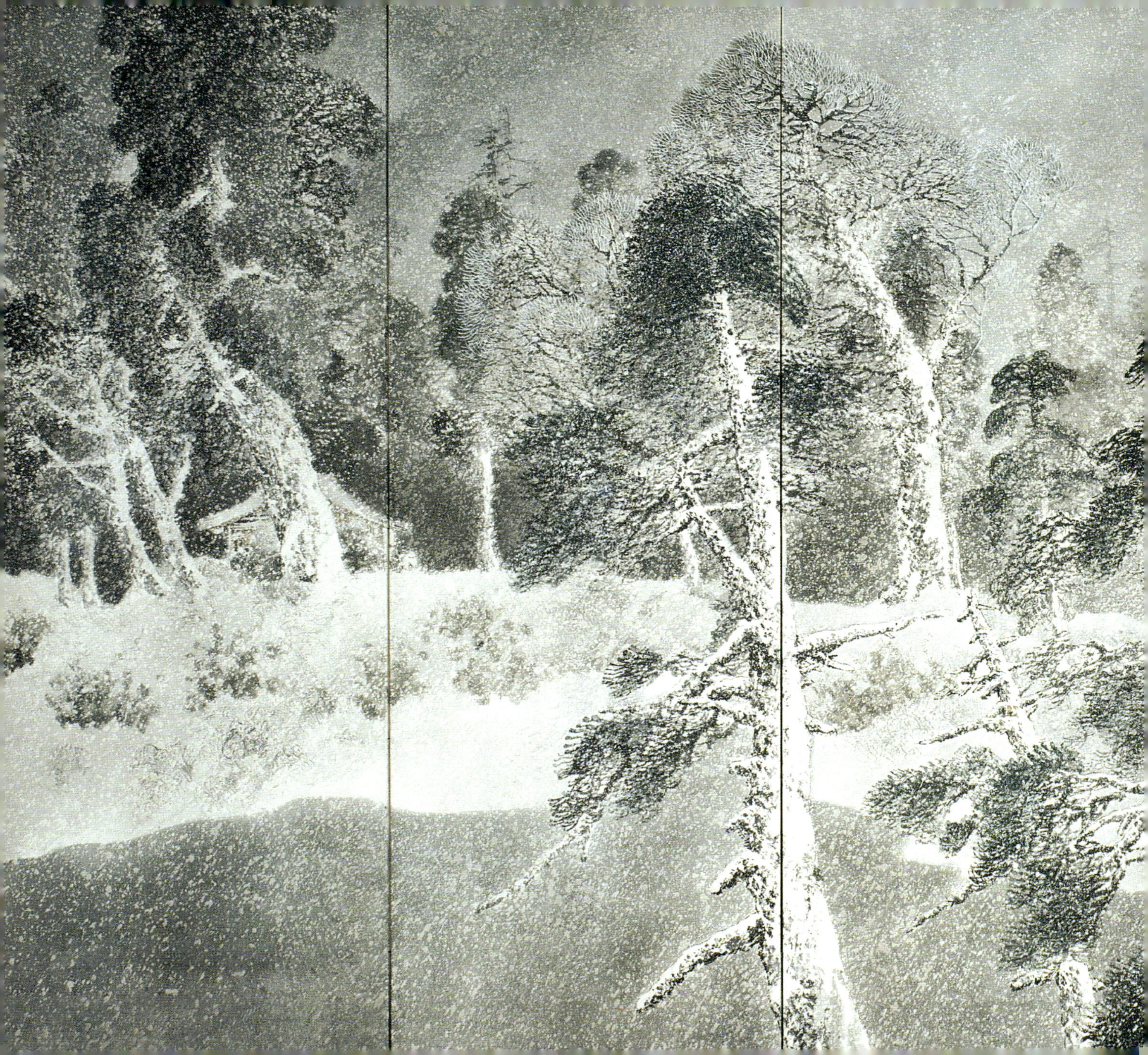

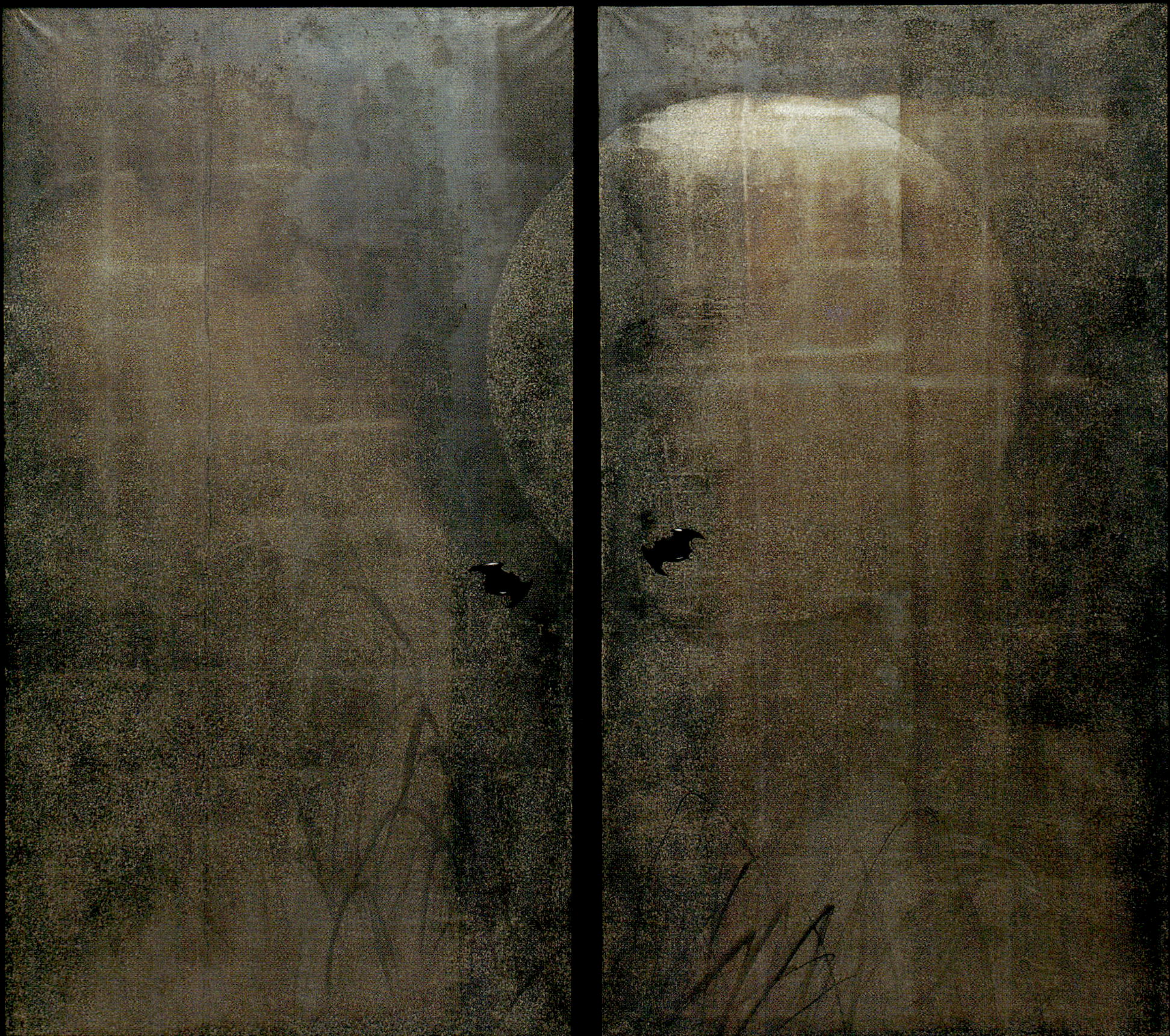

かげどう

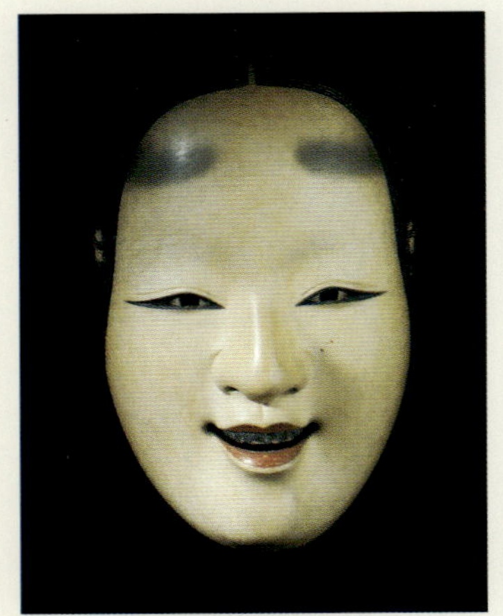

PAGE 3

Frontis Page: Mask for Noh, of *Ko-omote* type in the form of a beautiful serene young woman. Late Edo Period.

21.5 cm long x 14 cm wide x 8 cm deep.

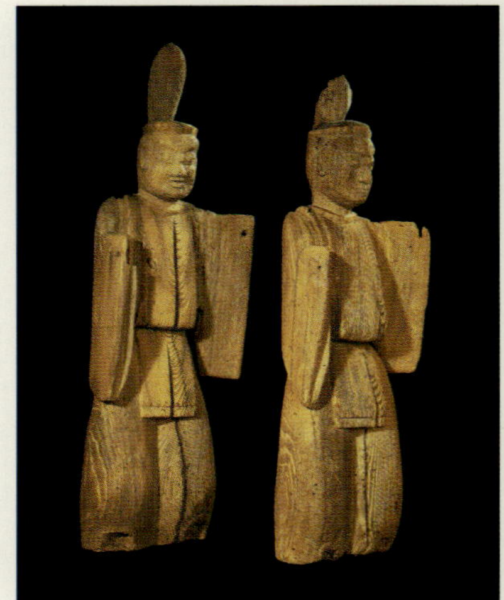

PAGE 13

1 ⟩ Pair of *Go-Shinzō* or images of Shintō gods, of carved cypress. Late Kamakura Period, late 13th–early 14th century AD.

Similar *Shinzō* are illustrated in Jūyō Bunkazai, volume 5, page 68, numbers 90 and 91, dating to the Heian and Kamakura Periods respectively.

72.7 cm high.
78.8 cm high.

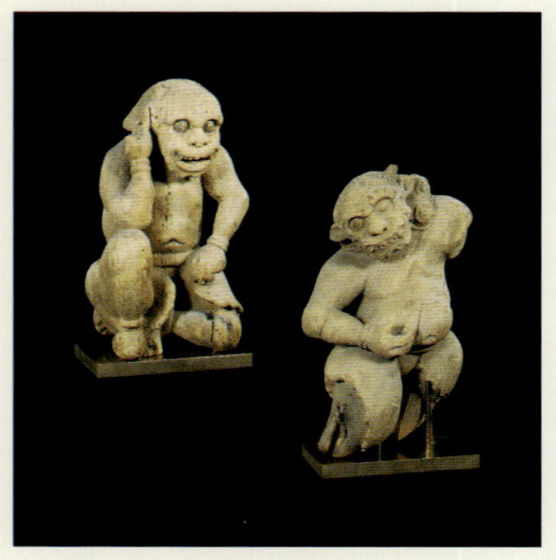

PAGE 14

2 ⟩ Pair of Buddhist architectural carvings in the form of Biranba and Niranba, the *oni* attendants of Bishamonten, the Guardian King of the North, of carved wood with traces of cinnabar applied directly to the wood. Kamakura Period, 13th–early 14th century.

For a comparison, see the Seattle Art Museum catalogue, A Thousand Cranes: Treasures of Japanese Art, number 13 on page 101.

27 cm high x 15 cm wide x 15.5 cm deep, with stand.
28 cm high x 17.5 cm wide x 12.5 cm deep, with stand.

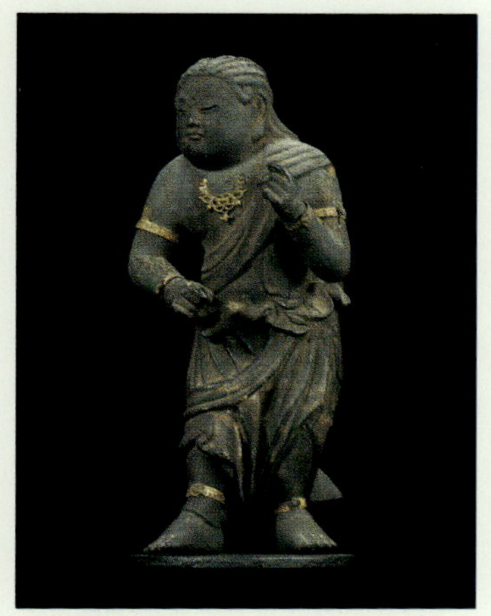

PAGE 15

3 ❭ Buddhist image of Kongara Dōji, an attendant of Fudō Myōō, of carved wood encrusted with incense, the eyes inlaid in crystal, and with applied gilt copper ornamentation. Late Kamakura Period, late 13th–early 14th century. Note: Edo Period, 18th century, restoration to feet.

26 cm high.

4 ❭ Pair of stone carvings of *shishi* or guardian lion-dogs from a Shintō shrine in Kyūshū. Muromachi Period, 15th–early 16th century.

These pieces were originally decorated with cinnabar pigment applied directly to the surface of the stone, traces of which can still be seen.

30.5 cm high x 39 cm long, each.

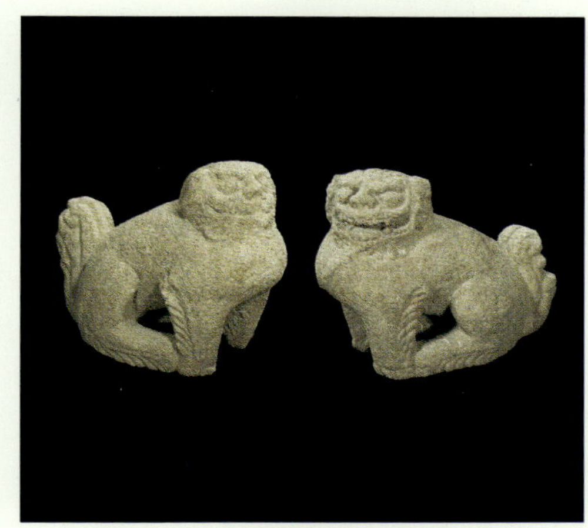

PAGE 16

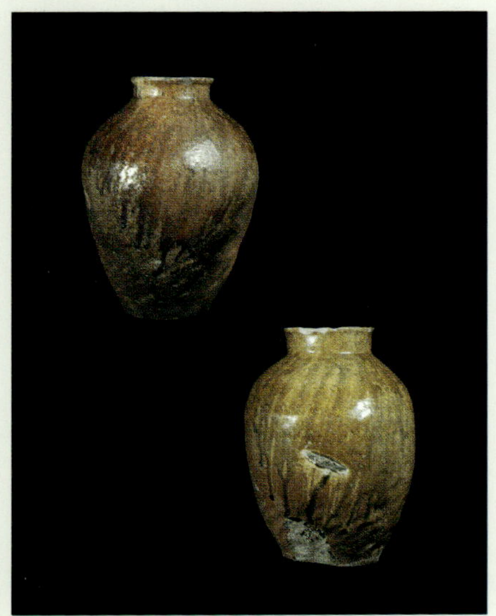

PAGE 17

5 ❭ Tokoname Ware stoneware *tsubo* or storage jar in a small ovoid form, with a natural ash caramel-brown glaze across one side. Late Muromachi Period, early 16th century.

Strong, rich example of Tokoname with the volcanic effects prized in Medieval jars.

33 cm high x 26 cm diameter.

6 ❭ Tokoname Ware stoneware *tsubo* or storage jar in a small ovoid form, with a natural ash green glaze cascading across one side. Muromachi Period, early 16th century.

33 cm high x 25 cm diameter.

For a comparison to these jars, see <u>A Selection of Japanese Art From The Mary and Jackson Burke Collection</u>, number 88.

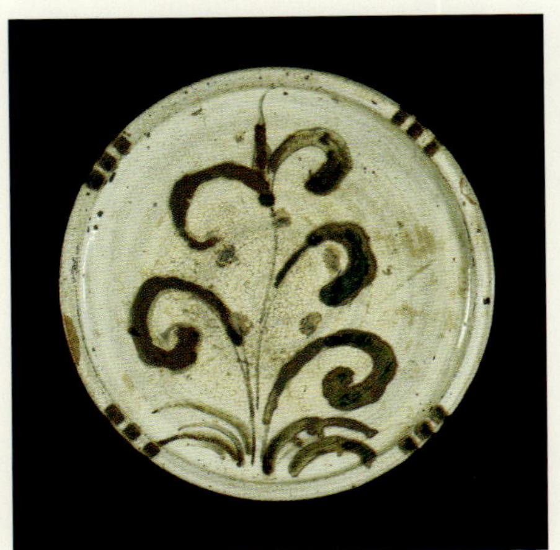

PAGE 18

7) Plate of Karatsu Ware in a circular form set on a split foot ring, the surface covered with a white slip and decorated in iron and copper oxides with a design of grasses. From Northwestern Kyūshū. Early Edo Period, circa 1610–1640. Note: minor gold lacquer repair to rim.

Almost none of this type of Karatsu has survived. An early and important example.

5 cm high x 26.5 cm diameter.

8) Mino Kasahara Ware large stoneware bowl, with a cream-colored slip ground painted over in iron oxide with a design of grasses. Edo Period, 17th century.

This utilitarian folk ceramic came to be used in the 19th century as a *Hira Mizusashi* or *Wide-mouthed Water Container* for summer *Matcha Tea Ceremony*. In the transformation it acquired a fine black lacquer lid and wood storage box. The base of the foot ring has softened and worn with long use.

For a comparison, see <u>Folk Traditions in Japanese Art</u>, number 98.

12 cm high x 37 cm diameter.

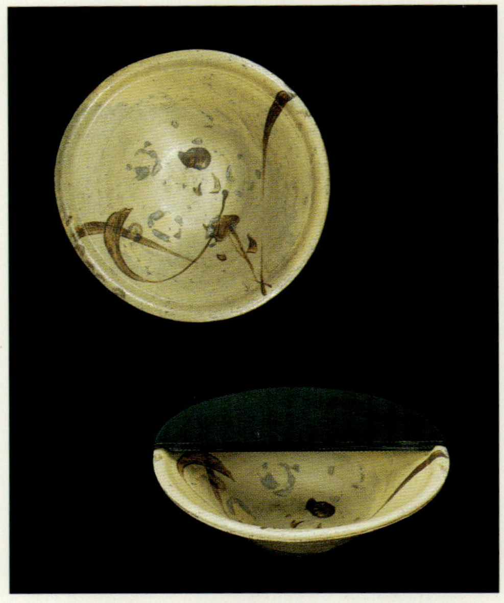

PAGE 19

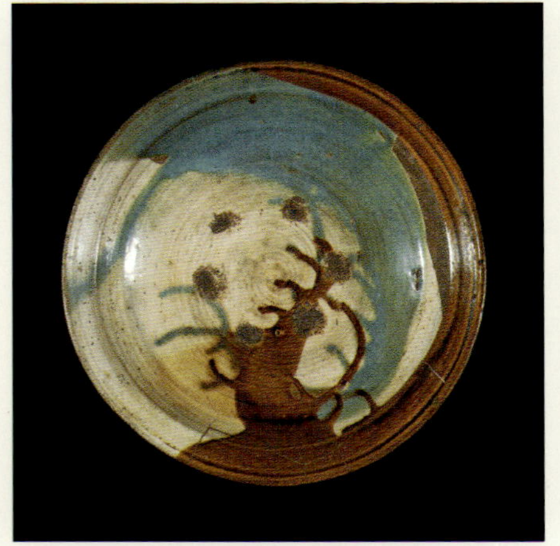

PAGE 20

9) Karatsu Ware stoneware bowl from the Takeo area kilns, in a shallow sloping form, the surface partly covered in cream-colored slip and then over splashed with iron oxide brown and copper oxide green glazes. Early Edo Period, 17th century. Note: gold lacquer repair to one side.

8.5 cm high x 32.5 cm diameter.

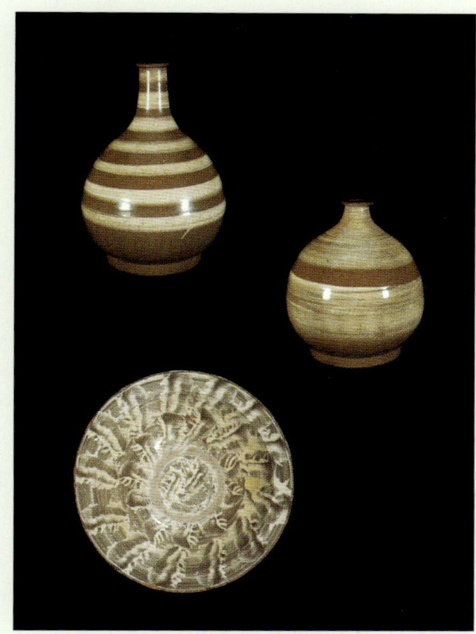

PAGE 21

10) Karatsu Ware stoneware *tokkuri* or *sake* bottle, in a globular form decorated with concentric horizontal bands of cream-colored *hakeme* (brushed slip). Edo Period, 18th century.

31 cm high x 22 cm diameter.

11) Karatsu Ware stoneware *tokkuri* or *sake* bottle, in a globular form brushed with concentric horizontal bands of thin cream-colored *hakeme* (brushed slip). Edo Period, 18th century.

24 cm high x 21 cm diameter.

12) Karatsu Ware stoneware bowl from the Takeo area kilns, in a rounded sloping form chatter brushed with cream-colored *hakeme*. Early Edo Period, 17th century.

12 cm high x 36 cm diameter

13) Yatsushiro Ware stoneware *tokkuri* or *sake* bottle in an octagonal faceted form, slip inlaid with playful variations on the character for *Kotobuki* or *Congratulations and Long Life*. The base is impressed with four shell form spurs resulting from firing on scallop shell supports in the kiln. Mid Edo Period, circa 1750. Note: small lacquer repair to edge of mouth on one side.

An early and very strong piece of Yatsushiro Ware.

19 cm high x 12 cm diameter.

14) Yatsushiro Ware stoneware *tokkuri* or *sake* bottle in a square form with a grey-green glaze, slip inlaid on each face with a flowering orchid, chrysanthemum, flowering plum, and bamboo. Edo Period, early 19th century. Note: minor silver lacquer repair to edge of mouth on one side.

20 cm high x 12 cm diameter.

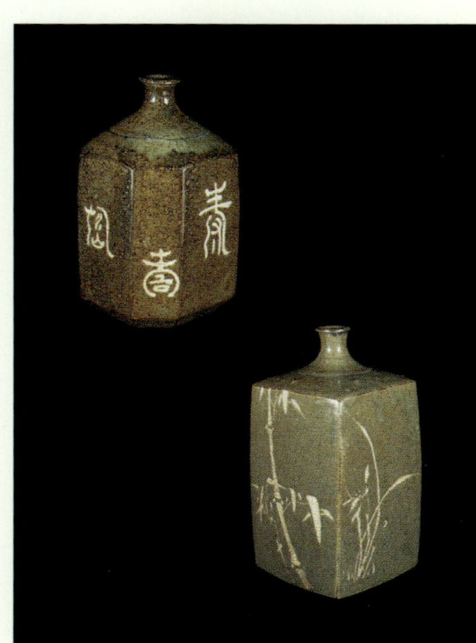

PAGE 22

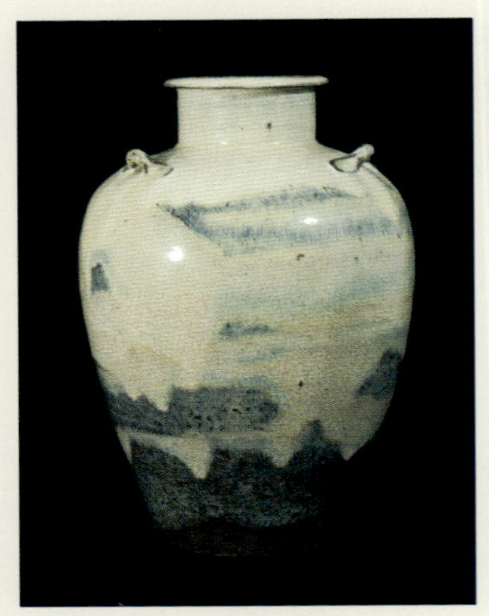

PAGE 23

15) Shōdai Ware stoneware *chatsubo* or tea storage jar, in a
baluster form with three applied lugs at the shoulder. The surface
is first decorated in an olive-green glaze and then thickly covered
with rice straw ash that clouds from white to blue with a fine
crackle. Edo Period, late 18th–early 19th century.

Classical Shōdai glaze effects, suggestive and cloudy.

31 cm high x 23 cm diameter.

16) Seto Ware stoneware *ishizara* plate, with a cream-
colored slip painted over in *gosu* blue with scattered maple
leaves and in iron oxide with a poem: *Storm Raging, Maple
Leaves of Mount Mimuro.* Mount Mimuro, near Nara,
is famed for maple viewing. The calligraphy ends without
the word for *momiji* or maple leaves, the poem's
completion being the whirling blue leaves scattered over
the plate. Edo Period, late 18th–early 19th century.

This is the rare, larger size in which *ishizara* were made.

6.5 cm high x 33 cm diameter.

17) Seto Ware stoneware *ishizara* plate, with a cream-
colored slip painted over in *gosu* blue and iron oxide with
the characters for: *Love is the Same in Any Country.*
Edo Period, late 18th–early 19th century.

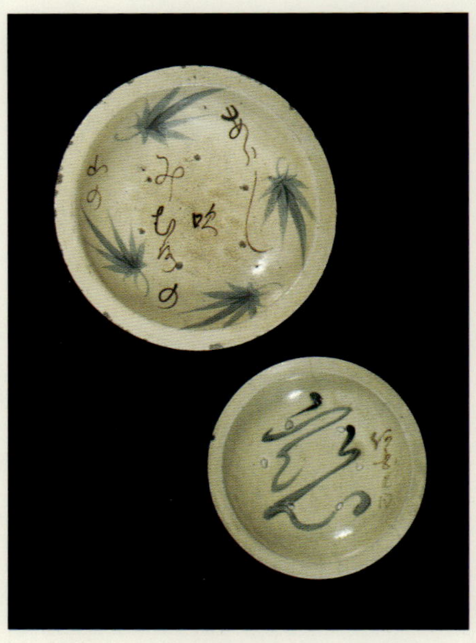

PAGE 24

At the time, *kuni* or *country* would have meant province,
though the feeling seems universal. A beautiful design
with fluid calligraphy.

5.5 cm high x 27 cm diameter.

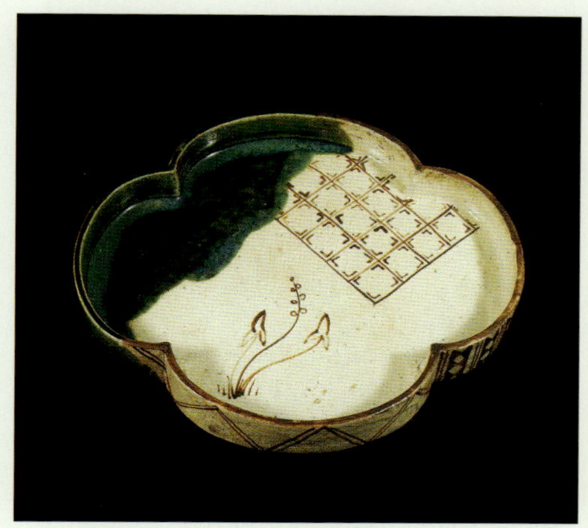

PAGE 25

18) Oribe Ware stoneware plate in a lobed form, with a cream-colored slip ground painted over with iron oxide designs of arrow-root and geometrics, then splashed with copper oxide. Edo Period, late 18th–early 19th century.

4.5 cm high x 31.5 cm x 27.5 cm.

19) Set of five *soba choko* or noodle sauce cups, of Arita Ware (Imari) porcelain hand painted in under-glaze blue with abstract water designs. Edo Period, circa 1800–1820.

6 cm high x 8.5 cm diameter, each.

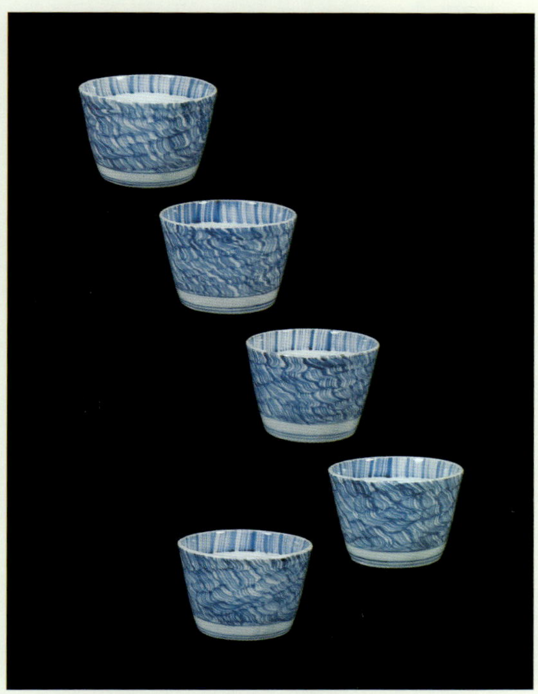

PAGE 26

20) Vase sculpted of ceramic in the form of an octopus jar encrusted with shells and sheltering a rock crab, by the artist Sasaki Niroku. Late Meiji Era, early 20th century. With the *tomobako* or signed original box.

Sasaki Niroku won awards at the 1903 fifth *Naikoku Kangyō Hakurankai* or Domestic Industrial Exhibition in Ōsaka. He worked in Ehime Prefecture, almost exclusively on a scale smaller than this piece. Most of his work consisted of miniature *Sencha Tea* and *sake* related serving pieces, suggesting that this vase may have been made for exhibition.

24.5 cm high x 16 cm diameter.

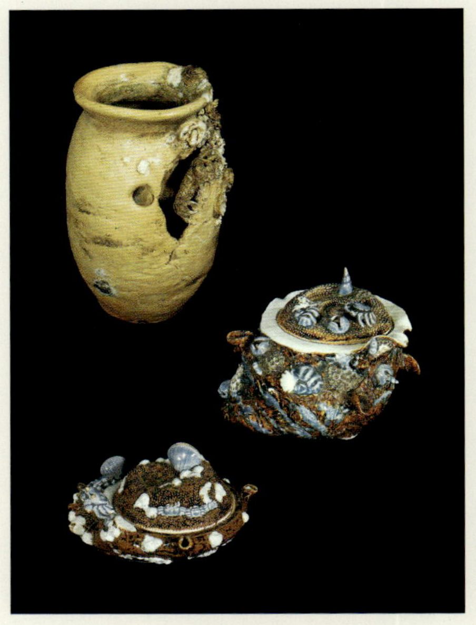

PAGE 27

21) Hirado Ware lidded dish, sculpted of porcelain in the form of a blue and brown *sazae* sea snail encrusted with shells and hosting a family of crabs (some of which have articulated parts). Meiji Era, late 19th century.

11 cm high x 22 cm diameter.

22) Hirado Ware *mizusashi* or water container for *Matcha Tea Ceremony*, sculpted of porcelain in the form of a large blue and brown *sazae* sea snail shell encrusted with corals, scallop shells, a crab, and barnacles. With the original box, the lid of which reads *Kai-gata Mizusashi* or *Shell Form Mizusashi*, and dated to Meiji 20, or 1887. Three of the barnacles are articulated. Note: the tip of one auger shell on the lid has been repaired in silver lacquer.

Numbers of Hirado serving dishes were made in this whimsical form, but we have never seen another *mizusashi* in a *sazae* form.

17 cm high x 22 cm diameter.

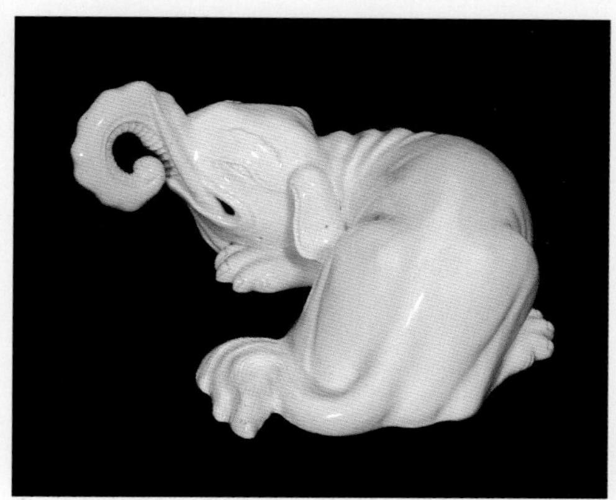

Page 28

23) Hirado Ware *kōro* or incense burner in the form of a recumbent elephant, sculpted in white porcelain. Edo Period, 18th century.

This is a *fusegōro* style *kōro* meant to be set over a small dish containing the burning incense.

10 cm high x 23 cm long x 21.5 cm wide.

24) *Kōro* or incense burner in the form of a crouching rabbit, of hand-sculpted white porcelain with touches of pink, the reticulated lid in the form of a Buddhist Jewel. The artist signed the reverse with an impressed seal, *Makuzu* (Makuzu Kōzan II, or Miyagawa Hanzan, 1859–1940). With the *tomobako* or original box, inscribed with the characters for: *Makuzu Kōzan Saku, Hakuji Gyokutō* or *Made by Makuzu Kōzan, White Porcelain Jeweled Rabbit*, and sealed. Late Taishō–early Shōwa, circa 1917–1940.

Another Makuzu Kōzan II piece in white porcelain bearing an identical impressed seal mark and calligraphic style on the box lid is illustrated in <u>Bridging East and West: Japanese Ceramics from the Kōzan Studio</u>, plate 26, page 50.

11 cm high x 13.5 cm long x 12 cm wide.

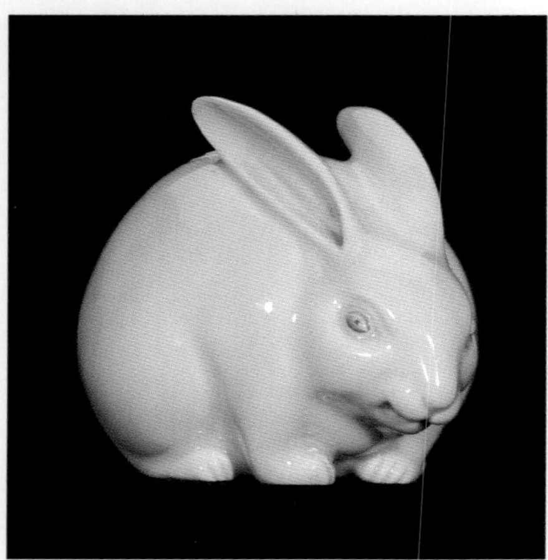

Page 29

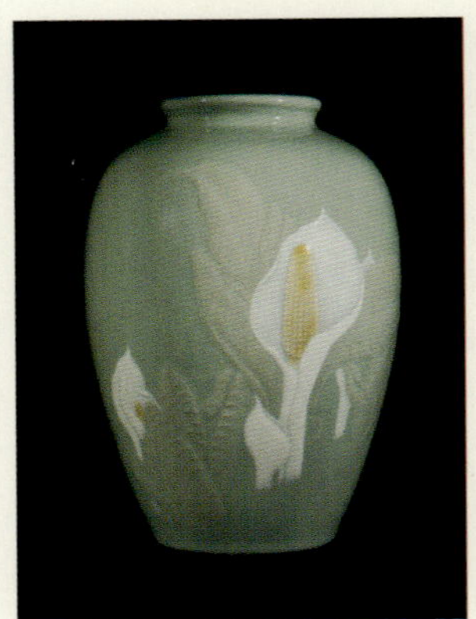

PAGE 30

25) Vase with a design of flowering *mizubashō*, sculpted in celadon and white porcelain with touches of yellow, signed by the artist on the reverse with an impressed seal mark which reads *Sōzan* (Sōzan II, Sōzan Torako) and with the *tomobako* or signed original box. The box lid exterior reads: *Seiji Kōryō Kamon Kabin* or *Celadon High Peak Flower Vase*, and the interior is signed *Sōzan* and sealed.

Sōzan Torako was born in Kanazawa in Meiji 23 (1890). In Meiji 25 (1892) she was adopted by her uncle, Suwa Sōzan (Sōzan I). Her ceramics resemble those of Sōzan I, but are considered to be more graceful and feminine. In Taishō 11 (1922), Sōzan I died and Sōzan Torako assumed the title, Sōzan II. Her work is represented in the Imperial Household Agency collections.

33 cm high x 23.5 cm diameter.

26) *Tsuitate* or standing screen of wood on a black lacquered base, the screen inset with a lacquer panel depicting a wood walkway over a marsh with flowering *mizubashō* and ferns. The panel is executed in *togidashi*, colored *takamakie*, *aogai* mother of pearl, and crushed egg shell. Shōwa Era, circa 1940–1950.

An Idemitsu Museum catalogue, <u>Hōan Hanzan Hakuyō Ten Zuroku</u>, plate 4, illustrates a writing box by the artist Takai Hakuyō (1895–1951) with a very similar design and made with the same techniques. Takai Hakuyō was a lacquer artist working in Niigata. He graduated from the Tokyo Fine Arts School and exhibited at the *Teiten* or Imperial Academy of Fine Arts Exhibition. This *tsuitate* came from a private collection in Niigata Prefecture and, although unsigned, it seems very possible that this may be the work of Hakuyō.

A paper label on the reverse of the stand indicates that this *tsuitate* was given in September of Shōwa 36 (1961) by the president of Tōhoku Kaihatsu Co. to the descendants of the *Daimyō* of Aizu Wakamatsu.

129 cm high x 164 cm wide.

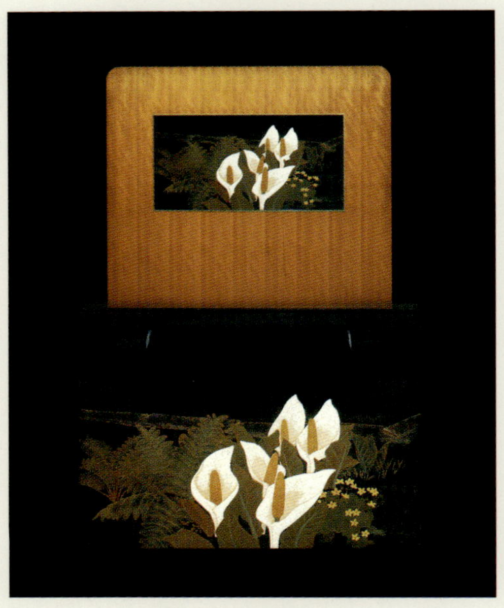

PAGE 31

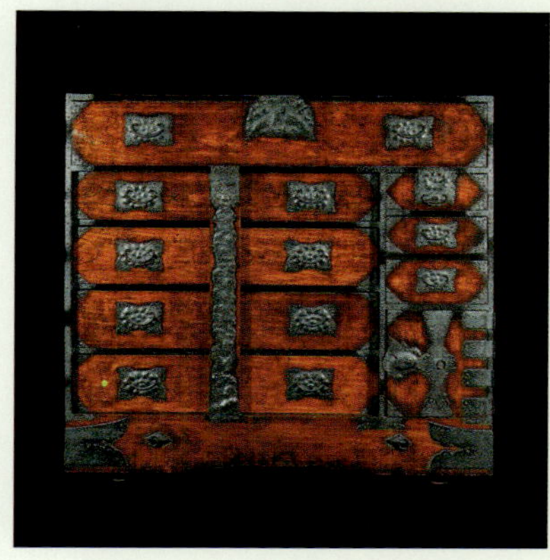

PAGE 32

Tansu or Japanese chests appeal to a modern aesthetic. Whether ornamented or plain, the overall design seems clean and linear, reflecting a basic concern for function. The makers prized wood grain and color. These often form the main ornament on a chest.

We can usually say with some precision where in Japan a piece was made. Since cabinet makers from one area shared a sense of how a chest should look, drawer configurations, hardware styles, and finishing preferences form a distinctive idiom. Over time these changed somewhat. While a later Sendai chest may be more refined than an Edo piece, it will still resemble the earlier *tansu*.

Rarity reflects a number of factors. Some regions produced many more chests than others. Fewer *tansu* were made in Edo than in Meiji. Sumptuary laws, a lower population level, and a smaller market economy played a part in this. Then earthquakes, fire, and war reduced the number of surviving examples.

Survival alone never guarantees condition. Many samurai families fell on hard times in the last 100 years, and furniture stored in decaying *kura* or family warehouses often met with hungry insects, the ravages of water, or simple ill use. Removable lock bars became inconvenient and many were thrown away or misplaced. During World War II, the Japanese government desperately needed metal for war materiel. Many chests were stripped of iron hardware to be melted down, a fate common to quantities of Edo Period bronzes as well. The older, less fashionable pieces seem to have suffered more, so great numbers of *tansu* were left missing hardware or their lock bars; others survived with damaged surfaces, or full of sawdust from the feasting of insects. These relics make up the bulk of the Japanese furniture market.

Therefore, *tansu* in excellent condition with their original hardware and surfaces command the highest prices. Of course some pieces were of better quality when they were made, built of finer woods, and lavished with more attention by the makers. Use of zelkova for cases as well as the drawer fronts was an extravagance. Some chests also developed richer color over time, greatly enhancing their value today.

These factors weigh against each other when looking at a chest. One might forgive minor worm damage in a piece with good age and color. However, hardware or lock bar replacements, the stripping of surfaces, and sunstruck or oxidized lacquer finishes destroy a chest's value.

27) *Kuruma-dansu* or wheeled chest of Iwayado type, of zelkova and cypress wood with a *kijiro* lacquer finish and hand forged and chiseled iron hardware. The lock bar is in a *shōchikubai* or pine, plum and bamboo motif, and the lock plates in a crane, tortoise and peony motif. From Iwate. Late Edo Period, early 19th century.

For a comparison in the Tokyo Furniture Museum's collections, see <u>Wa-dansu Shūsei</u>, plate 272.

111 cm high x 121 cm wide x 49 cm deep.

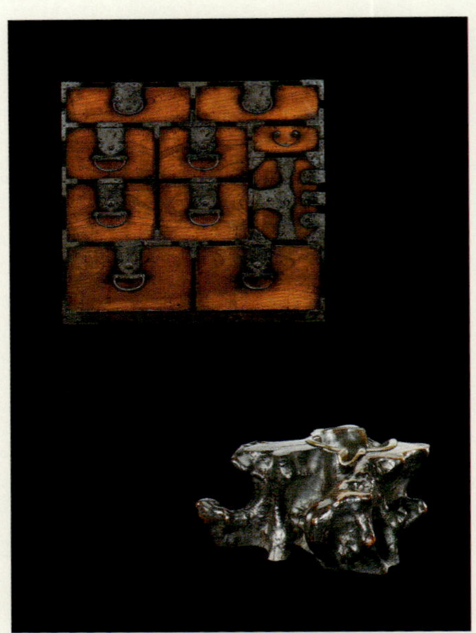

PAGE 33

28) *Chōba-dansu* or merchant's chest, of zelkova and cryptomeria wood with a *kijiro* lacquer finish and iron hardware. From the Yonezawa area. Inscribed on the back of one drawer by the maker, Murayama Tōshirō, a Buddhist altar carpenter, and dated to April of Meiji 13, or 1880.

83.5 cm high x 91 cm wide x 43.75 cm deep.

29) *Hibachi* or charcoal brazier, made from a gnarled section of natural hardwood tree trunk with a lacquered surface and a cast bronze ash container. Edo Period, early 19th century.

Exceptional color. This piece came from an estate house in Ōita Prefecture.

30 cm high x 70 cm x 58 cm.

30) *Tansu* or chest for clothing storage in three sections, of zelkova and cypress wood with a *bengara* red and *kijiro* lacquer finish, and iron hardware. The lower sections are configured with drawers and the top section with sliding panels. From the Mikuni area in Northern Fukui. Early Meiji Era, circa 1870.

169 cm high x 90.5 cm wide x 46 cm deep.

31) *Chōba-dansu* or merchant's chest with four drawers and central sliding panels, of zelkova wood and cypress with a *bengara* red and *kijiro* lacquer finish, and iron hardware. From Miyagi. Edo Period, early 19th century.

Both the case and drawer fronts are of zelkova. The lock plates are engraved with the character for *fuku* or *good luck*. The sliding panels ride on coins, allowing the owner to enjoy the sound of money every time they were slid.

91.25 cm high x 86.5 cm wide x 45 cm deep.

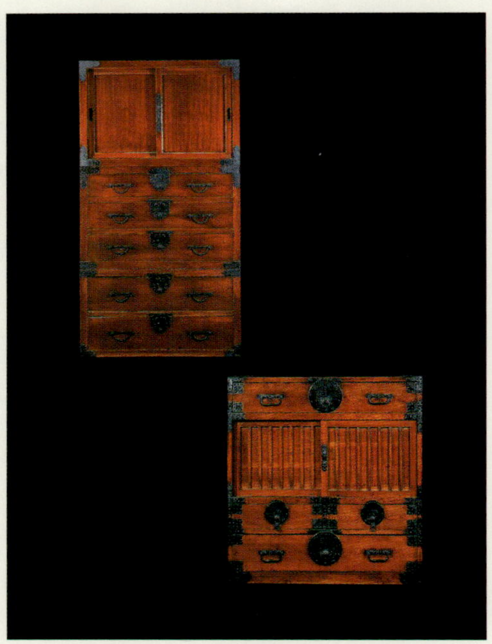

PAGE 34

138

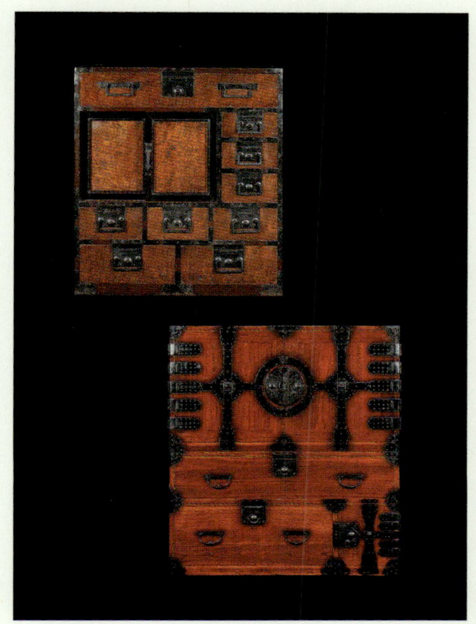

PAGE 35

32) *Chōba-dansu* or merchant's *tansu* chest with nine drawers and a sliding panel compartment, of zelkova burl and cypress wood with a *kijiro* lacquer finish, and iron hardware. From the Matsumoto area in Nagano. Early Meiji Era, circa 1870–1880.

For a comparison, see <u>Wa-dansu Shūsei</u>, plate 126.

87.5 cm high x 79.5 cm wide x 36.5 cm deep.

33) *Ishō kasane-dansu* or two section clothing storage chest in a *ryōbiraki* style. The top section configured with hinged doors behind which lie two sliding drawers, the lower section with two drawers and a *kinko* style safe compartment. Crafted of solid paulownia wood with a *bengara* red and *kijiro* lacquer finish, and iron hardware. From the Tokyo area. Early Meiji Era, circa 1870–1880.

Engraved on the central lock plate is a paulownia leaf *mon* or family crest.

109 cm high x 100 cm wide x 45.5 cm deep.

34) *Chō-bako* or merchant's document storage box, made of solid paulownia wood with iron hardware, the face with *ryōbiraki* style doors and an engraved central lock plate. The interior designed with eleven drawers bearing the original paper labels and open compartments at the top for storing ledgers. From the Shōnai Plain area in Yamagata Prefecture. Late Meiji Era, circa 1900.

77.5 cm high x 55 cm wide x 40.5 cm deep.

35) *Ishō kasane-dansu* or two section clothing storage chest with five drawers and a *kinko* style safe compartment. Built of paulownia and cypress wood with embossed iron lock plates depicting auspicious motifs. From the Shōnai Plain in Yamagata Prefecture. Meiji Era, late 19th century.

106.5 cm high x 88 cm wide x 42.5 cm deep.

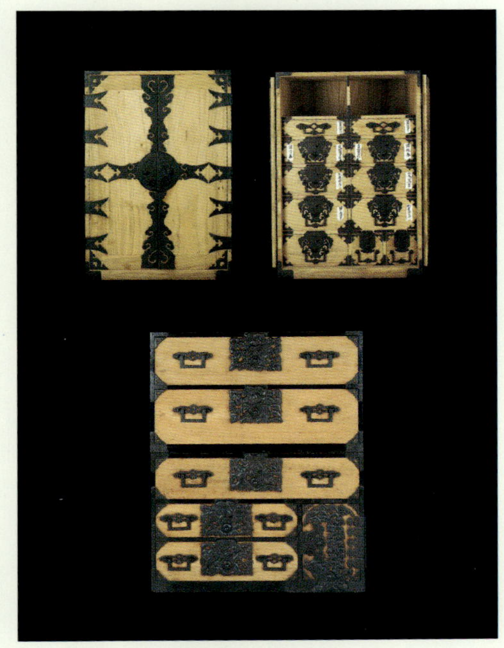

PAGE 36

139

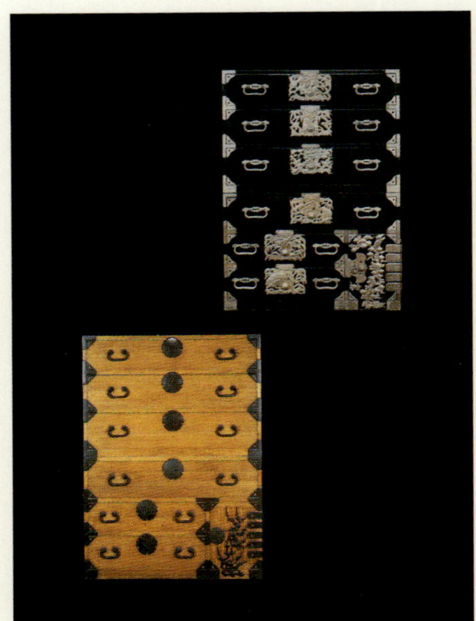

PAGE 37

36) *Ishō kasane-dansu* or two section clothing storage chest with six drawers and a *kinko* style safe compartment. Crafted of solid paulownia wood with snowflake style iron lock plates engraved with auspicious motifs. From the Shōnai Plain in Yamagata Prefecture. Meiji Era, late 19th century.

121 cm high x 89.5 cm wide x 45.5 cm deep.

37) *Ishō kasane-dansu* or two section clothing storage chest with six drawers and a *kinko* style safe compartment. Made of cryptomeria and paulownia wood, with a black *tame-nuri* lacquer finish on the face, and the case with a *kijiro* lacquer finish. The iron hardware deeply embossed with auspicious symbols (among them sparrows and bamboo, hawk and pine, tortoises and cranes). From the Shōnai Plain in Yamagata Prefecture. Meiji Era, late 19th century.

For a comparison, please see <u>Wa-dansu Shūsei</u>, plate 176.

120.5 cm high x 88 cm wide x 42.5 cm deep.

38) *Kuruma-nagamochi* or wheeled coffer-chest in one section, of lacquered zelkova wood with iron hardware. From Niigata on the Northwest Coast of Honshū. Edo Period, late 18th–early 19th century.

This was made for use in a *kura* or family warehouse, and the use of zelkova wood for such a chest was always extravagant. Beautiful rich color and condition.

95.5 cm high x 136 cm wide x 74 cm deep.

39) *Nagamochi* or lidded storage trunk with two drawers at the base, of solid paulownia wood with a *bengara* red and *kijiro* lacquer finish, and iron hardware. From Niigata Prefecture. Late Edo Period, mid 19th century.

Behind the small drawer lies a *kakushi* style secret compartment.

75 cm high x 85 cm wide x 42.25 cm deep.

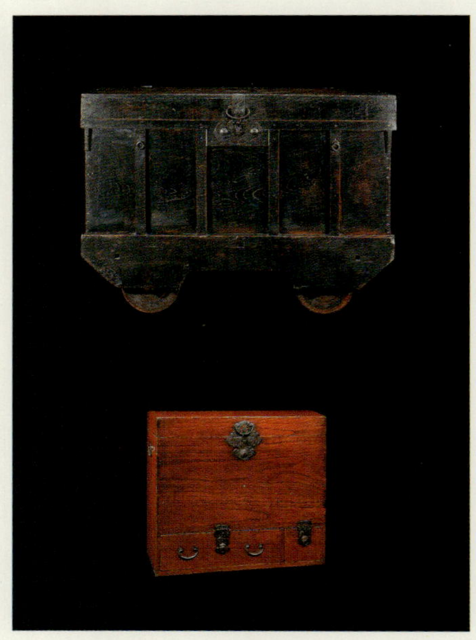

PAGE 38

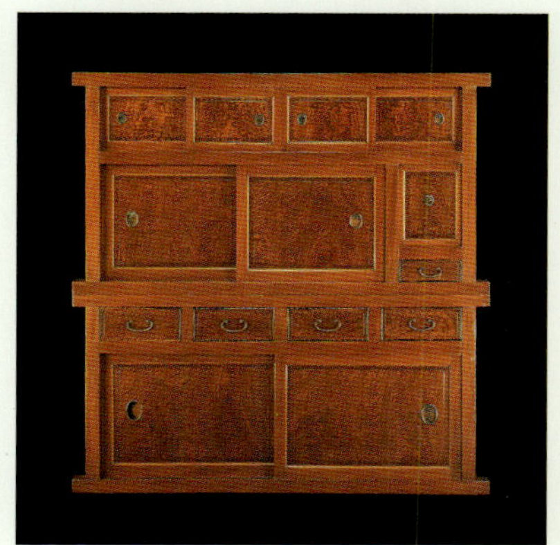

PAGE 39

40) *Mizuya* or kitchen area storage chest in two sections, configured with three sliding panel compartments, five drawers, and a drop fit panel. Made of zelkova burl and cypress wood with a *kijiro* lacquer finish and copper hardware. From an estate house in the Kaga area of Ishikawa Prefecture. Late Meiji Era, circa 1900–1910.

One of the most refined *mizuya* we have seen, with a zelkova case and burl front.

151.25 cm high x 150 cm wide x 45.5 cm deep.

41) *Mizuya* or kitchen area storage chest in two sections, with four sliding panel compartments and seven drawers. Crafted of cypress and zelkova wood with a red and black lacquer finish and copper hardware. From the Obama area in Southern Fukui. Early Meiji Era, circa 1870.

The lacquer surface on this chest has developed exceptional color.

176.5 cm high x 182 cm wide x 49 cm deep.

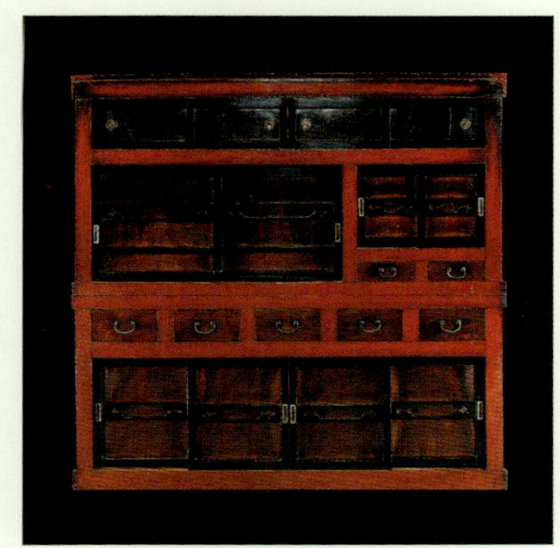

PAGE 40

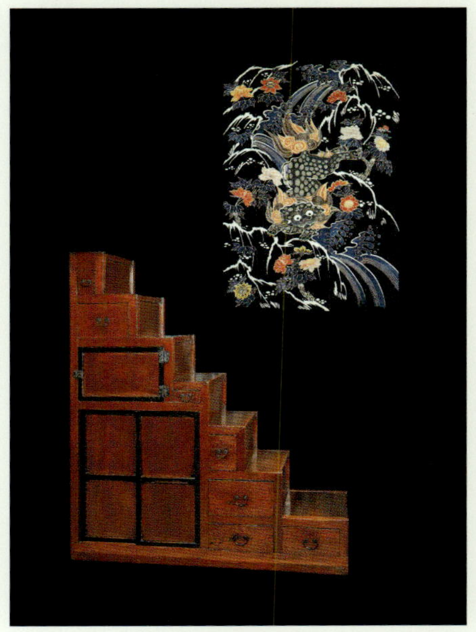

PAGE 41

42) *Kaidan-dansu* or stair-step chest in a single section. Crafted of zelkova and cypress wood, with a *bengara* red and *kijiro* lacquer finish, and iron hardware. From an estate on Awaji Island. Edo Period, mid 19th century.

Zelkova case and front.

198.5 cm high x 175.5 cm wide x 72.25 cm deep.

43) *Futonji* or bedding cover in five panels, of indigo dyed cotton with *tsutsugaki* paste resist-dyed designs of a *shishi* or lion-dog leaping down a cliff amidst a waterfall and peonies. From Kyūshū. Meiji Era, late 19th century.

215 cm high x 156 cm, exclusive of border.

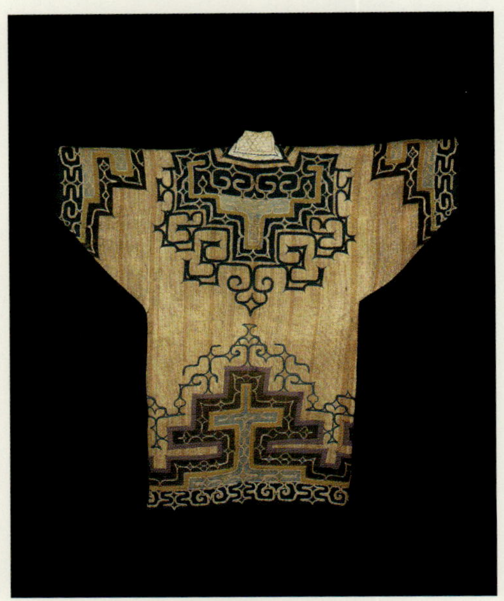

PAGE 42

44) Ainu robe from Sakhalin Island (*Aharushi*), woven of elm bark fiber (*ohyō*) cloth decorated with embroidery and appliqué. This decoration uses cotton and elm bark fiber thread, cotton cloth, velvet, and silk. Edo Period, early 19th century.

Several features of this robe are typical of Sakhalin area textiles; namely the tall white cotton collar, very narrow appliqué, and extensive use of imported trade fabrics. While the cotton fabric used here is certainly of Japanese origin, the velvet and silks probably came from the Continent. The use of couching stitches tends to be seen in earlier garments.

An exceptional and early Ainu textile.

120 cm high x 130 cm across sleeves.

45) *Katakuchi* or spouted *sake* server, of *negoro* lacquer over wood. Early Edo Period, early 17th century.

Intense red and black color.

18 cm high x 34 cm x 23.5 cm.

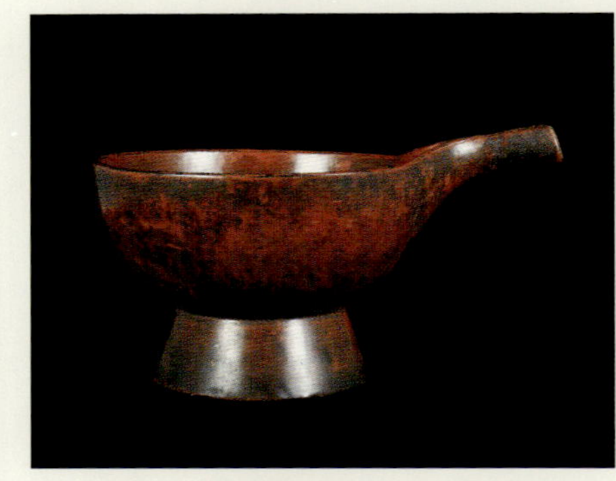

PAGE 43

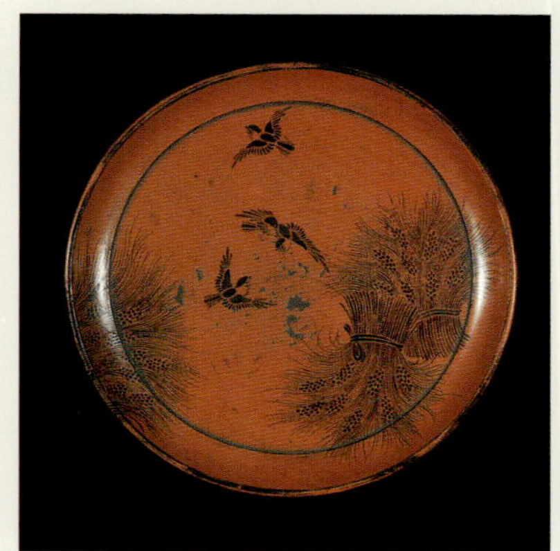

PAGE 44

46) Tray in a circular form, of wood with a design of rice sheaves and sparrows lacquered in red and black. Mid Edo Period, 18th century.

5 cm high x 43 cm diameter.

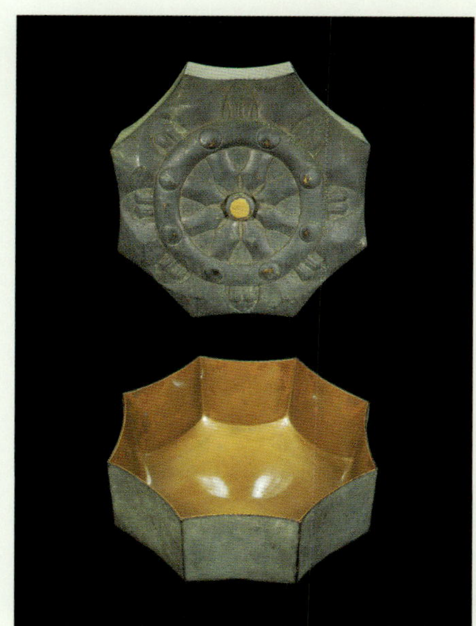

PAGE 45

47) *Kashiki* or container for tea sweets, the exterior a large gilt bronze temple *kugikakushi* or nail head cover dating to the Muromachi Period, early 16th century, and the interior lined with *sentoku* yellow bronze by Nakagawa Jōeki, 10th generation (Meiji 13–Shōwa 15, 1880–1940). Early 20th century. With the *tomobako* or original box, signed and sealed on the reverse.

The 10th generation Nakagawa Jōeki master had a talent for transforming beautifully aged objects into his work. Lining such a container in *sentoku* looks misleadingly simple.

8 cm high x 19.5 cm diameter.

48) *Kugikakushi* or nail head cover, in a large size from a Shintō shrine, of gilt bronze in the form of a camellia flower. Late Muromachi Period, 16th century. With a new bronze stand.

The camellia flower was a symbol for Suitengū shrines which were dedicated to the drowned child emperor, Antoku Tennō. The most important of these is located in Kurume City, Fukuoka Prefecture. Since this nail head cover also came from a private collection in Kyūshū, it is likely to have come from the same shrine complex.

18 cm high x 18 cm across, exclusive of stand.

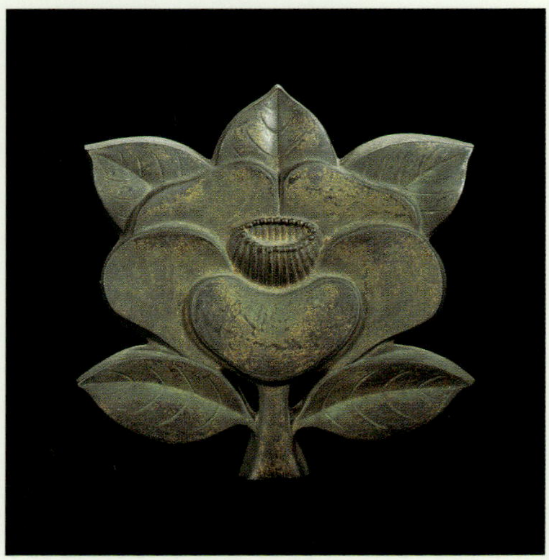

PAGE 46

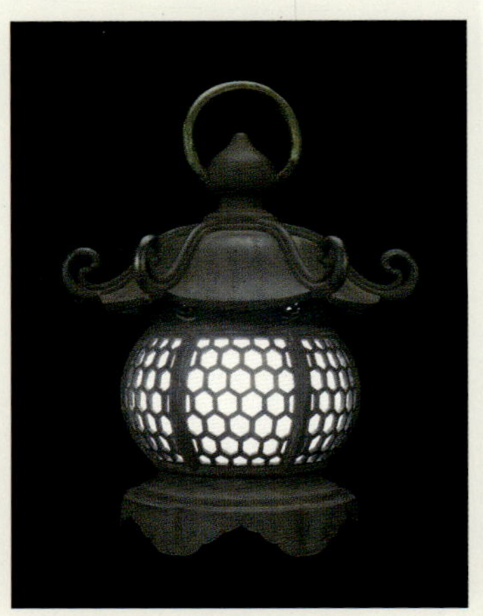

PAGE 47

49) *Tsuridōrō* or hanging lantern of heavily cast and engraved bronze. The lantern rests on a scalloped circular base, the globe form candle box fashioned in a pierce work net design (which can also be read as a tortoise shell or longevity motif), the gracefully curved roof ribbed with curling waves, and surmounted by a *giboshi* style finial and hanging ring. Originally the ends of the roof waves supported hanging bells. An inscription engraved across the roof reads: *Kii Province* (modern Wakayama), *Presented to the gods of Hi No Kuma Shrine in the First Year of the Kambun Era, (1661), A Lucky Day in September. Made by the Master of Buddhist Altar Fittings, Dōi.*

This massive hanging lantern was made as a memorial gift for an important shrine in Wakayama in 1661. The weight and scale are balanced by the pierce work and graceful curves of the roof and base. It casts stretching net shadows when lit.

60 cm high x 47 cm diameter.

50) Vase in a curving hexagonal form with animal mask ornaments at the neck, cast of *Karadō* or Chinese bronze and the surface with an applied rich *benidō* or mottled red patina. Unsigned, but with an attestation inscribed on the storage box by the 13th generation (present day) Kanchi master certifying that the vase was made by his ancestor, Miyazaki Kanchi I, who was active in the late 17th century and died in 1712.

The Kanchi family reside in Kanazawa and have always been famous metal casters, especially noted for their *chagama* or water boiling kettles for *Matcha Tea Ceremony*.

Graceful yet very strong sensibility common to Early Edo bronzes.

30 cm high x 14 cm diameter.

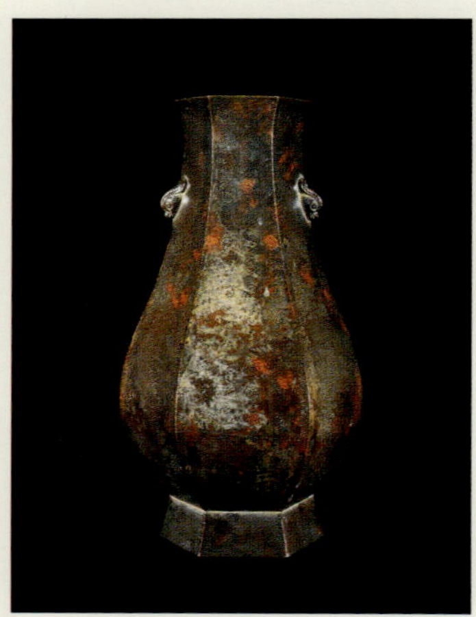

PAGE 48

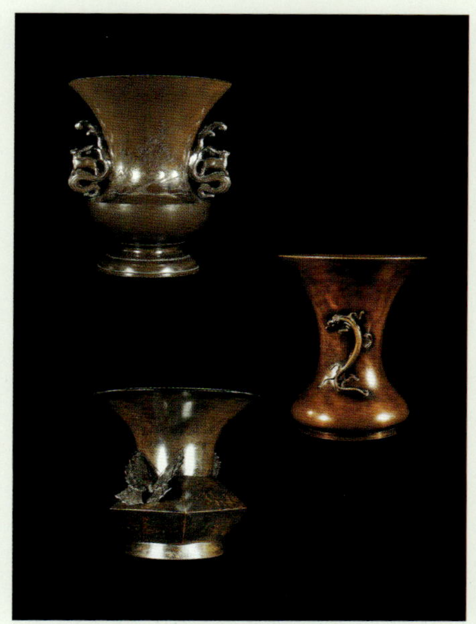

PAGE 49

51) Vase in an *Ikenobō* style with a flaring mouth and two applied handles in the form of rabbits and waves. The body is engraved with designs of water plants and waves. Early Edo Period, 17th century.

An early example with a charming motif.

32 cm high x 28.5 cm diameter.

52) Vase in an *Ikenobō* style with a hexagonal base and a round flaring mouth and two detachable side handles in the form of butterflies. Mid Edo Period, 18th century.

For a similar example, see plate 47 in <u>Flower Bronzes of Japan</u>. Beautiful mottled color.

29 cm high x 31.5 cm diameter.

53) Vase of cast bronze in an hour glass form with a flaring mouth, ornamented on the sides with two applied handles in the form of dragons. Edo Period, 18th century.

31 cm high x 26.5 cm diameter.

54) Pair of vases in tall squared forms, of cast bronze with relief designs of dragons and gold inlaid designs of clouds. The vases are signed with a chiseled seal, *Gorōsaburō*. The box bears an inscription stating that these were the collaborative work of both Kanaya Gorōsaburō and Hata Zōroku, and date to 1912.

33 cm high x 14 cm x 14 cm, each.

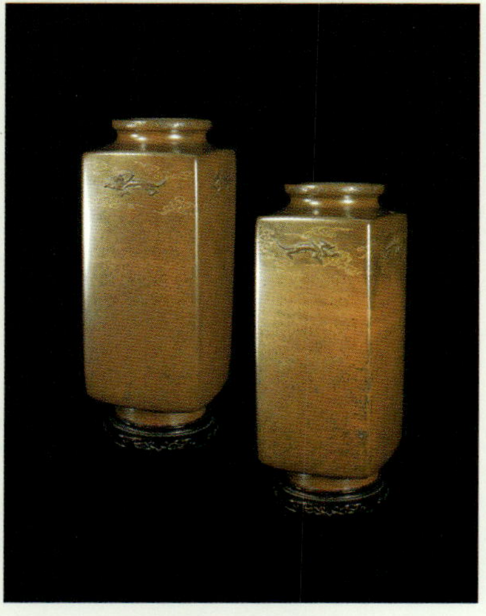

PAGE 50

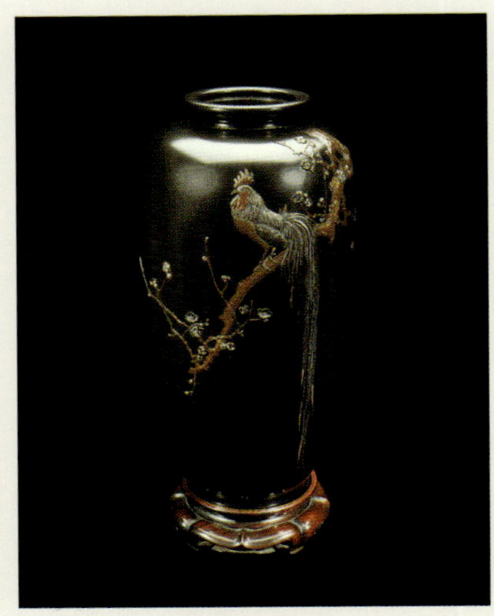

PAGE 51

55) Vase in a tall and massive ovoid form, of *shakudō* with a design of a cock on a branch of plum blossoms inlaid in silver, gold, *shibuichi*, *shakudō* and colored bronze. Sealed on the base with the Hattori mark and signed by the artist on the back, *Ichimoku*, and with a *kakihan*. Meiji Era, late 19th century. With the original rosewood stand, and the *tomobako* or signed original box.

Outstanding workmanship and quality in a classical Meiji design.

46 cm high x 24 cm diameter.

56) Vase of cast bronze with a high relief design of two lizards, the eyes inlaid in gold and *shakudō*. Signed on the reverse with an inlaid gold seal, *Nihon Koku Maruki Sei* or *The Country of Japan, Made by Maruki*. Meiji Era, late 19th century.

The Maruki Works Art Factory was one of the best studios during Meiji. Located in Tokyo, the studio employed many of Japan's finest artists.

20.5 cm high x 12 cm diameter.

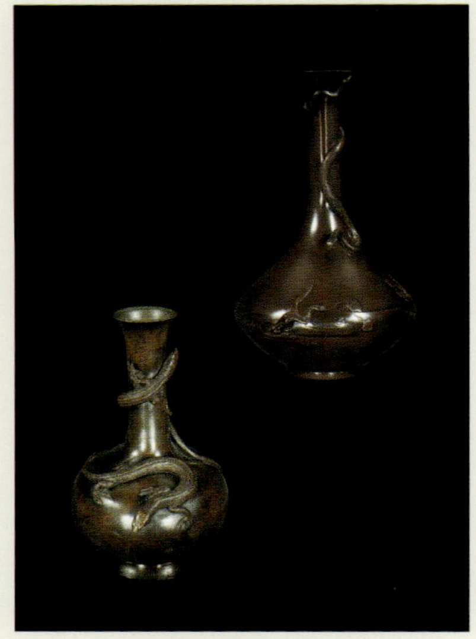

PAGE 52

57) Vase of cast bronze with a high relief design of an inquisitive snake avidly setting his sights on a neighboring frog. Signed on the reverse by the artist, Masayuki. Meiji Era, late 19th century.

A classical example of the lunch theme.

29 cm high x 18 cm diameter.

58) Vase of cast bronze with an applied high relief design of a *sentoku* bronze frog pursuing an inlaid *shakudō*, gold and silver wasp. Signed on the reverse by the artist, Yoshinori. Taishō Era, circa 1920.

The frog having chosen lunch is about to be surprised.

22 cm high x 8.5 cm diameter.

59) Vase of *sentoku* bronze decorated with an applied cast and cold chiseled bronze snail. The shell is inlaid with red bronze spots and the snail's trail is inlaid in *shakudō*. Signed to the right of the snail's track by the artist with chiseled characters, *Hokusen*, and with an inlaid red bronze seal, (Kitagawa Hokusen, 1846–1923). With the *tomobako* or original box, the box lid sealed by the artist and inscribed: *Yellow Bronze With Snail Design Single Flower Vase.*

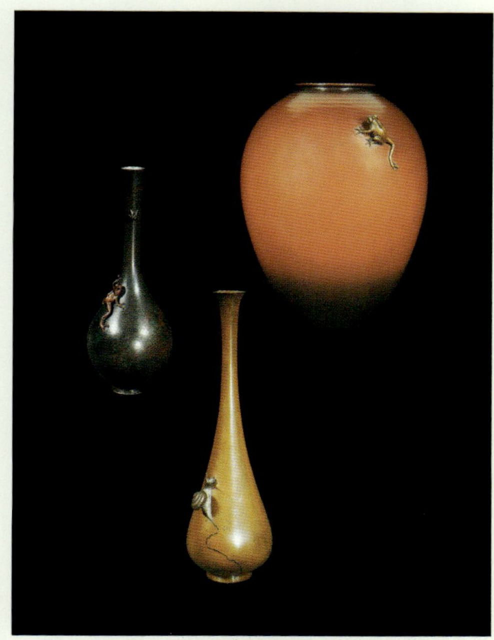

PAGE 53

Kitagawa Hokusen lived in Mito, and studied under Sekijōken Motozane. Later he taught at the Tokyo Fine Arts School. This vase dates from the Late Meiji or Taishō Periods. The extreme simplicity and elegance of the design is more typical of that era's turn away from overall ornamentation. Superb workmanship by a gifted artist.

26.5 cm high x 8 cm diameter.

60) Vase of cast bronze with a gradated patina of smoke to red, the side ornamented with an applied frog in *sentoku* yellow bronze. Signed by the artist, *Issai*. Taishō Era, circa 1920.

24.5 cm high x 19 cm diameter.

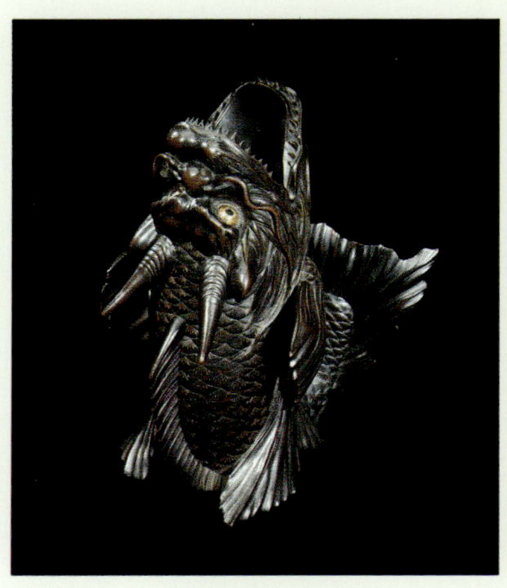

61) Vase in the form of a leaping dragon-carp of cast, assembled and chiseled bronze, the eyes inlaid in gold. Signed by the maker, Maruki. Early Meiji Era, circa 1870–1880.

26.5 cm high x 23 cm deep x 17.5 cm wide.

PAGE 54

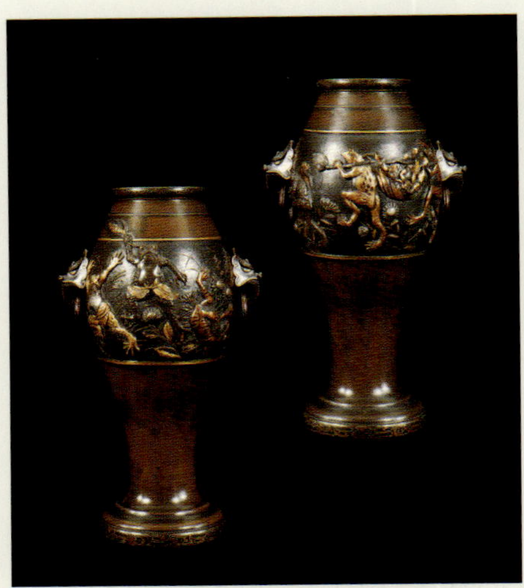

62) Pair of vases, of cast bronze inlaid in soft metal and gilt with designs of parading frogs. Signed on a gilt plaque by the artist, *Jugyokusai Kazuyoshi*. Early Meiji Era, circa 1870–1880.

Animal caricatures dressed as humans, engaging in amusing activities recur again and again in Japanese art. The subject dates from the Heian Period. Giving balloons to these Meiji Era frogs made them terribly up-to-date.

26.5 cm high x 12 cm diameter, each.

PAGE 55

63) Pair of Imperial presentation vases of silver, chiseled and inlaid in *shibuichi*, *shakudō* and gold with designs of landscapes. The necks inlaid in gold with the Imperial chrysanthemum crest. Each vase signed on the reverse by the artist with a chiseled signature, *Shimizu Nanzan Kinkoku* or *Carved by Shimizu Nanzan* (Shimizu Nanzan was the *Gō* or art name for Shimizu Kamezō). Late Meiji–early Taishō Era, circa 1900–1920.

Shimizu Nanzan was born in Hiroshima. He studied under Kanō Natsuo and Fujita Bunzō. Later he became an Imperial Household Artist and a member of the Imperial Academy of Fine Arts. In 1948 he died at the age of 73.

32 cm high x 15 cm diameter, each.

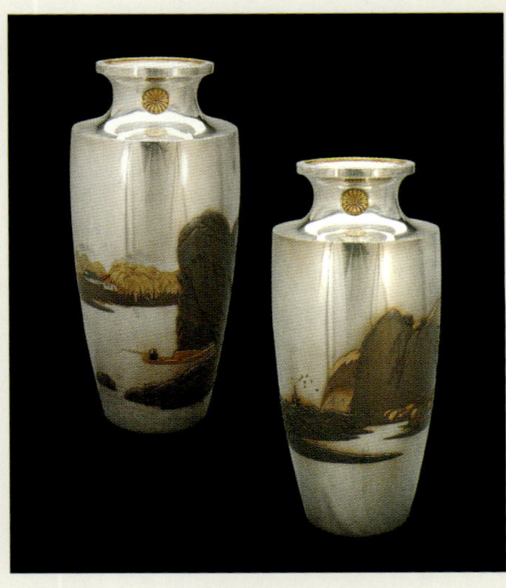

PAGE 56

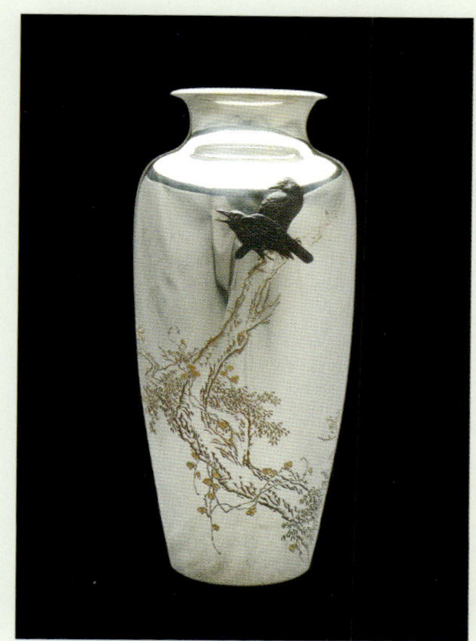

PAGE 57

64) Vase in a tall baluster form of silver, chiseled and inlaid in *shakudō* with a pair of ravens in an old tree encircled in ivy. The ivy leaves are inlaid in gold. Signed by the artist on the back with the chiseled characters, *Hōshūsō Shōmin Chin* or *Carved by Hōshūsō Shōmin*, and with an inlaid gold seal that reads *Sōin Hōshū* (Unno Shōmin, 1844–1915). With the *tomobako* or original signed and sealed box.

Shōmin was one of the most important Meiji metal artists, famous for painting with his chisels. He taught at the Tokyo Fine Arts School from 1894. In 1896 Shōmin became a *Teishitsu Gigei-in*, or an Imperial Household Artist. This piece dates from after Meiji 35 (1902), when Unno Shōmin changed his *Gō* or art name to *Hōshūsō Shōmin*.

35 cm high x 16 cm diameter.

65) Vase of cast bronze with a relief design of bamboo in snow, the snow in random flush silver inlay. Signed on the back by the artist with a chiseled signature and with an inlaid gold seal, *Masayoshi*. Meiji Era, late 19th century.

The random silver inlay was a difficult technique. Employed here, it transforms a conventional form into an object of beauty.

25 cm high x 9 cm diameter.

66) Vase of cast bronze in the form of a section of timber bamboo with applied leaves. Signed on the reverse with a chiseled signature, *Yoshihide*. Meiji Era, late 19th century.

10 cm high x 47 cm long x 10 cm wide.

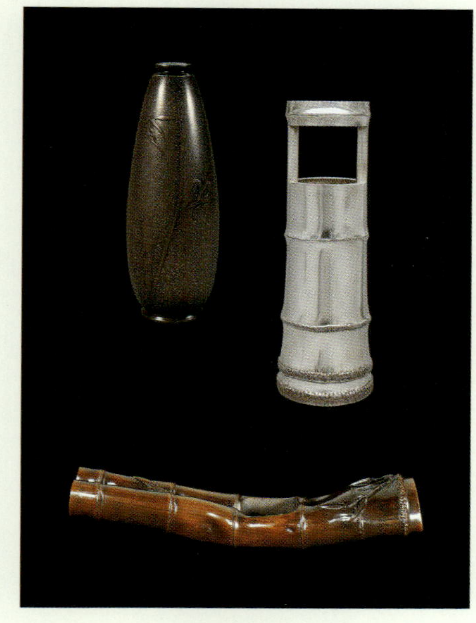

PAGE 58

67) Vase of hammered and assembled silver in the form of a cut timber bamboo flower container. Signed on the reverse with a seal by the artist, and with the *tomobako* or original box inscribed: *Heian Masami Saku* or *Made by Masami of Kyoto*, and titled *Pure Silver Bamboo Form Hitogire Okizutsu Style Flower Container*. Taishō Era, circa 1920.

37.5 cm high x 13 cm diameter.

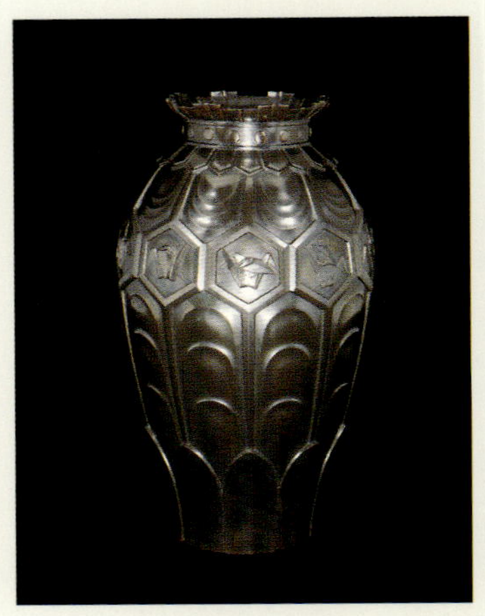

PAGE 59

68) Vase of cast and cold chiseled *shibuichi* with relief designs of stylized feathers and a band of hexagons (tortoiseshell motif) containing *origami* style cranes. Signed on the reverse with a cast seal by the artist, *Seihō*. Early Shōwa Era. With the *tomobako* or signed original box, the lid of which is inscribed: *Tsuru-Kame Kabin* or *Crane-Tortoise Vase*, signed *Seihō* and sealed. Included is an exhibition card from the Takaoka City Art Museum in Toyama Prefecture.

The crane and tortoise motif (*tsuru-kame*) signifies longevity, making New Year's an appropriate occasion for displaying this vase. The sentiment may be traditional, but the rendering is strikingly modern. Classical Japanese Deco.

29.5 cm high x 16 cm diameter.

69) *Suiban* style flower container of cast bronze, in a circular form with a flaring rim set with three stylized birds. Signed on the reverse by the artist with a chiseled signature, *Tetsushi* (Nagano Tetsushi, born 1901, now deceased; made *Ningen Kokuhō* or *Living National Treasure* in 1963). With the *tomobako* or signed original box, signed and sealed *Tetsushi* on the interior.

For additional information, see <u>The Enduring Crafts of Japan: 33 Living National Treasures</u>, pages 178–185, and page 228.

15 cm high x 35.5 cm diameter.

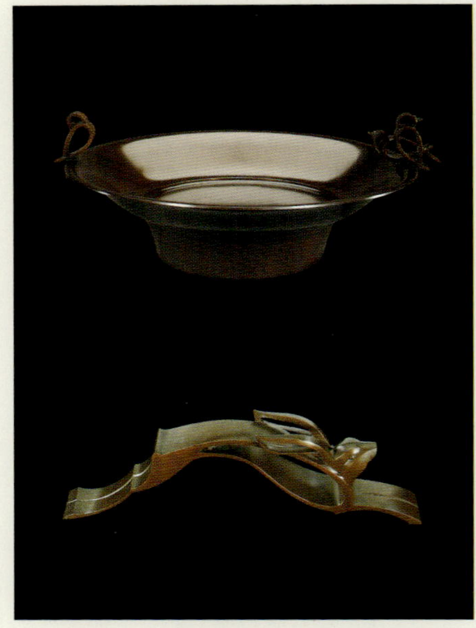

PAGE 60

70) *Okimono* of cast bronze in the form of a stylized rabbit leaping over waves. Signed by the artist on the reverse with a chiseled signature, *Torizō* (Morimura Torizō, died Shōwa 24, or 1949). Early Shōwa Era. With the *tomobako* or original box.

Morimura Torizō graduated from the Tokyo Fine Arts School.

Elegant modernist treatment of a classical theme in Japanese art. Here, Torizō moves beyond the Taishō Era preference for simplicity towards a stylized aesthetic similar to Art Deco in the West.

12.5 cm high x 40 cm x 5 cm.

71) *Okimono* in the form of a resting yet alert rabbit,
of hammered and lacquered iron, the eyes inlaid in copper.
Early Edo Period, 17th century.

7 cm high x 15 cm x 8 cm.

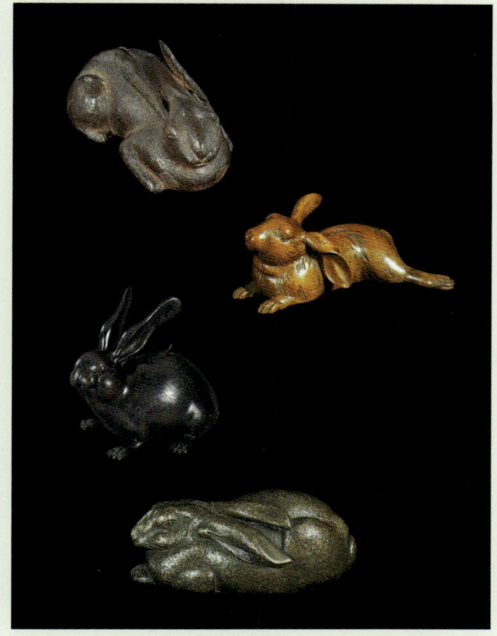

PAGE 61

72) *Okimono* in the form of a recumbent rabbit with
long floppy ears and outstretched legs, carved of
cypress wood. Signed on the reverse by the artist,
Hōsai. Meiji Era, late 19th century. Note: old repair to
the back leg.

7.5 cm high x 16 cm x 11 cm.

73) *Kōro* or incense burner in the form of a
quizzically aroused rabbit, of cast and cold chiseled
aka-gane bronze. Edo Period, early 19th century.

12 cm high x 14 cm x 11.5 cm.

74) *Okimono* in the form of a resting hare, cast of *hakudō* or
white bronze. Signed on the reverse with a cast seal mark by
the artist, *Kiyoshi* (Nakagawa Kiyoshi, died in Shōwa 52 or 1977,
at the age of 79). Shōwa Era, circa 1935. With the *tomobako* or
original box, signed *Nakagawa Kiyoshi* and sealed *Kiyoshi*.

Nakagawa Kiyoshi lived in Shiga Prefecture. He graduated from
the Tokyo Fine Arts School, won prizes at the Imperial Arts
Academy Exhibition, and was a judge of the *Nitten Art Exhibition*.

9.5 cm high x 24 cm x 12 cm.

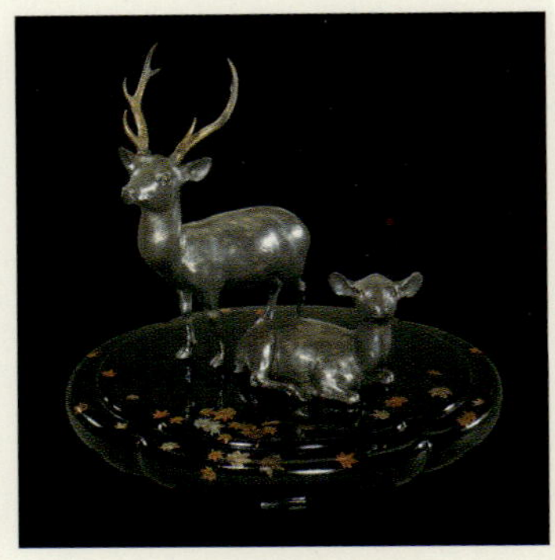

PAGE 62

75) *Okimono* in the form of a Stag and Doe resting on a black lacquer stand inlaid in *raden* mother of pearl and colored lacquers with scattered maple leaves. Both deer are cast of silver, their markings chiseled and inlaid in gold, the eyes in *shakudō* and copper, the stag's antlers of gilt bronze, and the hooves in *shakudō*. The artist signed both pieces on the reverse with a chiseled signature, *Takatoshi*, and on one of the stag's hooves, *Kanechikadō Tsukuru*, or *Made by Kanechikadō*. Each with its storage box. Late Edo–early Meiji Era.

Superb workmanship that captures the delicate feeling of the deer startled by the falling maple leaves.

39.5 cm high x 28 cm x 14 cm, Stag.
15 cm high x 24 cm x 12 cm, Doe.
7.5 cm high x 55 cm x 45 cm, Stand.

76) *Okimono* in the form of a Rooster and Hen, of cast and cold chiseled silver, the feathers inlaid in *shakudō* and *shibuichi*, the eyes inlaid in *shakudō*, and the feet and combs gilt. Signed on the reverse of the Rooster with a chiseled signature by the artist, *Katsuhiro* (Kagawa Katsuhiro, 1853–1917). With a wood box, inscribed and labeled with their provenance.

These *okimono* belonged to Arisugawa Tadako, the wife of Prince Arisugawa Taruhito (1835–1895). Prince Arisugawa was one of the most important figures during the Meiji

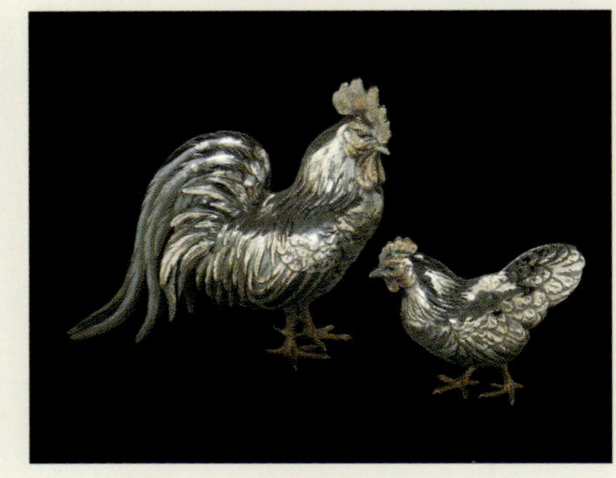

PAGE 63

Restoration. Upon Tadako's death, the *okimono* passed to her granddaughter, Arisugawa Mieko, who had become the wife of Tokugawa Yoshihisa (the youngest son of Tokugawa Yoshinobu, the last *Shōgun*).

Kagawa Katsuhiro taught metal work at the Tokyo Fine Arts School, and was one of the most respected metal artists of his time. In 1906 he achieved the rank of Imperial Household Artist. While numbers of silver chicken *okimono* were made during Meiji, this pair exhibits a soft, breathing grace far above the convention. The technique of inlaying the irregular *shakudō* and *shibuichi* markings, rather than merely overlaying the color, shows the hand of an accomplished artist taking the most difficult means to display his skill.

For another example of Kagawa Katsuhiro's work, see <u>Meiji No Takara: Treasures of Imperial Japan, Metalwork Part II</u>, number 132.

24 cm high x 27.5 cm x 11 cm, Rooster.
13 cm high x 18 cm x 7.5 cm, Hen.

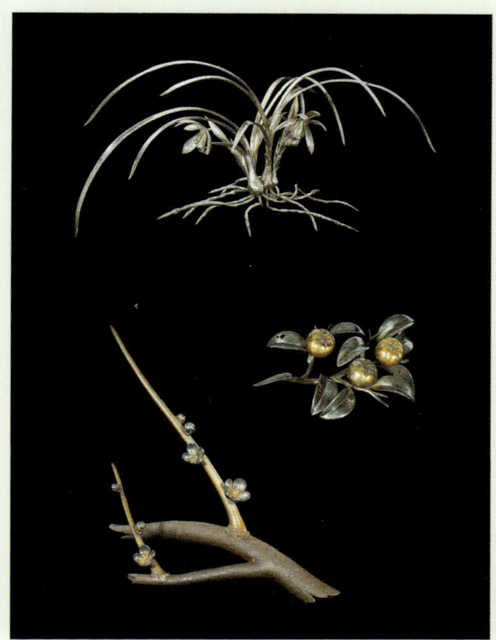

PAGE 64

77) *Okimono* in the form of orchids, of hammered silver. Signed by the Kyoto artist, *Kōzan*. Meiji Era, late 19th century. With the *tomobako* or signed original box.

17 cm high x 37 cm x 17.5 cm.

78) *Okimono* in the form of a branch of *tachibana* or mandarin orange, of cast and gilt silver. Meiji Era, late 19th century.

4 cm high x 15 cm x 9 cm.

79) *Okimono* in the form of a flowering plum branch, of iron, bronze, silver, gold and red bronze. Signed on the reverse by the artist with a chiseled signature, *Mitsunori Saku* or *Made by Mitsunori*. Late Meiji–Taishō Era. With the *tomobako* or original box, titled: *Sōbai Okimono* or *Early Plum Okimono*, signed *Mitsunori Saku* and sealed.

24.5 cm high x 29.5 cm x 10 cm.

80) *Okimono* in the form of an articulated model of a grasshopper, of cast, chiseled and assembled silver. Signed by the artist, *Kōzan* (of Kyoto). Meiji Era, late 19th century.

2.5 cm high x 8 cm x 3.5 cm.

81) *Okimono* in the form of a *semi* or cicada, the wings of tortoiseshell, the body of horn, and the legs of bronze. Signed by the artist, *Kaigyokudō* (Kaigyokusai, 1813–1892).

A rare study by a master *netsuke* carver.

2.25 cm high x 6 cm x 3 cm.

82) *Kōro* or incense burner in the form of a praying mantis, of cast bronze. Early Meiji Era, circa 1870.

9.5 cm high x 21.5 cm x 6.5 cm.

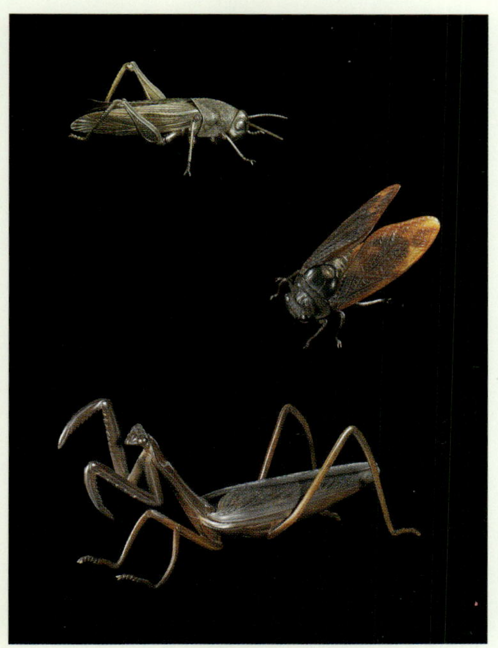

PAGE 65

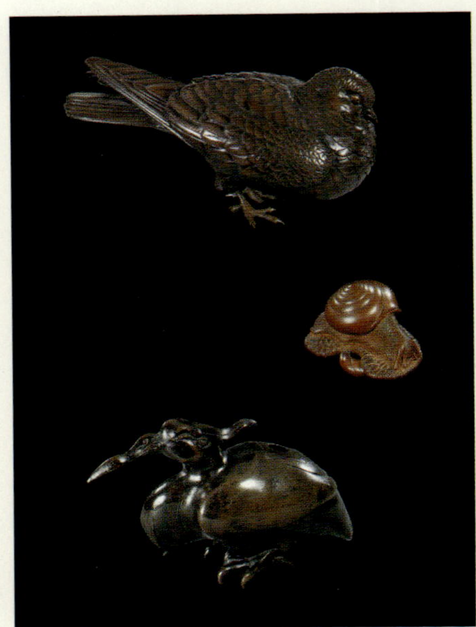

Page 66

_83_) _Okimono_ in the form of a plump dove, of cast and chiseled bronze, the eyes inlaid in gold. Meiji Era, late 19th century.

Similar studies of birds were produced by the Maruki studio during Meiji. For a comparison, see <u>Meiji No Takara: Treasures of Imperial Japan, Metalwork Part II</u>, number 103. Beautiful workmanship.

12.5 cm high x 25 cm x 11 cm.

_84_) _Netsuke_ or decorative toggle of carved boxwood in the form of a snail crawling on an upturned straw sandal. Signed by the artist, _Masanao._ 19th century.

3 cm high x 4.5 cm x 3 cm.

_85_) _Kōro_ or incense burner of cast bronze in the form of an odd, dozing bird. Edo Period, 18th century.

11 cm high x 18.5 cm x 7.5 cm.

_86_) _Okimono_ in the form of a hawk on a tree branch, of cast, assembled and cold chiseled bronze, the beak in _shakudo_, and the eyes inlaid in crystal. Signed with a cast seal mark on the underside of the hawk's tail feathers, _Yoshitani_, and on the back of the tree trunk. Meiji Era, late 19th century.

42 cm high x 17 cm x 22 cm.

_87_) _Okimono_ in the form of a sleeping cat, of cast bronze. Signed on the reverse with a chiseled signature by the artist (Asakura Fumio, died in Shōwa 39 or 1964, at the age of 81). With a fitted wood box, inscribed with the title: _Chō No Yume_ or _Dreaming of Butterflies_, and an attestation by the artist's daughter, Asakura Kyōko. Taishō–early Shōwa Era, circa 1920–1940.

Asakura Fumio was a member of the Imperial Arts Academy. As a modernist, he was little interested in Meiji realism. This study captures the essence of a dreaming cat.

4.5 cm high x 20.5 cm x 12.5 cm.

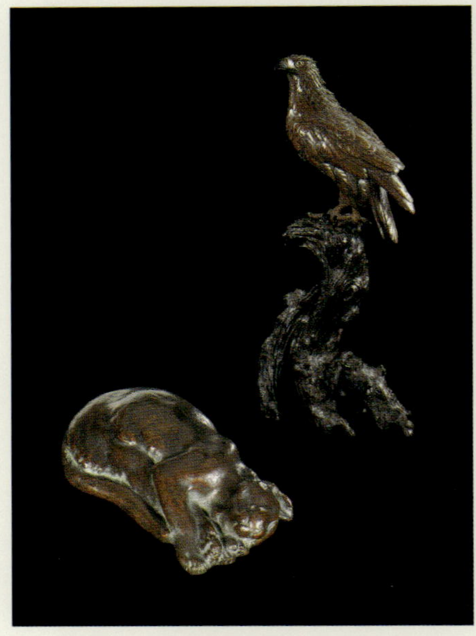

Page 67

154

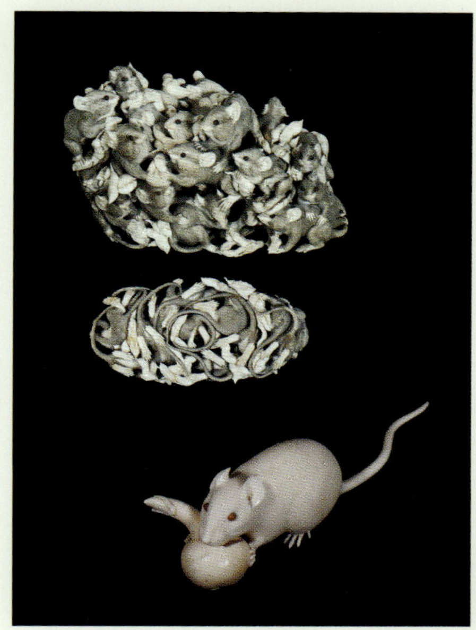

PAGE 68

88 *Okimono* in the form of a tribe of rats eating beans and nuts, of finely carved, assembled and stained ivory, the eyes inlaid in horn. Signed on the reverse by the artist, *Nobukazu*. Meiji Era, late 19th century.

Exceptionally beautiful study.

12 cm high x 20 cm x 9.5 cm.

89 *Okimono* in the form of a rat nibbling on a mountain potato, finely carved of ivory, the eyes inlaid in amber. Signed and sealed on the reverse by the artist, *Ryokuzan* (Andō Ryokuzan). Late Meiji Era–Taishō Era, early 20th century.

Ryokuzan was a member of the *Tokyo Chōkōkai Zōgebu* or *Tokyo Ivory Carvers Association*. He is listed as a member in Meiji 43 (1910), and for the years Taishō 9–11 (1920–1922) in the catalogue <u>Nihon No Zōge Bijutsu</u>, page 240.

5.5 cm high x 23.5 cm x 6 cm.

90 *Okimono* in the form of a pair of rats, one cast and cold chiseled in *shibuichi* with inlaid *shakudō* eyes, and the other cast and cold chiseled in silver with inlaid copper eyes. Signed by the artist on the reverse of the *shibuichi* rat with a chiseled signature, *Jōun Saku* or *Made by Jōun* (Ōshima Jōun, 1858–1940). With the *tomobako* or original box, the interior of the lid signed *Jōun Saku*, and sealed.

Ōshima Jōun was a professor at the Tokyo Fine Arts School, and famous for his skill in casting. One of his studies of swimming fish and waves is illustrated in <u>Meiji No Takara: Treasures of Imperial Japan, Metalwork Part II</u>, number 102.

8.5 cm high x 14 cm x 11.5 cm.

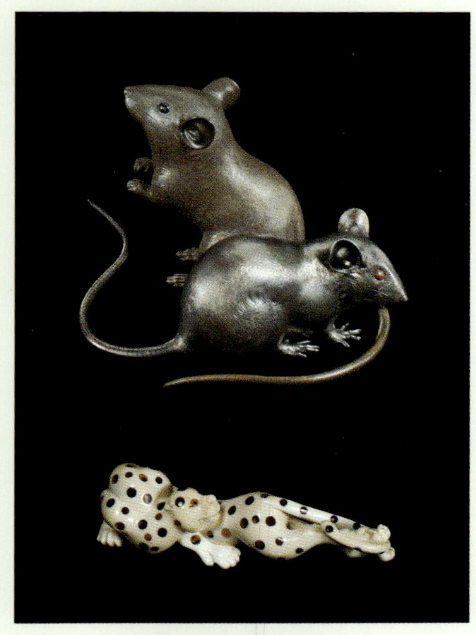

PAGE 69

91 *Okimono* (or possibly a *sashi netsuke*) in the form of a male leopard turning in mid-leap, carved of ivory with his spots inlaid in tortoiseshell. Signed on the reverse by the artist, *Enzan*. 20th century.

3.5 cm high x 12.5 cm x 3.5 cm.

92) *Okimono* in the form of a reclining tigress, carved of boxwood. Signed
on the reverse with a square seal by the artist, Nishimura Unseki. Meiji Era,
late 19th century. With the *tomobako* or original box, signed, *Nishimura
Unseki Tsukuru* or *Made by Nishimura Unseki* and sealed.

Nishimura Unseki lived in Hikone in Shiga Prefecture and was an
accomplished amateur carver of samurai descent. This *okimono* shows him
to have been well aware of trends toward realism in the painting and
depiction of tigers during the Meiji Era.

10.5 cm high x 15 cm x 8.5 cm.

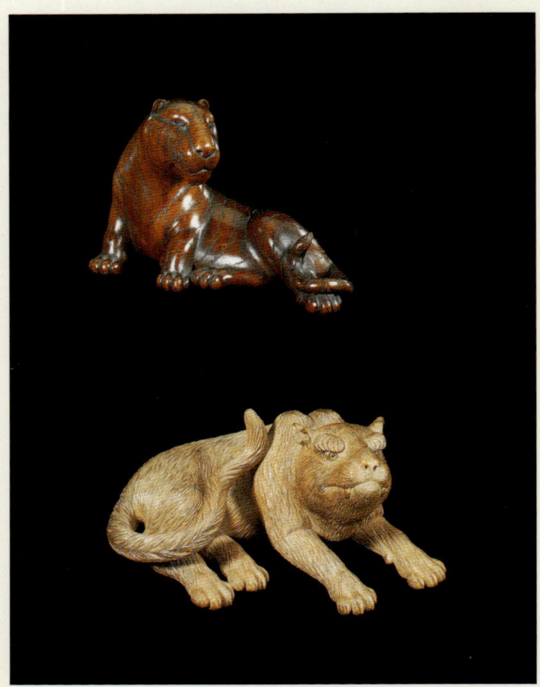

PAGE 70

93) *Okimono* in the form of an inquisitive recumbent tiger, of carved
boxwood. Signed by the artist, *Beishin Saku* or *Made by Beishin*. Edo Period,
early 19th century.

Beishin was a *netsuke* carver who worked in Niigata Prefecture. He was
born in the port town of Izumozaki.

15.5 cm high x 32.5 cm x 21 cm.

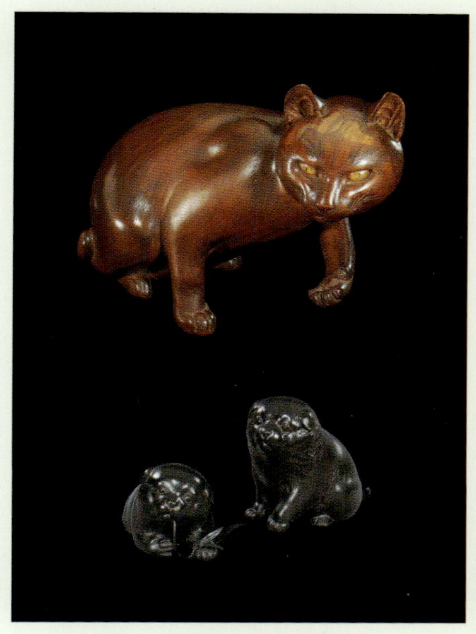

PAGE 71

94) *Okimono* in the form of a cunning calico cat, carved of a large piece of boxwood, the calico markings inlaid in mulberry wood, and the eyes inlaid in horn. Signed on the reverse by the artist, *Yōsetsu* (Yōsetsu was the *Gō* or art name of Nakanishi Daizen, who died in Taishō 11 or 1923). Taishō Era, early 20th century. Note: old age crack on reverse with inlaid repair.

Yōsetsu worked in Kumamoto Prefecture, and is famous for his carvings of Kannon Bosatsu, crabs, and catfish. He also carved *nyoi* or sceptres. *Okimono* of cats are quite rare, perhaps because the Japanese suspected them of criminal designs on their *tatami* and *shōji*. In any case, this cat clearly meditates something entertaining.

24 cm high x 36 cm x 16.5 cm.

95) *Okimono* in the form of a pair of puppies preoccupied with a piece of bamboo, of cast and chiseled bronze, the eyes inlaid in *shakudō*. Sealed on the reverse by the Tokyo School artist, *Ryōun* (Ryōun was a *Gō* or art name for Unno Moritoshi, 1834–1896). Meiji Era, late 19th century.

9 cm high x 16 cm x 12.5 cm, smaller puppy with bamboo.
14.5 cm high x 17 cm x 11 cm, larger seated puppy.

96) *Okimono* in the form of two *shishi* or lion-dogs on a rock form base, of cast and chiseled bronze and silver, the *shishi's* eyes inlaid in gold and *shakudō*. Signed on two inlaid silver plaques on the back of the base by the two Tokyo School artists, *Jōshun Saku* and *Kiuun Koku*. Jōshun was the caster, and Kiuun the artist who executed the chiseling and inlay. Meiji Era, late 19th century.

24 cm high x 30 cm x 18 cm.

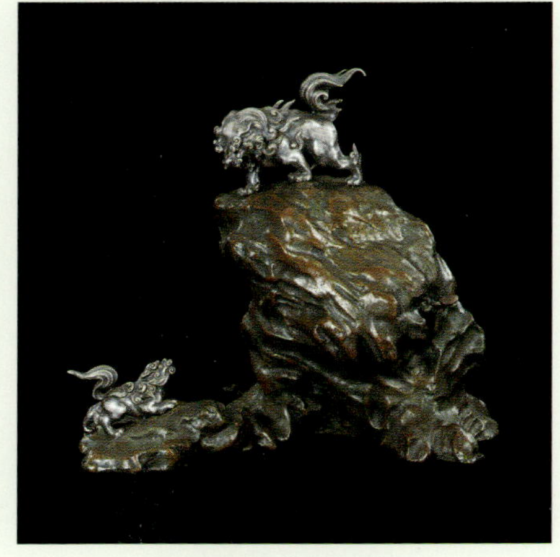

PAGE 72

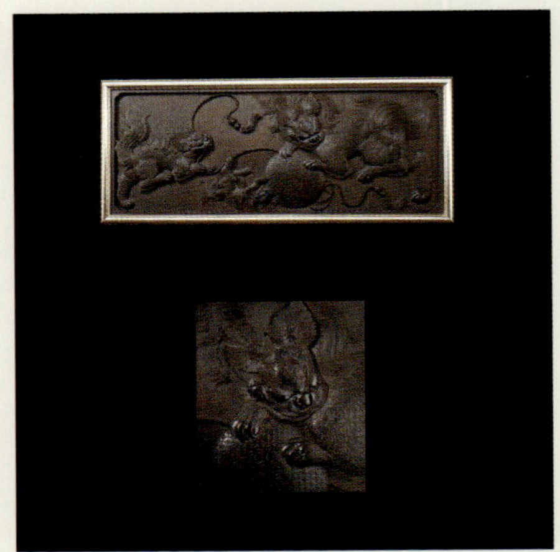

PAGE 73

97) Wood panel finely carved in relief with designs of *shishi* or lion-dogs playing with a thread ball, the *shishi's* eyes inlaid in ebony. Late Edo Period, mid 19th century. Set in a new gilt frame.

Though unsigned, the quality of the carving suggests the work of a *netsuke* artist.

47 cm high x 113 cm across, including frame.

98) *Okimono* in the form of two *oni* or demons holding up a glass ball, one *oni* cast and cold chiseled of *sentoku* and the other of *shibuichi*, both inlaid in *shakudō*, gold, silver, and copper. Unsigned. Meiji Era, late 19th century.

These are extremely similar to an *oni* supporting a crystal ball by Sano Takachika illustrated in <u>Meiji No Takara: Treasures of Imperial Japan, Metalwork Part II</u>, number 123. A close comparison of the workmanship, style and quality of the two pieces suggests that these may also be the work of Takachika.

19.5 cm high x 10 cm x 10 cm.

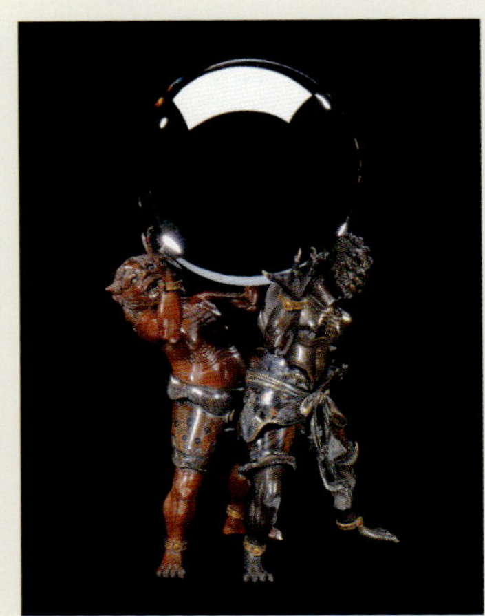

PAGE 74

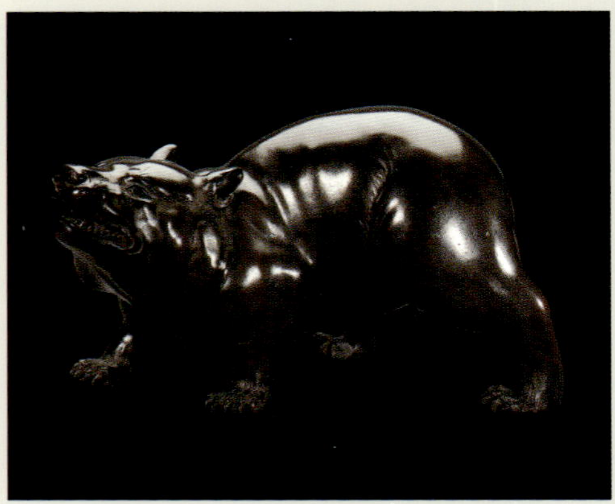

PAGE 75

99) *Okimono* in the form of a large snarling bear, of cast and cold chiseled bronze. Late Edo Period, early 19th century.

This powerful study of a bear seems to be partly related to a wild boar. The sensibility shares that of other quirky Edo bronzes, a view of nature decidedly different from Meiji realism.

18 cm high x 30 cm x 19 cm.

158

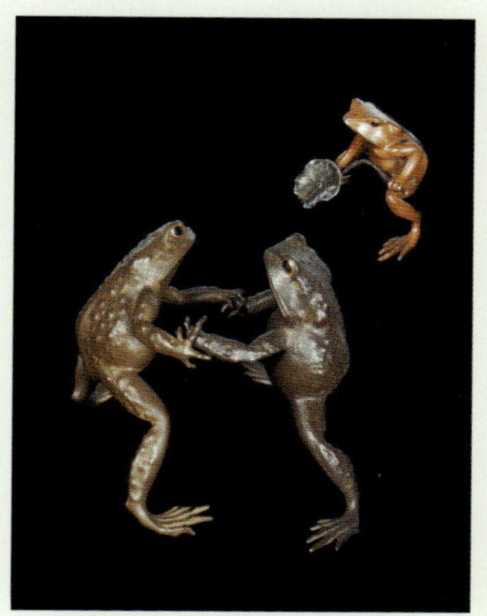

100) *Okimono* in the form of two *Sumō* toads with a *Sumō* frog referee, each toad in a different color of bronze and the frog of *sentoku* with a silver lotus leaf wand. All of the creatures' eyes are inlaid in *shakudō* and gold. Signed by the artist on the reverse of the frog with a chiseled signature and *kakihan, Harutoshi*. Taishō Era, early 20th century. With the *tomobako* or original box, signed and sealed on the interior of the lid.

7.5 cm high x 9 cm x 5.5 cm, frog referee.
9.5 cm high x 12 cm x 11.5 cm, brown and green toads wrestling.

101) *Okimono* in the form of a seated *Sumō* rabbit, triumphantly hoisting aloft a gold rice bale and Daikoku's magic mallet. Carved of boxwood with Shibayama style inlay of shell, ivory, lacquer, cloisonné, and crystal. Meiji Era, late 19th century.

Daikoku, the god of wealth and good fortune, traditionally stands on bales of rice holding a magic mallet which rings out gold coins when struck. This hare has apparently bested him in a *Sumō* wrestling match.

18.5 cm high x 10.5 cm x 8 cm.

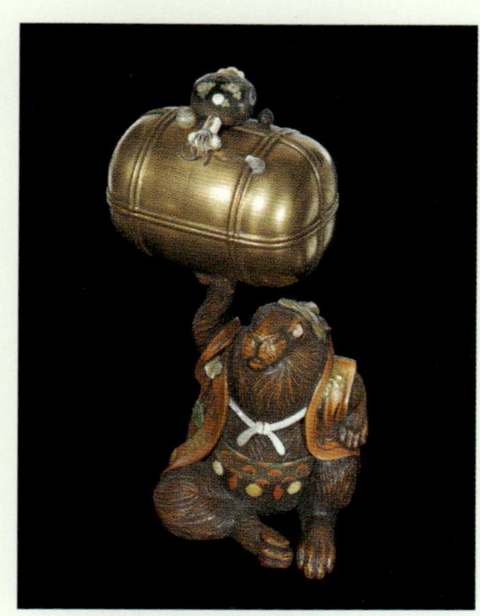

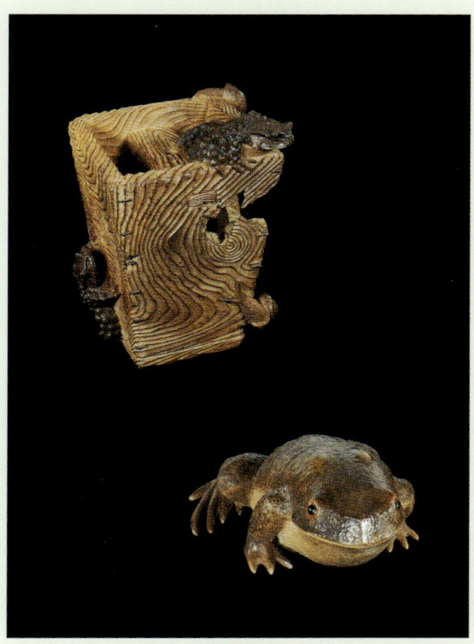

102) *Okimono* of carved cypress wood in the form of an old, decayed well pail over which two snails and two frogs are crawling. Even the exposed nails are carved and stained cypress. The artist signed the pail on the reverse, *Shunsen Saku* or *Made by Shunsen*. Taishō Era, early 20th century.

20.5 cm high x 16 cm x 16 cm.

103) *Okimono* carved of camellia wood in the form of a large frog, the eyes inlaid in horn. Signed on the reverse by the artist, *Sukeyuki*. Taishō–early Shōwa Era, circa 1920–1930.

7 cm high x 17 cm x 12.5 cm.

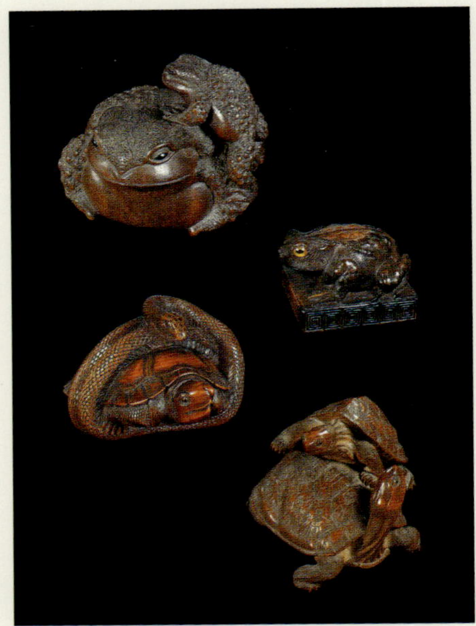

104) *Okimono* carved of wood in the form of two toads, the smaller crawling onto the larger's back, the eyes inlaid in ebony. Signed on the reverse by the artist, *Harumitsu*. Meiji Era, late 19th century.

6.5 cm high x 10 cm x 9 cm.

105) *Inkan* or seal of carved and lacquered bamboo surmounted by a crouching toad, the eyes inlaid in tortoiseshell and ebony. Early Meiji Era, circa 1870–1880.

4 cm high x 6.5 cm x 6 cm.

106) *Okimono* carved of boxwood in the form of a tortoise encircled by a foolish but hungry snake, the eyes double inlaid. Signed on the reverse by the artist, *Masatami Tō* or *Carved by Masatami*. Meiji Era, late 19th century.

Probably the work of Moribe Masatami, (1854–1928), a Nagoya School *netsuke* carver.

6 cm high x 9.5 cm x 7 cm.

107) *Okimono* carved of boxwood in the form of two playing tortoises, the eyes inlaid in horn. Meiji Era, late 19th century. Note: original inlaid signature plaque on reverse now lost and replaced with ivory.

7 cm high x 9 cm x 9 cm.

108) *Okimono* in the form of a large articulated model of a lobster, of cast, chiseled and assembled red bronze. Signed by the artist with a chiseled signature. Edo Period, early 19th century.

Very few articulated lobsters of such a large size were made. For a similar example, see <u>Meiji No Takara, Metalwork II</u>, number 112.

33 cm high x 58 cm x 56 cm, with antennae extended.

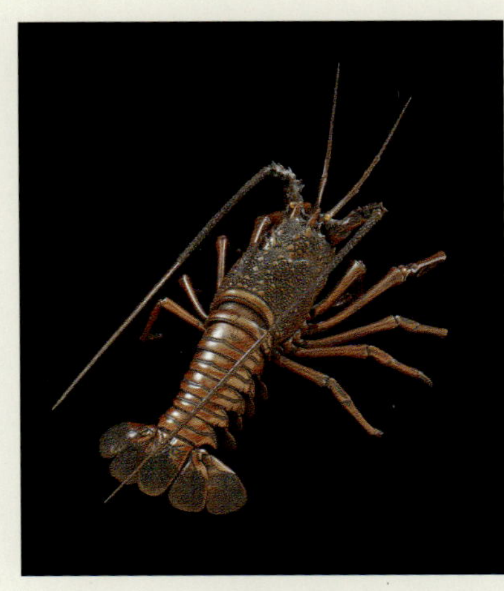

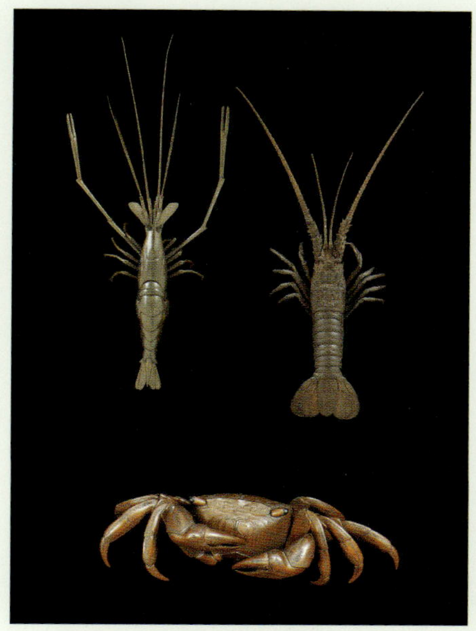
PAGE 81

109) *Okimono* in the form of an articulated model of a crayfish, of cast, chiseled and assembled *shibuichi*. Signed by the artist, *Kōzan* (of Kyoto). Meiji Era, late 19th century. With the *tomobako* or signed original storage box, inscribed *Kawa Ebi* or *Crayfish*, and signed and sealed on the interior, *Kōzan*.

3 cm high x 26.5 cm x 7.5 cm.

110) *Okimono* in the form of an articulated model of a rock lobster, of forged, chiseled and filed iron. Signed by the artist, *Myōchin Muneakira* (Myōchin Muneakira was a sword smith and armorer active circa 1673–circa 1745).

5.5 cm high x 26 cm x 16.5 cm.

111) *Okimono* in the form of an articulated model of a crab, of folded and engraved copper, the eyes of *shakudō*. Unsigned. Meiji Era, late 19th century.

Most articulated crabs were made of cast and assembled bronze. The folded *origami* technique required far greater skill.

5.5 cm high x 20 cm x 11 cm.

112) Vase with a design of a family of five crabs beneath a band of *jaku-kago* and rocks, of cloisonné enamels with silver mounts. The crabs executed in *moriage* relief, the river bank baskets in silver wire, and the rocks in *musen* or wireless technique. Sealed on the reverse with the Andō mark in silver wire. Taishō Era, circa 1915. With the original rosewood stand bearing the original Andō label on the reverse, and a double storage box. The interior *tomobako* inscribed: *Shippō Seitei Gun Kani Kabin* or *Perfect River Bank Crab Cloisonné Vase*, and signed, *Jūbei Tsukuru* or *Made by Jūbei* (Andō Jūbei) and sealed.

The paper label affixed to the base is printed in English: *J. Andō, Cloisonné Ware, Nagoya-Tokyo, Japan*, and with the Andō mark in red. It is printed in Japanese: *Kunaishō Goyōtashi* or *Purveyors to the Imperial Household Agency*, and *Nagoya Andō Shippōten* or *Nagoya Andō Cloisonné Company*.

The quality and double wood box suggest that this was made as an exhibition or presentation piece.

25 cm high x 18.5 cm diameter, without stand.

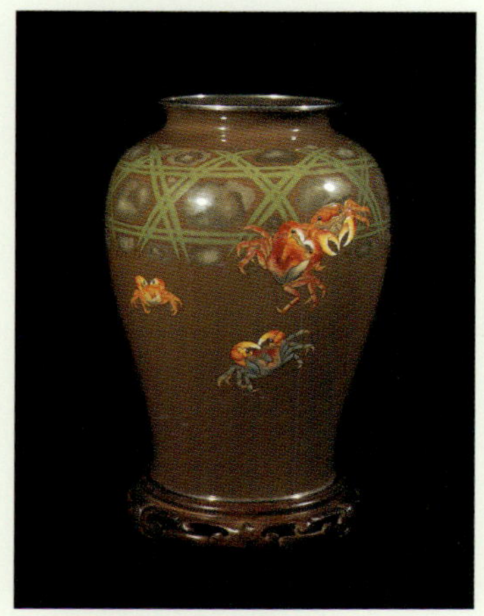
PAGE 82

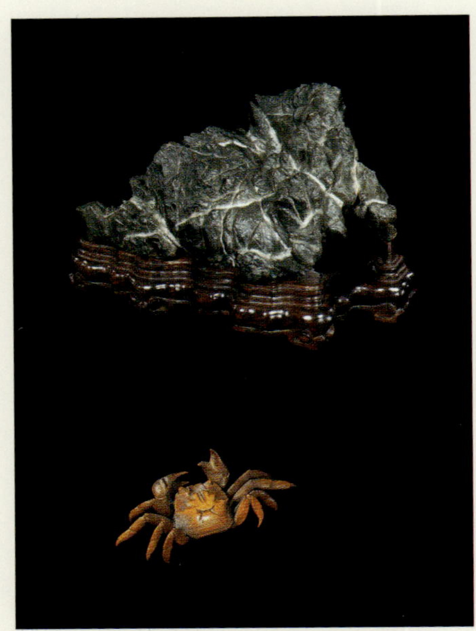

113) Scholar's table stone of Furuya type from Wakayama Prefecture, on a carved rosewood stand which is signed on the reverse by the carver, *Hōsen*. Accompanied by a collector's box inscribed: *Furuya Mei Seki Kumano Shūzan* or *Famous Furuya Stone from the Kumano Shūzan Area*. Late Meiji Era, circa 1900–1910.

Furuya stones are famous for their white veining. This example has a richer, denser black color than most and particularly dramatic white lines. The bottom of the stone is not carved, a rarity among Furuya *suiseki*. The base is beautifully carved to fit the stone, creating a window effect from the overhang.

16 cm high x 28 cm x 18 cm.

114) *Okimono* in the form of a small crab, of carved bamboo root, made to be used in *Sencha Tea Ceremony* as a stand for an incense container. Meiji Era, late 19th century. With the *tomobako*, inscribed: *Chikukoun Saku*, or *Made by Chikukoun.*

3 cm high x 9 cm x 3.5 cm.

115) Chinese scholar's table stone on a Japanese rosewood stand in a curling leaf motif. With a Japanese paulownia wood storage box, inscribed on the lid: *Reiheki Seki Ippin Unsōdō Chinzō, Shuboku Dai Tsuki*, and sealed *Chikudō*, or *Spirit Wall Stone, of Unrivaled Rarity, With a Redwood Fitted Stand*, and sealed *Chikudō*, (almost certainly the painter Kishi Chikudō, 1826–1897).

A similar type of stone is illustrated in <u>Arts From The Scholar's Studio</u>, number 9, page 46. The catalogue <u>Kernels of Energy, Bones of Earth: The Rock in Chinese Art</u>, plate 39 (No. 20), page 72, also illustrates a similar variety of stone.

20 cm high x 16 cm x 8 cm.

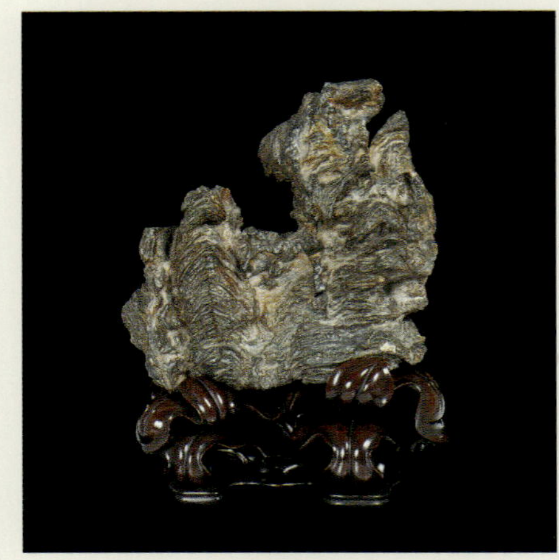

116) Chinese scholar's stone of *ying-shih* type, on an 18th century hardwood stand. The stone is grey with fine white veins or inclusions.

A very large stone with good tone and strong, powerful movement.

90 cm high x 29 cm x 26 cm.

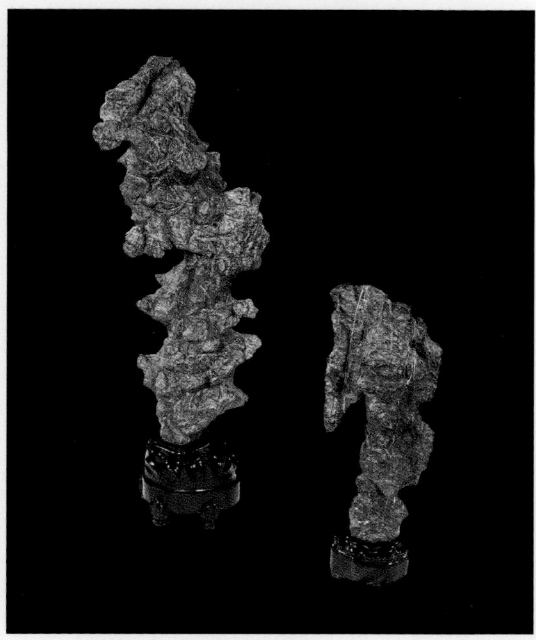

PAGE 85

117) Chinese scholar's stone of *ling-pi* type, in an upright vertical form with numerous overhangs, of dense black stone with brown-grey inclusions and vertical quartz veining, on an 18th century rosewood base. Ching Dynasty, 18th century.

Exceptionally dense stone with beautiful tone. This stone came out of a collection in the Okayama area in Japan.

55 cm high x 21 cm x 20 cm.

118) *Suzuri* or ink stone for calligraphy and painting, made from a flat, irregular section of polished slate. The lid shows light and dark patterns as one elevation wears down to the next. Late Edo–early Meiji Era, circa 1850–1870.

The tradition of scholar's taste both in China and Japan encompassed a type of object made from a natural form, often improved to bring out the spirit perceived to lie in the piece. This Japanese *suzuri* seems to have been lifted straight out of a mountain stream bed, bringing echoes of rushing water to the scholar's desk.

3 cm high x 25 cm x 15 cm.

119) *Suzuri* or ink grinder, made from a section of bamboo pinned with gold, the lid of *enju* wood. Meiji Era, late 19th century. With a storage box inscribed: *Mōsō Bamboo Suzuri, the beloved object of Teacher Fukada Naoki.*

Bamboo is a very rare material for a *suzuri* (stone and sometimes ceramic being typical). The literati felt very strongly about the ornaments of their desks and work, and often memorialized their appreciation on the storage boxes.

7 cm high x 15 cm x 9.5 cm.

120) *Suzuri* or ink stone made from a massive natural block of polished slate, inscribed on the reverse: *Dragon Valley, Made by Isseki.* The storage box inscription reads: *Famous Ink Stone From the Shinshū District Called Dragon Valley Stone.* Shinshū is in present day Nagano Prefecture. Taishō–early Shōwa Era, circa 1920–1940.

22 cm high x 28 cm x 14 cm.

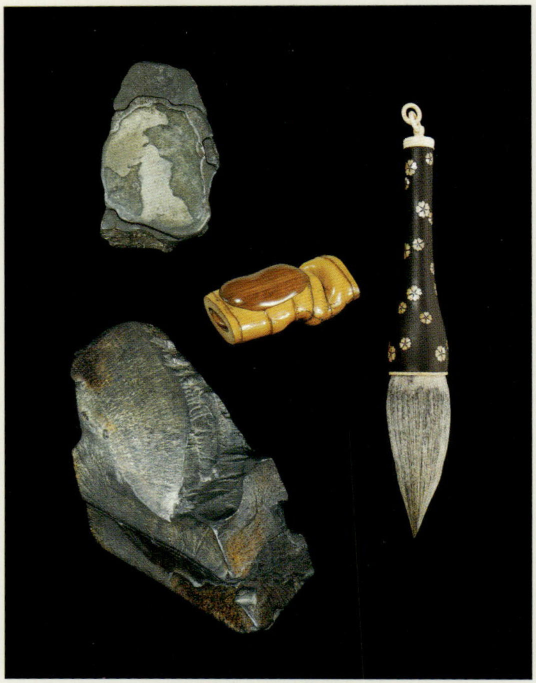

PAGE 86

121) Brush for calligraphy or painting, of lacquered wood inlaid in *raden* mother of pearl with a design of scattered cherry blossoms. The fittings of carved ivory, and the bristles of animal hair. Edo Period, early 19th century.

52 cm long x 7.5 cm diameter.

<u>122</u>) *Sake* gourd, ornamented in raised lacquer with a design of a *Kappa* water
demon and willow. Meiji Era, late 19th century.

29 cm long x 7 cm diameter.

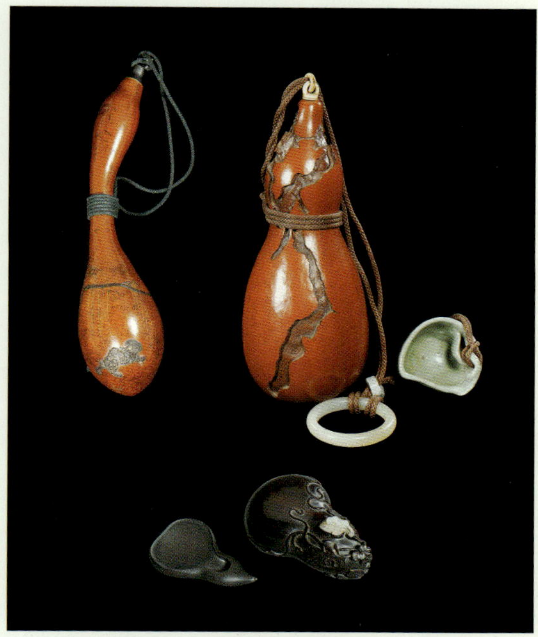

PAGE 87

<u>123</u>) *Sake* gourd elaborately carved with a *mushi-kui* or insect eaten motif,
with a Chinese peach form cup in a celadon green glaze, and jade toggles.
Edo Period, 19th century. With a *nijūbako* or double storage box, inscribed:
This gourd once belonged to Mr. Yanagihara of Fukui. It was given the name
Iku Senshū, meaning Many Thousands of Years, by Sanyō Sensei (possibly
Rai Sanyō, 1780–1832). Last year (1902, a cyclical date) in March, Fukui
experienced a large fire. The box turned to ashes, but miraculously the gourd
survived. Indeed the gourd proved worthy of its name.

The *mushi-kui* motif suggests the passing of time, and the changing
seasons.

28 cm long x 11 cm diameter.

<u>124</u>) *Suzuri* or ink stone delicately carved in the form of a small gourd,
of Duan type stone carved with a seal on the reverse. Fitted with a
rosewood case, the lid inlaid with a leaf form jade plaque, from China.
Ching Dynasty, 18th century. With a wood storage box and fitted period
silk bag, made by the Japanese collector.

5 cm high x 10.5 cm x 7.5 cm, with case.

125) *Nyoi* sceptre formed from a twisting rhizome of bamboo suggesting a *reishi* fungus, the surface lacquered. The end of the handle pierced and set with a bronze fitting for the attachment of a cord and tassel. Edo Period, 18th century.

Spectacular, rich color. *Reishi* (or *lingzhi* to the Chinese) are symbols of longevity, associated with the Daoist Immortals.

32 cm long x 8 cm x 7 cm.

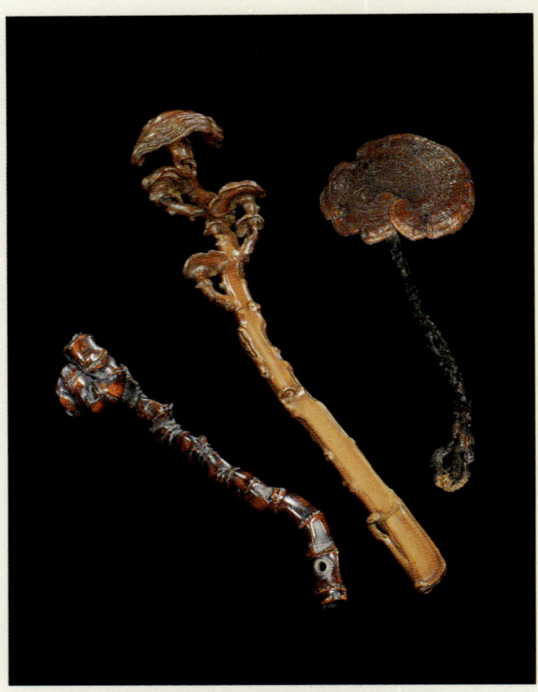

PAGE 88

126) *Ruyi* sceptre carved from bamboo in the form of *lingzhi* fungus, of rich golden brown color. Minute age cracks in places. Chinese, 17th century. With a Japanese collector's box inscribed: *Old Bamboo Reishi Sceptre*, the interior with an inscription by Kōkoku: *In the Fall of the First Year of Meiji (1868) I Received this Wonderful Rare Gift.*

For a comparison, see <u>Arts From The Scholar's Studio</u>, number 67, page 106. This *ruyi* sceptre has beautiful balance and movement.

43.5 cm long x 8 cm x 8 cm.

127) *Nyoi* sceptre made from two sections of lacquered *reishi* fungus, the end of the handle signed in red lacquer *Reishi* with a *kakihan*. With a *tomobako* or original box, inscribed: *Reishi Ensen* or *Reishi Circle Fan* and signed on the reverse of the lid, *Reishi* with a *kakihan*. Early Meiji Era, circa 1870.

During Late Edo into Meiji, objects in *Sencha* taste were occasionally made from *reishi* fungus. We have seen *kadai* or art display stands, *tonkotsu*, and tea room *kanban* inscribed with calligraphy all made from *reishi*. To represent the object with itself seems an elegant idea.

30.5 cm long x 13 cm x 3.5 cm.

128) *Nyoi* sceptre in the form of a stylized *reishi* on which rests a lizard, carved of rosewood, the lizard's eyes inlaid in bronze. Signed by the artist, *Yoshitoki Tō* or *Carved by Yoshitoki*. Meiji Era, late 19th century.

Perhaps the *mushi-kui* or insect eaten motif has attracted the lizard. Classical Meiji idea and workmanship.

50.5 cm long x 6 cm x 4 cm.

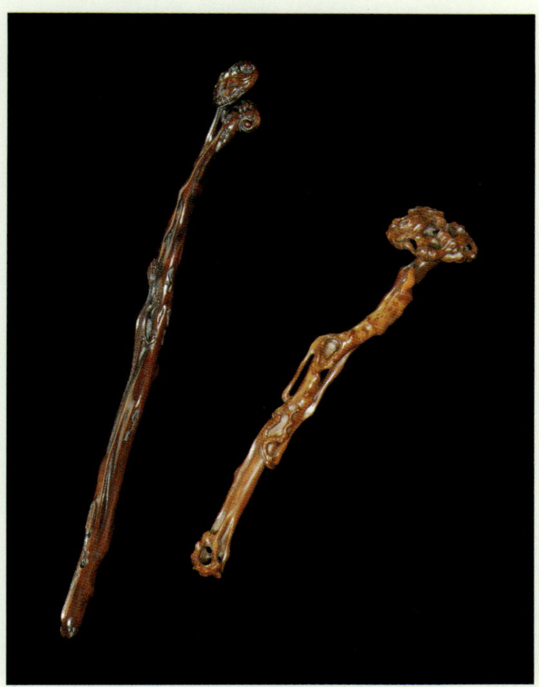

PAGE 89

129) *Ruyi* sceptre in the form of *lingzhi* fungus, carved of boxwood. Ching Dynasty, late 18th–early 19th century.

Note: at one point the sceptre cracked through below the head, and the Japanese collector had it repaired with a boxwood butterfly pin on the back, and a crawling boxwood slug on the front. The style of this repair suggests the Meiji or Taishō Era, the taste following very closely the aesthetic of the above lizard sceptre (number 128).

36.5 cm long x 8 cm x 7 cm.

The late 19th century *Sencha* taste for natural burls and materials suggestive
of other forms flowered in the work of a few studios that produced pieces
such as these *okimono*. Seeing something in the natural form, the artist
would carve and encourage the essential nature to reveal itself. Pieces were
sometimes assembled, and the surfaces lacquered. As much as possible the
idea was to allow the found object to speak for itself. The *Sencha* tradition
is linked intimately to the Chinese scholar's taste for natural burls.

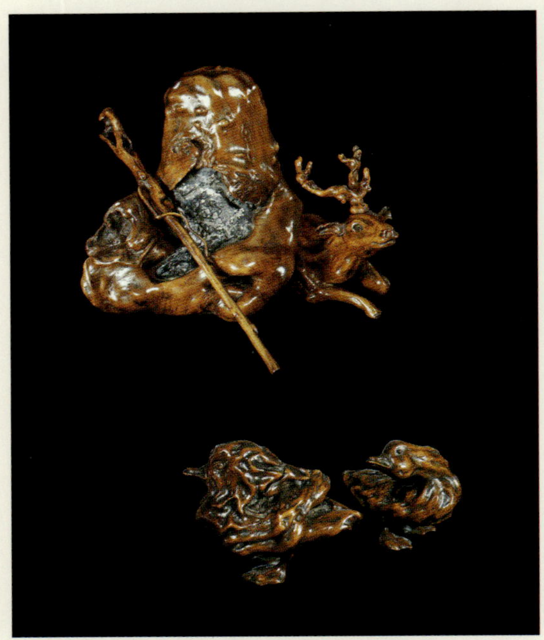

PAGE 90

130) *Okimono* in the form of Jūrojin, the god of longevity, dozing with his
attendant stag, of lacquered burl and stone. Meiji Era, late 19th century.

19 cm high x 25 cm x 15.5 cm, approximate overall dimensions.

131) *Okimono* in the form of a pair of mandarin ducks, of lacquered burl,
the male's body encasing a dark stone. Meiji Era, late 19th century.

Like Daruma, ducks and geese were an archetype often seen in burls.
The bearing and personality of this pair, and their rich color put them
above the rest of the flock.

11 cm high x 14 cm x 7 cm, male.
10.5 cm high x 12 cm x 8.5 cm, female.

132) *Okimono* in the form of a crane standing on a fallen tree and gazing towards the heavens, of lacquered burl wood. Meiji Era, late 19th century. With a double *tomobako* or storage box, the interior box lid titled and sealed and with a *sumi-e* painting on the interior depicting the *okimono*; the two sides of this box inscribed with four separate appreciations.

Sencha Tea and the aesthetic that developed with it came as a reaction by the literati to the stiff formality of life under the Tokugawa. By the beginning of the 19th century, *Matcha Tea Ceremony* was perceived as rigidly formal. Drinking *Sencha* with one's friends became an elegant part of the scholar's life, an expression of informal hospitality involving the appreciation of art. These quiet gatherings sometimes drifted on *sake* instead of tea, but the ideal of camaraderie integrated with the enjoyment of art remained the same. This *okimono's* box records this way of life, as well as the high opinion in which this crane was held.

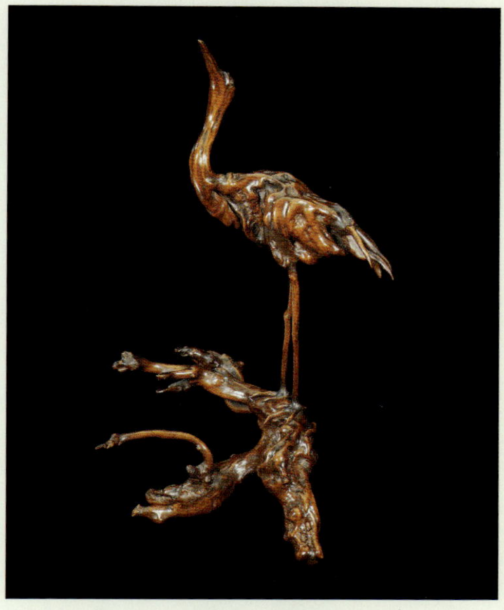

PAGE 91

Cranes were symbolic of long life, having been thought to live for a thousand years. Like mandarin ducks, they were images of conjugal felicity. The crane seems to look upward, poignantly searching for its companion.

Cranes became a genre of burl *okimono* often made in pairs, typically awkward and stiff. Bearing little relation to that common stereotype, we see here a masterpiece of balance and form, perfectly expressing the natural elegance of a crane.

44 cm high x 26.5 cm x 20 cm.

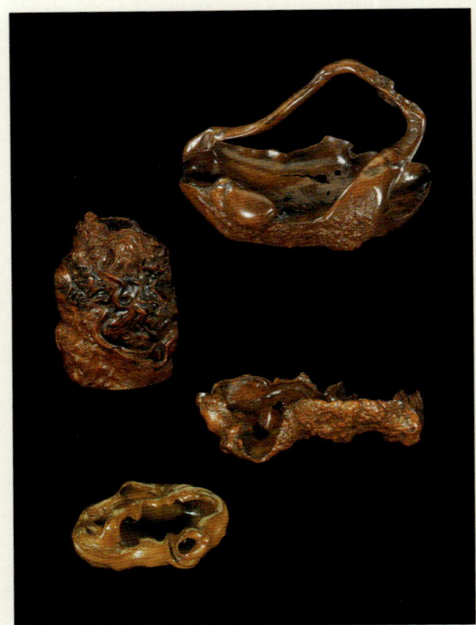

133) *Moribon* or tray for displaying seasonal fruit, carved of curling burl wood in a large scale with a bold handle jogging diagonally across the top. Meiji Era, late 19th century.

32 cm high x 56 cm x 41 cm.

134) Vase made from a section of natural burl with intensely swirling cloud-like wood grain. Meiji Era, late 19th century.

31 cm high x 23 cm diameter.

135) *Moribon* or tray for displaying seasonal fruit, of an exterior section of curled burl wood echoing the naturally curving contours of the tree, the interior carved to a smooth surface. Late Edo Period, mid 19th century.

12 cm high x 41 cm x 20 cm.

136) *Kashiki* or small tray for tea sweets hollowed out from a tightly curled burl to leave a fluid section of handle across the top. With a lacquered surface. Meiji Era, late 19th century.

9 cm high x 20.5 cm x 15 cm.

Kadai or display stands such as these were meant for setting off a flower arrangement, a piece of art, or an incense burner.

137) *Kadai* or display stand, carved of a large section of burl wood in an irregular form echoing the shape of the tree trunk, with a lacquered finish. The underside is carved to resemble twisting sections of root wood. Meiji Era, late 19th century.

7.5 cm high x 70.5 cm x 46.5 cm.

138) *Kadai* or display stand, carved of a large section of burl wood in an irregular form echoing the shape of the tree trunk. The surface is lacquered and the underside carved to resemble twisting sections of root wood. Meiji Era, late 19th century.

6 cm high x 71.5 cm x 55 cm.

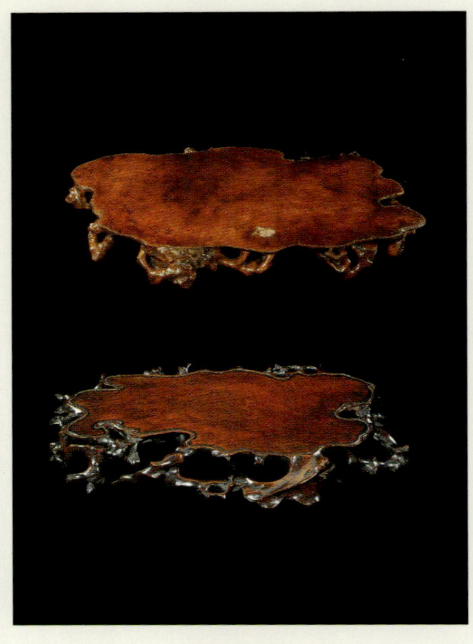

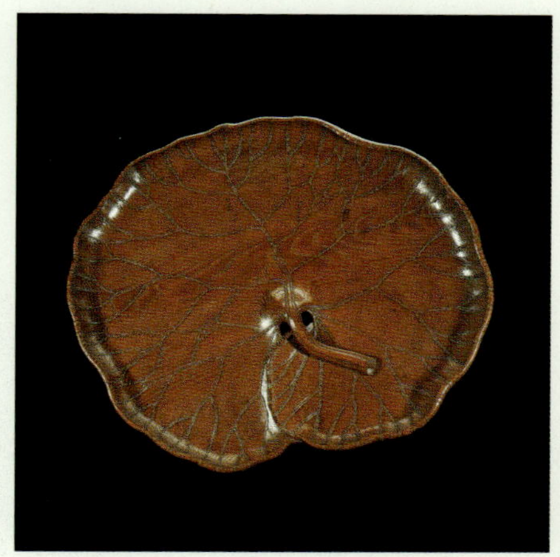

PAGE 94

139) Tray in the form of a large *akitabuki* or giant butterbur leaf, carved of chestnut wood. Dated on the reverse to Meiji 14 (1881) and signed by the carver, *Kido Konroku* (Kido Konroku was the *Gō* or art name for Kido Seibei, 1810–1882), with a wood storage box.

Kido Konroku lived in the town of Ōmi in Shiga just north of Kyoto. He was famous for his wood carvings, garden designs, and flower arranging. His talent extended to *haiku* poetry, and apparently an inclination to collect antiques— an inclination his work continues to foster.

5 cm high x 61 cm x 51 cm.

140) Tray in the form of a large grape leaf overlaid with grapes, carved of a section of burl wood. Meiji Era, late 19th century.

A paper label on the box indicates that this tray was carved of camphor wood in the form of wild mountain grapes, and was meant to be used during late summer when the fruit was in season.

5 cm high x 63.5 cm x 56 cm.

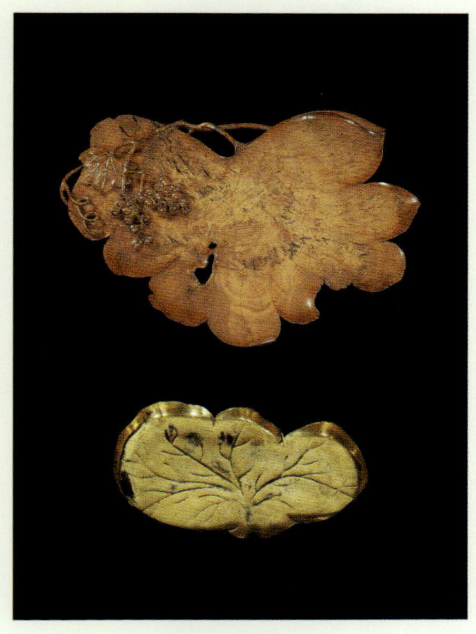

PAGE 95

141) Tray in the form of a curling lotus leaf, of black and gilt lacquered wood. Edo Period, late 17th–early 18th century.

4 cm high x 37 cm x 27 cm.

171

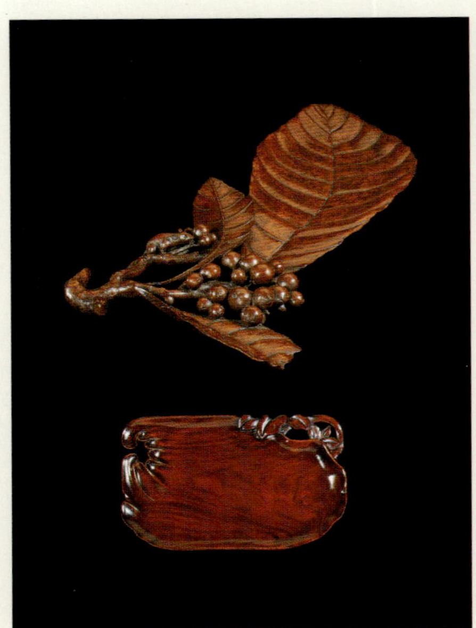

142) Tray in the form of a branch of loquat fruit with an inquisitive mouse, of carved and lacquered wood. Meiji Era, late 19th century.

4 cm high x 59 cm x 26.5 cm.

143) Tray in the form of a finger citron, carved of lacquered rosewood. Taishō Era, circa 1920.

2.5 cm high x 41 cm x 24.5 cm.

144) Tray in the form of a bird perched on the edge of a tattered leaf, carved of hardwood. Edo Period, late 18th–early 19th century.

3 cm high x 50 cm x 19 cm.

145) *Okimono* in the form of a small finger citron, delicately carved of boxwood. Late Meiji Era, circa 1900. With the *tomobako* or original box, signed by the artist, *Shōchikusai Shūdō Saku* or *Made by Shōchikusai Shūdō.*

Shūdō worked during the Meiji Era and lived in Himeji in Hyōgo Prefecture. This piece was made to be used as a rest for a *kozutsu* or incense container. In Japan this type of citron is commonly referred to as a *Buddha's Hand Citron*, imbuing this study with universal as well as seasonal overtones.

5.5 cm long x 3 cm diameter.

146) *Okimono* in the form of a large finger citron, carved of hardwood. Meiji Era, late 19th century.

20 cm long x 7 cm diameter.

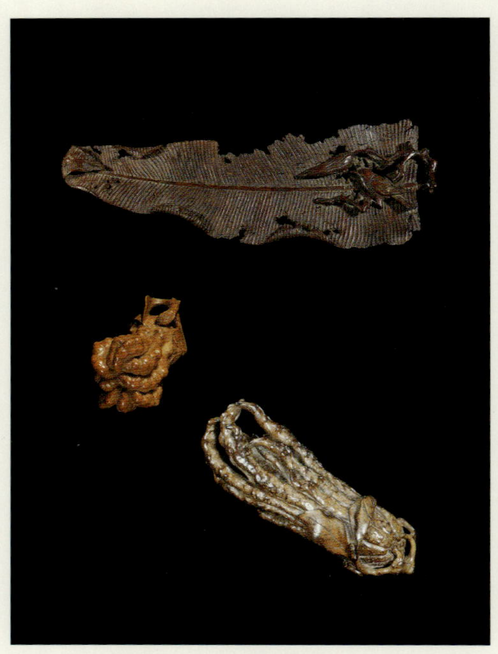

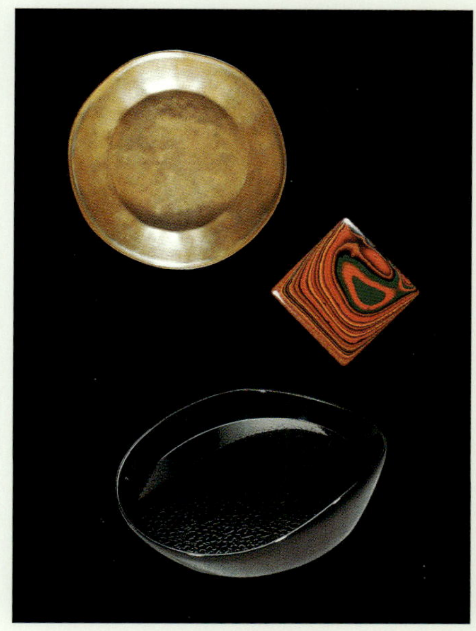

PAGE 98

147) *Kashiki* or tray for tea sweets of silver lacquer with an abstract rippled surface. With the *tomobako* or original box, signed on the interior: *Nuri-shi Hyōami Zō* or *Made by the Lacquerer Hyōami* (Tanaka Hyōami, the Kyoto lacquer artist), and sealed. Taishō Era, early 20th century.

The storage box also bears a title: *Blue Sea Tray.*

3.5 cm high x 26 cm diameter.

148) *Kōgō* or incense box of layered colored lacquer with an abstract pattern. From the Aizu-Wakamatsu area in Fukushima. Late Meiji–Taishō Era, circa 1900–1920.

2 cm high x 4.5 cm x 4.5 cm.

149) *Kawari-bon* or irregularly shaped tray in a curling, folding shape of black lacquer, the reverse with an imitation sharkskin design. 20th century. With the *tomobako* or original box signed on the interior of the lid by the artist *Masachika,* and sealed *Masa.*

9 cm high x 44 cm x 34 cm.

150) Set of five nesting lidded boxes for serving food, of *Wakasa-nuri* lacquer. Each box executed in a slightly different technique and abstract design. Meiji Era, late 19th century.

For other examples of this lacquer, see the Victoria And Albert Museum catalogue, <u>The Toshiba Gallery: Japanese Art and Design</u>, pages 198–199.

10.5 cm high x 26 cm x 22.5 cm, largest box.
8 cm high x 20 cm x 16 cm, smallest box.

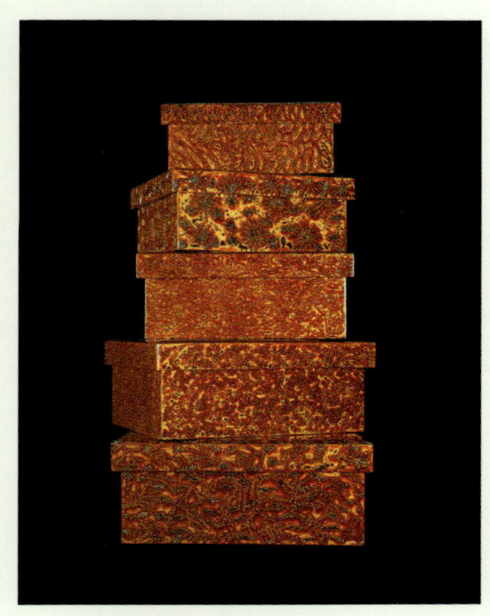

PAGE 99

151) *Tonkotsu* or portable tobacco container of paulownia wood inlaid with a design of a crab and grasses. Inlaid materials include silver, mother of pearl, boxwood, ivory, horn, and ebony. Signed on an inlaid ebony plaque by the artist, *Ichio,* and with a carved and inlaid seal signature. Meiji Era, late 19th century.

6.5 cm high x 9 cm x 5.5 cm.

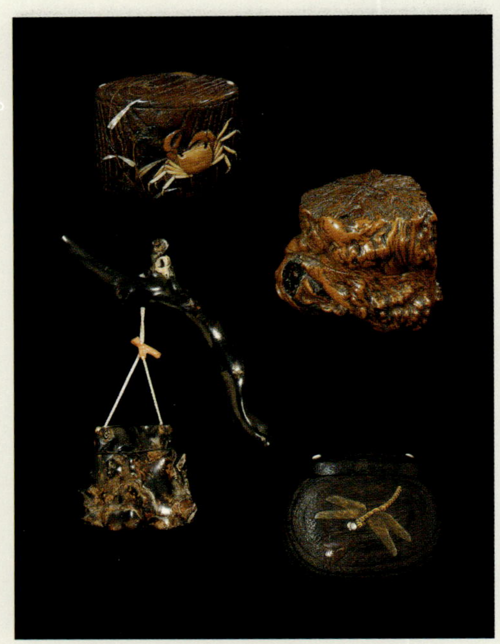

Page 100

152) *Tonkotsu* or portable tobacco container and *kiseru-ire* or pipe holder carved of *umimatsu* or black coral. Meiji Era, late 19th century.

Beautiful use of natural material. The shell inclusions are quite rare.

9 cm high x 9.5 cm x 6 cm.

153) *Tonkotsu* or portable tobacco container of burl wood carved with a lotus motif. Late Edo–early Meiji Era, circa 1850–1870.

7.5 cm high x 10 cm x 7.5 cm.

154) *Tonkotsu* or portable tobacco container of paulownia wood inlaid with a design of a dragonfly and moth on one side, and a spray of mandarin oranges on the other. Inlaid materials include mother of pearl, ivory, coral, tortoiseshell and hardwood. Signed on an inlaid mother of pearl plaque by the artist, *Shibaichi.* Meiji Era, late 19th century.

7 cm high x 8.5 cm x 4.5 cm.

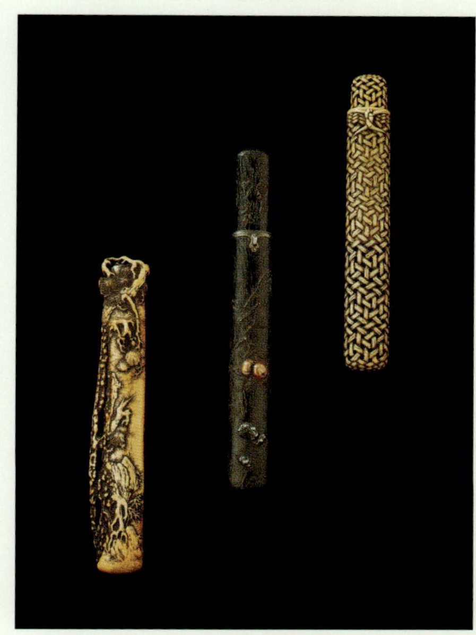

PAGE 101

155) *Kiseruzutsu* or portable pipe case, of stag antler carved with a design of pine and rock formation. Signed by the artist, *Chika-aki*, and with a *kakihan*. Edo Period, late 18th–early 19th century.

The natural texture of the stag antler has been brilliantly utilized by the carver to suggest the bark of the pine tree.

21.5 cm long x 4 cm wide.

156) *Kiseruzutsu* or portable pipe case of ebony carved with a proverb, *Hyakuji Nyoi* or *100 Things Come True As You Wish*, and with a persimmon branch inlaid in gold and silver to suggest lichens. The case is inlaid with persimmon fruit in *sentoku* bronze and silver, and lily roots in silver. Signed on a silver plaque by the artist, *Kaikō*. Meiji Era, late 19th century.

Persimmon and lily roots typically are linked with the proverb *Hyakuji Nyoi*.

23 cm long x 3 cm wide.

157) *Kiseruzutsu* or portable pipe case of carved ivory in a reticulated basket motif. Signed on an inlaid gold plaque by the artist, *Hokusai*. Meiji Era, late 19th century.

19 cm long x 3 cm wide.

158) *Inrō* or portable medicine case of rosewood with a *takamakie* design of a mouse looking at chili peppers and *sanshō* or Japanese pepper, the reverse with its footprints. Meiji Era, late 19th century.

It may be that the imagery on this *inrō* refers to the famous Edo Period folk hero, Nezumikozō Jirokichi. He was a thief renowned for stealing from *Daimyō* residences, lionized by the townsmen and hated by the Shogunate. His name begins with the word for mouse (*nezumi*); *sanshō* and footprints were linked with thieves; and chili peppers were considered an exotic import, associated with treasure.

9 cm high x 4.5 cm wide.

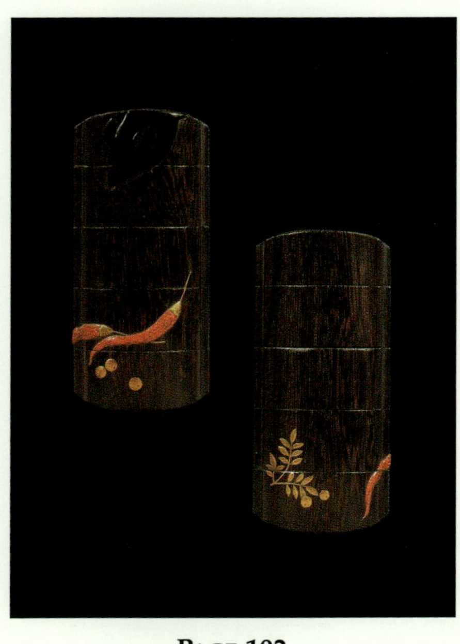

PAGE 102

175

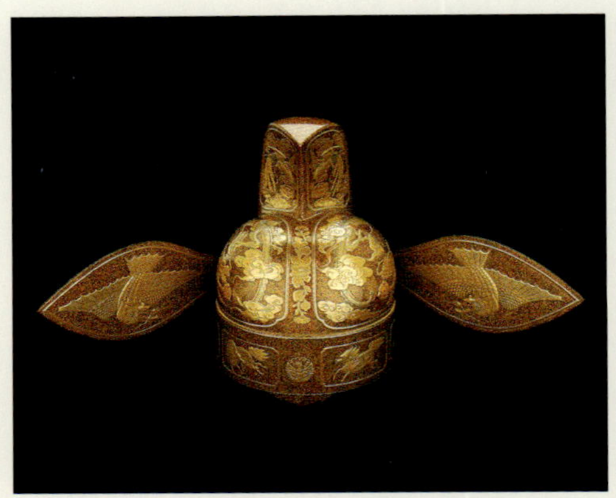

PAGE 103

159) *Okimono* in the form of a *kanmuri* or formal winged court hat worn by ancient Chinese officials, and in Japan used in Noh drama by the *kami* or gods. Made of lacquered wood decorated in dense *nashiji* gold flake lacquer and with colored and gold *takamakie* in congratulatory designs of dragons in clouds, *kirin*, dragon-carp, phoenix and floral designs. With an elaborate wood storage box. Meiji Era, late 19th century.

16.5 cm high x 31 cm x 10 cm.

160) *Kōro* or incense burner of red bronze inlaid in *shakudō, shibuichi*, gold, silver and bronze with a design of butterflies. The pierce work lid in a floral motif of *shibuichi* inlaid in gold and *shakudō*. Signed on the reverse with a chiseled signature by the artist, *Seihō Tsukuru* or *Made by Seihō*. Meiji Era, late 19th century. With a wood storage box.

8 cm high x 11 cm diameter.

161) *Te-aburi* or hand warmer of *sentoku* bronze with chased and gilt floral roundels. Meiji Era, late 19th century.

23 cm high x 16 cm diameter.

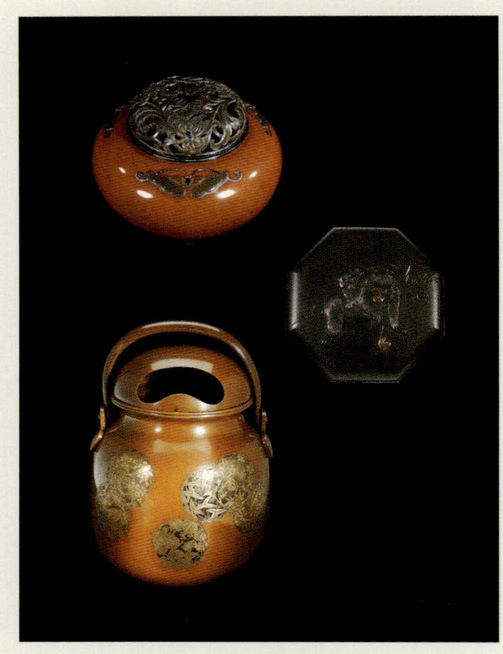

PAGE 104

162) *Kōgō* or incense box of iron with applied silver rims, the lid with a design of two monkeys teasing a crab with grasses, inlaid in silver, copper, and gold. Signed on the reverse with a cast seal form signature. Meiji Era, late 19th century.

3.5 cm high x 8.5 cm diameter.

176

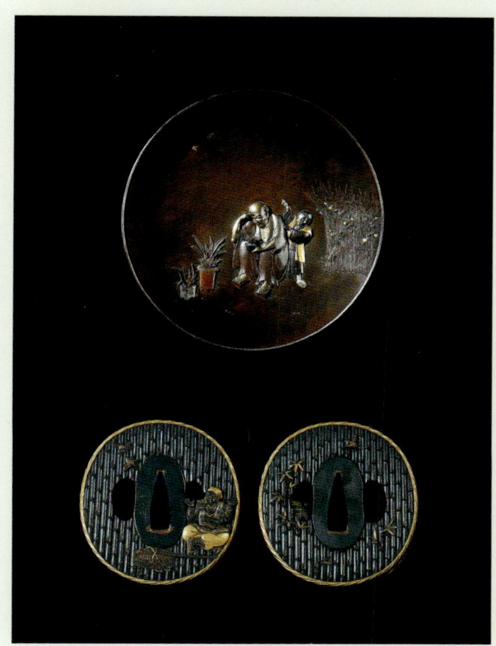

PAGE 105

163) Charger of cast bronze inlaid in gold, *shakudō*, silver, copper and *shibuichi*, with an exceptionally deep relief design of a *bonsai* teacher and his grandson. Meiji Era, circa 1880–1890.

4 cm high x 36.5 cm diameter.

164) *Tsuba* or sword guard, of *shakudō* inlaid in soft metals with a design of a peddler and sparrows against a bamboo ground. Signed *Masutoshi*. Late Edo Period, circa 1850.

Extraordinary Mito School workmanship, illustrating the story of the Cut-Tongue Sparrow.

7.3 cm high x 7 cm wide x .5 cm.

165) *Mizusashi* or water container for *Matcha Tea Ceremony*, made from a Muromachi Period, 15th–16th century, *yamagane* or mountain bronze well pail with deep plum color. The interior now lined in silver foil and with a contemporary fitted silver lid.

20 cm high x 22 cm diameter.

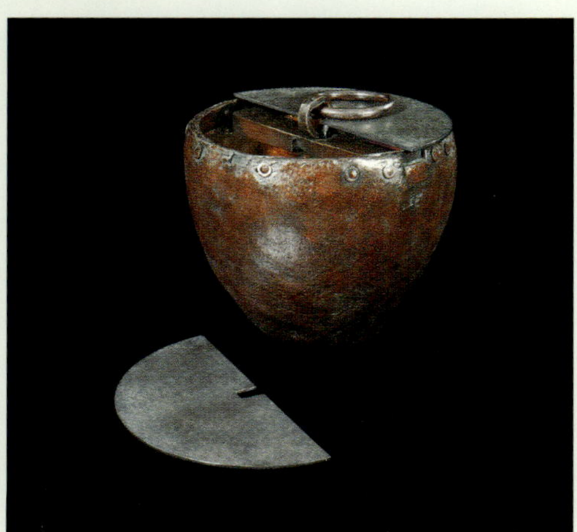

PAGE 106

Drinking tea in Japan has long had associations with a formal world of ritual and ceremony, and with objects treasured for both their beauty and utility. Powdered green tea whisked in small ceramic bowls, the type still prepared for *Matcha Tea Ceremony*, was for centuries the only tea drunk in Japan. Water for *Matcha* was boiled in kettles called *chagama*. One took water from the top with a bamboo dipper. By the late 17th and early 18th century, formal schools were established dictating rules for every aspect of the way tea should be made.

Chinese émigrés fleeing the new Ching Dynasty brought a different style of tea to Japan and it was taken up by their *Bunjin* or Literati hosts. The *Bunjin* also reacted against the formality and stifling prevalence of rules associated with *Matcha*. They associated the new style of infused tea, called *Sencha*, with a personal informality and hospitality. *Sencha* required no formal tea house or room. It was more spontaneous, and seemed to allow for more personal choice than the tea of the schools. This style of infused tea, made in small ceramic or bamboo *kyūsu* or infusing pots, and served in very small cups, required a smaller kettle for heating the water. The *tetsubin*, a small hand held kettle, came into use to meet this need. By the Tempo Era (1830–1844), traditional casters of *chagama*, such as the Ōnishi and Kanchi families, were producing *tetsubin* in small quantities. In Kyoto, the second Ryūbundō master (Shikata Yasunosuke, died 1841) and his descendants became famous for lost wax cast *tetsubin*. Ōkuni in Ōsaka, Kinryūdō in Nagoya, Kibundō and Baisen in Shiga also made beautiful *tetsubin*. A less polished tradition of *tetsubin* grew up in the Nambu iron rich region of Iwate in Northeastern Honshū, producing kettles often used in *minka* farm houses and now often associated with *Mingei* or folk art.

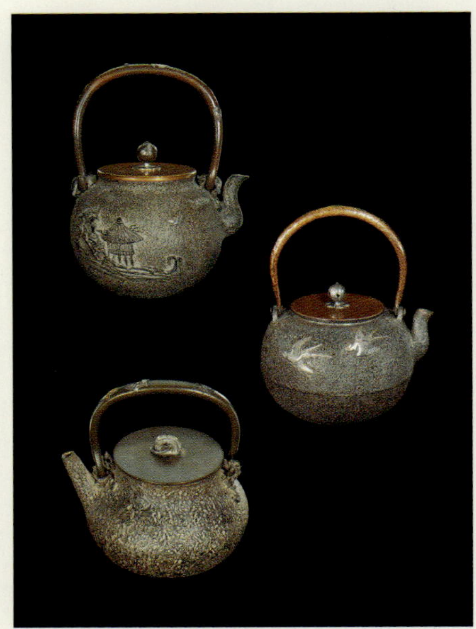

PAGE 107

Tetsubin owe a marked debt to *chagama*, and to some extent to *chōshi* or hand held *sake* servers. Unlike *chagama*, *tetsubin* show a freedom of design, a creative exuberance that probably reflects their association with *Sencha*. The personality and whims of the owners were of greater importance than with the conventions of *Matcha*. Up until the Second World War this lively tradition produced one of Japan's most varied and beautiful of the practical arts.

Chōshi or *sake* servers, and *ginbin* or water ewers, are related forms that share much of the design tradition of *tetsubin*. *Chōshi*, however, always have an open spout and *ginbin* are always of silver.

166) *Tetsubin* or tea pot of cast iron with relief designs of a pavilion in a landscape with flying geese inlaid in silver on one side, and on the other with a country hut in a landscape with the moon inlaid in silver. The surface of the iron is textured an unusual grey and black. The handle supports are in the form of rain dragons, and the handle is of bronze inlaid in silver with lucky treasures (Daikoku's mallet, the magic rain cape, a coin, and a Buddhist jewel). The lid is of *sentoku* yellow bronze with a silver and *shibuichi* knob inlaid with a butterfly. Below the handle support on the back is a square reserve with relief characters for the maker's signature, *Nihon Baisen* or *Baisen of Japan*. On the reverse is another square reserve with the characters for *Biwako No Higashi, Ōmi Hachiman* or *East of Lake Biwa,* (the town of) *Ōmi Hachiman*, referring to the city in Shiga where Baisen worked. Late Meiji Era–Taishō Era, early 20th century.

Baisen was a famous pupil of Hatano Shōhei Kibundō (1812–1892), who also worked in Ōmi Hachiman, and this *tetsubin* shows a marked stylistic debt to Kibundō pieces.

24 cm high x 19 cm x 16 cm.

167) *Tetsubin* or tea pot of cast iron inlaid in silver with three flying swallows with gold eyes. With the *tomobako* or original box signed by the maker, *Kinjūdō*. The bronze lid is surmounted by a silver lobe form knob and signed on the reverse, *Kinjūdō Saku* or *Made by Kinjūdō*. The handle is formed of hammered copper folded and pinned with silver staples. Meiji Era, late 19th century.

Kinjūdō was perhaps the most famous metal house in Kyoto specializing in *tetsubin*. The technique of chiseling and inlaying the silver sparrows was developed by sword makers and required great skill. A lyrical design.

20.5 cm high x 16.5 cm x 15 cm.

168) *Tetsubin* or tea pot of cast iron with a *mushikui* surface meant to suggest antique insect eaten wood, the handle supports in the form of stylized dragons. Signed on the body behind the back handle, *Nihon Ryūbun*, and with the *tomobako* or original box, also signed by the caster, *Shōhei* (Hatano Shōhei Kibundō, 1812–1892, when he worked with Ryūbundō Yasuhei). The bronze lid was designed to suggest an ancient Chinese seal, the circular silver knob with a stylized *taotie* mask in relief, holding a simple silver ring. Scattered across the bronze handle are butterflies inlaid in gold and silver. Late Edo–early Meiji Era, circa 1850–1870.

The *mushikui* texture and the *inkan* or seal style lid suggest that this *tetsubin* was made for someone familiar with the tradition of tea ceremony taste, and the scholarly tendency to favor restraint and references to antiquity. The exuberance of the butterflies on the handle indicates the tea pot may have been made for spring and summer usage, and contrasts beautifully with the restraint of the body. The spout is in an unusual *Teppō-gata* or matchlock style, a reference appropriate for someone of upper-class Samurai background.

This is one of Ryūbundō's more sophisticated pieces, likely ordered by a client of upper-class, rather than merchant origins.

19 cm high x 17 cm x 16 cm.

169) *Ginbin* or water server of hammered silver in the form of lotus leaves with crabs crawling out from the edges, their eyes inlaid in gold. Signed on the back in a rectangular reserve by the artist, *Izumi Kōshō*. Meiji Era, late 19th century.

20 cm high x 17.5 cm x 14 cm.

170) *Ginbin* or silver water server in a miniature size with relief designs of chrysanthemums. Sealed on the base by the maker, *Chikutō*. Late Meiji–Taishō Era, circa 1900–1920.

10.5 cm high x 8.5 cm x 6.5 cm.

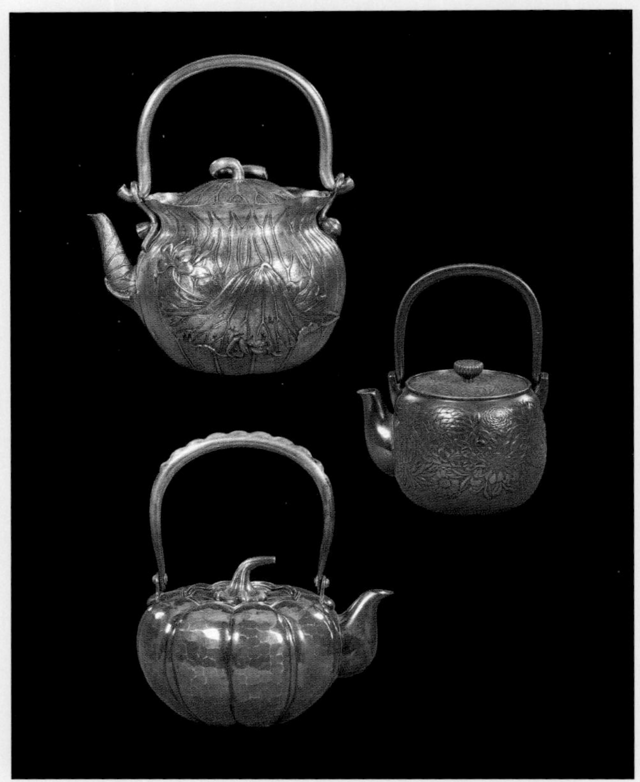

PAGE 108

171) *Ginbin* or silver water server in the form of a pumpkin. Sealed on the reverse, *Jungin* or *Pure Silver* and *Shōeidō*. With the *tomobako* or original box, signed and sealed *Shōeidō*. Taishō Era, circa 1920.

15.5 cm high x 13.5 cm x 11 cm.

172**)** Pair of *chōshi* or sake servers of spun *sahari* bronze in circular forms with strong angular spouts and graceful lobed handles, the lids with a plum bud finial. Late Edo Period, mid 19th century.

Though unsigned, these may be the work of the Ōnishi family, Ōsaka specialists in the casting of iron and bronze. The Ōnishi were noted for their *chagama*, *tetsubin*, and *chōshi*. We have had a number of their *chōshi*, the pieces like these usually unsigned, but often with signed storage boxes.

22 cm high x 28 cm x 21 cm, each.

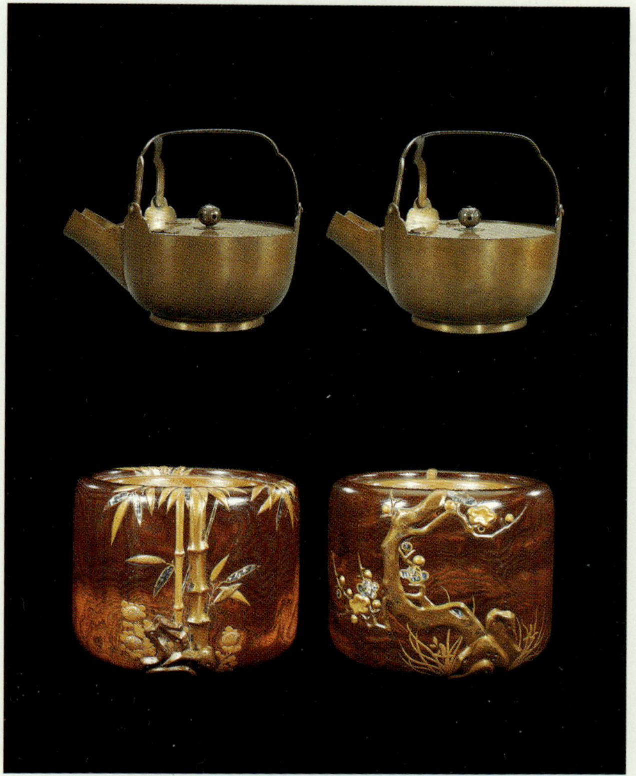

PAGE 109

173**)** Pair of *hibachi* or hand warmers in cylindrical form, of carved chestnut wood decorated with raised lacquer, *kirikane* inlay, and *aogai* shell with designs of flowering plum, orchids, bamboo and chrysanthemums, the interiors lined with copper. From the Kanazawa area. Meiji Era, circa 1870–1880.

21 cm high x 26.5 cm diameter.

Prior to the Meiji Era, basket makers were craftsmen, mostly anonymous and of humble status. They made folk tools, essentially utilitarian even when beautiful. However, a number of these artisans wove flower baskets and trays for use in the tea ceremony and in upper class homes. This connection with *Matcha Tea* and *Ikebana* created a level of patronage which allowed them to devote to their work a great deal of time and creativity. During Meiji, the best of these weavers began to exhibit at the national craft and art exhibitions. By 1910, they consciously saw themselves as artists, signing their baskets, competing with each other at exhibitions, and stretching the horizons of their own work. Still, the folk tradition from which this art form branched and flowered did not completely disappear. Provincial weaving areas such as Beppu in Ōita survived, and produced quantities of work for the growing *Ikebana* market. These baskets rarely reached the level of their more sophisticated cousins, though certain provincial weavers transcended the folk tradition. Sometimes signed, the best of these regional baskets are flower containers of beautiful balance and complexity, meriting a place next to the studio baskets made by artists in Ōsaka, Kyoto and Tokyo.

Looking at a basket we see a piece of sculpture in bamboo, created from a sophisticated vocabulary of techniques. Ornamental knots are often repeated in one piece, sometimes slightly altered in form or size, and chosen to contrast with the plaiting and other knotting in the architecture of the basket. While unnecessary to a feeling for its form, understanding the structure of the basket deepens our appreciation for the weaver's art.

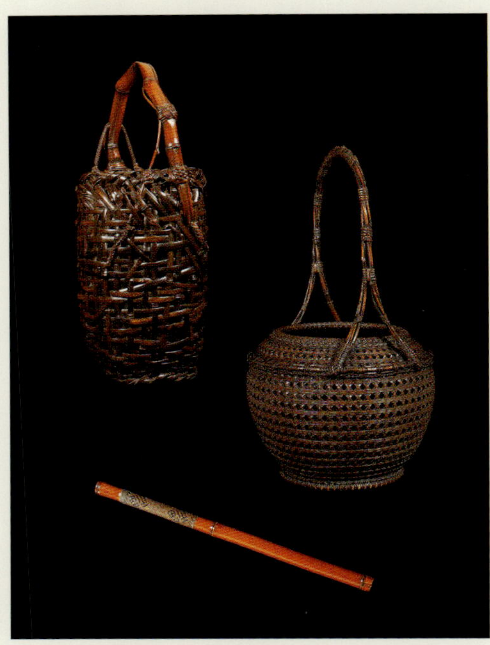

PAGE 110

174) Flower arranging basket of split bamboo in a roughly cylindrical form with a natural bamboo loop handle. The body is woven in an abstracted, loose version of square plaiting. A strong section of branch bamboo bent at the top forms the handle. A number of ornamental knotting techniques join the handle to the body: insect wrapping (*mushi-maki*) used in varying sizes, a large double interlocking V knot, and complex cross knots (*jūji musubi*). The artist signed the piece on the reverse, *Chikuunsai Tsukuru* or *Made by Chikuunsai* (Tanabe Chikuun, 1877–1937). With the *tomobako* or original box, the lid inscribed on the exterior: *Purple Bamboo Flower Basket Named Abundant Harvest;*

and on the interior: *Sakai Fu Nansō, Chikuunsai Tsukuru,* or *Sakai City, A House Facing South, Made by Chikuunsai,* and sealed with two seals.

The title and strong plaiting probably suggested a rough winnowing basket. By increasing the size of the ornamental knotting, Chikuunsai complements the large abstract plaiting of the body and the strong scale of the handle. Rich color and exceptional handle treatment.

47 cm high x 20 cm diameter.

175) Flower arranging basket of split bamboo with a globe form body and a tall loop style handle formed from two intertwined bundles of root bamboo (rhizomes). Another bundled group of root bamboo overlays the shoulder. The body is plaited with repeating bands of twining (*nawa-ami*) which circle the body in graduated widths, overlaying an openwork simple hemp leaf weave. Ornamental knotting techniques included are: insect wrapping (*mushi-maki*), and series of interlocking V knots (*kunoji-musubi*). The artist signed the basket on the reverse, *Chikuunsai Tsukuru* or *Made by Chikuunsai* (Tanabe Chikuun, 1877–1937). With the *tomobako* or original box, the lid exterior inscribed: *Bamboo Root Handled Flower Basket,* the interior signed *Chikuunsai Tsukuru* or *Made by Chikuunsai,* and sealed.

52 cm high x 31 cm diameter.

176) *Kōzutsu* or container for stick incense with the characters for *Fuku* or *Good Luck* woven into the body of the bamboo, the surface lacquered. With the *tomobako* or original box signed by the artist, *Chikuunsai Tsukuru* or *Made by Chikuunsai* (Tanabe Chikuun, 1877–1937), and inscribed: *Fukuji Monyō Ami Senkōzutsu* or *Incense Container Woven with a Design of Fuku Characters.*

Rather than employ the simple technique of overlaying the basketry work, Tanabe Chikuun used an extremely difficult approach. He split the bamboo cylinder in order to weave through the body of the bamboo. This represents a tour de force of workmanship by one of the most important bamboo artists of the early 20th century.

40.5 cm long x 2 cm diameter.

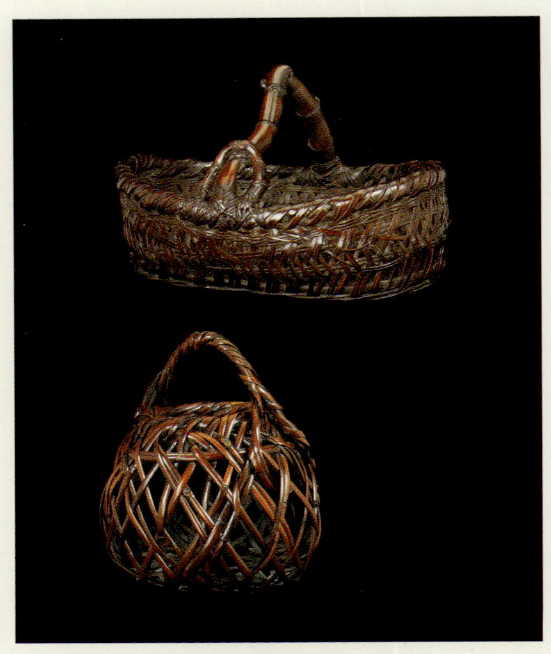

177) Flower arranging basket of split bamboo in the form of a stylized Treasure Boat. The body is woven in a loose, abstracted hemp leaf pattern (*asa-no-ha*), and the base in a formal hemp leaf pattern. Two sections of branch bamboo form the handle. Joining the single large branch end to the body is a double interlocking V knot, and on the opposite side the handle sections are tied to the body by insect wrapping (*mushi-maki*). The artist signed the basket on the reverse, *Shōkōsai Tsukuru* or *Made by Shōkōsai*. With the *tomobako* or signed original box, inscribed with the Early Shōwa Era date, Winter of 1932, and the signature of the 4th Generation Hayakawa Shōkōsai.

Treasure Boat motif baskets were meant to be displayed at New Year's, the most important festival in the Japanese calendar. Often the theme was executed in a common, mass-produced style that looked far more realistic, more like an actual model of a boat than this piece. Shōkōsai took this genre and, using classical weaving techniques on a large scale, created a vessel for flowers far surpassing the ordinary. The variegated bamboo of the body has a rich purple color that makes a beautiful foil for the massive twisting handle.

30 cm high x 44 cm x 36 cm.

178) Flower arranging basket of red-brown split bamboo in a rounded form, the handle made from intertwined strands of some of the split bamboo plaiting the sides. A loose, abstracted lozenge pattern makes up the body of the basket. The artist signed the piece on the reverse, *Sōunsai Tsukuru* or *Made by Sōunsai* (Sakaguchi Sōunsai, 1902–1970).

Sōunsai was born in Ōsaka and studied there under Chikuun I (Tanabe Chikuun). In Shōwa 4 (1929), he exhibited at the *Teiten* or Exhibition of the Imperial Academy of Fine Arts. In Shōwa 20 (1945), Sōunsai moved to the small city of Fukuchiyama in Hyōgo. After the War he exhibited widely, showing at both the *Bunten* (The Ministry of Education Art Exhibition) and the *Nitten* (Japan Art Exhibition).

This basket's fluid, almost informal weaving style contrasts with the richly polished color of the bamboo.

38 cm high x 34 cm diameter.

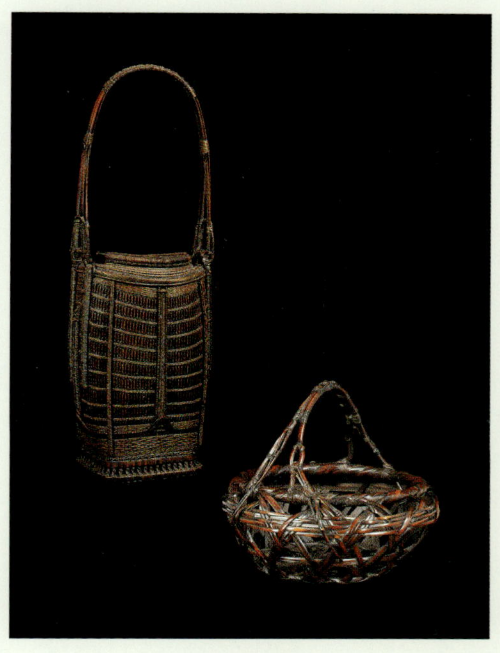

PAGE 112

179) Flower arranging basket in a rounded rectangular form set on a squared base and with an oval mouth. Four sections of split and curved bamboo tied together form the handle. The body is woven in a hemp leaf pattern (*asa-no-ha*) set on its side and divided into bands by very fine lines of insect stitch (*mushi-kagari*). Backing the hemp leaf weave is another plane of finely split bamboo in twining (*nawa-ami*) technique. Other weaving techniques include: butterfly knots (*chō-musubi*), insect wrapping (*mushi-maki*), simple wrapping (*bō-maki*), and turtle shell knots (*kame-no-kō-musubi*). The artist signed the piece on the reverse, *Chikuhōsai Tsukuru* or *Made by Chikuhōsai* (Maeda Chikuhō, 1872–1950). With a wood storage box (*awasebako*).

Maeda Chikuhō and Tanabe Chikuun were among the most important basket weavers working before the War. Of the two, Chikuhō had the greater range, creatively working in countless numbers of styles. This is likely a piece made for exhibition, or for one of Chikuhō's more important patrons. He takes one type of knotting or wrapping, and then echoes it in variation after variation. A spectacular example of weaving, using a wide vocabulary of techniques.

55 cm high x 19 cm x 15.5 cm.

180) Flower arranging basket of dark red split bamboo in a low compressed globe shape. Two sections of branch bamboo splitting into finger branches form the loop style handle. The body consists of an openwork hexagonal weave made up of four split bamboo strips ranked together. Ornamental knotting techniques include: double interlocking V knots, insect wrapping (*mushi-maki*), and double bound simple wrapping (*bō-maki*). The artist signed the basket on the reverse, *Chikuhōsai* (Maeda Chikuhō, 1872–1950). With the *tomobako* or original box, the exterior of the lid inscribed: *Rough Woven Flower Basket*, and the interior: *I Made this Natural Bamboo Handled Basket with Ancient Kinmei Bamboo from Izumo*, and dated *Shōwa 19* (1944), *a day in Autumn*; and inscribed with the location of his studio in Sakai, *Senyō Kuze Sato*, then signed *Chikuhōsai Tsukuru* or *Made by Chikuhōsai*, and sealed.

A number of other baskets by Maeda Chikuhō exist with similarly inscribed boxes, all dating from 1941–1945, and all apparently woven from bamboo taken from houses in different parts of Japan. It seems that at this time in his life, already famous and at the peak of his career, Chikuhō traveled to different parts of Japan and stayed with distinguished families in old houses. His hosts allowed Chikuhō to take some of the bamboo built into the house as material for his art. This rafter bamboo had developed heavy encrustation from smoke and oils over time. When polished, this material revealed beautiful color.

The delicate elegance of the handle and its attachments contrast superbly with the coarser open work of the body.

32 cm high x 35 cm diameter.

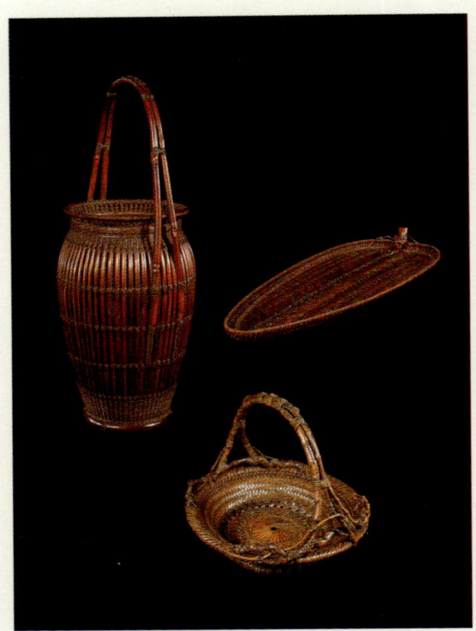

181) Flower arranging basket of split bamboo in a tall ovoid form with an out-turned lip, the handle formed of two sections of bent branch bamboo. The body of the basket is formed of split sections of small branch bamboo, gently curved and aligned in vertical series. Five rows of cross knots (*jūji musubi*) tie the vertical slats to a ring of split bamboo on the interior, breaking the vertical lines and strengthening the structure. Other techniques used include: interlocking V knots (*kunoji-musubi*), simple double interlocking V knots, mat plaiting (*gozame-ami*), stitched insect wrapping (*kakemushi-maki*), and simple wrapping (*bō-maki*). The artist signed the basket on the reverse, *Chikuhōsai Tsukuru* or *Made by Chikuhōsai* (Maeda Chikuhō, 1872–1950). With the *tomobako* or original wood storage box, the exterior lid of which is inscribed: *Armor Form Flower Basket*; the interior lid with an inscription to the effect: *Made in the Autumn of the 2600th Imperial Year* (1940), and signed *Chikuhōsai Tsukuru* and sealed.

We have seen a number of baskets with titles such as this one, with references to armor or to arrows. Some actually incorporate split lacquered arrows into the fabric of the basket. They generally have a gently curving face, and a structure of vertical stays as a defining characteristic, features that suggest the breast plates in traditional Japanese armor. Chikuhō treats the theme gently, using split bamboo that suggests arrows rather than actual arrows.

51 cm high x 20 cm diameter.

182) Leaf shaped basket tray, the face woven of split purple bamboo in a basic twill plaiting with the nodes of the bamboo lined up in series to form the central vein of the leaf. A bent section of branch bamboo with three small finger branches forms the stem. Among the techniques used to create this piece are: stitched insect wrapping (*kakemushi-maki*), cross knots (*jūji musubi*), and spiral cross knots (*jūji-usumaki-musubi*). The artist signed the tray on the reverse, *Chikuhōsai Tsukuru* or *Made by Chikuhōsai* (Maeda Chikuhō, 1872–1950). With an *awasebako* or unsigned wood storage box.

This is a rare figural *morikago* or fruit display basket of a type that could also have been used in *Sencha Tea* as a tray for an incense box. This leaf represents a form we have never seen duplicated and must have been a special commission, or a piece woven for exhibition.

6.5 cm high x 67 cm x 29 cm.

183) *Morikago* or basket tray for displaying seasonal fruit, woven of variegated gold and brown split bamboo in a shallow circular form, the tall loop handle made from branch and twig bamboo. The body is woven in basic twill plaiting of alternating types of bamboo. Ornamental knot types include: double interlocking V knots (some including an elaboration of braiding), insect wrapping (*mushi-maki*), and double bound simple wrapping (*bō-maki*). The artist signed the basket on the reverse, *Chikuhōsai Tsukuru* or *Made by Chikuhōsai* (Maeda Chikuhō, 1872–1950).

36.5 cm high x 42.5 cm x 39.5 cm.

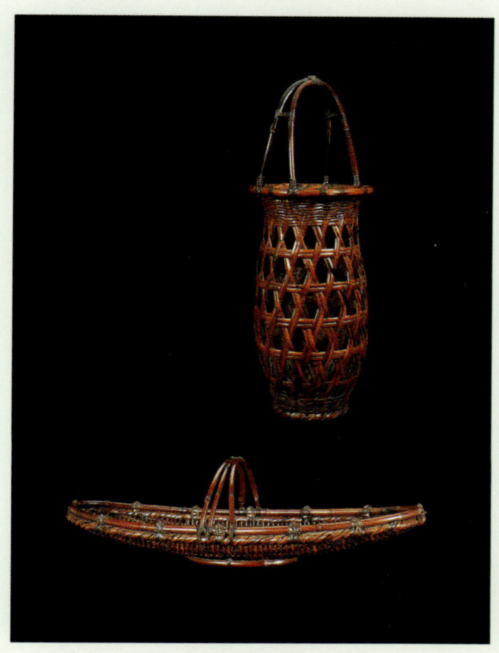

184) Flower arranging basket in the form of a long oval stylized boat, the body woven in mat plaiting. Edging the rim is a strong half-inch diameter section of branch bamboo bound to the body with repeating double interlocking V knots. The loop style handle is formed of two sections of twig bamboo, one of which splits into a third branch at the top. The base is formed by a section of twig bamboo curled into an oval that mirrors the upper rim and which is bound to the body at four points with simple wrapping. Inscribed on a section of split bamboo inserted on the reverse at the center of the basket is the artist's signature, *Chikushinsai Tsukuru* or *Made by Chikushinsai*. Early 20th century.

This is an elegant basket, very much in the style of what the Ōsaka–Kyoto artists were making in the 1920s and 1930s. A minimalist, severe rendering of a Treasure Boat.

17 cm high x 60 cm x 21 cm.

185) Flower arranging basket of red split bamboo in a tall ovoid shape with an out-turned rim and a loop handle. Two sections of branch bamboo form the handle (one dark red and the other black-red) tied together at the top with one large ornamental double interlocking V knot. Sections of insect wrapping (*mushi-maki*) tie the handle to the mouth, which is formed of another section of lighter red branch bamboo bent into a circle. Simple wrapping (*bō-maki*) in split black-red bamboo ties this mouth section to the basket, and contrasts with the lighter red of the rim and body. A section of twining (*nawa ami*) binds the top and bottom of the piece, the balance of which is woven in large double strands of hexagonal plaiting. The artist signed the basket on the reverse, *Chikushinsai Tsukuru* or *Made by Chikushinsai*. Taishō–early Shōwa Era, circa 1920–1940.

The use of red bamboo for the body, and the darker bamboo for the handle and rim knotting, give this basket a dramatic quality, emphasized by the large plaiting and tall overall scale. Chikushin made the color of the material itself an important element of the design.

60.5 cm x 23 cm diameter.

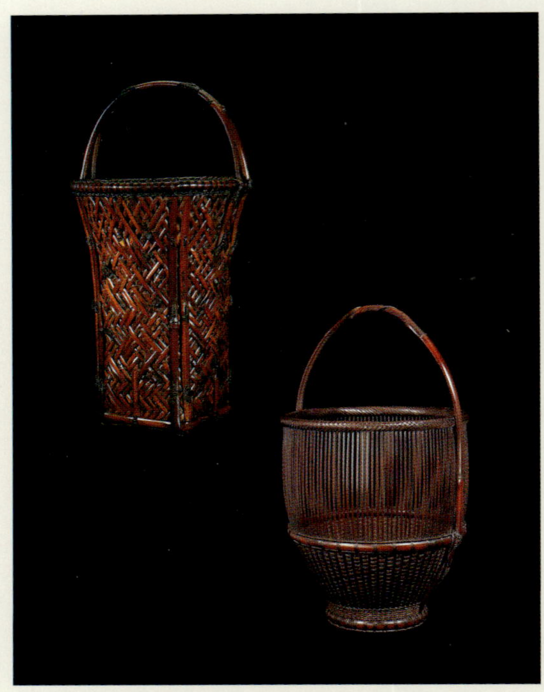

Page 115

186) Flower arranging basket, woven of split bamboo in a tall square form gently swelling to a round mouth, the rounded handle of two sections of branch bamboo joined at the top. The weaver formed the body with basic twill plaiting made irregular by skipping over stays. Wider sections of split bamboo overlay the corners and base. Ornamental knot types include: insect stitch (*mushi-kagari*), insect wrapping (*mushi-maki*), stitched insect wrapping (*kakemushi-maki*), spiral cross knots (*jūji-uzumaki-musubi*), and double interlocking V knots. The artist signed the piece on the reverse, *Chikuami Tsukuru* or *Made by Chikuami* (Morita Chikuami was the *Gō* or art name for Morita Shintarō). With the *tomobako* or original box, the lid inscribed: *Suehiro Gata Hanakago* or *Unfolding Fan Shaped Flower Basket*, and the interior signed, *Chikuami Tsukuru* or *Made by Chikuami*, and sealed. Early 20th century.

Morita Chikuami is recorded as winning a prize for his work at the fifth *Naikoku Kangyō Hakurankai* (Fifth Domestic Industrial Exhibition) in Meiji 36 (1903). He lived in Kyoto and was active as late as Shōwa 2 (1927). His grandson continues to weave baskets today.

This basket's *Suehiro* form would have been perceived as auspicious and congratulatory, appropriate for a special occasion such as New Year's. Morita Chikuami chose bamboo with angularly cut branch nodes, and scattered these as ornamentation across the faces of the basket.

48 cm high x 25 cm diameter.

187) Flower arranging basket, woven of split bamboo in a tapering cylindrical form, with a loop handle formed from a single section of split bamboo twisted over on itself at the top. The lower part of the body is woven in a simple square plaiting overlaid with vertical stays. Skipping in sequence behind successive stays creates a rising diagonal line through the front face of this plaiting. The waist is overlaid with a section of split bamboo similar to that forming the handle. Vertically set strips of bamboo arranged in openwork series form the balance of the body. Ornamental knot types include: flattened insect wrapping (*mushi-maki*) at the rim, elaborate cross knots (*jūji-musubi*), and stitched insect wrapping (*kakemushi-maki*). The artist signed the basket on the lower side of the handle section, *Chikuami Tsukuru* or *Made by Chikuami* (Morita Chikuami was the *Gō* or art name for Morita Shintarō). With the *tomobako* or original box, signed, *Chikuami Tsukuru* or *Made by Chikuami*, and sealed.

An elegant basket by the same artist as number 186 above.

40 cm high x 24 cm diameter.

188) Flower arranging basket, woven of baleen in two colors in a bag like form, the interior lined in red copper. The body is woven in a square plaiting for the lower third, then shifts into a basic twill plaiting. Overlaying this are heavy braids covered in insect wrapping (*mushi-maki*). The same technique covers the circular rim. Late Edo Period, early 19th century.

Basketry woven from baleen is very rare in Japan. This piece was made in Ishikawa Prefecture, probably in Kanazawa, and was said to have come out of a house in the Noto Peninsula. This basket shows a classical Edo Period sensibility in form and ornament.

22 cm high x 32 cm x 30 cm.

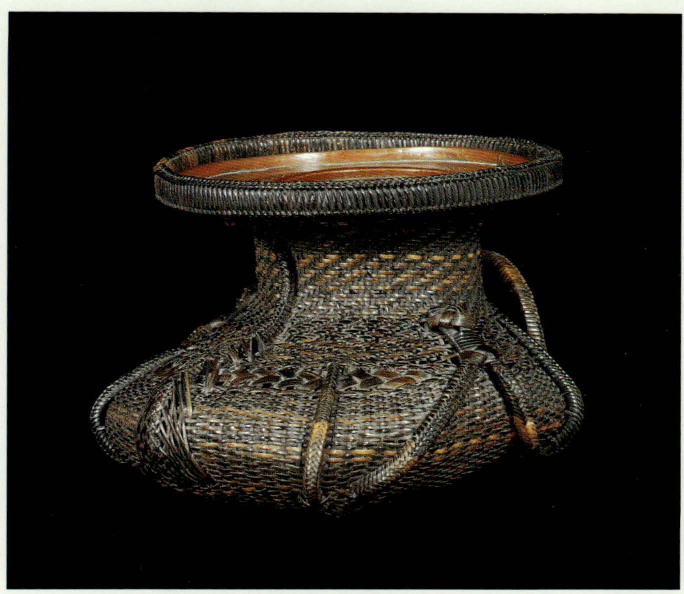

PAGE 116

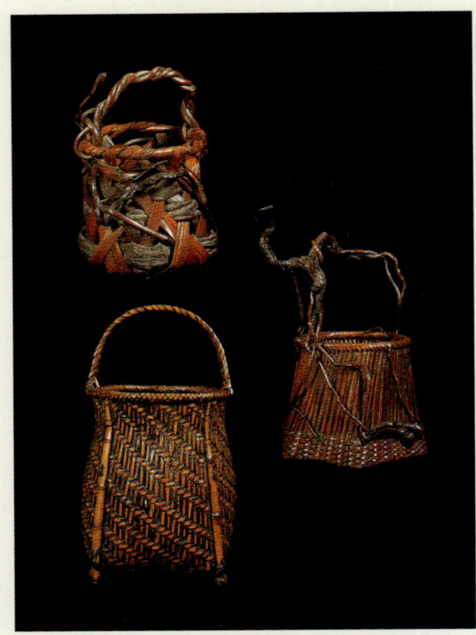

PAGE 117

189) Flower arranging basket, woven of split bamboo and sections of cherry bark in a roughly cylindrical form, the handle formed of three twisting sections of wisteria vine interwoven with a section of natural branch on one side. The body is woven in a rough hemp leaf pattern (*asa-no-ha*). Unsigned. Meiji Era, late 19th–early 20th century.

With its cousins, this flower basket was probably made in Central Honshū, relatively close to Kyoto. This is the only part of Japan where this type consistently appears. Shiga Prefecture is the most likely source. The basket has a rough, handsome quality due to the exuberance of the plaiting and spontaneity of the handle treatment. Fine color and an intuitive balance distinguish this basket.

39.5 cm high x 28 cm diameter.

190) Flower arranging basket, woven of variegated split bamboo in a tapering hexagonal form, the handle formed from long sections of natural branch that stretch completely around the body of the basket. The lower quarter of the body is woven in a simple square plaiting, the upper portion consists of the twisting vertical stays of this plaiting rising to a circular rim. Unsigned. Meiji Era, late 19th–early 20th century.

This basket is a cousin to number 189 above. It may even have been woven in the same workshop. While the plaiting technique remains very simple, and the only ornamental knotting is a flattened version of stitched insect wrapping (*kakemushi-maki*) binding the mouth, the weaver had an intuitive sense of balance. Beautiful color and movement.

44 cm high x 29 cm diameter.

191) Flower arranging basket of split bamboo in a large bag shape, with a diagonal plaiting in the body and a square plaiting on the base. Four tapering sections of cut branch bamboo form the corners and the feet. Attaching these corner pieces are rice-character stitches (*kome-no-ji-dome*) and insect stitches (*mushi-kagari*). The handle is formed from two sections of bundled split bamboo tightly covered and bound together at the top with simple diagonal wrapping. Unsigned. Meiji Era, late 19th century.

This is an earlier flower basket in the *Mingei* tradition. The spiral weave lends a lively movement to what would have been a solid and static form. This type of weave and the rich gold and black color are usually only seen on *sumi-kago* or charcoal baskets for tea rooms. Very possibly the shape is also meant as a reference to the treasure bag carried by Daikoku, the god of wealth.

49 cm high x 27.5 cm diameter.

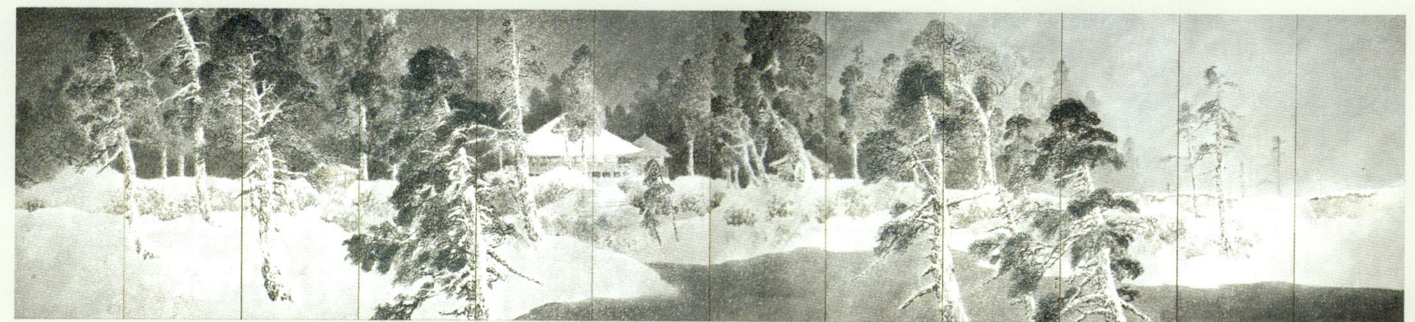

PAGES 118–123

192) **Page 118:** Detail of *byōbu* pictured on pages 119–122.

Pages 119–122: Pair of six panel *byōbu* or folding screens painted in *sumi* ink, *gofun* or clam shell gesso, and mineral pigments with a view of Mount Kōya in a snow storm. One screen sealed and signed, *Baikyū*, and the other sealed (Kawashima Baikyū, Meiji 29 or 1896–?). Taishō Era, circa 1918–1919.

A paper label affixed to the reverse of one screen is dated December of Taishō 8 (1919), and titles the screens: *Kōya San Yuki No Hara* or *Mount Kōya—Field of Snow*. The label states that these were painted by Kawashima Baikyū of Kyoto, for display at the *Teiten* or annual Exhibition of the Imperial Academy of Fine Arts.

Kawashima Baikyū lived in Kyoto. He studied painting under Shōda Kakuyū (1879–1947), a professor at the Kyoto School of Painting and noted landscape painter.

A spectacular pair of screens by Kawashima Baikyū. Famous for its ancient Shingon temples and haunting forests, Mount Kōya is one of Japan's most sacred places. Baikyū quiets this landscape with a snow storm, stressing the ascetic isolation of the mountain. Winter is a season to turn inwards, to think of endings. The association with Kōya suggests Buddhist themes of mortality and the eternal.

The white *gofun* gives the snow texture and thickness. To achieve depth of field, Baikyū mixed *sumi* ink in varying degrees with the *gofun* to produce differing shades of snow. A wide range of brush work was employed to create subtle differences in the snowflakes.

170.5 cm high x 376 cm, each six panel screen when unfolded flat.

Page 123: Detail of *byōbu* pictured on pages 119–122.

191

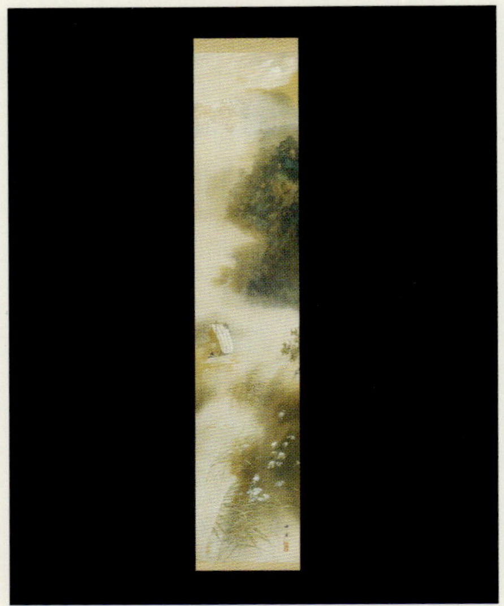

PAGE 124

193) Painting in natural pigments on silk mounted as a hanging scroll, depicting a river scene with reeds in the foreground, a figure sailing a small boat in the middle ground, and hills with clouds in the distance. Signed *Baikan*, and sealed (Kawashima Baikan, died at 75 years of age in 1977). With a *tomobako* or original box, inscribed and sealed by the artist: *Shūfū Sōrai* or *The Autumn Winds Come Quickly*. Early Shōwa Era, circa 1930–1940.

Baikan was a Nihonga School painter noted for his landscapes and paintings of flowers and birds. He studied under Yamamoto Shunkyo (1871–1933). This painting is an evocative meditation on the passage of time.

128.5 cm high x 27.5 cm wide, painting exclusive of mounting.

194) Painting on silk mounted as a hanging scroll, in *sumi* ink and mineral pigments, depicting a waterfall in the mist. Signed and sealed by the artist, *Sekka Hitsu* or *Brushed by Sekka* (Kamisaka Sekka, 1866–1942).

The artist worked in Kyoto, in the traditions of the Rimpa School. A very lyrical, and impressionist painting. For other examples of his work, see: <u>Kindai No Rimpa: Kamisaka Sekka</u>.

116 cm high x 19.5 cm wide, painting exclusive of mounting.

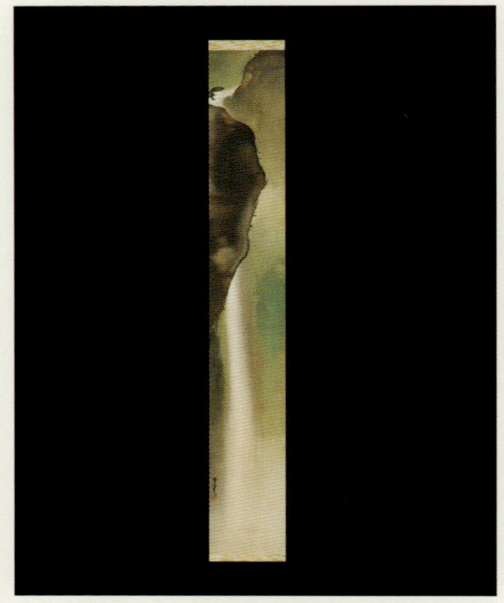

PAGE 125

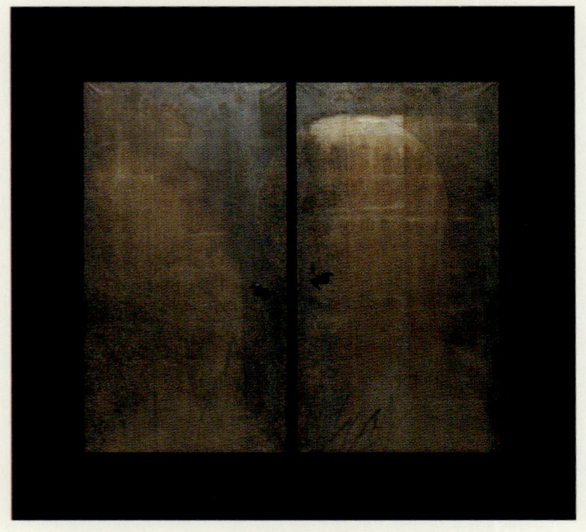

PAGE 126

195) Pair of *fusuma* or sliding doors with paintings in *sumi* ink and mineral pigments on silver foiled paper with a design of grasses and the moon, the *hikite* or door pulls in the form of flying bats. Taishō–early Shōwa Era, circa 1920–1940.

173 cm high x 193 cm wide, fit together.

Bibliography

Arts, P.L.W. *Tetsubin: A Japanese Waterkettle*. Groningen: Geldermalsen Publications, 1988.

Conant, Ellen P. *Nihonga: Transcending the Past: Japanese-Style Painting, 1868–1968*. Saint Louis: Saint Louis Art Museum, 1995.

Earle, Joe. *Flower Bronzes of Japan*. London: Michael Goedhuis Ltd., 1995.

Earle, Joe, ed. *Japanese Art and Design*. London: The Toshiba Gallery, Victoria and Albert Museum, 1986.

Emerson-Dell, Kathleen. *Bridging East and West: Japanese Ceramics from the Kōzan Studio*. Exhibition Catalogue. The Walters Art Gallery, Baltimore, December 3, 1994–April 9, 1995 and Ashmolean Museum, Oxford, May 3–July 2, 1995. Baltimore: The Walters Art Gallery, 1994.

Hauge, Victor and Takako. *Folk Traditions in Japanese Art*. Tokyo, New York and San Francisco: Kodansha International Ltd., 1978.

Hay, John. *Kernels of Energy, Bones of Earth: The Rock in Chinese Art*. Exhibition Catalogue. China House Gallery, New York, October 26, 1985–January 26, 1986. New York: China Institute in America, 1985.

Heineken, Ty and Kiyoko. *Tansu: Traditional Japanese Cabinetry*. New York and Tokyo: Weatherhill, 1981.

Idemitsu Museum of Arts. *Hōan Hanzan Hakuyō Ten Zuroku*. Exhibition Catalogue. Tokyo: Idemitsu Museum of Arts, 1980.

Impey, Oliver; and Fairley, Malcolm, eds. *The Nasser D. Khalili Collection of Japanese Art*. Vol. 2: *Meiji No Takara* (Treasures of Imperial Japan: Metalwork Part II). London: The Kibo Foundation, 1995.

Kiuchi, Takeo; Shionoya, Hiroharu; and Abe, Domyo. *Wadansu Shūsei* (Japanese Chests). Tokyo: Kodansha, 1982.

McCallum, Toshiko M. *Containing Beauty: Japanese Bamboo Flower Baskets*. Los Angeles: UCLA Museum of Cultural History, 1988.

Ministry of Education and Agency for Cultural Affairs. *Jūyō Bunkazai*. Vol. 5: *Chokoku* (Important Cultural Property: Sculpture). Tokyo: Mainichi Shinbunsha, 1974.

Moss, Paul; and Harkins, Brian. *When Men and Mountains Meet: Chinese and Japanese Spirit Rocks*. London: Sydney L. Moss Ltd., 1995.

Nagatake, Takeshi, et al. *Nihon Yakimono Shūsei*. Vol. 11: *Kyūshū I* (Japanese Ceramics: Kyūshū Part 1). Tokyo: Heibonsha, 1980.

Negishi, Hideyuki, ed. *Bijutsu Nenkan 1996* (Art Annual 1996). Tokyo: Bijutsu Nenkansha, 1996.

Okamura, Kichiemon. *Famous Ceramics of Japan*. Vol. 4: *Folk Kilns II*. Tokyo, New York, and San Francisco: Kodansha International Ltd., 1981.

Sakakibara, Yoshio. *Kindai No Rimpa: Kamisaka Sekka* (Modern Rimpa: Kamisaka Sekka). Kyoto: Kyoto Shoin, 1981.

Seattle Art Museum. *A Thousand Cranes: Treasures of Japanese Art*. Seattle and San Francisco: Seattle Art Museum and Chronicle Books, 1987.

Sugimura, Tsune; and Ogawa, Masataka. *The Enduring Crafts of Japan: 33 Living National Treasures*. New York and Tokyo: Weatherhill, 1968.

The Shoto Museum of Art. *Nihon No Zōge Bijutsu* (History of Japanese Ivory Carving: Gebori-Okimono and Shibayama of Meiji Period). Tokyo: The Shoto Museum of Art, 1996.

Tokyo National Museum. *A Selection of Japanese Art from The Mary and Jackson Burke Collection*. Exhibition Catalogue. Tokyo, May 21–June 30, 1985. Tokyo: Tokyo National Museum, 1985.

Tsang, Gerard; and Moss, Hugh. *Arts from the Scholar's Studio*. Exhibition Catalogue. Fung Ping Shan Museum, University of Hong Kong, October 24–December 13, 1986. Hong Kong: Oriental Ceramic Society of Hong Kong, 1986.

KAGEDO JAPANESE ART - Catalogue Price List

Frontis Piece	$ 9,500.	27	$ 24,000.	54	$ 12,000.
1	$ 40,000.	28	$ 18,500.	55	$ 22,000.
2	$ 18,000.	29	$ 5,500.	56	$ 8,500.
3	$ 14,000.	30	$ 11,000.	57	$ 8,500.
4	$ 12,000.	31	$ 11,000.	58	$ 8,500.
5	$ 7,500.	32	$ 9,500.	59	$ 12,500.
6	$ 7,500.	33	$ 6,800.	60	$ 3,800.
7	$ 28,000.	34	$ 6,600.	61	$ 12,500.
8	$ 12,500.	35	$ 7,200.	62	$ 15,000.
9	$ 9,500.	36	$ 11,000.	63	$ 28,000.
10	$ 9,500.	37	$ 14,000.	64	$ 56,000.
11	$ 4,200.	38	$ 8,800.	65	$ 8,500.
12	$ 9,500.	39	$ 5,200.	66	$ 9,500.
13	$ 14,000.	40	$ 15,000.	67	$ 7,600.
14	$ 12,000.	41	$ 15,000.	68	$ 11,000.
15	$ 8,800.	42	$ 22,000.	69	$ 11,000.
16	$ 9,500.	43	$ 8,200.	70	$ 8,500.
17	$ 6,800.	44	$ 32,000.	71	$ 8,500.
18	$ 5,200.	45	$ 22,000.	72	$ 4,500.
19	$ 3,800.	46	$ 7,500.	73	$ 3,600.
20	$ 9,500.	47	$ 6,800.	74	$ 4,500.
21	$ 2,400.	48	$ 8,500.	75	$ 65,000.
22	$ 4,600.	49	$ 32,000.	76	$ 50,000.
23	$ 11,000.	50	$ 12,000.	77	$ 4,500.
24	$ 9,000.	51	$ 12,000.	78	$ 3,600.
25	$ 18,000.	52	$ 6,200.	79	$ 6,500.
26	$ 32,000.	53	$ 7,500.	80	$ 4,500.

81	$ 11,000.	108	$ 28,000.	135	$ 2,800.
82	$ 6,500.	109	$ 8,500.	136	$ 1,600.
83	$ 8,500.	110	$ 22,000.	137	$ 5,200.
84	$ 4,800.	111	$ 6,800.	138	$ 5,200.
85	$ 4,600.	112	$ 62,000.	139	$ 9,500.
86	$ 11,000.	113	$ 5,200.	140	$ 18,000.
87	$ 8,200.	114	$ 3,200.	141	$ 9,500.
88	$ 32,000.	115	$ 26,000.	142	$ 11,000.
89	$ 15,000.	116	$ 15,000.	143	$ 3,200.
90	$ 15,000.	117	$ 7,500.	144	$ 7,800.
91	$ 3,600.	118	$ 4,500.	145	$ 4,800.
92	$ 9,500.	119	$ 2,800.	146	$ 4,800.
93	$ 8,500.	120	$ 3,200.	147	$ 6,800.
94	$ 9,500.	121	$ 5,200.	148	$ 2,400.
95	$ 6,500.	122	$ 6,500.	149	$ 4,500.
96	$ 11,000.	123	$ 9,500.	150	$ 7,200.
97	$ 14,000.	124	$ 5,600.	151	$ 4,500.
98	$ 12,000.	125	$ 6,500.	152	$ 5,200.
99	$ 18,500.	126	$ 11,000.	153	$ 2,850.
100	$ 22,000.	127	$ 3,200.	154	$ 2,800.
101	$ 22,000.	128	$ 7,500.	155	$ 8,500.
102	$ 11,000.	129	$ 4,200.	156	$ 7,600.
103	$ 4,200.	130	$ 9,500.	157	$ 6,500.
104	$ 6,800.	131	$ 5,200.	158	$ 7,500.
105	$ 4,800.	132	$ 14,000.	159	$ 25,000.
106	$ 8,500.	133	$ 4,800.	160	$ 6,200.
107	$ 8,500.	134	$ 4,800.	161	$ 3,200.

162	$ 8,500.		189	$ 4,500.
163	$ 7,600.		190	$ 4,500.
164	$ 6,800.		191	$ 3,800.
165	$ 11,000.		192	$145,000.
166	$ 2,800.		193	$ 6,800.
167	$ 4,500.		194	$ 9,500.
168	$ 4,800.		195	$ 9,500.
169	$ 5,500.			
170	$ 2,100.			
171	$ 3,200.			
172	$ 5,200.			
173	$ 7,500.			
174	$ 8,800.			
175	$ 6,500.			
176	$ 6,500.			
177	$ 7,500.			
178	$ 4,200.			
179	$ 8,500.			
180	$ 8,500.			
181	$ 6,500.			
182	$ 8,500.			
183	$ 6,800.			
184	$ 4,600.			
185	$ 3,200.			
186	$ 6,200.			
187	$ 5,800.			
188	$ 8,500.			